D0916929

SKILL IN READING ALOUD

SKILL IN READING ALOUD

JOSEPH F. SMITH AND JAMES R. LINN
University of Hawaii

HARPER & ROW, PUBLISHERS

New York and Evanston

SKILL IN READING ALOUD

Library of Congress catalog card number: 60-7020

To
Ruth and Kay

Contents

TO JOIN YOUR HEARERS

TO END AND TO BEGIN

Preface

Skill in Reading Aloud is intended for a one-semester beginning course in the oral interpretation of literature. Almost inevitably it is addressed to the intelligent student who doesn't especially like Lit. and who rather mistrusts Interp.; he has the most to gain from such a course, and he is very much in the majority, not only on campus, but in committee room and capitol, in laboratory and on testing ground. Poets may be, as Shelley claims, the unacknowledged legislators of the world; but in the age of the bomb, it behooves us in the liberal arts to incline somewhat toward those whose power is more direct. Fortunately, in helping the nonliterary to read more critically, to experience more deeply, and to communicate more effectively, this textbook may perform an additional and valuable service for the potential major in speech or English: it may provide him with a specific basis for some of the smoother abstractions in his professional jargon. For although we offer no radically new approach to our subject, we do make a basic assumption which even the most recent of our predecessors do not.

Most of the better textbooks in oral interpretation assume that the student who does not like literature usually does not understand it and that he does not understand it because he does not see its relevance. We are not sure that the second assumption necessarily follows—or at least that it follows immediately. After all, any quiz program will reveal the student's mind to be crammed with useless information; he learned it and retained it, relevant or not. And so we make an intervening assumption: we assume that he does not understand literature because *he does not know what to look for.* When he learns how it works he will see its relevance.

Accordingly we question the value of assuring him cheerfully that literature is that which he already likes. At best this postpones the inevitable, and at worst he sees clearly the salesman's foot in the door. Nor is there much point in merely urging him—or warning him—to be sure to discover the mood or attitude or tone. We doubt the effectiveness even of strings of quotations if they are introduced by no more than "Notice the mordant irony in the following." Definitions help little, however carefully phrased; his problem, we think, is not "What is tone?" for example, or even "Why am I concerned with tone?" His problem is "How do I find the tone of this selection?" This textbook tries to show him *what to look for.*

Therefore, the pattern of most of the sections of Chapters Two, Three, Six, and Seven—those which deal with gaining a clear impression—is roughly this: the introduction of some new aspect of meaning—attitude, say, or metaphor or dramatic irony—a discussion of its relevance to the oral reader; *an explanation of the common clues to that aspect;* an analysis of a sample passage; and, in later chapters, some discussion of the problem of presenting such specific clues to an audience.

The assumption that underlies the chapters on expression is somewhat closer to that which guides the more outstanding of recent textbooks in the field: when the student's presentation of material is unconvincing, we assume not that he isn't thinking of what he is saying, but that he isn't making total use of the procedures which nature and society have placed at his disposal. If he does not recognize these procedures he must be taught them. (Whether they feel natural to him at first is of course quite beside the point: we remind him that he stopped acting completely natural when he learned to lie in a crib instead of on his head.) Chapters Four and Nine use simplified linguistic notation to help him begin to analyze vocal patterns; further they contain detailed discussions of some of the possibilities implicit in sample passages. Chapter Five, without quarreling with the think-the-thought method, explains eight "techniques" to supplement that method. The techniques are not new—each has appeared in some form in one or another of the standard textbooks of interpretation or acting; what is new is the inclusion of eight within one volume. The chapters on expression, like those on impression, reflect our determination to spell things out in specific detail.

This textbook, then, is a sort of academic how-to, in that it tries throughout to show the student clearly what the problem is, what his resources are, how to use those resources, and (where we can avoid the loftier aesthetic speculations) why he must solve the problem. But it does not attempt to blueprint the arts either of literature or of interpretation. We thoroughly subscribe to the belief that in the arts *degree* is all important and that the validity of any element is determined by the whole. So much the more reason, we feel, for trying to explain as explicitly and concretely as possible just what those elements are. To talk about Form or Mood without even mentioning how they may be created is surely *more* atomistic than our "clues" and "techniques"; to the student Form and Mood are mysterious, inviolable *entities*, whereas anything so specific as our "clues" must obviously be combined.

But the teacher—to whom, naturally, falls the responsibility of securing the effective combination of these elements—will be relieved to find that we have not pushed our hunch very far. Just as this textbook goes into finer detail than most, so it must take greater precautions against atomism. One such is its rather elaborate system of cross reference: many pieces of practice material are assigned at least twice, to be approached whether in analysis or synthesis from at least two different viewpoints. Further, it insists again and again upon the need for a totality of response; again and again it reminds the student that details and techniques are capable of many combinations and that each new combination will introduce a new modification of the detail or technique; it never introduces a "mechanical" technique as anything more than a way of getting started; and whenever it can do so economically, it relates those techniques to the overall problem of meaning.

If this book achieves its purpose, the teacher should find that he spends less time in the explanation of isolated elements and more in the discussion of their effective combination. He should spend less time filling the gaps in the background of the individual student, for we have rarely hesitated to explain the "obvious." And most important, he should be able to devote more time, both in class and in conference, to the supervision of student practice.

Because it treats oral interpretation in such detail, this book cannot venture far into voice science or the anthologizing of literature. There is a very brief appendix which offers the student practical suggestions for better understanding of the commoner voice problems (and—we hope—stimulates interest in going further) and there are abundant practice materials in other parts of the book; these we hope will satisfy all but those who believe the major goal of oral interpretation to be the cultivation of voice. We are pleasantly surprised at the number and variety of the practice materials which we have included, because our goal was, if anything, the opposite of an anthology: we wanted selections which would pose at least two "unrelated" problems—by which we meant that when the student attempted to solve one of them he would not be unduly handicapped by his inability to solve the others; and that after he had encountered the same selection from two or three viewpoints he would see that the problems were interrelated after all. Such cumulative practice, we believe, is extremely valuable; but in fairness to the teacher who has to listen to these multiple attempts, we have avoided selections which have been done to death and those of questionable literary merit. And to allow maximum classroom participation, we wished to restrict most of them to less than four minutes' running length. We have, however, included a fair number of longer selections. In view of these rather special criteria, the fact that our selections are fairly representative of the major genres and periods is a source of some pride.

A word should be said about the typography. The page has been designed so that teacher and student can tell at a glance the purpose of the matter. Textual discussion is printed full page width; analysis of selections is in smaller type, and set to a narrower measure; selections illustrating principles are indented; selections to be read and practiced orally are set in bolder face and indented. Format therefore immediately proclaims textual discussion, literary analysis, illustrative selections, material to be read aloud.

The chapters have been kept as self-contained as is consonant with the need for cumulative experience; hence other sequences are possible: One, Two, Three, Six, for example, or One, Four, Two, Three.

Although this book is the result of the closest collaboration throughout, Chapters Four, Eight–Eleven and the appendix are basically Smith's; Chapters Two, Three, Five–Seven basically Linn's; Chapter One is thoroughly joint.

We seem never to have mentioned our distinguished predecessors except to differ with them, but we feel that this book is too close to the central tradition of oral interpretation to allow us to minimize our debt to them. To all of them we owe our profoundest thanks, not only for their ideas which we have shamelessly borrowed, but for the inspiration which they provided. Linn wishes to thank Dr. Orland S. Lefforge of the University of Hawaii for his perceptive comments on two of the chapters. Both of us are not only very grateful but deeply indebted to Miss Lousene Rousseau, of Harper & Brothers, for her patience and understanding and, indeed, for her dogged persistence. And to Mrs. Carole Yukitomo we owe not only a world of thanks, but at least a month of holidays which she devoted to typing the manuscript.

J. F. S.
J. R. L.

February, 1960

TO GET UNDER WAY

Preview

Wherein Lies Skill?

Skill in oral reading is what this book is about. *Oral reading,* we think, is plain enough; let us try to make what we mean by *skill* just as plain.

We can begin in solid standard fashion by quoting *The American College Dictionary:* "Skill. n. 1. The ability that comes from knowledge, practice, aptitude, etc., to do something well. 2. Competent excellence in performance; expertness, dexterity."

With this as a guiding generalization let us look for as many elements of skill as we can find.

Let's start with piano playing.

We all will agree that expert piano playing entails skill. To achieve renown as a concert pianist entails great skill. But skill must be scanned. Whatever the elements of pianistic skill may be and however many of them there are, they can become piano playing only by way of the keyboard and the pedals of a piano—a strictly mechanical contrivance. So, ultimately, skill in piano playing, in all its aspects, consists of striking piano keys with the fingers and pushing down pedals with the feet. Obviously there is no part of pianistic skill which does not entail keyboard or pedal operation. But there are ways and ways *and* ways of poking keys and pushing pedals.

Not so long ago, when Ignace Paderewski and Josef Hofmann were the two great pianists in the concert world, their respective merits were frequently topics of conversation and indeed of argument. Comments like the following were common: "Hofmann's technique is greater. (Did you ever see anything to compare with his left hand?!) He is more accurate than Paderewski; Paderewski hits more wrong notes. But Paderewski is the greater pianist. Hofmann may be more skillful but he is cold. Paderewski plays with more warmth, more understanding, more soul."

3

Let's consider these comments. "Hits wrong notes" is fairly specific; "technique" is vague; "understanding" is provocative; "warmth and soul" are pretty hazy; but they *all* report recognition of differences in the playing of the two men. These differences—often very subtle, some wholly ineffable—could be heard; some of them could be seen; but ultimately they all point to the different ways in which Hofmann and Paderewski struck keys with their fingers and pushed pedals with their feet. So far as the piano itself was concerned, Paderewski's "soul" was just as mechanical as Hofmann's "technique." Paderewski's "understanding" was as integral a part of key poking as was Hofmann's digital dexterity. Each required its own set of neural patterns and muscular tensions.

Although it is inescapable that the pianist's only pianistic contact with the piano is through his hands and feet, he is, of course, not just hands and feet. He is arms and shoulders and torso and thighs and legs, to say nothing of lungs and glands and nerves—and, mind you, brain. How he will strike a certain note, incorporate it into a chord or phrase, will depend on tensions in arms, shoulders, torso—yes, and possibly even legs as they push pedals. This astonishing complex of tensions is made possible in the well-practiced organism by "understanding," by "emotional grasp," by "soul," if you must.

Does not the statement, "Hofmann had the greater skill, but Paderewski was the greater pianist," indicate a lack of understanding of pianism? Does it not exclude from "skill" some of its most important and basic elements? Of two pianists, A and B, playing the same score, each striking all the keys in the same linear sequence in which the notes are written, A's playing is "cold," "unmoving," whereas B's has "warmth," "emotional depth," "understanding," etc. Whose technique is better? Again, X plays with "understanding" but he hits so many wrong notes his errors are distracting; Y is "cold" but he is more "accurate." Who in this case is the more skillful? And since we have used the word, what does "accuracy" entail? Is playing F sharp for F any more "inaccurate" than playing a note fortissimo that should have been played pianissimo? Are not errors in accent and phrasing, and indeed in "mood," "tone," and "spirit," inaccuracies? Is it not an egregious error to bang out a prelude from Bach's "Well Tempered Clavichord" as if it had been written by Rachmaninoff for a 1920 Steinway? Why?

All knowledge essential to pushing keys down properly is inescapably an integral part of the skill of piano playing. Remember the dictionary definition of skill: "The ability that comes from knowledge, practice, aptitude, etc., to do something well." The pianist lacking that knowledge is deficient in skill because he cannot push the keys down properly no matter how fast he can make his fingers fly over a keyboard. As we suggested a moment ago, knowledge requisite for pianistic ability may well include some history of instruments. And how may knowledge of acoustics modify a pianist's key pushing? We must not exclude from *skill* any knowledge which may contribute to ability.

The necessity for extensive and intensive piano practice is too apparent to need extended comment at this point. It is enough to say that encyclopedic knowledge will not make a pianist of a person who never goes near a keyboard. Moreover much essential knowledge can be acquired only at the keyboard. Knowledge directs practice; practice produces necessary physical facility and increases knowledge. Skill cannot be independent of pertinent knowing. Digital dexterity, important as it is, does not in itself make a pianist.

We hear a lot about dichotomies these days. Physicists are bit by bit dissolving in the public mind the dichotomy of space and time. Psychologists are struggling with mind and body. Some speech teachers and artists still go haywire on form and content. And some art critics exclude from their notions of skill or technique those elements without which consummate skill is an impossibility.

Although it may be convenient—our language being what it is—to talk of elements, of knowledge and performance, and even of form and content, let us be quite clear that we do not want even remotely to suggest that such elements are mutually exclusive; that performance is independent of knowledge; or that form is not an aspect of content. Whatever contributes to a pianist's particular key striking and pedal pushing is part of his pianistic skill. So, where is the lesson for improving oral reading skill?

Like the pianist, the interpretative reader must operate an instrument. The former has one advantage in this matter: if he has enough money he can buy a good instrument and can hire a tuner to keep it in good condition. The reader is his own instrument—an instrument which, as human bodies go, may be of superior or inferior quality, etc. However, barring unusual abnormality, the reader can improve his instrument.

Like the pianist, the reader has to interpret a score or text. This requires study, analysis, knowledge—in short, understanding. Understanding determines greatly "how it will come out." Understanding is the appropriate sensory-neuromuscular response to the black marks on the paper—the printed text.

Like the pianist, the reader must turn the sensory-neuromuscular patterns, which are his understanding, into appropriate sound waves—sound waves set up by his operation of his particular instrument. But here the reader has an added responsibility: unlike the pianist his communication, by its very nature, is aimed at two senses instead of just one—seeing as well as hearing.[1] We watch a reader because he is speaking; from the beginning of mankind seeing has been an inte-

---

[1] It is true, of course, that a pianist's visible behavior may enhance or detract from his playing, but persons go to piano concerts chiefly to listen, and as for seeing, they like to watch the pianist's hands. (We wonder if they would not *get* more if they would watch his face?)

gral part of communication by speech. So the reader must transmit his understanding of his text simultaneously on two wave lengths—light and sound. So much are both transmissions bound into a single communicative act that absence of appropriate visible behavior can actually be *heard* as vocal deficiency! The reader's audience depends not only on hearing the results of the tensions but on seeing them overtly.

Like the pianist's, the reader's behavior must be appropriately total. If certain tensions clear down in the pianist's legs are necessary for accurate key pushing with his fingers, how equally important it is for the oral reader to have the necessary total tensions! His body is his instrument and it must work and be worked skillfully in order that vocal and articulatory mechanisms shall set up the appropriate noises.

Like the pianist, the reader must practice long and hard. Indeed, in the matter of practice the reader has the greater responsibility: he has the job of improving his instrument. He must bring all his pertinent knowledge to bear upon his practice and he must increase his knowledge through his practice.

In summary, then, effective rendition is a matter of skill. Skill, for the most part, has been much too narrowly defined. For fully skillful interpretative reading, the reader must make of his body a good instrument; he must learn to make it respond instantly and exactly as he wants it to respond. He must study his text and ultimately evoke in himself a complete, satisfactory, and defensible response to the text, and finally he must transmute the energy of that response into sound waves and light waves within a given situation, so that those sound and light waves impinging upon the ears and eyes of an audience will be retransmuted into responses comparable to and compatible with his own.

That is a large and very complex order indeed, but we will take it bit by bit.

"What Do I Shoot At?"

We do not know precisely why you are taking a course in reading aloud. Your reason may lie anywhere between resentful compliance with requirements and enthusiastic determination to become a top-flight interpretative reader. It can be assumed that since you are pursuing some sort of higher education you can hardly escape situations, even beyond your present course, which will demand your reading something aloud. That reading, whatever the situation and whatever the text, should be completely appropriate; it should be crystal clear; it should fulfill your purpose in reading.

So, whether you are starting out merely with the desire to avoid a failing grade in a required course or with the intention of becoming an interpretative reader of note or with the hope of something in between; whether you will face situations which call for your reading of the minutes of the last meeting, of a poem by William Blake, of the day's "lesson" in church, of testimony in a courtroom, of a mathematical disquisition in a seminar, of the part of Othello in the theatre, or of a story just for fun, your goal is "appropriate" communication—a reading which "fits" the text being read.

Obviously a "reading" which is appropriate to Othello will not be appropriate to the minutes of the last meeting. But we had better emphasize the point anyway because ignoring it can lead to all sorts of artiness. We have no patience with the sentimental moan that many persons affect in the presence of "high art," and we certainly hope you have none either. If you are reading a treatise on mathematics you want to sound like an alert, interesting mathematician. Oral interpretation, then, is neither mooing Milton nor mumbling minutes; it is the reading of material in such a way that the material "hangs together"— that what is read fuses satisfactorily with how it is read.

The bare minimum of appropriateness, then, will be reading which has at least three qualities: (1) it will be logically defensible—it will make sense; (2) it will be psychologically convincing—it will present the attitudes and reactions of a credible human being, such reactions as he might conceivably experience in the given circumstances, (3) it will compel favorable attention. This bare minimum has nothing to do with artiness, but it has a very great deal to do with art. And it represents a far larger order than appears at first glance.

In Act II of Shakespeare's most famous play, Hamlet requests an actor to recite a speech which recounts the grizzly death of King Priam and the resulting grief of Queen Hecuba. The actor complies, reciting so effectively that Polonius remarks: "Look whe'er he has not turned his colour and has tears in's eyes," and Hamlet himself, contemplating his own ineptitude, thinks:

> Is it not monstrous that this player here,
> But in a fiction, in a dream of passion,
> Could force his soul so to his own conceit
> That from her working all his visage wanned,
> Tears in his eyes, distraction in's aspect,
> A broken voice, and his whole function suiting
> With forms to his conceit?

By "conceit" Shakespeare means conception, understanding: "Is it not astonishing that an actor, having arrived at a particular understanding of Hecuba's grief through his study and learning of a text, could so control his entire body during the reciting of the text that his face grew pale, tears came to his eyes, his voice broke with apparent grief?" Here is oral reading skill of a high order. Again compare it with piano playing.

The pianist's aim is to gain a proper concept of his score and then to "force his soul so to his own conceit" that his whole function will supply suitable forms—piano playing—which will reveal his "conceit" to his audience.

Our purpose in this book is to help you to achieve penetrating concepts of written texts and to present principles of presentation—"forms"—which will help you to force your own soul so to your conceit that you can read the texts aloud and reveal your "conceits" to your audience.

This two-way process—appreciative intake (concept) and persuasive outpouring (execution)—is what we mean by *interpretation*.

To answer your question, "What do I shoot at?" even more specifically: ever deepening apprehension of the literature you read to yourself; increasingly effective portrayal of whatever you may have to, or desire to, read aloud to others. Bear in mind that getting through college depends in very great measure on your apprehension of what you read; whatever your "major," you will meet occasions where reading aloud is "indicated."

"What Is My Range?"

We have drawn an analogy from piano playing not only to make clear what we mean by skill but also to point out a particular difficulty often encountered in trying to improve reading.

No one whatsoever expects a person to become an accomplished pianist in a single one-semester course in college. Everyone readily agrees that skill in interpreting the "literature" for the piano requires long and profound study and long and intensive practice. However, many, many persons assume that "there isn't much to this reading business." After all, they learned to read down in the grammar grades. They can "quickly recognize the words on a page and pronounce them correctly and with fair fluency so that listeners can recognize the words." To these we say nothing. Many others realize that their reading can be greatly improved but fail to realize what oral reading skill involves. Some of these are likely to reply to our piano analogy, "I don't intend to be a professional performer; I'll be satisfied if I can develop a reading skill comparable to playing easy pieces or easy accompaniments." If by chance you are one of these, we would say three things: (1) "Very well; expect to put fully as much time and effort on your reading as is necessary for whatever degree of skill you have in mind." (2) "Are you really willing to limit yourself to the caliber of literature comparable to the piano pieces you are talking about?" (3) "If not, are you willing to do to Shakespeare, or Shelley, or Shaw, what your analogical piano ability would do to Bach, Beethoven, or Brahms?"

Since you have willy-nilly stepped into this oral reading business, we assume that you will try at least to shoot at the "target" heretofore described. Note carefully that we have described the target as a continuum. In clarifying what we meant by appropriate reading we did not suggest that you shoot at "deep apprehension and effective portrayal of literature," but at *"ever deepening* apprehension and *increasingly effective* portrayal of literature."

Here, maybe, we should say a word about "literature." If you are not shooting very high, for instance, only as high as effective reading of the minutes, you may wonder "Why bother with literature?" Well, if you can read "literature," you can read anything. After all, literature treats of everything, and in all sorts of ways. Learning to read "literature" appropriately will take care of your reading of the minutes and, furthermore, will allow you to go as high up the ladder of the art of reading as you choose to go, within your capabilities.

As you start out, the target may appear to be a fixed point, even as railroad tracks appear to converge at an exact spot. As you travel the road (and it requires attentive going!) the target is forever ahead. Discouraging? Not a bit of it! You can arrive at the spot where the target first appeared to be (you can read the minutes very well indeed!); you can know that you have traveled in the right direction, that you have arrived at new insight and greater communicative accomplishment; maybe best of all, you can be thrilled at the vista ahead which you never could have seen save for the distance you have traveled.

The range open to you is two-dimensional: the literature you read and your "reading" of the literature. The scope of the first is the whole field of English letters, including English translations from other languages. The scope of the second is determined by your purpose, talent, and industry.

Obviously, you will have neither reason nor occasion to read aloud by far the greater part of what you read silently to yourself. Even so, as you increase your oral reading skill, you will find more and more literature that seems to be unfulfilled without appropriate utterance; you will find your mind's ear hearing that utterance even as you read silently. Furthermore, it is axiomatic that increasing ability to do brings with it more frequent opportunity for doing. He who reads aloud well lacks neither opportunity nor audience, be he teacher, preacher, lawyer, doctor, or parent. One of the present authors remembers vividly and gratefully hearing a great surgeon read some letters written by a famous English clergyman, Sydney Smith. The surgeon knew he read well; the listener was, in a way, a captive auditor, since he was framed (literally) in a hospital bed where he had been put following a chassis overhaul by the surgeon. Certain conversations with the patient had called Reverend Smith's letters to the surgeon's mind. Had not the surgeon been widely read, had he not been able to read well, the patient would have been denied a very enriching and indeed therapeutic experience. Looking back upon it through the light of his own reading experience, the patient knows that the surgeon enriched himself even as he read.

You cannot fully predict when, where, and how oral reading skill will be to your advantage. Your scope will be what you make it. As you increase your skill, you will widen your scope.

Our business now is to set up a program.

WHAT DO I HAVE TO DO?

When you glanced at the Table of Contents, you may have noticed that the title of Chapter Four is "The Bare Essentials: Clear Expression." We rather hope that this elicited a strangled cry, "What!! Three chapters before we get down to brass tacks!" Some such remark would indicate that you enjoy one advantage over your fellows: you react to what you read.

If this were a class in public speaking, we could start your practice immediately, recognizing that you have been speaking with some success for the past fifteen years or so and using that foundation to build on. But here we must lay a new foundation. Indeed, it is hardly too much to suggest that half of this course will be devoted to getting you to a comparable point at which you begin a course in public address—and in the process we shall treat of many problems analogous to those of the public speaker, so that by the end of this course you should have attained a proficiency at least as great as his at the end of *his* course.

The first problem is your lack of previous experience. The average college student has done very little reading aloud. An occasional letter, an interesting or funny paragraph in a magazine, maybe a few children's stories while baby sitting, and perhaps a written report or two in high school—it hardly adds up to the amount of talking you would do in a normal day.

But, you may say, surely a lack of experience can be easily compensated. After all, instead of having to grope for words, as in public address, the reader finds all the words lined up on the page before him. There is, of course, the problem of turning the black squiggles of ink into sound waves (and that, as we will find, is none too easy, if we wish to convey ideas and not mere words) but once this fairly mechanical trick is accomplished, what more can there be? More important, why wait for three chapters before getting to it? This question brings us to the major handicap imposed upon the beginning oral reader.

In a sense, oral reading requires you first to move backwards through the normal process of expression. Ordinarily we speak because we have gone through a complex pattern: something has induced a tension in the nervous system; the body has taken up an anticipatory attitude or set; the tensions have induced the formation of a private, ineffable conception; a communicable concept has been abstracted from this inexpressible conception; and we finally find words to symbolize the concept. You may observe much of this cycle being traced in painful slow motion during an impromptu speech, but more commonly the process is unconscious, if not automatic: tension, set, conception, concept, word. And often the words are the least important part of the cycle. Consider this exchange:

"Where did you put my book?"
"You mean your pen?"
"Yes, that's what I said."
"I put it on the thingamijig."
"Oh, thanks a lot."

And so, even though the oral reader has all the words in advance, he does not really have very much. He must move from the printed words backward through the cycle until he has induced the relevant tension, and then forward again to the spoken word. The inept reader, who moves from printed to spoken word, and the slick reader, who moves from printed word to concept to spoken word, never manage to persuade us that they are credible human beings engaged in real talk. The tension, the set, the conception—the human elements, if you like—are missing. The beginning speaker, however painful his groping for words, enjoys this great advantage over the beginning reader: he already has the tensions, the set, the conception—*he knows his meaning.*

For this reason we advise postponing your initial practice until after you have had some training in close analysis, such as is offered here in Chapters Two and Three. But your teacher may wisely consider that another order is better suited to your particular needs. Moreover, you may feel that some particular problem demands immediate attention—how to choose material, or what to do about stage fright, for instance.

WHAT SHALL I READ?

In a beginning course this question may not often arise. Your teacher will doubtless assign most of your trial readings in an attempt to give you the kind of graduated practice you need. Occasionally, however, you may be turned loose to find your own material. Such free assignments may become increasingly necessary as you move through this book because we have deliberately limited the number and length of practice materials. Let us therefore help solve a problem for which we are in part responsible.

Probably your first big question is, "Where do I look for material?" Bibliographies and sample reading lists are not as helpful as they seem because your schedule rarely allows you time to venture into completely unknown territory:[2] besides, as we shall suggest, such published lists introduce new dangers.[3] Your best bet is to recall material which you have encountered previously. What have you read in your literature courses, either in college or high school? What about your casual reading; what scenes from what novels impressed you? What plays or movies do you remember vividly? Who are your favorite authors? Is there any chance that a swift survey of their works would elicit two or three selections? In short, consult your memory first and *then* the library.

If your search is still undirected, consult anthologies of the type of literature you seek; there are anthologies compiled on almost every conceivable principle of choice. Fortunately many of them are available in inexpensive paperback editions; but do not neglect the card file in your library. A practical tip here is: generally avoid collections entitled *One Hundred Readings for Every Occasion* or some such; there are a few reputable anthologies of material designed specifically for oral reading, but to date most of them are trash.

If all else fails, consult your teacher—who will doubtless give you the same advice that we have, but who may with his questions prod you into following it!

Let your search for material be guided by a few important considerations— criteria similar to those used in determining the subject of a speech: purpose, speaker, speech, audience, time, and occasion. Assuming that the purpose of the assignment has been set by the teacher, let us turn to some of the other considerations to bear in mind.

Consider Yourself

This priority is deliberate. Too many beginners handicap themselves by concentrating exclusively upon "What does the teacher want?"

CONSIDER YOUR LIKES AND DISLIKES.   This cardinal rule is not inspired by the sardonic reflection that if you follow it you will be sure that one person in the room is interested. We suggest it rather because you will be less easily bored

---

[2] Colleges commonly define a credit hour as "three hours of satisfactory work per week." Two hours of preparation time can be easily squandered in vain search.

[3] You can, however, find bibliographies in Otis J. Aggertt and Elbert R. Bowen, *Communicative Reading,* Macmillan, 1956, chap. 2; Martin Cobin, *Theory and Technique of Interpretation,* Prentice-Hall, 1959, *passim;* Lionel Crocker and Louis M. Eich, *Oral Reading,* 2nd ed., Prentice-Hall, 1955, appendices I–XI.

during rehearsal and less likely to become inhibited in presentation and because there is a strong chance that you will be responding, perhaps unconsciously, to its form, its mood, and to similar facets difficult to analyze. In short, if you like a selection, you can more easily make it a part of you.

The corollary principle—do not read what you dislike—is offered with more hesitation. Most of us dislike, or at least mistrust, what we do not understand. If you use this principle in order to save yourself the trouble of understanding something, you will never widen your horizons. But if, after a thorough and sympathetic analysis, you find that the material leaves you cold, turn to something else. Do not sacrifice your self-respect simply because the selection enjoys great prestige or because you think your teacher likes it. Life is too short, and literature too much fun, to turn either into drudgery.

CONSIDER YOUR OWN TALENTS.   Read what you are good at. This common-sense advice assumes that you will not be graded on your practice readings; in practice readings, by all means concentrate upon the kinds of reading that give you most trouble. But where there is a penalty for failure you are obviously ill advised to attempt material beyond your scope. One other consideration enters here, however: most of us, including your teacher, *are more deeply impressed by a gallant failure than by an easy victory.* Your wisest course is to choose material which is as difficult as you can reasonably hope to encompass; aim, at worst, for a near miss.

Consider the Intrinsic Worth of the Material

The following criteria are especially difficult for the beginner to apply and can easily lead to misunderstanding, so we must be careful here.

CONSIDER YOUR OWN SENSE OF VALUES.   Choose material you think is worth while, and avoid material *you think* is trash. Notice the emphasis upon what you think. Our concern here is not with "Good Taste"—a vexed subject, to which we shall turn in a moment; right now we are offering hard-headed practical advice. Contrary to popular belief, trash is not easy to read aloud: you get bored too early in rehearsal. More important, you find that the author is letting you do all the work. And finally, you find that the additional work does not much increase your chance of success. Trash makes hard work and yet gives you no sense of accomplishment.

CONSIDER THE CANONS OF SOCIAL GOOD TASTE.   Here we come to the tricky part; and before we explain what we mean, we must point out that we do not mean that you are to pay much attention to the canons of *literary* good taste.

Among the most devastating and, in our opinion, unfair weapons that can be used against a beginner are the "Canons of Good Taste." In offering to public view something you have chosen, you are offering something of yourself; when you are criticized for that choice, you feel, quite rightly, that your intelligence or your system of values—that which is most intrinsically you—is being called into question. And when the charge is as vague as "Good Taste" you have no reply. Ignore such criticism if you can. Reflect that the development of taste—i.e., the ability to discriminate values—is perhaps the chief goal of education; to claim that your literary taste is poor is merely to charge you with having "failed" to complete your education—a charge which all but the smug can cheerfully grant.

There is of course some value in sticking to acknowledged masterpieces, to works that have stood the test of time. But few beginners can use these touchstones to test new material, and too often they reject anything that lacks a seal of approval. Be more courageous than that. As you deepen your analytical ability in this course, and as performance makes you more deeply appreciative of a job well done, you will learn to distinguish between the worth while, which repays your efforts, and the inferior, which does not. By sticking to safe works and great authors you avoid the challenge but miss the opportunity. Furthermore, as even a superficial knowledge of literary history will show, few works and fewer authors are safe for very long. Wordsworth turned out an astounding amount of trash, and even Shakespeare could be pretty bad at times. Pope was idolized in the eighteenth century and damned in the nineteenth; Shelley, worshipped a hundred years ago, often seems flabby today. Or think of the "revivals" that have occurred within your lifetime: James, Fitzgerald, Melville, Twain—and now, as you read this, who is the current rage? Playing safe, in short, is not as safe as it seems.

In matters of literary taste we see little reason to abandon our earlier position: choose material that *you* think is worth while. But listen carefully to those who can show in detail where they think you are wrong.

Social good taste is a different matter, and here we can offer some specific tips. Remember first that one's public behavior is usually more guarded than private; expressions and situations which we accept calmly enough in silent reading may embarrass us when we read them or hear them read in public. Perhaps more important, such frankness or indelicacy can remind us sharply that we *are* in public, so that even though we may not be embarrassed, we look around to see who is. The four-letter words in the more hysterical war novels and the quasi-poetic parades of sexual intimacies are cases in point. They pose essentially the same problem, though on a somewhat higher level, as we face in telling a risqué joke in mixed company. As you have probably learned through experience, the question is not only whether the company will feel embarrassed, but whether they will feel that they *ought* to feel embarrassed.

We have said enough, perhaps, to render our next point superfluous, but some will need it spelled out: Do not bother trying to shock your teacher. He has heard it all before, and if he does not resent your impertinence, he will be amused by your naïveté.

In addition to an ordinary regard for convention, call upon your sense of fair play. Your classmates may not give you their courteous attention, but at least they do not answer you back; so do not exploit the advantage by reading material which might be expected to give them pain. Attacks on racial or religious groups, especially those represented in your audience, are always to be avoided. It is not necessary to truckle to the hypersensitive: to interpret every reference to "Jew" or "Jap" or "nigger" as a religious or racial slur is to ignore the changes in social usage, if not indeed to succumb to the very bigotry which every sensible person is trying to eliminate. In this troubled matter we advise you to rely less on social tact—which can be pretty nebulous at times—than on your own sense of fair play. After all, it is only good sense to consider social convention and to play fair whenever you choose or are asked to read aloud. You can develop your literary taste by hard-headed experiment.

CONSIDER THE SELECTION'S ADAPTABILITY TO ORAL PRESENTATION. Some selections which look promising in written form may prove disappointing when read aloud. For example, the oral reader has few visible or audible equivalents of spelling or typography: he probably cannot communicate those Elizabethan lyrics that are printed in the shape of a butterfly or a heart; and some of e.e. cummings' and even Dylan Thomas' typographical experiments may prove equally incapable of oral translation. Too, the oral reader cannot easily render homonyms (e.g., to, two, and too; vein, vain, and vane, etc.) and therefore must avoid literature which exploits such ambiguities; certain passages in James Joyce's novels, and some contemporary poetry, must be *seen* to be appreciated.

But although these two principles may be self-evident, many a beginning reader neglects to apply them to the more popular levels of art—specifically to material written in "dialect." He seizes gleefully upon some such sentence as this:

> He wuz awweez sayn sumpm about we hafta get it straightent out

and discovers, too late, that none of the words sounds as peculiar as it looks; with the possible exception of "sumpm," the effect of semiliteracy resides more in the spelling than in the pronunciation. Hence we must be suspicious of any material that renders colloquial dialect. Unless the pronunciations are peculiar, or the diction and syntax contribute largely to the effect—unless, in short, it *sounds* like "dialect"—we should urge our friends to read it for themselves. For this reason we must regretfully abandon many of the adventures of Don Marquis' archy and mehitabel, many of Arthur Kober's delightful phone conversations, and even some of Rosten's H*Y*M*A*N* K*A*P*L*A*N*.

An obvious further limitation is imposed by the difficulty of the material. Note that some excerpts require too much preliminary explanation to be worth while. By the time you have finished explaining unfamiliar terms or previous incidents in the plot, the audience has lost all sense of pleasant anticipation. You would have been wiser to choose material that was more nearly self-contained.

Consider the Audience

Obviously we must give careful thought to the target of our oral reading. Chapter Ten will be devoted to discussing audience, but since reading aloud is, after all, aimed at an audience of some kind, and since, therefore, audience of some kind is inescapably a crucial part of communication by oral reading, it will be well to say a few words about it right now.

The ambiguity implicit in the phrase "audience of some kind" may help us to avoid exaggerating or denying the importance of the listeners in front of us. We know that history rarely vindicates the artist who ignores his contemporaries, that the "artist ahead of his time" is largely a myth; but we know too that those artists who were most conscious of their audience have often sunk to second rank. Apparently art and communication are not quite the same thing, so in the sections that follow we must avoid easy generalization.

CONSIDER THE INTERESTS AND CAPACITIES OF YOUR AUDIENCE. Choose material that will appeal not to the average, but to the most sophisticated, the most mature, and the most sensitive members of your audience. (We defend this advice in Chapter Eleven; and if you are now planning to face an audience beyond the classroom, perhaps you should refer to page 417 immediately.) For the present let us assume that your problem is to satisfy a classroom assignment, and our advice is based upon more immediate, and perhaps more cynical, grounds than is presented later. Practically, your success in class depends not upon how your reading affects your friends, especially nonliterary friends, but upon how it affects the person who gives the grades. Your own self-respect will preclude you from catering to your teacher's likes and dislikes—and the attempt would probably not succeed—so the soundest compromise is to choose material that will appeal to the upper reaches of the class.

One further practical tip: Do not choose material that has been worn thin by too frequent reading, unless you are sure that *your* reading will restore its luster. Avoid pieces that you have heard *ad nauseam:* "Under the Spreading Chestnut Tree," "The Children's Hour," "The Tell-Tale Heart," Henry's "Liberty or Death" address, "What Is a Boy?" "Curfew Shall Not Ring Tonight," "By the Shores of Gitchee Gumee," Antony's funeral oration—their very mention can conjure visions of grammar school and shrill little boys and girls primly reciting pieces. Your own experience will warn you away from others; but here are a few that your teacher has probably heard too often: Noyes' "The Highwayman," Browning's "My Last Duchess," Lowell's "Patterns," Service's "The Cremation of Sam McGee," Thayer's "Casey at the Bat," Blandings' "The Cruise of the Spun-Glass Ship," Marullus' speech from *Julius Caesar* I, i, Field's "Little Boy Blue," Sandburg's "Chicago," and Markham's "The Man with the Hoe." We do not condemn these favorites of yours (we like some of them too, and we have included others in this book); we merely suggest that your teacher has probably heard them over and over. Not only do you risk boredom; your version, however fresh, may be competing with an ideal version which he has formed, perhaps unconsciously, after years of tinkering with students' misreadings. He has too great a head-start.

This doesn't mean that you should seek out the recondite—merely avoid the opposite. If *you* like the material, if you have a strong hunch that the most intelligent of your classmates will like it, and if you've no reason to believe that they've heard it too often, then you can embark upon rehearsal with confidence.

WHAT IF I'M SCARED?

You probably will be. We hope so. And if you are, be grateful for it; you're normal. Unless you are keyed up you are not likely to arouse much excitement in your audience. However, the way you feel may be relatively unimportant—the important matter is how the audience feels.

This approach to stage fright is not as unsympathetic or as frivolous as it may seem. There is a valid distinction to be drawn between the symptoms you feel and those which the audience can detect. The latter are surprisingly few: we cannot see the butterflies in your stomach; we rarely can see the trembling of your hands and knees or the perspiration on your palms. Furthermore, if you turn your attention to the audience, you will not only be less keenly aware of the symptoms, but you will find that most of them diminish.

Lest this seem easier said than done, we propose to give an account of stage fright and to suggest some practical ways of controlling it. One plausible theory holds that stage fright is the result of conflict between two parts of the nervous system: the autonomic nervous system, controlling the heart and other internal organs that keep us alive, automatically prepares for activity which is rejected by the central nervous system, comprising the brain and the nerves of the skeletal musculature.

When the cave man saw a saber-toothed tiger, he did not have time to ponder, "Ah, a tiger, subfamily Machairodontinae. I had better prepare to fight. No, perhaps it would be better to head for the hills." His reactions had to be automatic: the moment the message was received a short circuit into the autonomic system triggered the release of adrenalin and other glandular secretions; these hormones caused the liver to release extra sugar as fuel and accelerated the heartbeat so that air would be available for combustion; to channel this extra energy the digestive processes slowed—the stomach stopped work, the surface blood vessels contracted, the pupils of the eye dilated, and a number of other phenomena, all designed for efficient tiger fighting, occurred immediately. We are closely related to the cave men whose autonomic nervous systems worked well, and our common inheritance frequently saves our lives as when we dodge a bus. In physical emergencies we don't have time to think; we react automatically or not at all. But not all "emergencies" are physical. Facing an audience can be an emergency, and our autonomic nervous system prepares us to fight or run away, while our central nervous system tells us we cannot do either. We are all fueled up with nowhere to go. Moreover, the autonomic nervous system is receiving emergency messages from the very organs it has mobilized; therefore it works harder and consequently receives more signals; if the process continues unchecked we go into a state of shock. (Classes are always dismissed for the funeral.)

Despite the macabre results that are theoretically possible, stage fright can be a valuable asset to a reader. It provides extra "emergency" energy which, if harnessed intelligently, can be turned into enthusiasm, stamina, force, and perhaps even inspiration. One of the occupational hazards of teaching is that we stop feeling stage fright, and our lectures become dull; good teachers and good actors welcome a little stage fright, and they pace the halls and the wings attempting to induce it.

But having warned you not to avoid it completely, we still have not solved the problem. Obviously we must find some way to dampen the emergency signal, reëstablish control by the central nervous system before the vicious circle begins, break the vicious circle at some point, or use up the superfluous energy. The procedures below will accomplish most of these tasks. Now that you understand the nature of stage fright perhaps you can think of others.

First of all, be well prepared. Thorough preparation may not be enough to eliminate the emergency signal; even the most experienced are never satisfied that their preparation is absolutely complete. But the alternative, the consciousness of inadequate preparation, is almost certain to create an emergency; thorough preparation is, at very least, a form of insurance.

Next, look coldly at the entire situation. Is it an emergency? The audience wants you to succeed; they lose if you don't; unlike the public speaker, the reader almost never faces a hostile audience. And what, after all, is the worst that could happen? Probably that your reading will be dull or hard to follow, and you've sat through too many such readings to think them grave misfortunes. Lastly, and most important in this connection, look closely at the audience before you start. No matter what effort it costs you, get your eyes off the text and look carefully at this shape that hovers somberly beyond the rim of your eyelids; you will find that this unseen terror is just a group of people—probably the very classmates who bored *you* a moment ago! Furthermore, the mere process of looking at them will remove the chasm which formerly yawned between you and give you instead the impression of being part of their circle. Never read to an audience until you have taken time to survey it.

Act confident. This is not just a form of autosuggestion; it is an application of a theory about the very nature of emotion. You have seen a child *work himself into* a tantrum: by maneuvering his muscles into the position they would assume if he really were angry, he managed, in a surprisingly short time, to be nearly insane with rage. You can work yourself into confidence in the same way by arranging your muscles into a pattern of confidence. Act as if you owned the place, and you will begin to feel that you might, after all.

Focus your attention upon your purpose in reading and upon the reaction you hope to secure from the audience. Groping for symptoms within your psyche will merely unearth more symptoms, if indeed it doesn't engender them. (For this reason do not gossip about symptoms with your friends.) Get to work on the job to be done.

Some of the foregoing hints will perform the additional function of reëstablishing control by the central nervous system; here are some further procedures which have this as their prime objective. First of all, take your reading position, whatever it is—at the front of the classroom, on a platform, or in a chair—deliberately and firmly; adjust your book or manuscript; look your listeners in the eye; assume the posture that will help you communicate. Do anything that has conscious purpose and does not distract your listeners. Try not to do anything unconsciously. If you simply must smooth your hair or pull your nose or lick your lips, do so carefully and deliberately—with intent; you are not helping your reading much with this irrelevant activity, of course, but at least your central nervous system is assuming control.

Needed relaxation, that is, reduction of undue tension, can be secured by deliberately avoiding muscular rigidity: getting to your reading position with free, easy movements; taking a deep breath as you go and fully exhaling; managing your book without hurry and with easy precision; looking at your listeners really to see them and to invite their attention. DO NOT under any circumstances giggle or grimace apologetically. Make whatever comment you deem appropriate easily and directly. Throw yourself boldly and deliberately into the first few lines of your text; most beginners use too little volume in the opening, and you will thereby avoid a common fault as well as use some of your extra energy. Remember, deliberate activity is the m.o. for properly relaxing to your reading job.

And again, *be well prepared.* Probe your text deeply, study the principles of oral reading involved, practice intensively. This reëmphasis on preparation as the first step in harnessing stage fright would seem superfluous were it not for the authors' experience with the ubiquitous lazy student.

So, what if you are scared? You have proof that your organism is ready to work for you. Protect yourself in advance by being well prepared, act confident, take your time, relax with deliberate and purposeful physical activity, turn your attention fully to getting your listeners to get from your reading what you have got from your text. As a final reassurance, the one thing that research into stage fright has established is that stage fright lessens with practice. The oftener you read aloud to people, the less your stage fright, until you run the risk of losing it entirely. Not another word about stage fright.

And now, to get down to work in earnest.

TO GET UNDERSTANDING

What's in a Word?

WE ARE NOT going to make much headway in this course until we realize that in literature the words really count. That realization is not as easy as it might seem: most of us never strive for any great precision in our use of words; we do not need to. We use them loosely and read them uncritically, so that we are rarely surprised to encounter such self-contradictions as "Frigidaire Range" (i.e., stove) or "Hotpoint Refrigerator" or "Superette." Most of us are capable of saying something like "Come and see what you can hear." A few, like the Sweet Singer of Michigan, can easily write it. And so our basic premise is far more heretical than it appears; a much more popular assumption is contained in the following question.

What Is the Author Trying to Say?

This helpful hint, frequently offered to perplexed students by their teachers or classmates, suggests that the author has tried to convey a meaning but failed. We might legitimately conclude that if his words are not clear we should look for clues elsewhere—perhaps in his deeds. Or it may picture an author weakly signaling through the mists of time. Our obvious course then is to plug into another circuit—to contact a critic, or perhaps a historian.

Now of course there are many ways of approaching literature. You can comb through it in search of the Great Thoughts. You can find in it signs of social evolution and group it with the kitchen middens of a vanished civilization. You can consider it a special branch of history and trace sources and analogues in this writer or that. You can consider it as data for the psychoanalysis of its authors. Or you can turn your attention solely to its authors and use literature as evidence to confirm or deny an amorous intrigue. Each of these approaches has its value, each requires discipline, and each can be fun. But because of the special nature of our task, we must take a different approach to literature. We must read it. Not as evidence for this theory or that, not for the insights it provides into the creative process or into the personality of the author, but because it is valuable in and of itself.

Part of that value resides, of course, in the problems it poses, the associations it arouses, the speculations it engenders. Part of the fun of inspecting the newest Fords may lie in trying to detect the influence of foreign cars, in gauging the possibility of a price war, or in predicting the shape of next year's models. But if we were given a Ford and told to turn it into a tractor, we would quickly cease speculating upon what the Ford Motor Company had in mind when it made this car. We would concentrate upon learning how a car is put together and how a tractor is put together. Then we would try to figure out how to turn this particular Ford into that particular tractor. The analogy is none too strained. As oral readers, we must take literature apart, translate it into another medium, and then make it work.

The Author Said What He Meant

When you face an audience, proposing to re-create something called "Bright Star, Would I Were Constant as Thou Art," you have absolutely no way of knowing what Keats "really" intended. Furthermore, no amount of information about his relations with Fanny Brawne, no statistics about the T.B. rate in 1820, and no theories about the characteristics of Romanticism will determine whether you do or do not succeed. And so, at the very outset, we may as well make a towering assumption: that the sonnet is *there* to be re-created. As we shall soon point out, ultimately that sonnet exists only within your nervous system. But try inserting into it a couple of lines from *The Pirates of Penzance* and you will learn, from your audience's reaction, that in a very real sense Keats' sonnet exists as a thing apart. Exactly the right words were put into exactly the right place to give us a unique experience. (What Keats was thinking as he labored over it may well have been unprintable!) And even if some scholar should unearth a later revision of the sonnet—something closer to what Keats "really meant"—we would still have the option of choosing the one which seemed the better (just as, in point of fact, we have done with the four versions which Fitzgerald prepared of the *Rubáiyát*).

Let us now cease thinking continually of those who were truly great and concentrate instead upon the evidence of their greatness. For the next nine chapters, you are cordially invited to forget about what the author "meant" and what the critics say he meant. The author built something out of words; let us concentrate on them.

THE NATURE OF MEANING

This section sets forth a number of basic assumptions upon which to build a method of analysis. Since it is very important that you understand these principles, we shall avoid technical terms wherever possible and point out the immediate practical applications of each. In the following section we shall discuss the specific influences upon the meaning of a word—or, from your point of view, the clues to seek in determining its meaning. But first the assumptions.

Meaning Is Never Objective

Any basic general semantics textbook will cite examples of our superstitious use of words, as if by changing the word ("died" to "passed away") we can change the nature of the thing itself. But whatever our practice, it is obvious that the word is not the thing for which it stands. A moment's thought will make it equally obvious that subjectivity can never be entirely removed from a word. The word is transmitted by an organism, generally human; it is perceived by an organism, generally human; its relation to a thing or event is established by an organism, generally human; and the thing or event must be perceived by an organism, generally human. Somewhere in the process—and often many times during it—there will almost certainly occur modification, if not distortion.

Nevertheless, when we compare the words "Hallelujah" and "Na_3PO_4," we see that some words are more "objective" than others. Some words contain little editorial comment, little detectable bias. Unless you have an almost pathological aversion to chemistry you accept "Na_3PO_4" with detachment; even though bitter experience may have invested trisodium phosphate with unpleasant associations, you probably have little emotional reaction to Na_3PO_4. On the other hand, Hallelujah, in its common usage, does not clearly refer to any thing or event in external reality; it is largely the verbalization of an emotional state.

That part of a word's meaning which refers to a thing or event in external nature we shall call its *denotation,* or its extensional meaning; that part of its meaning which indicates bias, attitude, emotional reaction, or mental association we shall call its *connotation,* or intensional meaning. The meaning of Na_3PO_4 is largely denotative; the meaning of Hallelujah is largely connotative.

Generally the more concrete a word is—the more specifically it refers to something we can do or see or feel, etc.—the greater its denotation and the more limited its connotation; the more abstract the word is, the more things or events it may embrace, the greater its proportion of connotation to denotation; and the more familiar a word is, the more personal associations we have attached to it, and therefore the richer its connotations.

Ordinary expository writing is concerned only that the denotations all mesh—or at least that they do not contradict each other. But in literature not only the denotations, but the connotations as well must fit together to produce a harmonious effect.

Meaning Is Ultimately Personal

Since we apprehend reality only through our senses, and since no two persons have exactly the same sensory apparatus, it is unlikely that two persons ever form the same picture of reality. Furthermore, since we attach meaning to these unique experiences only by fitting them into the pattern of our previous experience, and since no two people ever have exactly the same pattern of experience, it is extremely unlikely that any two people attach exactly the same meaning to any one word.

In the sense that all experience is personal and unique, so is all meaning. Therefore the hard-headed literal and practical student may as well abandon his search for the one absolute and unequivocal meaning—even in a message as comparatively impersonal as $(a + b) (a - b) = a^2 - b^2$.

To the diffident, uncertain student this should be a liberating idea. Ultimately the meaning of a literary selection—indeed, the meaning of anything—is whatever you can find in it. Whatever you find will be unique, and no one else will ever entirely agree with you. By the time the poet has finished building his poem he himself will find a new meaning in it (almost certainly different from the one he "intended"), the critic will find another meaning in it, your teacher will find another, and your classmate still another; and, as we can never even compare those meanings, it is foolish to assume that yours is wrong. Your interpretation will always be at least unique, even if you try to adopt your teacher's explanation of his interpretation. Cling to your own until *you* see that it won't fit, won't square with the words in the selection.

Meaning Is Societal

If the previous paragraph seems to have turned communication into chaos, we had better lodge a stabilizing qualification right now: ultimately, meaning is whatever you can find; practically, meaning is whatever your audience can find. If the hard-headed literalist in search of the one absolute meaning is on the wrong track, so is the diffident student who assumes his teacher to have the correct meaning; but even more seriously astray is the intense young lady who simply loves all poetry and uses it as a sort of Rorschach Inkblot into which she can project her own well-worked emotions. The others are looking for a precision that makes communication possible; she, alas, is not.

Obviously we cannot arbitrarily juggle the *denotations* of words without blocking communication; to persist in calling a dog "a cat" causes needless confusion. But apparently it is not so obvious that *connotations* are public property as well; too many students of interpretation believe that "the emotional meaning, that is, the connotative meaning, is found in your memories, your imagination, your heart."[1] We think it is found where denotations are: in the dictionary, in conversation, in writing. Just because you dislike calf's liver intensely you cannot use "calf's liver" as a cuss word and expect to be understood. And if, just because you were once scratched by a cat, you think the connotation of "cat" is "sharp claws," sooner or later you will find yourself being treated for a phobia, and perhaps locked up.

We believe, then, meanings must be public property if communication is to occur. Although each of us has probably formed a unique and private conception of a given thing, we have learned, through listening and reading, the extent to which our conceptions agree with those of other people. We discover an area of agreement, an overlap, a *concept,* which we can abstract out of our total conception.[2] This concept will be shared by all people who have had approximately the same experiences, both direct and vicarious, and who live in roughly similar cultures in roughly similar historical periods. Each person who receives the concept will dress it in his own private conception and hence receive a unique "meaning"; but communication demands that this conception fit the concept without greatly distorting it.

Meaning "Resides" in the Text

Perhaps now you understand our impatience with questions about what the author was "trying" to say. They point in the wrong direction. According to our assumptions, the author started with a private ineffable conception—which we can *never grasp.* Hence it is irrelevant whether this conception arose from

---

[1] Charles H. Woolbert and Severina E. Nelson, *The Art of Interpretative Speech,* 4th ed., Appleton-Century-Crofts, 1956, p. 181. This view is common to textbooks in the field; you must realize that ours is heretical.

[2] See Susanne K. Langer, *Philosophy in a New Key,* Harvard Press, 1942; or, in paperback, M25 in Mentor Series. Our debt is clear.

a personal experience or whether he made it up.[3] The point is that, because he was well versed in the concepts of people around him and extraordinarily adept in securing words to symbolize those concepts, he was able to abstract from his inexpressible conception a public communicable concept and to clothe that concept in words which reasonably well-trained people could understand.

Granted, even the best of authors can fail. Sometimes his conceptions are unique, and there exist no public concepts which he can mobilize; his task then becomes one of forging a new language, of so marshaling old concepts that new ones are formed, and of providing us with experiences so intense that we form new conceptions. During the transition period, while the rest of us catch up with the author, there is bound to be some confusion. But you will find that editors usually provide some explanatory notes to such "new" works as Yeats' "Sailing to Byzantium" or Eliot's *The Wasteland*. (As an oral reader you may well question the adaptability of works that require a lot of explanation.) Sometimes, too, an author fails through carelessness; "the worthy Homer nods" at times, Shakespeare "is many times flat, insipid," and Keats can confuse Balboa with Cortez. Certainly we should never forfeit our right to tear a selection to bits—if we can.

But our initial working assumption should always be that the "meaning" is there in the text before us, to be ferreted out by methods available to all. When an accepted author seems especially obscure we should *first* assume that the obscurity is there for a detectable purpose or that it carries an especially heavy freight of meaning. Our first problem is not to translate it quickly into simpler and more forthright English, or to speculate upon the historical intent of its author, but rather to discover the full complexity and full intensity of the message. The primacy of our own reactions must yield to the necessities of communication, and our interpretation, like all sane behavior, must be in broad accord with that of any other well-trained rational person. But whatever we find will be unique, and no one will agree with us fully.

THE DETERMINANTS OF MEANING

The foregoing discussion should at least suggest that there is nothing initially mysterious about literature. Complicated, perhaps: a given passage can pose an intellectual challenge to equal any problem in chess; it can be a puzzle tougher than crossword or jigsaw. More than the average detective story, it can test your

---

[3] Inasmuch as experience is distorted by the very act of perception, and as imagination can only recombine the data of experience, the difference between "experiencing" something and "making it up" is less than might be supposed.

inductive skill, your ability to follow a hunch, and your power of concentration. Perhaps its only mystery lies in the emotional wallop it packs; but that wallop can come early or late, and it usually comes unbidden. At the outset we need aim only for intellectual understanding and the appreciation of a job well done; in deepening our understanding we prepare for the total realization.

An obvious first step toward gaining that understanding is to look up all the unfamiliar words in a dictionary—one of collegiate size at least. We assume that you already know that technique, though we shall probably nag you about it from time to time. However, your main difficulties are more likely to come, not from the unfamiliar words, but from those which are so familiar that you hardly ever think of them any more. We shall therefore devote the rest of this chapter to spelling out techniques for analyzing words you think you already know.

Ultimately those techniques pose a single question, pointing to the central clue in word analysis: *What is gained by using this word instead of its possible alternatives?*

Meaning Is Largely Contextual

No doubt you learned at an early age that dictionaries were not as necessary as teachers seemed to think them, that you could often infer the meaning of a word by studying the words around it—by studying *the context in which it occurred*. If you repeated this process whenever you encountered that word again, you can skip the next three or four pages because you already possess what is doubtless the most important single clue to meaning: the contexts in which a word *frequently* occurs. But if you were like most of us, you concerned yourself only with the *immediate present* context. That technique is usually safe enough for ordinary expository prose, but the resultant impressions are too vague for the complete understanding of literature. Furthermore, literature often uses words in unique ways, and so the immediate context may be misleading. Better read the next few pages after all—just in case.

THE WORD IN ITS FREQUENT CONTEXTS. Let us repeat: the contexts in which a word frequently appears provide the most important single clue to its meaning. Dictionary makers apply this principle above all others; to discover the meanings of a word they compile long lists of quotations in which it appears, seek the thread which runs through these quotations, and hence infer the meanings— particularly connotative meanings.

You are well advised to use a similar method, though perhaps less systematically. When the dictionary does all the work for you, you learn only words about words; but in recalling contexts in which *you* have frequently observed the word, you get the feel of the word—you learn its connotation. Form the habit of asking yourself "Where have I seen this word, and how was it used then?" Compare words with their synonyms: ask "What can be such-and-such but not so-and-so?" Most important, ask "What are some common expressions or stock phrases that contain this word?"

Here is a simple example of the process at work:

> We wish to be brusque, and we wish to be paid; do we ask for "cash" or for "money"? It is not enough that to us "cash" *seems* harsher; as author or reader we must know what will "seem" harsher to the audience. And so we consider some common expressions which our audience probably knows: "cash on the line," not money on the line; "cold hard cash," not cold hard money; "to cash in one's chips," where money may not even be implied; "cash-and-carry"; "cash on hand"; etc. And on the other hand: "the moneyed interests"; "a run for one's money"; "to get one's money's worth"; "it's money in the bank" (meaning, often, "it's an advantage"); "it takes money to make money"; etc. If we then compare the two series, we see that the first never gets very far away from the idea of business, business in its most impersonal form. The second series often does not refer to business at all, and when it does ("it takes money to make money," "the moneyed interests"), the attitude is mixed or perhaps mildly favorable. Now, if we believe that our audience uses these same expressions, we know which word will seem more brusquely businesslike to them. Similarly, as readers who encounter one or other of these words, we know which set of connotations is appropriate to the text.

Let us turn to a more literary example. Again we shall be interested in apparently simple words, because it is upon such little words that complex meanings can turn. We assume that you will turn to your dictionary when you encounter "antidisestablishmentarianism" or other such unusual polysyllables; but unless we nag you about it, you will rarely slow down for a familiar word like "sever," though its connotations provide a valuable clue to the interpretation of the poem on page 36. Here are the relevant lines:

> Love not me for comely grace,
> For my pleasing eye or face,
> Nor for any outward part;
> No, nor for my constant heart,—
> For these may fail, or turn to ill,
> So thou and I shall sever:

Why "sever"? Why not "part"? Surely it is more romantic. Well, what severs? A knife (he severed his bonds); a saw (he severed an arm); etc. What parts? A comb (he parted his hair); etc. What can be severed but not parted? Consider the frequent contexts: severance pay; he severed himself from all society; till death do us part; I just can't bear to part with it; parting is such sweet sorrow; never more to part; *partir, c'est mourir un peu;* etc. Do you see two fairly distinct patterns forming, in spite of the exceptions that always seem to turn up? One pattern implies something slow and perhaps reluctant; the other is abrupt and impersonal.

"I am tracing her." "I am tracking her." Which of these sentences refers more appropriately to a female bankrobber? Which to a lost sweetheart? Why?

Searching your memory for the contexts in which a word often occurs is your most valuable clue to connotation. Apply this technique liberally, concentrating upon the familiar words whose meanings, as we suggested, may be largely connotative.

THE WORD IN ITS PRESENT CONTEXTS.   By present context we mean the words surrounding a word at the time you meet it. You have inferred the meaning of many a word from the general sense of a phrase or sentence—from present context. However, in addition to its *immediate* present context, a word often partakes of a *larger* present context—the general meaning of a paragraph or chapter or book. Consider this simple illustration:

Just look at all those cats!

This seems straightforward enough; but there would be some change in its meaning if we had learned, three pages before, that the scene was a zoo, or an excavation, or a sewing circle.

If I water the stock, I'll make lots of money.

If the large context is cowpunching, the sentence is not the same as if it is finance; the difference is roughly ten years!

In the following passage, why is the word "scrupulously" used instead of "accurately"?

SLANDER
... His enemies beat him temporarily, not by bending his will, but by wrecking his health. Christmas 1757 saw him on leave after

a physical collapse which looked very like an attack of consumption, involving hemorrhage, fever, and a *certain* hollowness of the chest which never quite left him. He *bore up* as well as he could under the barrage of slander which his enemies *poured in* upon him, including the *foulest* of all, that he was accepting graft; but he had been ill for months when he finally broke down. (Years later, when he was appointed Commander-in-Chief, he was offered a regular salary, but *refused* to accept it. Instead, he asked Congress to pay his expenses; he kept the accounts *scrupulously;* and he presented them without extras at the end of the war. Slanders are always *raised* about great men; but this one slander was never *leveled* at Washington again.)[4]

— Gilbert Highet, "The Old Gentleman" (1953)

Our first step in determining why "scrupulously" is used and not "accurately" is to compare frequent contexts: accurate as the stars; unerring accuracy; he works slowly but accurately; an accurate shot; he has no scruples; an unscrupulous rogue; she was scrupulous in her housework. We see that one has a moral quality that the other lacks. Now, when we consider only the immediate context, we may conclude that "accurately" is the better term because it focuses more narrowly on the idea of "no mistakes" and introduces fewer unrelated ideas. But in the larger context, Washington has been accused of accepting graft; a moral issue has been raised, and "accurately" is not enough to settle it. "Scrupulously" is needed to link the two contexts, with its implication of accuracy plus morality.

Analyze the other words we have italicized. Why "a certain hollowness"; why not "a sort of hollowness," "a kind of hollowness"? Why "he bore up . . . under" instead of just "he bore"? Why "foulest"; why not "meanest," "most inaccurate"?

Why is slander "poured in" in one immediate context, and "raised" in another? When slander is finally "leveled," do we need just the immediate context, or the whole passage, to explain it?

The Word Is Sometimes Equivocal

Whether or not you agree that the pun is the lowest form of humor, you must admit that it is a good way of saying two things at once. The Elizabethans, and such "metaphysical" poets as Donne and Marvell, pun fairly often; but ordi-

---

[4] From *People, Places and Books*, Oxford. Italics added.

narily serious writing secures its double and triple meanings through the use of the related but subtler device of ambiguity.[5] Ambiguity results when a context includes a unit with more than one meaning that fits the context. By capitalizing upon the fact that a word may be equivocal—or better, multivocal—a writer can greatly enrich a passage, and you will miss much if your interpretation restricts each word to a single meaning.

When, in our analysis of the Highet passage on page 32, we decided that "scrupulously" contributed more than "accurately" would have, we did so because "scrupulously" includes among its accepted meanings "accurately" as well as "as if having scruples." The word fitted into the context in more than one way and so enriched the meaning. Similarly we argued that "cash" contributed more meanings to a peculiar context than did "money"; again we seized the opportunities provided by ambiguity.

If it seems surprising that you were penalized for ambiguity in your freshman compositions and are now urged to admire it in literature, perhaps we should try to distinguish between artistic and inartistic ambiguity. What you were alleged to have done was to insert into your composition a term one of whose senses disrupted the context. When read one way, your term made the wrong kind of sense; at very least it blurred the meaning of the passage instead of making it sharper. Since expository prose aims not only to be easily understood but also to eliminate any possible misunderstanding, your ambiguity need not have been very serious in order to blur the meaning. Most literature, however, is concerned less with the avoidance of misunderstanding than with the unification of widely disparate elements. Ordinarily it tries to compress a wealth of ideas into the shortest possible time; hence it often "says two things at once," using ambiguous terms whose multiple meanings contribute to the context.

In so doing literature takes chances, of course. Some of the peripheral meanings of a word may blur the context; but so long as the central ones reinforce it our attention need not wander too far. For example, consider these familiar simple lines from a familiar simple poem:

> . . . all at once, I saw a crowd,
> A host, of golden daffodils.

How does "host" give depth to this straightforward statement? Insofar as it means "a large number" it merely restates

---

[5] A related device, irony, which results when a context is manipulated so that a unit means the contrary of what it ostensibly means, is discussed in Chapter Three, pages 90–93. Dramatic irony, which is even more clearly contextual or structural, appears in Chapter Six, pages 215–219.

the idea of "crowd"; but let us discuss two additional meanings: those which allow the word to be used in the contexts "an armed host" and "host and hostess." Inasmuch as an armed host may be dangerous, the poem has introduced a misleading ambiguity; but inasmuch as an armed host is a fine spectacle, a parade, the meaning may reinforce that of "golden," and the ambiguity is valuable. "Host and hostess" may imply snobbishness, and so mislead us; but it may imply dancing, gaiety, and generosity—and so reinforce the context. ("In sprightly dance," "such a jocund company" and "What wealth the show to me had brought"—all these occur later in the poem; see page 182.)

In seeking out these secondary, apparently irrelevant meanings, give free rein to your imagination; indulge in some word play yourself.

For example, when you were weighing the words "track" and "trace" in the exercise on page 31 you might legitimately have asked the apparently irrelevant question "What runs on tracks?" The answer might have suggested the inflexibility of railroad tracks, or the irresistibility of tank tracks; by comparing either or both with the suggestion of slackness in "harness traces" you might have found one more distinction between the two words.

In a celebrated analysis, one modern critic sets forth about a dozen meanings to be found in the Shakespearean line "Bare ruin'd choirs, where late the sweet birds sang." Without making literature simply a means of testing your own ingenuity, you should be prepared in analysis to turn your imagination loose, to let word associations come freely. Later on you can check your impressions for objectivity by citing frequent contexts; but free association is one way of getting the impressions in the first place.

Meaning Is Often Merely Implied

Since literature usually tries to achieve its effects economically, it has little time for laboring the obvious. We in turn welcome the chance to solve a puzzle, provided it is not too hard for us; furthermore we get an increased sense of personal involvement, perhaps even of proprietorship, when we have contributed some of the work.

Rather than spelling a thing out in explicit detail, literature will often marshal its resources of rhythm, cadence, rhyme, structure, and sound in order to suggest much that it leaves unsaid. Chapters Six and Seven are devoted to the problem of reading "between and around the lines"; here we shall concern ourselves with two facets only: inferential meaning and allusion.

INFERENTIAL MEANING.   Since many times an unexpected word will suggest a whole new situation, one which the context has not previously hinted at, we must maintain a constant lookout for such clues. Odd as it may seem, the hardest part of this detective work is to see that something has gone wrong.

One clue we can watch for is *too much* of a thing. In the first four paragraphs of Poe's "The Tell-Tale Heart," there are four explicit denials of insanity. Even Hamlet's shallow mother knows when she has been nudged too pointedly: "The lady protests too much, methinks."

Here are the opening lines of a sonnet:

> Since there's no help, come, let us kiss and part;
> Nay, I have done; you get no more of me.
> And I am glad, yea, glad with all my heart
> That thus so cleanly I myself can free.

Nothing suspicious here, perhaps, until we remember dimly that a sonnet has only fourteen lines in which to create an effect. Why waste the third line? Why repeat "glad"? Surely if the speaker is trying to be more emphatic, he has chosen a flabby way of doing so: repeating the original weak word and intensifying it with a cliché. And why try to be emphatic anyway; if he is so glad, why does he not just leave? Whom is he trying to convince?

Once we ask these questions, we begin to suspect that he is not glad at all. Turn to page 68 for the whole sonnet, and see if this hunch is correct.

The difficult part of the process here was to see that one "glad" was superfluous. What is meant by "too much"? The only advice we can give you is this: *always be suspicious whenever a passage repeats itself.* Do not settle for the easy answer, "It's there for emphasis"; ask instead, "Why bother to emphasize this? And why do it so obviously?"

An even subtler clue to inferential meaning is *too little* detail. What is not said or not done that we would expect to be done or said? In a given situation we expect a certain type of behavior; if that behavior is not forthcoming we should begin to ask questions.

LOVE NOT ME FOR COMELY GRACE

Love not me for comely grace,
For my pleasing eye or face,
Nor for any outward part;
No, nor for my constant heart,—
For these may fail, or turn to ill,
So thou and I shall sever:
Keep therefore a true woman's eye,
And love me still, but know not why—
So hast thou the same reason still
To dote upon me ever!

—Anon. (1609)

At first glance, this may seem to be the sort of thing that Elizabeth Barrett Browning did so well:

If thou must love me, let it be for nought
Except for love's sake only.

A man is saying, "Don't love me for my good looks" (but note that they *are* good looks, not merely looks!). We expect him to base his claim upon the deeper things: his constant heart, his devoted soul. But no, that constant heart "may fail, or turn to ill." And incidentally, what about *her* pleasing face; when does he start praising her?

And what will happen if face and heart do change? Any fear of the consequences, any anticipation of pain? No; they will simply sever (and as we saw before, there is a difference between severing and parting). And what if she does follow his advice; what reward can she expect? His undying love? No; she will gain—what? The privilege of doting (not loving, mind!), doting upon him forever.

Can you see now the absolute necessity of asking yourself over and over, *what does this add up to?* What has been left out that I would normally expect to find? Why stop to emphasize this point; why get so excited? Once you have become suspicious, it is often relatively easy to infer the meaning.

ALLUSION.   An allusion is an undeveloped reference to some thing or event outside the selection; in literature such references are usually to persons, places, or events in mythology, history, or literature. It is sometimes used as a brief example or parallel; more often its purpose is to secure, economically, some of the intensity of the original. To reduce the number of technical terms we include in the category of allusion a related device which aims at the same effects: the device of echoing a famous literary passage.

Insofar as allusion is an attempt to conjure up quickly vivid associations which cluster around the original, there is not much point in telling you to track it down in a reference book.

> He dreamed of Thebes and Camelot
> And Priam's neighbors.[6]

When you encounter these lines, the associations either come immediately or they do not come at all. Looking up "Priam" may net you the information that he was the legendary king of Troy and father of Hector; but what have you gained? Unless you happen to have read the last book of the *Iliad,* with its moving account of his pathetic but dignified negotiation for the body of his son, you will almost certainly miss the ironic juxtaposition, "Priam's neighbors."

Nevertheless, a little is better than nothing. At worst your research will show you that these names are significant, and you may read them in such a way that the more fortunate of your audience are free to get the associations. At best, when you notice the same people and places turning up again and again, you may become curious enough to read the originals; in frequent allusion you will discover an anthology of "the world's best literature" compiled not by some educator or other but by the makers of literature themselves.

Fortunately such research is rarely difficult. Good reference books are available in any worth-while library, and the staff of the reference department are almost always eager to help. Furthermore, adequate reference books are turning up in inexpensive editions; for example, the best mythology on the market, Graves', is available only in paperback.[7] Do not forget the dictionary, or the Gazeteer of Geographical Names and Biographical Dictionary found at the back of some dictionaries. A book of common quotations—Bartlett's will do—can sometimes help you to trace echoes of other works, as for example in this pastiche, written by one of the authors for a colleague who was departing for England on sabbatical leave. Can you identify five of the nine works echoed?

---

[6] Reprinted by permission from E. A. Robinson, "Miniver Cheevy," in *The Town Down the River,* Charles Scribner's Sons, 1910.

[7] Robert Graves, *The Greek Myths,* vols. 1 and 2, Penguin Books, 1955, #1026, 1027.

THE COLD FAMILIAR FACES

To one who's long been in Hawaii pent,
(With brightness *always* falling from the air),
'Tis sweet to travel on the Continent
And steam a season in wool underwear.

Oh to be in England, now that winter's there!
Or whan Aprille and the London soote
Drencche hem to the boote—
And back and side go bare
Nevaire!

Then once more into breeches, friends, once more
Create thee stately mukluks for thy sole;
Prepare, of course, to warm both hands before
The fires of life. But just in case, take coal.

—J. R. L.

The Word Is Often Figurative

In treating figures of speech we must proceed cautiously, because the subject is full of confusion. We meet slangsters who do not make a dozen coldly literal statements per year but who expect literature to "mean what it says"; at the other extreme there are those who profess to find a pulsating personification in the phrase "foot of the stairs." Maybe we should offer a few broad principles before getting down to specifics.

The chief purpose of figurative language is rarely ornamentation. Tastes change, of course. Sometimes a significant body of enduring literature is produced by schools or periods that prize decoration hugely (the epic and the Elizabethan are examples), but by far their more frequent product is a mass of literary curiosities. To illustrate what happens, a homely example will serve; how many of the following 1957 slang terms are still current when you read them: egg-head, real gone, don't knock the rock, real George, cube? We predict (with perhaps some malice) that those whose purpose is to make speech vivid will have been worn out and discarded; those which contribute new insights to experience may survive.

The chief purpose of figurative language is to deepen meaning by comparing one concept with another. Far from being ornamentation, simile and metaphor and symbol are ways of thinking. In *simile* the concepts are compared as distinct entities (A is like B); in *metaphor* the comparison is compressed to an equation (A is B); in *symbol* the comparison has been further compressed to substitution (A is B). Knowledge can thus be synthesized, and new experience can take on some of the connotations of the old. To sum up with an example, probably the main reason for using the phrase "All hands on deck" is not that "hands" is more vivid than "men" or "sailors," but that it contains additional relevant implications—manual labor and manual dexterity, to mention only two.

Vividness is, however, necessary; figurative language must achieve some degree of surprise. Surprise—your surprise—is the criterion we must use if the category "figurative language" is not to become well-nigh all-inclusive. If during analysis you are reading carefully enough to detect, say, ambiguity, you may safely treat as a routine problem in word analysis any figurative language that is not vivid enough to draw itself separately to your attention. This rules out of consideration buried metaphor, which must be excavated by etymologists,[8] and dead metaphor, which has been assimilated into common speech so thoroughly as to have lost its original impact—"the hands of a clock," "rush into print." By basing our distinction upon your surprise we increase the likelihood of your neglecting passages that have become overfamiliar through frequent quotation. But that is not an unmixed danger: to gauge the comparative originality of, say, "all the world's a stage" and "the marriage of true minds" requires a considerable literary background; lacking such background, you will perhaps be making a more honest and, in our opinion, more relevant response if you rely on your own surprise rather than on the research of literary historians.

Figurative language, then, is that which expresses or implies a comparison, usually not literal. Its function is to deepen meanings by introducing new associations. Although it must be vivid enough to draw itself to our attention as a separate entity, vividness or embellishment are not usually its chief purpose. In this course we shall not attempt to distinguish between such tropes as meiosis, synecdoche, oxymoron, hendiadys, etc.; let us consider only simile, metaphor, and symbol.

SIMILE AND METAPHOR. As you know, a simile states a comparison ("My luve is like a red, red rose"), and a metaphor implies one by compressing it into an equation ("There is a garden in her face"); but the major problems facing us as readers are the same for both: Why make a comparison at all; why not use a more precise word? Why make this particular comparison rather than another?

Expressed in these terms, the questions almost dictate the procedure by which we find their answers. We cast about in our minds for a more precise word: "He

[8] For a contrasting viewpoint, see Dorothy Kaucher, "Interpretation and the Etymon," *Quarterly Journal of Speech*, 38 (October, 1952), 300.

travelled like a typical executive" becomes "He was driven to the airport by his chauffeur," and we detect flabbiness. If we agree that a comparison is necessary, we look for one more appropriate. We search the context for clues to the alleged resemblance; "all the world's a stage," for example, occurs in this context:

> And all the men and women merely players;
> They have their exits and their entrances,
> And one man in his time plays many parts,
> His acts being seven ages:

We try to find other resemblances for ourselves. And then we test the connotations of the figure and of its possible alternatives by recalling the contexts in which the key terms appear. (The key terms here are obviously "world" and "stage.") And to prod our imaginations, we look for possible ambiguities.

In thus discovering the new associations contributed by simile and metaphor, we may encounter two additional problems: mixed metaphor and bizarre metaphor.

Mixed Metaphor: A rapid shift from one metaphor to another may cause the denotations to clash, often with puzzling or ludicrous results: "I take that alleged chiseling upon my own head, and let the chips fall where they may!" Mixed similes are less frequent, perhaps because the fact of comparison is more insistent; we include mixed similes within the category "mixed metaphor."

In expository prose, mixed metaphor is usually so obvious that it presents little problem to analysis; unless the ludicrous effect is intentional, the blunder simply should not be there. But in more evocative literature the comparisons are sometimes so daring and so closely juxtaposed that we may wonder whether they are the result of carelessness or whether they are legitimate metaphors unusually compressed and highly charged. For example, what are we to make of this?

> . . . to suffer
> The slings and arrows of outrageous fortune,
> Or to take arms against a sea of troubles,
> And by opposing, end them.

> Does this suggest a fully accoutered Quixote striding manfully into the surf? Or is it the product of a mind flashing from association to association with the clarity as well as the speed of lightning? Is it a powerful compression of this argument: Should I battle my troubles? My troubles are (as wide as, as

deep as, as powerful as, as relentless as, as unchanging as) the
sea; a battle also is like the sea (as in such common phrases as
"the tide of battle," "the battle surged," "the third wave of the
attack," "we were swamped")?

This problem can easily take us beyond the process of analysis—of determining what is there—and into the process of evaluation—of deciding whether
"what is there" is worth while. Although the distinctions are hard to maintain at
this point, we prefer to confine our discussion of evaluation to Chapters One and
Eleven. Here we suggest only that for analytical purposes you consider mixed
metaphor to be a *sign of emotional intensity* and look *immediately* for other clues
which will confirm or deny that diagnosis.

> MOCK ON, MOCK ON, VOLTAIRE, ROUSSEAU
> Mock on, mock on, Voltaire, Rousseau:
> Mock on, mock on: 'tis all in vain!
> You throw the sand against the wind,
> And the wind blows it back again.
>
> And every sand becomes a Gem
> Reflected in the beams divine;
> Blown back they blind the mocking Eye,
> But still in Israel's paths they shine.
>
> The atoms of Democritus
> And Newton's Particles of light
> Are sands upon the Red Sea shore,
> Where Israel's tents do shine so bright.
> —William Blake (1809)

In this example we find a number of corroborative clues—the repetitions of
"mock on," the intensives, and the loaded adjectives—and so we can safely conclude that the mixing of metaphors indicates high feeling. If, however, we find
no such confirmation, we must conclude either that the intent is humor or that a
blunder has been made.

Bizarre Metaphor: Even more difficult to weigh is bizarre metaphor (or simile)
—metaphor that calls strong attention to itself, metaphor for metaphor's sake. If
the metaphor is not vivid, of course, it may escape notice; but if it is extremely
vivid it attracts so much notice that we neglect the context.

Bizarre metaphor may be a sign of extreme tension. The overwrought Macbeth, contemplating murder, delivers these famous lines:

> . . . his virtues
> Will plead like angels, trumpet-tongu'd, against
> The deep damnation of his taking-off;
> And pity, like a naked new-born babe
> Striding the blast, or heaven's cherubin hors'd
> Upon the sightless couriers of the air,
> Shall blow the horrid deed in every eye,
> That tears shall drown the wind.
> —William Shakespeare, *Macbeth* (1606?)

Far more often bizarre metaphor is simply decoration. Temporarily our attention is being withdrawn from the subject at hand and focused instead upon a fanciful digression, or perhaps upon the skill of the speaker. There is almost certain to be some loss of sincerity—at times a valuable clue in itself: for example, when Macbeth "discovers" the body of the slain Duncan, he refers to

> His silver skin lac'd with his golden blood.

But the comparative insincerity may be simple exuberance, not necessarily to be scorned in an art that can take itself too seriously. Given the long tradition of lovers' sighing like furnace, is there anything to be said for toying with the subject of love?

THERE IS A GARDEN IN HER FACE

> There is a garden in her face
> Where roses and white lilies grow;
> A heavenly paradise is that place
> Wherein all pleasant fruits do flow.
> There cherries grow which none may buy,
> Till "Cherry ripe" themselves do cry.

> Those cherries fairly do enclose
> Of orient pearl a double row,
> Which when her lovely laughter shows
> They look like rosebuds filled with snow;
> Yet them nor peer nor prince can buy,
> Till "Cherry ripe" themselves do cry.

> Her eyes like angels watch them still,
> Her brows like bended bows do stand,
> Threatening with piercing frowns to kill
> All that attempt, with eye or hand,
>   Those sacred cherries to come nigh
>   Till "Cherry ripe" themselves do cry.
>   —Thomas Campion (1617)

The question is, of course, whether the charm of the conceit can so control our reaction that we do not think automatically—and in this case disastrously—of spades and hoes and fertilizer.[9]

In making such judgments—and we are now clearly in the realm of evaluation—we will be aided greatly by awareness of Tone. In the two selections following, try first to decide whether the similes and metaphors are in fact bizarre; then try to decide whether the showing off—if it is such—is justified.

> The One remains, the many change and pass;
> Heaven's light forever shines, Earth's shadows fly;
> Life, like a dome of many-colored glass,
> Stains the white radiance of eternity,
> Until Death tramples it to fragments. . . .
>   —Percy Bysshe Shelley, "Adonais" (1821)

> . . . A boy is Truth with dirt on its face, Wisdom with bubble gum in its hair and the Hope of the future with a frog in its pocket.
>
> A boy has the appetite of a horse, the digestion of a sword-swallower, the energy of a pocket-size atomic bomb, the curiosity of a cat, the lungs of a dictator, the imagination of a Paul Bunyon, the shyness of a violet, the audacity of a steel trap, the enthusiasm of a firecracker, and when he makes something he has five thumbs on each hand.
>   —Alan Beck, *What Is a Boy?* (1949)

SYMBOL. There are two senses in which a word may be a symbol. As the arbitrary representative or equivalent of a concept, a word is a symbol for that concept. But a word may also be a literary symbol, and it is with this second sense of the term that we are now concerned.

---

[9] See Gail Boardman, *Oral Communication of Literature,* Prentice-Hall, 1952, p. 87, for a highly unfavorable criticism based on the assumption that it cannot so control our reaction.

A literary symbol is a comparison which has been so compressed as to seem a substitution, of the order ($A \not{is} B$), in which one half of the equation has disappeared. But since there is rarely a one-to-one correspondence—there are usually many A's for one B—it may be more profitable to consider a symbol to be a word or phrase referring to some thing or event around which are gathered a vast number of associations, opinions, attitudes, and beliefs. Consider the meanings that gather around two sticks arranged thus: +. The cross can suggest Jesus, Redemption, Christianity, the Roman Catholic Church, the Crusades, the Inquisition, St. George, Switzerland, the International Red Cross, plus a host of others—plus all the multifarious associations, opinions, attitudes, images, and beliefs that cluster around each of these concepts. What meanings are associated with the cartoon character Uncle Sam? With the statue in New York harbor? With a red star? With this: $$$$$? With the terms "Wall Street" or "brass"?

Often the meanings to be assigned to the literary symbol are dictated not by convention but by the context of the work in which it appears. Maeterlinck's Blue Bird is a familiar example; so is the albatross in "The Rime of the Ancient Mariner." You might look up Elmer Rice's *The Adding Machine* for another clear example.

The major problem raised by the symbol—other than those discussed in the section on simile and metaphor—is that of clarity. We generally cannot look for a simple translation, a one-to-one correspondence; Coleridge's albatross is not simply another way of saying "fate." Usually many associations are attached to a symbol, some of them tenuous indeed. What is the significance of "Byzantium" in the following?

SAILING TO BYZANTIUM

That is no country for old men. The young
In one another's arms, birds in the trees
—Those dying generations—at their song,
The salmon-falls, the mackerel-crowded seas,
Fish, flesh, or fowl, commend all summer long
Whatever is begotten, born, and dies.
Caught in that sensual music all neglect
Monuments of unageing intellect.

An aged man is but a paltry thing,
A tattered coat upon a stick, unless

Soul clap its hands and sing, and louder sing
For every tatter in its mortal dress,
Nor is there singing school but studying
Monuments of its own magnificence;
And therefore I have sailed the seas and come
To the holy city of Byzantium.

O sages standing in God's holy fire
As in the gold mosaic of a wall,
Come from the holy fire, perne in a gyre,
And be the singing-masters of my soul.
Consume my heart away; sick with desire
And fastened to a dying animal
It knows not what it is; and gather me
Into the artifice of eternity.

Once out of nature I shall never take
My bodily form from any natural thing,
But such a form as Grecian goldsmiths make
Of hammered gold and gold enamelling
To keep a drowsy Emperor awake;
Or set upon a golden bough to sing
To lords and ladies of Byzantium
Of what is past, or passing, or to come.[10]

—William Butler Yeats (1927)

The use of free association is perhaps the best approach to the symbol; test the relative subjectivity of your conclusions by citing other contexts. The technique does not always work easily, however; since modern authors in particular must manufacture their own symbols, we sometimes have to read a number of their works in order to gain a context large enough to limit the possible associations that might attach to a major symbol. Fortunately editors and anthologists generally make some attempt to explain such semi-private symbols; Yeats' poem is often printed with a footnote referring to intellectual beauty, or to the pleasures of the intellect as opposed to those of the body. Our task consists of

[10] From William Butler Yeats, *Collected Poems,* Definitive Edition, copyright, 1956, by The Macmillan Company, and used with permission of The Macmillan Company.

verifying such hints by close study of the selection, and by tracking down other selections to which editors refer.[11]

Meaning Is Often a Function of Sound

About twenty-five years ago it was fashionable to compile lists of the Ten Most Beautiful Words in the Language; by striking coincidence these beautiful words almost invariably referred to "beautiful" things, and it is now generally agreed that the search for words of intrinsic beauty is a profitless task. Furthermore, most authorities now deny that any one sound in English is indicative of any one emotion or mood, although there is still some argument on the matter.

Nevertheless, we do not have to read "Jabberwocky" to realize that in a well-managed context a skillful combination of sound will greatly reinforce meaning. We shall venture deeper into the subject in Chapter Seven; for the present we shall consider only a few simple facts about the sounds of English, in the hope that you will increase your enjoyment of literature by reading with your ears as well as eyes.

Have you noticed, for example, that plosive consonants—*p, b, t, d, k, g*—because they cannot be prolonged, give a slightly abrupt effect to the words in which they appear? Or that a vowel followed by a voiced consonant—*b, d, g, v, th, z, m, n, ng*—will take longer to say than if followed by a voiceless or "whispered" consonant and that it will take even longer to say if it is followed by no consonant at all? (Compare vowel length in base, bays, bay; leaf, leave, lee.) Have you noticed that, where context permits, some vowels usually take longer to say than others? ("Bit" is usually shorter than "beat," "but" is generally shorter than "bat," and "took" is shorter than "talk.")

Begin to assess words for the appropriateness of their sound to their meaning. Notice that you can almost literally spit out the word "spit," that you can snap "snap," and crash "crash." (If you are tempted to talk in sound effects, let us remind you that even onomatapoetic words are far from realistic: a polylingual rooster would say "cock-a-doodle-doo" in English, "kee-keree-kee" in German, "koe-kay-koe-koe" in Japanese, and "koe-koe-ree-koe" in French!)

Watch for consonant clusters, "tongue-twisters," used to slow down a line. "Now, at the last gasp of Love's latest breath," page 68, is a good example; exaggerate the reading and discover what your tongue must do in order to say it: "last gasp" requires you to go from *s* to *t* and back to *g*, whereupon you must

---

[11] For example, you may gain additional insights by studying Yeats' "Byzantium" and others of his poems written during the late 1920's. Most of them appeared in *The Tower,* Macmillan, 1928, and *The Winding Stair,* Macmillan, 1933.

drop to *a* and swing up to *s* again. What happens on "Love's latest"? On "latest breath"?

Study the movements of your tongue, lips, and throat and try to discover how this tour de force of Pope's gains its effects:

An Echo to the Sense

'Tis not enough no harshness gives offense;
The sound must seem an echo to the sense:
Soft is the strain when Zephyr gently blows,
And the smooth stream in smoother numbers flows;
But when loud surges lash the sounding shore,
The hoarse, rough verse should like the torrent roar:
When Ajax strives some rock's vast weight to throw,
The line too labours, and the words move slow;
Not so, when swift Camilla scours the plain,
Flies o'er th' unbending corn, and skims along the main.
  —*Essay on Criticism* (1711), II

Meaning Is a Function of Structure

The explanation of the principle that meaning is a function of structure must wait until Chapters Six and Seven; here we will do little more than remind you of knowledge gained laboriously in freshman composition—that there are meanings implicit in the way in which words are assembled into sentences.

SENTENCE LENGTH.   We tend to shorten sentences when we have something important or complex to communicate. Short sentences, then, may be a sign of emphasis or of complexity; and if the matter turns out not to have warranted the treatment, we may infer a tone of naïveté or pedantry. Again, since breathing rate quickens during excitement, short sentences may imply intensity or haste. Finally, they may imply a reluctance to use "unnecessary" words; we may infer a laconic tone, or a cryptic one, or curtness, etc.

This is enough to get you started again. Note that these principles may apply to clauses and phrases as well; you may be misled by long meandering sentences whose phrases and clauses are nevertheless abrupt. When in doubt read the sentence aloud; your ear may detect rhythms which are lost to the eye.

INVERSION.   Generally the most emphatic part of a sentence—or a phrase or clause—is at the end, and the second most emphatic at the beginning. Hence an inversion—a departure from normal English order, subject, verb, and object—

may subtly indicate an emphasis. Compare, for example, the two sentences following:

> There is something that doesn't love a wall.

> Something there is that doesn't love a wall.

Unless we are curious about inversions we shall miss a subtle but important clue to Robert Frost's "Mending Wall," page 222, which begins with the second sentence above. Why, we ask, should a word as vague as "something" receive such emphasis? If the idea is so important, why does Frost not use a more precise word? By searching for additional clues, especially in lines 10, 18, 36–37, 40–43, we suspect that the something is so mysterious that it cannot be labeled.

We might go further and, recalling *The New Yorker's* parody of *Time* magazine, "Backward ran the sentences until reeled the mind," note the hint of literary affection in an inversion. Does the formality of Frost's first line help to keep the subsequent informality within bounds, so that it does not seem rambling?

> Almost thou persuadest me.

> Thou almost persuadest me.

Which should Agrippa have said to Paul, and why?

SUSPENSION.   A sentence is suspended when a separate grammatical unit—for example, this clause you are reading—is inserted between subject and verb or verb and object. Frequently a suspension serves chiefly to vary the rhythm, but sometimes it provides a direct clue to meaning. Anything that can deflect a strongly motivated statement must have had an even stronger motivation; therefore we should first examine the interruption to discover why it is so important. Second, and perhaps more useful, by delaying the solution an interruption can create suspense and thus emphasize the conclusion; or, by forcing us to pause it can in effect make the preceding material into an emphatic "end of a sentence."

In an intense passage, then, a suspension probably contains valuable material, and we look closely at the interpolation; in sentences that do not carry a strong emotive charge, we should look closely at the material that surrounds the interruption. Sometimes neither option is productive, and we may conclude that the suspension was used to vary the rhythm.

BALANCE.   Balanced sentences are those in which contrasting ideas have been given similar and often parallel constructions and approximately equal length. To illustrate briefly, instead of at length, a sentence is balanced, or else it is not. Our illustration is far too neat—it comes close to the chime of verse; but in other authors, or indeed in the present sentence, the balanced elements may not be so conspicuous.

Obviously balance is a way of pointing contrasts, and thereby of refining the meanings of each of the contrasted elements. Often too it is a way of increasing the formality of a statement, so that the tone is somewhat more impersonal.

Meaning Is a Function of Time

This highfalutin heading is intended to impress you with the solemnity of the obvious fact that meanings change. Most of us know that "charity" once meant "brotherly love" and make the necessary adjustment in our interpretation of the familiar lines:

> Though I speak with the tongues of men and of angels, and have not charity, I am become as sounding brass, or a tinkling cymbal.
> —Corinthians I, 12:i

In a line quoted a few pages back, "Now, at the last gasp of Love's latest breath," few of us would need a dictionary to tell us that "latest" means "last." And yet how many students accept uncritically Pope's line, "And the smooth stream in smoother *numbers* flows"?

A spectacular opportunity for misinterpretation occurs in Act I of *Hamlet,* in which Horatio and Marcellus try to prevent Hamlet from following the ghost; Hamlet's reply, "I'll make a ghost of him that lets me!" uses a verb that meant in 1600 precisely the opposite of what it means today. Portia's line "So shines a good deed in a naughty world" is not quite as priggish as the modern meanings of "naughty" would suggest. And as little as a hundred years ago Dickens could use the phrase "brave in ribbons."

Therefore we must emphasize the necessity of special care when you are studying a selection that does not seem modern. To remove part of your burden at the beginning, in this textbook we include with each practice selection the date either of composition or of first publication; but when you choose works outside you may have no such hints. You can, of course, look up the author's birth and death dates in any reasonably complete dictionary of biography; but ordinarily you can find some trick of construction or punctuation which suggests that the style is not contemporary. Here are some quotations from the practice materials in the first four chapters; what hints do you find to suggest that they are not modern?

So thou and I shall sever.

And every sand becomes a Gem.

Yet them nor peer nor prince can buy.

And I am glad, yea, glad with all my heart.

With suppliant knee, and deifie his power.

Mighty and dreadfull, for, thou art not soe.

Like corpses in a charnel.

Whenever you find such hints keep a dictionary handy.

Here too we should emphasize the necessity of using a *good* dictionary; the more complete, the better. The small "handy vest-pocket size" presents a double danger: not only does it give inadequate definitions for such words as it does attempt to define, but for your purpose, it fails to limit sufficiently the other possibilities. If you look up a word in an unabridged dictionary, and find no definition which fits the context you are studying, you know you have a puzzle on your hands: you might suspect a coinage, or a unique use of the word; or you might find that you have misread the context. But if you look the word up in a push-and-shove dictionary (in which "push" is defined as "shove" and "shove" as "push"), you have no such assurance.

SUMMARY

In summary, the key to successful word analysis is the question: WHAT IS GAINED BY USING THIS WORD INSTEAD OF ITS POSSIBLE ALTERNATIVES? It should be asked not only of the unfamiliar words but of all the important words in the selection. Whether you answer it with the aid of a good dictionary or infer it from the frequent contexts in which the words occur, you will have to answer it, and in some detail.

EXERCISES AND ASSIGNMENTS

The Role of the Author

1. Do you agree or disagree with the following statement? "The details we might glean from biography are as likely to mislead as to help." Defend your answer with specific examples.

2. Shakespearean love sonnets XVII–CXXVI were pretty certainly written to a man; does this fact help to explain the viciousness of the bedchamber scene in *Hamlet,* or does it explain it away?

3. With information gleaned from other courses discuss the ways in which the life of each of the following individuals sheds valuable light upon specific works of theirs. In what ways are such data completely misleading? Wolfgang Amadeus Mozart, Frédéric Chopin, Richard Wagner; Paul Gauguin, Vincent van Gogh, Francisco Goya; Christopher Marlowe, Alexander Pope, Robert Burns.

4. Scene familiar to moviegoers a few years back: author (composer, painter) yearns toward sweetheart, squints at ceiling, dashes off masterpiece; "It's beeyootiful!" she breathes. Was this Hollywood cliché merely an exaggeration of the usual method of composition, or was it completely false? Before you answer, consider the following items:

> Your own experience in composition classes.
>
> The evidence in exercise 4 under The Community of Meaning, page 54.
>
> Coleridge's claim that "Kubla Khan" came to him in a dream.
>
> Your knowledge of Hollywood's production methods.
>
> The evidence gained from a comparison of the 1597 and 1625 versions of Bacon's "Of Studies," or the 1899 and 1920 versions of Markham's "The Man with the Hoe."
>
> Fitzgerald's four versions of the *Rubáiyát.*

5. If exercise 4 interested you, read Brooks and Warren, *Understanding Poetry,* rev. ed., "How Poems Come About: Intention and Meaning," chap. IX; or Thomas and Brown, *Reading Poems,* Oxford, 1941, "The Creation of Poems," part VIII.

ADDITIONAL EXERCISES

[*Note:* For what seem to us eminently practical reasons we have taken the unusual position that you should ignore the author until the very last stages of preparation. We certainly do not favor the kind of "compromise" that would send you immediately to a pony. But as teachers in the liberal arts, we do not want you to accept our judgment uncritically. Hence the following questions are more discursive, and less closely connected with oral interpretation, than those in the rest of this book.]

1. If any of your classmates is a senior or a graduate majoring in English literature, ask for an extemporaneous report upon one of the following topics: The Image of the Author in the Eighteenth and Nineteenth Centuries; The Influence of Romanticism upon Popular Literary Theory; The Moderns Versus the Romantics; Critical Views of Shelley; The Romantic Ideal in Textbooks of Oral Interpretation.

2. Buffon said *"Le style c'est l'homme."* Milton believed that "he who would . . . write well, . . . ought himself to be a true poem," and Quintilian claimed that an orator must first and foremost be a good man. Do you agree or disagree? Is it possible to admire an author but dislike his works, or vice versa?

3. If your answer to exercise 2 was "No," how do you account for the following?

a. Francis Bacon supported Essex and then became special counsel to secure his execution. He wrote an essay "Of Friendship." He pleaded guilty to accepting bribes as lord chancellor; he wrote a number of essays upon government, honor, and reputation, etc.

b. Elizabeth Barrett Browning's happy domestic life is as well known as are Burns' infidelities; Burns' love songs seem the more sincere.

c. Southey supported Coleridge's family as well as his own; the ridicule he received from Byron, Moore, and Carroll is generally conceded to have been deserved.

d. Out of a rather unsavory affair with the wife of his patron came Wagner's *Tristan und Isolde*.

e. Dryden celebrated Cromwell's Protectorate and Charles II's Restoration; he wrote satires for and against the Church of England; critics often comment upon the manliness, reasonableness, and independence of his poems and essays.

f. Apparently Milton and Beethoven were, in their domestic life, singularly unpleasant people.

4. If your answer to exercise 2 was "Yes," how do you account for the concept of "skill" as set forth in Chapter One, or for the view that in order to read well you must make the material a part of you?

5. Is the relationship between the artist and his work similar to the relationship between the public and that work? Necessarily so? Necessarily not so?

Connotation and Denotation

1. Elaborating upon a quip of Bertrand Russell's, *The New Statesman and Nation* offered prizes for the best "conjugations" of "irregular verbs." Some of the entries cited in the June 5, 1948, issue were:

I am unfortunate. You are careless. He is asking for it.

I am beautiful. You have quite good features. She isn't bad looking, if you like that type.

I am fastidious. You are fussy. He is an old woman.

I day dream. You are an escapist. He ought to see [a psychiatrist].

I have about me something of the subtle, haunting, mysterious fragrance of the Orient. You rather overdo it, dear. She stinks.

a. "Conjugate" the following:
I think for myself.
I have a normal interest in boys (girls).
I try to contribute to class discussions.
My readings are lively.
I expect my date to show me a little courtesy.

b. Bring to class "conjugations" of six of your own "irregular verbs."

2. Account for the differences among the various *Iliad* translations on pages 153–156.

3. Discuss in class the meanings of such "flavoring particles" as: well now, it seems to

me, indeed, of course. Do those classmates who have studied German have any advantage here?

4. For a detailed examination of the way in which connotations may reinforce each other, see the sample analysis of a poem by Keats, pp. 197–200.

5. Which do you think will ordinarily contribute more to the meaning of a word, connotation or denotation? Why?

The Uniqueness of Meaning

1. Study the chapter on "perception" in your psychology textbook. Can any two people even "see" the same event?

2. Compare the readings of familiar scenes from *Hamlet* as recorded by Barrymore, Gielgud, and Olivier. To what extent do the differences arise out of minor tricks of style?

3. To one allomorph of humanity, geraniums have a delicate pleasant odor; to another they smell like mold. To which class do you belong? How will the two interpret Eliot's lines in "Rhapsody on a Windy Night":

> The reminiscence comes
> Of sunless dry geraniums
> And dust in crevices.[12]

How could the former possibly understand them?

4. On page 63 is the statement that "it is doubtful that you completely understand anything if you cannot express it, however falteringly, in your own words." Is this oversimplifying? Are we completely wrong?

The Community of Meaning

1. Read the chapters on attitude and prejudice in your psychology text to test this statement from Gardner Murphy and Rensis Likert, *Public Opinion and the Individual,* Harper, 1948:

> . . . it now appears clear that the individual usually acquires his prejudices against a minority group *not* primarily from contact with this minority group but from contact with the *prevailing attitude toward this minority group.*

What research is cited to confirm or deny this conclusion? What are the implications for the claim that connotation is largely societal?

2. To what extent is the following parody the logical extension of Woolbert and Nelson's position as reported on page 27? Where is the *non sequitur,* if any?

THE MEANING OF GLORY

". . . There's glory for you!"

"I don't know what you mean by 'glory,' " Alice said.

---

[12] From *Collected Poems 1909–1935* by T. S. Eliot, copyright, 1936, by Harcourt, Brace and Company, Inc., and reprinted with their permission.

Humpty Dumpty smiled contemptuously. "Of course you don't—
till I tell you. I meant 'there's a nice knock-down argument for you!' "

"But 'glory' doesn't mean 'a nice knock-down argument,' " Alice
objected.

"When *I* use a word," Humpty Dumpty said, in rather a scornful
tone, "it means just what I choose it to mean—neither more nor less."

"The question is," said Alice, "whether you *can* make words mean
so many different things."

"The question is," said Humpty Dumpty, "which is to be master—
that's all."

Alice was too much puzzled to say anything; so after a minute
Humpty Dumpty began again. "They've a temper, some of them—particularly verbs: they're the proudest—adjectives you can do anything
with, but not verbs—however *I* can manage the whole lot of them!
Impenetrability! That's what *I* say!"

"Would you tell me, please," said Alice, "what that means?"

"Now you talk like a reasonable child," said Humpty Dumpty, looking very much pleased. "I meant by 'impenetrability' that we've had
enough of that subject, and it would be just as well if you'd mention
what you mean to do next, as I suppose you don't mean to stop here
all the rest of your life."

"That's a great deal to make one word mean," Alice said in a thoughtful tone.

"When I make a word do a lot of work like that," said Humpty
Dumpty, "I always pay it extra."

—Lewis Carroll, *Through the Looking Glass* (1872)

3. What is Pater's position in "Style and the Man," p. 157?

4. We have suggested that as the author struggles to embody his meaning in words
his original concepts, if not his conceptions, will doubtless be modified. Here are
three drafts of a passage in "Lycidas." Which of Milton's concepts changed; which
remained constant?

a.   Bring the rathe primrose that unwedded dies
collu colouring the pale cheeke of uninjoyd love
and that sad floure that strove
to write his owne woes on the vermeil graine
next adde Narcissus y^t still weeps in vaine
the woodbine and ye pancie freak't w.th jet
the glowing violet
the cowslip wan that hangs his pensive head
and every bud that sorrows liverie weares
let Daffadillies fill thire cups with teares
bid Amaranthus all his beautie shed
to strew the laureat herse &c

b. Bring the rathe primrose that forsaken dies
the tufted crowtoe and pale Gessamin

the white pinke, and ye pansie freakt wth jet
the glowing violet   the well-attir'd woodbine
the muske rose and *the garish columbine*
wth cowslips wan that hang the pensive head

                                    ×   weare   ×   weares
and every flower that sad escutcheon ˄ *beares* imbroidrie *beares*
2 &*let* daffadillies fill thire cups wth teares
1   bid Amaranthus all his beauties shed
to strew &c.

c.   Bring the rathe Primrose that forsaken dies.
           The tufted Crow-toe, and pale Gessamine,
           The white Pink, and the Pansie freakt with jeat,
           The glowing Violet.
           The Musk-rose, and the well-attir'd Woodbine,
           With Cowslips wan that hang the pensive hed,
           And every flower that sad embroidery wears:
           Bid *Amaranthus* all his beauty shed,
           And Daffadillies fill their cups with tears,
           To strew the Laureat Herse where *Lycid* lies.[13]

5. Compare the 1899 version of "The Man with the Hoe," p. 186, with that of the 1920 version, to be found in almost any anthology of comparatively recent poetry.

ADDITIONAL EXERCISES

1. For an enlightening discussion of the work habits of a number of authors, see Brooks and Warren, *Understanding Poetry,* rev. ed., chap. IX.
2. For further study of the meaning of meaning, see some of the following:
Ayer, A. J., *Language, Truth and Logic,* Oxford, 1936.
Chase, Stuart, *The Tyranny of Words,* Harcourt, Brace, 1938.
Hayakawa, S. I., *Language in Thought and Action,* Harcourt, Brace, 1949.
Hayakawa, S. I. (ed.), *Language, Meaning and Maturity,* Harper, 1954.
Hayakawa, S. I. (ed.), *Our Language and Our World,* Harper, 1959.
Langer, Susanne K., *Philosophy in a New Key,* Harvard Press, 1942. (Also in paperback: M25 in Mentor Series.)
Mead, George H., *Mind, Self and Society,* University of Chicago Press, 1934.
Ogden, C. K., and Richards, I. A., *The Meaning of Meaning,* 3rd ed., Harcourt, Brace, 1930.
Richards, I. A., *Practical Criticism,* Harcourt, Brace, 1929. (Also in paperback: HB 16 in Harvest Books.)

---

[13] From *Milton's Poetical Works,* vol. 1. Reprinted by permission of The University of Illinois Press.

Richards, I. A., *How to Read a Page,* Norton, 1942.

Sapir, Edward, *Language,* Harcourt, Brace, 1921. (Also in paperback: HB7 in Harvest Book Series.)

Using the Dictionary

1. As a group project, compare the resources offered by the following: *The American College Dictionary; Century Dictionary; Dictionary of American English; Concise Oxford Dictionary; Funk & Wagnalls New College Standard Dictionary; Webster's New Collegiate Dictionary; Webster's New International Dictionary; Webster's New World Dictionary.*

2. Using your own dictionary, distinguish between the following pairs: infer, imply; Troy, Troyes; *mutatis mutandis, modus operandi;* like, as; Areopagus, Aeolian; verge, edge; *esprit,* élan; Castalia, Castlereagh; *Weltanschauung, Weltschmerz;* xenophobe, Xenophon.

3. Where does your dictionary list the following words—in the main text or in a separate section? Which words are still considered foreign? How does your dictionary indicate such words? Which words are misspelled? longeur, chauffeur, di penates, gemutlich, gnothi seauton, carpi deum, semplice, regina, de gustibus, valet.

4. Which words in the two preceding exercises are customarily given an American pronunciation? In which do we try to preserve the original pronunciation?

5. What is the derivation of the following words? Do the derivations clarify their current use or do they mislead? constable, stewardess, recalcitrant, incur, manganese, pejorative, congregate, coil, talisman, commend.

6. Without consulting the dictionary, distinguish between the following pairs of words by listing their frequent contexts: vast, great; doctor, physician; book, volume; trip, journey; holiday, vacation; labor, work; quick, fast; air, atmosphere; boat, ship; friend, companion.

7. Use your dictionary to check your answers to the foregoing exercise. Which tool, dictionary or frequent context, gave you a more vivid sense of the meaning?

ADDITIONAL EXERCISES

"Style and the Man," p. 157; "Mrs. Malaprop and Captain Absolute," p. 312; "The Psychosemanticist Will See You Now," p. 442.

Allusions, Archaisms, Ambiguities

1. As part of a class project, report on one of the library's standard reference works. Take careful notes on your classmates' reports.

2. In your library, locate and thumb through one of each of the following to determine its potential usefulness: an atlas; a concordance; a collection of reviews; a dictionary of biography; a dictionary of some special subject; an encyclopedia; a foreign language dictionary; a literary magazine such as *Kenyon Review, Sewanee Review,*

Poetry; the *Reader's Guide* or the *Times Index; The Saturday Review* or *Sunday Times Literary Supplement,* current issue; a who's who of some special field.

3. Trace all the references in "Mock On, Mock On," p. 41; in "Chapman's Homer," p. 197; in "The Death of Victoria," p. 101.

4. Which of the following poets was *not* echoed in the jingle on page 38? Lamb, Keats, Nashe, Browning, Coleridge, Chaucer, Shakespeare, Holmes, Landor?

5. So that you will not be baffled when you encounter such practice in other books, we have printed some selections in their original spelling and punctuation. In the following are there any problems you are unable to solve with the aid of a dictionary and a little ingenuity? "Mock On, Mock On," p. 41; the three drafts from "Lycidas," pp. 54–55; "Satan's Defiance," p. 96; "Death Be Not Proud," p. 97.

6. Here is a familiar selection, which you are invited to *study* for perhaps the first time.

STUDIES

Studies serve for delight, for ornament, and for ability. Their chief use for delight is in privateness and retiring; for ornament, is in discourse; and for ability, is in the judgment and disposition of business. For expert men can execute, and perhaps judge of particulars, one by one; but the general counsels, and the plots and marshalling of affairs, come best from those that are learned. To spend too much time in studies is sloth; to use them too much for ornament is affectation; to make judgment wholly by their rules is the humour of a scholar. They perfect nature, and are perfected by experience: for natural abilities are like natural plants, that need pruning by study; and studies themselves do give forth directions too much at large, except they be bounded in by experience. Crafty men condemn studies, simple men admire them, and wise men use them; for they teach not their own use; but that there is a wisdom without them, and above them, won by observation. Read not to contradict and confute; nor to believe and take for granted; nor to find talk and discourse; but to weigh and consider. Some books are to be tasted, others to be swallowed, and some few to be chewed and digested; that is, some books are to be read only in parts; others to be read, but not curiously; and some few to be read wholly, and with diligence and attention. Some books also may be read by deputy, and extracts made of them by others; but that would be only in the less important arguments, and the meaner sort of books; else distilled books are like common distilled waters, flashy things. Reading maketh a full man; conference a ready man; and writing an exact man. And therefore, if a man write little, he had need have a great memory; if he confer little, he had need have a present wit: and if he read little, he had need have much cunning, to seem to know what he doth not.

—Francis Bacon, "Of Studies" (1597, 1625)

a. What are the meanings of the following: privateness, expert, plots, humour, give forth directions too much at large, except, curiously, meaner?

   b. In the last two sentences are "writing" and "conference" used in their modern sense?

   c. Do their contexts make you suspicious of the following phrases: "simple men *admire* them"; "there is a wisdom *without* them"; *"distilled* waters"?

7. What were the originals from which these titles are quotations: Hemingway's *The Sun Also Rises, For Whom the Bell Tolls;* Hellman's *The Little Foxes;* Huxley's *Eyeless in Gaza, After Many a Summer, Time Must Have a Stop;* O'Neill's *Ah, Wilderness!;* Shaw's *Arms and the Man;* Waugh's *A Handful of Dust, Decline and Fall.*

8. Whose lines are echoed in "let us stop thinking continually of those who were truly great," p. 24; "lovers' sighing like furnace," p. 42; "does he promise us a tale that will freeze our young blood and make our two eyes like stars start from their spheres," p. 87?

9. Pope's "The Dunciad" is a mine of stylistic echoes, particularly of Milton and Shakespeare. Look it up some time. And if you like, or dislike, Hardy and the Brontës, read Stella Gibbons' *Cold Comfort Farm.*

ADDITIONAL EXERCISES

"The World Is Too Much with Us," p. 62; "I Am Born," p. 145; "An Important Omission," p. 158; "Medical Strategy," p. 65; "The House of Usher," p. 72; "Expression of Opinion," p. 104; "Cloistered Virtue," p. 106; "Education," p. 106; "Harry's Address at Harfleur," p. 175; "Cromwell Our Chief of Men," p. 354.

What's in the Text?

IN THE previous chapter, in which we discussed words as words, as if each of them had an entity of its own, we were constantly referring to context. We could not avoid such reference because the context in which a word occurs will greatly determine its meaning. Of course, the process works both ways: the context is determined largely by the words which comprise it. But the meaning of the whole text will usually be greater—and more exact—than the total of the appropriate meanings of the separate words; certainly it will be different. As an illustration of this principle, you may recall the man who tried to learn about Chinese metaphysics. He looked up the encyclopedia articles on China and on metaphysics, and simply combined the two. We cannot afford to be so naïve; after we have analyzed and added up the meanings of the separate words we shall expect to find that the overall message is different from the sum of its parts. Indeed, even after we have taken this second step and have analyzed the overall message, we shall expect to go back to a study of the relations between the parts, to an analysis of the way the selection has been put together.

In this chapter we shall concern ourselves with the overall message—that extra something that emerges from a simple addition of all the parts. We shall break that extra something into Sense, Mood, Attitude, Social Intent, and Tone. In the next two chapters we shall discuss *how* to express the "intellectual" and the "emotional" components of a selection—*after* you know *what* you're trying to express. Then in Chapter Six, "Between and Around the Lines," we analyze the relation between the parts of a selection—in short, we analyze Form or Structure.

Even a simple addition of the word clues will yield us a surprisingly complex message. The "extra something" we are seeking may easily be too large or too elusive to grasp quickly. Accordingly we shall have to look at it from a number of viewpoints. Fortunately, the first aspect is familiar to you and may provide a fairly painless introduction to the others.

THE FAMILIAR ASPECT: SENSE

Sense is the pattern formed by the denotative elements; it is the detailed logical argument of the selection, the answer, on the most concrete and impersonal level, to the question "What does this say?" As we have noted in the previous chapter, meanings are never completely objective; there is always a connotative element present. Therefore Sense is never entirely free of the other components we shall discuss presently—of Mood, for example, or of Attitude. Nevertheless, we shall not get very far toward understanding a selection, or interpreting it adequately to an audience, until we have made some attempt to come as close to the Sense as we can: to penetrate the bias and the personal reactions, and to understand the impersonal relations between the objective details that are reported in the selection. We must know what is happening.

This obvious first step is not always as easy as it sounds. All of us tend to make "stock responses" whenever confronted with our favorite stereotypes, or whenever we encounter words that set off a chain of personal associations. Some words have been used so often in emotionally loaded contexts that their denotations are almost completely blurred. We are slightly shocked at the headline MOTHER OF THREE SLAYS POSTMAN—as if the mere fact that a human female had been thrice wheeled out of an obstetrical ward could make her incapable of killing. And what is the precise denotation of "Jew" or "nigger" or "un-American"? Propaganda abounds in appeals to stereotypes; but they also turn up in what purports to be literature; and most of us are not hard-boiled enough to dig them out. Perhaps you have been embarrassed by a rereading of some sentimental poem you enjoyed in early adolescence. If not, look up a copy of "I think that I shall never see / A poem lovely as a tree," and try to figure out what that singularly gymnastic tree is doing: at one moment her branches are presumably feet; at the next, arms; then hair, and then bosom. And just how did "God" get into the poem? Is the reference prepared for? And does it make the tree any lovelier, or any less messy, for wearing birds' nests in her hair?

On the other hand, note carefully the fine detail in the following:

It was a crisp and spicy morning in early October. The lilacs and the laburnums, lit with the glory fires of autumn, hung burning and flashing in the upper air, a fairy bridge provided by kind Nature for the wing-less wild things that have their home in the tree tops and would visit together; the larch and the pomegranate flung their purple and yellow flames in brilliant broad splashes along the slanting sweep of the wood-land; the sensuous fragrance of innumerable deciduous flowers rose upon the swooning atmosphere; far in the empty sky a solitary oesophagus slept upon motionless wing; everywhere brooded stillness, serenity, and the peace of God.

A graphic description of nature, lovingly drawn and sensitive to the smallest detail? Better read it again. But before you do, just what is an oesophagus? And when did lilacs last in the dooryard bloom?

Do not feel chagrined if the passage fooled you; it took a Mark Twain to do it. Furthermore, the passage is not as foolish as it might have been: for our students, we have frequently inserted a second sentence to the effect that "The broad sun, resplendent in scarlet and gold, sank slowly in the west"—and *still* have fooled 95 per cent of them! So you are in good company. But please do take the selection as evidence of the fact that Sense can sometimes be so completely buried by non-Sense as to become nonsense;[1] and that the detection of Sense—apparently an obvious precaution in analysis—is by no means as obvious as it seems.

We know of no foolproof way of getting at the Sense, but the following procedures should help: paraphrase, itemization of detail, grammatical analysis, and précis making. If you master these procedures in this class, for the purposes of this class, you may find them even more valuable in later life—when you have to study the fine print on a mortgage or an insurance policy, for example.

Paraphrase

A paraphrase is a translation of the selection, line by line, into your own words. A paraphrase does not attempt to summarize; it does not try to describe the selection (e.g., "This is the story of Bill's struggle to get rich"); it does not try to state the theme or the "deeper meanings" (e.g., "This is an account of the struggle between youth and age"); all a paraphrase tries to do is to express the meaning of each word and line in your own words. Since the paraphrase will

---

[1] This footnote will be our only attempt to convince you that connotation usually contributes more to meaning than does denotation.

doubtless carry over some of the author's bias—and perhaps add some of your own—it will not give you the pure undistorted Sense. But if you have been reasonably careful to be accurate and impersonal, you will have come as close to the Sense as you need to in this course. Indeed, some authorities prefer not to speak of Sense at all; they use the safer term, "Paraphrasable Content."

A paraphrase should provide an excellent test of your grasp of the Sense of a selection. When you have finished writing it out, examine it for logical consistency. If the paraphrase does not make sense, you must conclude either that it is an inaccurate paraphrase or that the selection itself does not make sense. Needless to say, the former is much more likely than the latter. Next, examine it to make sure that it satisfactorily accounts for every word of the original selection. This is very important. Your paraphrase may make excellent sense, but if you have ignored some of the words of the original, it will make the wrong kind of sense, and your oral reading will almost certainly embody the misinterpretation.

Here is a familiar selection; write out your own paraphrase of the first four lines, before looking at the samples which follow.

THE WORLD IS TOO MUCH WITH US; LATE AND SOON

The world is too much with us; late and soon,
Getting and spending, we lay waste our powers:
Little we see in Nature that is ours;
We have given our hearts away, a sordid boon!
5   This sea that bares her bosom to the moon;
The winds that will be howling at all hours,
And are up-gathered now like sleeping flowers;
For this, for everything, we are out of tune;
It moves us not.—Great God! I'd rather be
10   A Pagan suckled in a creed outworn,
So might I, standing on this pleasant lea,
Have glimpses that would make me less forlorn;
Have sight of Proteus rising from the sea;
Or hear old Triton blow his wreathèd horn.
                    —William Wordsworth (1807)

Which of the following paraphrases of this poem are not paraphrases at all? Which make no logical sense? Which do not satisfactorily account for all the words in the original? Which most adequately translate the original? Which is nearest to your own?

1. In these melancholy lines, Wordsworth bemoans the Industrial Revolution. In these days of technological progress we should try to get back to the old simple virtues and remember "what availeth it a man if he gain the whole world and lose his own soul?" No truer words were ever written.

2. The world is too much with us all the time. Getting and spending we lay waste our powers. We don't see much in Nature that is ours. We have given our hearts away, a sordid boon.

3. We're too busy with the daily grind. Day and night we burn ourselves out in the rat-race. Natural beauty holds nothing for us. We've sold out—and a sorry bargain it was.

4. The world is too complicated for us, late and soon. We waste our natural resources; after all, we don't own them. We've given away our life's blood, a vulgar bunch.

5. The world is too much for us. We have wasted our strength by too much spending. Fortunately, Nature doesn't belong to us, or we would have given our very hearts away.

6. We are overly concerned with mundane things. In everlasting commerce, we destroy our personal resources. We find little identification with Nature; we have made a vulgar gift of our capacity to feel.

Before we abandon this exercise, we might remark that although the last sample is probably acceptable enough, it is not the one we prefer.

Since it is doubtful that you completely understand anything which can be put into words if you cannot express it, however falteringly, in your own words, and since it is equally doubtful that you can communicate to an audience much that you do not understand, paraphrasing provides one test of your readiness to appear before an audience. Perhaps you should completely paraphrase every selection you intend to read aloud; even the "easy" parts may be trickier than you suspect. But we are trying to be realistic in our advice, and so, having reminded you that even the self-evident passages may contain subtle traps, we suggest this compromise: Write out, in your own words, a line-by-line translation of all the sections that seem to you to be vague, or questionable, or difficult. In short, save paraphrase for the tough spots. And then hope against hope that you have not missed any.

Grammatical Analysis

Grammatical analysis is often an excellent tool for those who have the ability to parse a sentence; after all, grammar serves to indicate the relationships between the words in a sentence, and therefore, indirectly, between the ideas symbolized by those words. Unfortunately, most of us have only the vaguest recollections of our sixth grade grammar and so cannot use the weapon to full advantage. But even if we have forgotten how to diagram a sentence completely, we should be able to find its subject and its predicate, to trace the referent of every pronoun and to discover the antecedent of every phrase or clause. If we cannot, we will not know who is doing what.

We suggest, then, that if necessary you refresh your knowledge of at least the rudiments of formal grammar. Borrow a good composition text,[2] and read over the sections on subject and verb, reference of pronouns, restrictive and nonrestrictive clauses, dangling modifiers, and subordination. Relearn at least enough so that you can trace the bare skeleton of a complex sentence. Then when you encounter a tough spot in a selection you will be able to figure out the who, what, where, when, and how of the matter.

Itemization

Sometimes a selection will contain sentences—even entire paragraphs—which have so many clauses within clauses, so many suspensions of structure, and so many departures from normal word order that our attempts to paraphrase break down in a welter of words. We have lost the beginning before we reach the end. Grammatical analysis is sufficient here for some students, but probably a more useful tool is the simple itemization of all the details. We merely draw up a list—preferably written—of all the pieces of information contained in the puzzling passage.

Here, for example, is a sentence from Henry James:

> I remember vividly every element of the place, down to the intensely Londonish look of the grey opposite houses, in the gap of the white cur-

[2] One of the following may help: Porter G. Perrin, *Writer's Guide and Index to English,* Scott, Foresman, 1959; Cleanth Brooks and Robert P. Warren, *A Modern Rhetoric,* Harcourt, Brace, 1956; Donald J. Lloyd and Harry R. Warfel, *American English in Its Cultural Setting,* Knopf, 1956; Paul Roberts, *Understanding English,* Harper, 1958.

tains of the high windows, and the exact spot where, on a particular afternoon, I put down my tea-cup for Brooksmith, lingering an instant, to gather it up as if he were plucking a flower.

—Brooksmith (1892)

Struggling with a paraphrase, we might educe that "I" remembered the gap in the curtains, or that "I" was lingering; further, the verbosity of our paraphrase might prevent us from detecting the error. But a simple listing of the "facts" allows us to check for accuracy against the original.

> I remember every detail of the place vividly.
> I remember that the houses across the street were typical of London.
> They were grey.
> They could be seen between the white curtains.
> The curtains were on the high windows.
> I remember where I placed my tea-cup one afternoon.
> I placed it there for Brooksmith to remove.
> Brooksmith was waiting for it.
> Brooksmith was not waiting long.
> He was waiting to pick it up like a flower.

Now that we have it out in the open, we can see where the real problem in this sentence lies (and perhaps the only part that requires paraphrase): "on a particular afternoon." Does this mean "one afternoon," or "any afternoon you care to mention"?

Note, then, that itemization, like grammatical analysis, is not usually a substitute for paraphrase. Rather, it is most often a preliminary step of clarification, taken in order to simplify the process of paraphrase.[3]

Which of the foregoing—paraphrase, grammatical analysis, or itemization—is most helpful to you in clarifying the following passages? Which could you dispense with?

MEDICAL STRATEGY

To say the truth, Mr. Allworthy's situation had never been so bad as the great caution of the doctor had represented it; but as a wise general never despises his enemy, however inferior that enemy's force may be, so neither doth a wise physician ever despise a distemper, however in-

---

[3] If you have been trained in public address, you will be able to cast many of your lists into the form of outlines and thereby gain a valuable tool in the detection of subordination.

considerable. As the former preserves the same strict discipline, places the same guards, and employs the same scouts, though the enemy be never so weak, so the latter maintains the same gravity of countenance, and shakes his head with the same significant air, let the distemper be never so trifling. And both, among many other good ones, may assign this solid reason for their conduct, that by these means the greater glory redounds to them if they gain the victory, and the less disgrace if by any unlucky accident they should happen to be conquered.

—Henry Fielding, *Tom Jones* (1749)

ALL THESE BLESSINGS

Kindly separated by nature and a wide ocean from the exterminating havoc of one quarter of the globe; too high-minded to endure the degradations of the others; possessing a chosen country, with room enough for entertaining a due sense of our equal right to the use of our own faculties, to the acquisitions of our industry, to honor and confidence from our fellow citizens, resulting not from birth but from our actions and their sense of them; enlightened by a benign religion, professed, indeed, and practiced in various forms, yet all of them including honesty, truth, temperance, gratitude, and the love of man; acknowledging and adoring an overruling Providence, which by its dispensations proves that it delights in the happiness of man here and his greater happiness hereafter; with all these blessings, what more is necessary to make us a happy and prosperous people?

—Thomas Jefferson, *First Inaugural Address* (1801)

VITAL EXPRESSION

When I hear the hypercritical quarrelling about grammar and style, the position of the particles, etc., etc., stretching or contracting every speaker to certain rules of theirs,—Mr. Webster, perhaps, not having spoken according to Mr. Kirkham's rule,—I see that they forget that the first requisite and rule is that expression shall be vital and natural, as much as the voice of a brute or an interjection: first of all, mother tongue; and last of all, artificial or father tongue.

—Henry David Thoreau, *Journal,* January 2, 1859

The Précis

A précis is a condensation of the selection. At most it will be about one-third the length of the original, and for longer selections it will be proportionately shorter. Rarely will it extend to more than a page, and usually it will be a short paragraph. In the précis you try to state generally and abstractly the central logical argument—the main thread—in your own words. You omit the specific detail and the minor qualifications, and frequently you suppress even the large subordinate elements. When you are through you have a miniature of the original, a rough sketch of the main logical design.

We suggested that the paraphrase, the grammatical analysis, and the itemization of detail were optional weapons to be used for the difficult parts of a selection; we believe the précis to be far more important. Indeed, we advise you to write out a careful précis of any selection you propose to read aloud. We do so for three reasons. First, a précis is more economical than the others; you do not waste time with the self-evident. More important, since it forces you to evaluate the paraphrasable content—you must pick out the essentials—it therefore provides an excellent test of your understanding of the Sense of the selection. And perhaps most important, it forces you to concentrate on the main thread—you must discover "where the selection is going." Later, when you come to read the selection aloud, you will be less likely to become bogged down in detail; you stand a better chance of making the selection hang together. For example, the selection on page 36, "Love Not Me for Comely Grace," will present fewer oral difficulties after you have reduced it to a précis somewhat like this:

> Don't love me for my inner or outer qualities, because neither may be permanent. Continue to love me without knowing why, and then you can love me forever.

Later on, you may find the précis a useful tool for further analysis, but in the meantime three reasons are enough. Write out a careful précis of every selection you propose to read aloud.

One difficulty you may encounter in précis writing is the temptation to produce a description or a report. If, instead of trying to condense the main idea of the original, you attempt to describe what happens, you will not be able to check the result for accuracy. If, for example, we try to summarize "Love Not Me for Comely Grace" in the following words:

> This man said that he didn't want his wife to love him for his inner or outer qualities because both of them might change, and instead he said to love him without knowing why because then she could love him forever.

we have not only created a wordier product, not only introduced a number of unnecessary ambiguities, but we have increased the difficulty of testing our précis against the original.

Remember, then, that in writing a précis you are trying to abstract or condense the original; you are neither describing nor reporting at secondhand. Therefore, retain the grammatical person (I, you, he, she, etc.) and thus the viewpoint; retain the verb tense; and, unless you are very sure of yourself, retain the sequence in which the ideas are presented. You may have to add material that is not explicitly stated in the text, as we have done ("man", "woman") in our first sample hereafter; but you had better indicate such additions clearly, to remind you to be suspicious of them.

Here is a sonnet we have referred to a number of times (pages 35, 46–47). Try to make a précis of it before looking at our samples, which follow it.

SINCE THERE'S NO HELP

Since there's no help, come let us kiss and part;
Nay, I have done, you get no more of me,
And I am glad, yea, glad with all my heart
That thus so cleanly I myself can free;
5   Shake hands forever, cancel all our vows,
And when we meet at any time again,
Be it not seen in either of our brows
That we one jot of former love retain.
Now, at the last gasp of love's latest breath,
10   When, his pulse failing, passion speechless lies,
When faith is kneeling by his bed of death,
And innocence is closing up his eyes,
Now, if thou wouldst, when all have given him over,
From death to life thou mightst him yet recover.
    —Michael Drayton, *Idea* (1619)

Apparently a large part of the difficulty lies in lines 9 to 12; if your précis begins to get vague at that point, try paraphrase, or itemization of detail, or even grammatical analysis. To what or whom does "his" refer? Who is doing what? Check your own précis against the original once more, and then compare it with the ones below.

> (Man) One more kiss? (Woman) No, we're through and I'm glad of it. (Man) Well, let's shake hands. (Woman) No, from now on, pretend you don't even know me. (Man) When I'm dead and gone you'll wish you could recover my love.

Very well, if nothing can be done, let's say goodbye. From now on, we'll pretend to be strangers. But even now, when our love is almost extinct, you could revive it if you so desired.

Farewell, cruel world, I am glad to bid you adieu. Soon I will be in heaven, and will not even recognize my sorrows. Dear God, as I lie on my deathbed, I offer You my love and innocence, and pray You will recover my soul from death to eternal life.

This woman is remembering how her sweetheart left her abruptly, and comforts herself with the thought that she will see him after death.

Notice that the last of these samples is not a précis at all—it is a report or description and therefore cannot be checked against specific parts of the original. The others can be so checked and are consequently of greater value to analysis; we should be able to reject two of them with confidence.

To summarize, a précis is an abstract of the central logical argument of a selection; it retains the viewpoint and the grammatical relations of the original, but omits the specific detail and the minor qualifications. It is used chiefly to impress upon us the central thought of the selection, so that our oral reading does not lose itself in a maze of detail.

But having counseled you to write a précis of every selection you intend to read in class, we had better make sure that you do not expect too much of it. Some students—and some teachers—think that a précis gives them the selection in a nutshell. Here is a good statement of their viewpoint:

> . . . [to reduce it to a précis,] you boil it down to about a third its original size; or, to change the figure, you squeeze the water out of it, retaining its original form and proportion. . . . The finished précis should say all that the original says, but should say it much more briefly.[4]

We disagree. Such boiling and squeezing, we think, is a little like head-shrinking: to do it at all, you have to remove something of value.

As you should suspect from our discussion of connotation, we think that a précis can't possibly say all that the original says. It does not even give you the "essence." You have *not* stripped away the gingerbread and the decoration and got to the heart of the matter. At very best, you will have discovered the dominant pattern of the simple denotations; you will have abstracted, and generalized, the Sense.

[4] W. M. Parrish, *Reading Aloud*, 3rd ed., Ronald, 1953, p. 43; but see p. 258 also.

But the Sense is not necessarily—or even usually—the heart of the matter. If someone calls you a fool, his Sense is plain enough, but you are sophisticated enough—and prudent enough—to realize that his *meaning* may depend, not on Sense, but on his mood, or on his attitude toward you, or on his intention. Furthermore, you will want to know *how* he called you a fool. In Chapter Six, we shall try to show that how a thing is said is an aspect of what is said; but even here we can offer a simple illustration of the point:

"Hey! Gimme a cuppa coffee!"

"Coffee. Hot. And fast."

"Hi gawjis, sling us some mud, wi' ya?"

"Doo caffay, see voo play."

"Hi Rosie. Same as usual."

"Hey! Can't a guy even get a cuppa coffee in this dump?"

"Excuse me—may I have a cup of coffee, please?"

"Black."

A précis of each of these might well be "I want some coffee"; but even on this simple level of utterance you can readily see that each contains additional meanings—and will get a different response from Rosie.

The précis as described will test your grasp of the main thread of the Sense, just as a paraphrase will test your grasp of the detailed Sense; but Sense is only one of the aspects of the total meaning. A précis, indeed, is useful in subsequent analysis only insofar as it raises the problem: "Why did the author write the selection his way instead of mine; why didn't he write my précis?" Or more specifically: "What are the extra meanings, which my précis cannot encompass?"

The rest of this chapter will point the direction in which to look for the answers to these questions.

FOUR OTHER ASPECTS OF OVERALL MESSAGE

In a well-constructed work every element contributes to a total effect of unity. We cannot put this unity into words—except by quoting verbatim the original passage. Since it is ineffable, we shall come closest to it, not by simplifying it or "boiling it down," but by studying it from a number of different angles or viewpoints.

The problem is a little like studying a person's head. No matter how hard we try, we can't see it all at once. So we study it from a variety of angles, see a number of aspects of it, and then combine our impressions of those aspects. Note that we can study it from any of an infinity of viewpoints, but probably we'll settle for three or four. Note too that the aspects we see from those viewpoints won't necessarily be mutually exclusive; indeed, the chances are that they'll blur into one another. When we look at him full-face, his nose will contribute to the aspect we see, and that same nose will contribute to all the other aspects we see until we view him from three-quarters profile—and if he has a long nose, it will pop up in that aspect too!

We have already looked at the total meaning from one viewpoint and have seen the aspect of Sense. Now let us shift our viewpoint a few times, and try to see four other aspects—any one of which may be more important than Sense in a particular selection. Note that these are not THE aspects of meaning; we could look for any one of perhaps a million aspects, but we choose to look for these four: Mood, Attitude, Social Intent, and Tone.[5] Note too that we can expect to find the same elements popping up in different aspects; indeed, Mood and Sense, for example, shade easily into Attitude, and Attitude and Social Intent will largely determine Tone.

To return to our analogy for the last time: if we are trying to study a head, it probably isn't tremendously important that we draw fine distinctions between full-face and 1/100th profile; the important thing is to know afterwards what the head looks like. Similarly, you probably need not worry about the subtle distinctions between, say, Mood and Attitude. Your job is to learn to see a selection from more than one viewpoint.

Let us turn now to the aspects that emerge when we shift our viewpoint from a strict regard for Sense.

MOOD

Mood we shall define as the major feeling or emotive response that is evoked in us by a selection. It is the aspect of meaning which is least susceptible of analysis. Ordinarily it strikes us immediately (as, for example, we were struck by the Mood of the Mark Twain selection, on page 60); subsequent analysis

---

[5] For example, I. A. Richards, *Practical Criticism,* Harcourt, Brace, 1929 (also available in paperback, Harvest Books, HB 16) uses these four categories: sense, feeling, tone, and intent. Our debt is obvious.

may deepen the Mood, but we know of no foolproof way of finding it in the first place. However, since Mood is usually the first aspect to emerge, we can suggest only that your first step in the preparation of a selection be to read it intently but uncritically a couple of times. Then ask yourself, "What has the selection done to me?"

THE HOUSE OF USHER

During the whole of a dull, dark, and soundless day in the autumn of the year, when the clouds hung oppressively low in the heavens, I had been passing alone, on horseback, through a singularly dreary tract of country, and at length found myself, as the
5   shades of the evening drew on, within view of the melancholy House of Usher. I know not how it was—but, with the first glimpse of the building, a sense of insufferable gloom pervaded my spirit. I say insufferable; for the feeling was unrelieved by any of that half-pleasurable, because poetic, sentiment with which the
10   mind usually receives even the sternest natural images of the desolate or terrible. I looked upon the scene before me—upon the mere house, and the simple landscape features of the domain—upon the bleak walls—upon the vacant eye-like windows—upon a few rank sedges—and upon a few white trunks of decayed trees—with an
15   utter depression of soul which I can compare to no earthly sensation more properly than to the after-dream of the reveller upon opium—the bitter lapse into everyday life—the hideous dropping off of the veil.

—Edgar Allan Poe, *The Fall of the House of Usher* (1839)

"What has the selection done to me?" Having asked this question, you may find some difficulty in pinning down an answer. We need words or pictures in order to fix something in our memory; and English has a limited and imprecise vocabulary of mood. Nevertheless, the attempt may be worth while. One textbook contains a fairly comprehensive "Vocabulary of Attitudes" which may help,[6] or you might look through the section on "Sympathetic Affections," in *Roget's Thesaurus*. On the other hand, you may give the Mood a rough, tentative label—anger, longing, carnival, indignation, etc.—and trust that subsequent analysis will clarify it.

Having spontaneously found the Mood, however vaguely, we can do much to deepen and intensify it by conscious analysis. To find the Mood, we asked, "What has the selection done to me?" Now, to corroborate our findings, we ask,

[6] Parrish, *op. cit.,* pp. 70–72.

"How did the selection do it to me?" Put another way, our guiding question is, "How was this effect obtained?"

> If we study, for example, the Poe selection above, we notice immediately the large number of adjectives and adverbs. Upon further examination, we notice a pattern emerging from them: dull, dark, soundless, oppressively, alone, singularly dreary, melancholy, etc., etc. While attempting to write a précis of the Sense, we will be struck by the absence of specific detail: when did this happen?—in the autumn; where?—in a dreary tract of country; where was the house?—within view; what kind of house was it?—not until line 13 or 14 do we find such relatively specific details as "vacant eye-like windows" or "rank sedges." The imprecision is deliberately reinforced by such apologies as "I know not how it was" and "which I can compare to no earthly sensation more properly than"; the speaker is suggesting that he is imprecise because he has to be. We note too the mannered, formal style—"I know not" instead of "I do not know"—and the apparent hairsplitting—"I say insufferable"—and we infer that this is no spontaneous utterance; the speaker seems to have taken great pains with what he has to say, so that his failure to be precise is all the more persuasive. He manages to suggest that he is imprecise not only because he has to be, but because anyone with such an experience would have to be.
>
> Analysis, then, has confirmed our original reaction of vague foreboding. And insofar as we have detected some hint of frustration at the impossibility of uttering the inutterable, analysis has reinforced our original reaction.

Often analysis of Mood must delve deep into the subtleties of connotation. Poe's adjectives and adverbs fell almost too easily into a pattern; close analysis was hardly worth while. But what happens when a pattern is slow to emerge?

I HEAR AN ARMY

I hear an army charging upon the land,
And the thunder of horses plunging, foam about their knees:
Arrogant, in black armor, behind them stand,
Disdaining the reins, with fluttering whips, the charioteers.

They cry unto the night their battle-name: 5
I moan in sleep when I hear afar their whirling laughter.

They cleave the gloom of dreams, a blinding flame,
Clanging, clanging upon the heart as upon an anvil.

They come shaking in triumph their long, green hair:
10   They come out of the sea and run shouting by the shore.
My heart, have you no wisdom thus to despair?
My love, my love, my love, why have you left me alone?[7]
—James Joyce (1907)

No matter how hard we try, we are not going to make complete "sense" out of this poem—we cannot reduce it to a statement of cold fact. Presumably it embodies an experience beyond the realm of everyday logic. Later on, we can make a précis; we can create a rough outline of what goes on and thus assure ourselves that it makes Sense. But the chief value of the poem—its chief meaning—is to be found in the feelings it evokes in us, in its Mood.

Read the poem again; read carefully but uncritically. What Mood do you find? Terror, wild excitement, a kind of frozen panic, remote dread? As we suggested earlier, do not worry about attaching a precise name to it. The important thing is to become aware of your initial reaction. Next, we must attempt a critical reading. How was this effect obtained?

Doubtless our impressions are contradictory. We note that the charioteers carry whips—an implication of viciousness and danger; but we note too that the whips flutter—like butterflies, or birds, or pennants. We feel the charging effect of the strong metrical beat at first; yet we may feel that the charge peters out, and (after we have studied prosody in Chapter Six) we may attribute it to the six-foot lines. We note the frequent suspensions in the second clause; the charging comes in short spurts, so that when the charioteers finally "arrive" much of the impetus has disappeared. We see that the riders clang clang upon the heart; but a moment later they are off in the distance, running by the shore.

Having made some of these observations, we had better dig into the connotations. Space precludes our analyzing the entire poem; we shall leave that to you. But let us examine, as our sample, a line which at first sight does not seem to be rich in implications: line 5, "They cry unto the night their battle-name."

[7] From *Collected Poems* by James Joyce. Copyright 1918 by B. W. Huebsch, 1946 by Nora Joyce. Reprinted by permission of The Viking Press.

The word "cry" may connote screams and yells and other such sounds of battle; but it may also carry the implication of defenselessness—babies and birds and small animals cry. Why has an ambiguous word, with an aura of weakness, been used instead of the more forthright "shout" or "roar"? What about "unto"; what contexts does that occur in? The Bible? The church? And is the implication one of remoteness, or ritual, or both? "Night" might be one of the standard props in horror stories, much as Poe's adjectives were; but here it also reinforces the later references to sleep and dreams. "Battle-name" is peculiar; we expect "battle-cries." What kind of ritual prompts these warriors to don special names for battles; and what stranger ritual compels them to announce these magic names? Usually, among primitive people, the publicizing of a ritual name destroys the magic; do these rituals cancel each other out? Lastly, whence are these cries directed? Unto the night. Does the night's emptiness reinforce the ineffectuality of the cries; or does the mystery of the night reinforce the mystery of the ritual and the antiquity of the charioteers?

Continue this analysis until the poem clicks together. Be especially alert to connote all terms that surprise you, given your early reaction to the poem. If, for example, you had decided that the Mood was one of wild terror, you would have to explain "clanging, clanging" in line 8. How dangerous is clanging? What impression does it make on an anvil?

Do not be disappointed if, after the most intensive analysis, you still cannot quite put your finger on the Mood. (We chose the Joyce selection partly to illustrate that point.) All you should expect from analysis is to confirm your original reaction (or to show you where you were mistaken) and perhaps to intensify that reaction. That is about as far as intellect alone will take you. You will discover, later on, that probably the best fixative of Mood is to read the selection aloud.

ATTITUDE

An attitude is an enduring predisposition toward a certain action with respect to a certain thing; it is what someone is set to do about something. More loosely, it is bias, prejudice, "opinion about." Since it has an emotional component, it will distort the thing which calls it forth; for example, in the selection below we have no clear idea of the facts of the case, even though the speaker raves, ostensibly about those facts, for twelve lines.

A GLASS OF BEER

The lanky hank of a she in the inn over there
Nearly killed me for asking the loan of a glass of beer;
May the devil grip the whey-faced slut by the hair,
And beat bad manners out of her skin for a year.

5   That parboiled ape, with the toughest jaw you will see
On virtue's path, and a voice that would rasp the dead,
Came roaring and raging the minute she looked at me,
And threw me out of the house on the back of my head!

If I asked her master he'd give me a cask a day;
10   But she, with the beer at hand, not a gill would arrange!
May she marry a ghost and bear him a kitten, and may
The High King of Glory permit her to get the mange.[8]
                                                —James Stephens (1954)

Some such distortion is inevitable; the object is an "objective correlative" of the attitude, in that it is the psychological equivalent of the attitude—the attitude and the object are so mixed in the person's mind as to be almost interchangeable.[9] To some extent, then, Attitude is a combination of Sense and Mood. As such, it is a more complex and yet often a more convenient aspect to seek in most literature. Let us consider two reasons.

In the first place, a search for Attitude instead of for Sense may preserve the message in a form more useful for reading aloud. After all, rarely is Attitude as intense as in the Stephens selection above; more commonly it is even subtler than in the following examples, perhaps unwitting, which have been taken from textbooks in the field.

> . . . T. S. Eliot, born an American, but choosing to become a subject of the British king . . .[10]

These persons have not read thrillingly real poetry. Perhaps sometime they have read a poem written in the Elizabethan style or in the seventeenth century school of highly artificial language, or "conceits." But

---

[8] From James Stephens, *Collected Poems.* Copyright 1954 by The Macmillan Company, and used with their permission.

[9] If this seems unduly mystical, reflect that the anti-Semite does not see the same Jew that you see. The object of his bias has been so distorted by the bias that to him it is self-evident that Jews are blank-blank. He has only to look at one to "prove" his case against them.

[10] C. C. Cunningham, *Making Words Come Alive,* Brown, 1951, p. 18.

let them read Millay's "Renascence," Frost's "Birches," "Mending Wall,"
. . . or any other real, red-blooded poetry. If they are intelligent, sensitive,
and fair minded, they will agree that poetry is a part of every human being's need.[11]

. . . even more seriously astray is the intense young lady who simply loves
all poetry and uses it as a sort of Rorschach Inkblot into which she can
project her own well-worked emotions.[12]

You may test this for yourself by sitting down for an hour with the
monotonous "rocking-horse" couplets of Alexander Pope, say in his
translation of the *Iliad*.[13]

Assuming that in our paraphrase or précis we do manage to remove the slanting from the individual words (and that will require a nice talent for splitting
hairs), we must still make Sense out of the fact that "born an American" has
been contrasted with "choosing to become a subject," or that Elizabethan poetry
and red-blooded poetry have been placed in two mutually exclusive categories.
We must account for the "say" in the last example, and yet ignore the implication that the evidence most convenient to the thesis has been chosen at random.
And even if we do manage to reduce these messages to impersonality, what will
we have accomplished, beyond testing our ingenuity? When we come to read
these passages aloud, we must certainly re-create the animus that impelled them,
and we are just as likely to do so before a Sense analysis as after. Indeed, given
our tendency to think of Sense as somehow more "basic" than the other aspects,
perhaps we are *more* likely to do a good job if here we do not seek it separately.

Secondly, besides being less artificial than Sense, Attitude is more flexible than
Mood. Attitude is focused on details and can change as the details change; Mood
is pervasive. Hence the search for Mood can present two dangers to oral readers:
we may cling to our original impression and ignore or distort any clues that
won't fit, or we may claim that the Mood has been "shattered" by the intru-
sion of some detail we did not expect to find. A familiar passage will illustrate
the point:

> It was roses, roses, all the way,
> With myrtle mixed in my path like mad:
> The house-roofs seemed to heave and sway,

---

[11] Gail Boardman, *Oral Communication of Literature*, Prentice-Hall, 1952, pp. 117–118.
[12] See above, p. 27.
[13] Parrish, *op. cit.*, p. 195.

The church-spires flamed, such flags they had,
A year ago on this very day.

The air broke into a mist with bells,
The old walls rocked with the crowd and cries.
Had I said, "Good folk, mere noise repels—
But give me your sun from yonder skies!"
They had answered, "And afterwards, what else?"

    Most of us, if we had to read this aloud, would attempt to convey the joy and the triumph implicit in the occasion described. If we analyzed the connotations of the major words, we might find a few—mad, heave, sway, flamed, rocked, repels—that suggest a boisterousness beyond the usual. If we analyzed the relation between the parts, we might find one line a little disturbing: "A year ago on this very day" doesn't quite fit, it doesn't clearly relate to the others. But these may be minor lapses, if any, and we should doubtless conclude that we were correct in our attempts to express joy, triumph—and perhaps a somewhat savage exultation. Now, what happens when we read the whole selection?

THE PATRIOT
AN OLD STORY

It was roses, roses, all the way,
With myrtle mixed in my path like mad:
The house-roofs seemed to heave and sway,
The church-spires flamed, such flags they had,
5   A year ago on this very day.

The air broke into a mist with bells,
The old walls rocked with the crowd and cries.
Had I said, "Good folk, mere noise repels—
But give me your sun from yonder skies!"
10   They had answered, "And afterwards, what else?"

Alack, it was I who leapt at the sun
To give it my loving friends to keep!
Naught man can do, have I left undone:
And you see my harvest, what I reap
15   This very day, now a year is run.

There's nobody on the house-tops now—
Just a palsied few at the windows set;
For the best of the sight is, all allow,
At the Shambles' Gate—or, better yet,
At the very scaffold's foot, I trow.   20

I go in the rain, and, more than needs,
A rope cuts both my wrists behind;
And I think, by the feel, my forehead bleeds,
For they fling, whoever has a mind,
Stones at me for my year's misdeeds.   25

Thus I entered, and thus I go!
In triumphs people have dropped down dead.
"Paid by the world, what dost thou owe
Me?"—God might question; now instead,
'Tis God shall repay! I am safer so.   30
                                    —Robert Browning (1845)

> Many a student attempts to maintain the "happy mood"
> right up to the very scaffold's foot; and then abruptly becomes
> mournful and full of self-pity. Little use to point out the psy-
> chological improbability of such a sudden switch; any other
> reading, they feel, would violate the Mood of the first stanza.
> But the moment the question becomes one of Attitude—even
> on the purely speculative level of "What would his attitude
> probably be?—the problem almost resolves itself. The bother-
> some clues in the first stanza snap into place (and, inciden-
> tally, a Mood which *can* be maintained is established). Specu-
> lative questions about probable attitude are, of course, un-
> necessary; close attention even to the connotations of "it was"
> and "all the way" might indicate that lines 1 and 2 were full
> of smug self-satisfaction, at very brightest, but it would hardly
> support the thesis that they were firmly joyful.

In suggesting that the search for Attitude is often more practical than the
search for Sense and less deceptive than the search for Mood, we do not mean
to imply that you should use it to the exclusion of the others. Attitude will
not unravel a complicated phrasing; we might guess at the patriot's attitude
to his bonds, but we still have to figure out the Sense of lines 21 and 22. Excessive preoccupation with isolated details may reveal countless shadings of
Attitude; but unless we hold firmly to the Mood, the pervading emotional

response, our reading will fall apart, and our audience may think we are talking in sound effects. Therefore, we suggest you use all three aspects; research into the one may help to solve problems in the other two.

Having discussed the nature of Attitude and indicated some of its values and limitations, let us turn to the problem of detecting it. Here our major question is: "What is the speaker's—i.e., the author's, the narrator's, or the character's—reaction to the details he is presenting?" And we shall find our answer in the details themselves: in what details he has chosen and what omitted; in what words he has used to present them; in what words he has used as modifiers and predicates; and in what other details he has linked them with.

Chapter Two has already indicated the way in which we examine the words used to present the details or to modify or predicate them; we are to weigh the connotations of each major word in an attempt to answer the question: "Why use this term instead of its possible alternatives?" Let us consider other useful questions. First we can ask: "What has been suppressed? What is the other side of the coin?" This consideration will not only help us to detect the common propaganda trick of card stacking—of giving only one side of an issue—but it will also give us considerable insight into the Attitude. "Love Not Me for Comely Grace," page 36, didn't make much Sense until we noticed the omission of most of what we would expect to find in a love song.[14]

A second valuable question, to aid in answering the major question, is this one: "Why emphasize this point?" In other words: "Why repeat this detail; why elaborate upon this item; why restate this idea? Why not go on to something new?" The answers "For emphasis" or "Because it's important" both beg the question; we must press further and ask, "Why, out of all the ideas that *could* have been emphasized, was this one chosen?" Obviously that particular idea bothered the speaker more than did the others; and we must search the context to determine why. We saw this process at work in "Since There's No Help," page 68, which contains the line "And I am glad, yea, glad with all my heart." Here is a somewhat more obvious example:

THE EVIL EYE

True!—nervous—very, very dreadfully nervous I had been and am! but why *will* you say that I am mad? The disease had sharpened my senses—not destroyed—not dulled them. Above all was the sense of hearing acute. I heard all things in the heaven and

---

[14] Did you notice, while examining "The Patriot," page 78, that the first stanza omits a detailed description of the triumph, but that the second stanza includes it? Does the Attitude change somewhat?

in the earth. I heard many things in hell. How, then, am I mad? Hearken! and observe how healthily—how calmly I can tell you the whole story.

It is impossible to say how first the idea entered my brain; but once conceived, it haunted me day and night. Object there was none. Passion there was none. I loved the old man. He had never wronged me. He had never given me insult. For his gold I had no desire. I think it was his eye! yes, it was this! One of his eyes resembled that of a vulture—a pale blue eye, with a film over it. Whenever it fell upon me, my blood ran cold; and so by degrees—very gradually—I made up my mind to take the life of the old man, and thus rid myself of the eye for ever.

Now this is the point. You fancy me mad. Madmen know nothing. But you should have seen *me*. You should have seen how wisely I proceeded—with what caution—with what foresight—with what dissimulation I went to work!

—Edgar Allan Poe, "The Tell-Tale Heart" (1843)

Yet a third additional subquestion is: "Why interrupt the selection to insert this detail?" "Why go off on a tangent here?" We must realize that when the flow of directed thought is interrupted, the disruptive element must have been stronger than the original flow. For this reason, a tangent, a sudden change of subject, a switch in the main line of thought, may prove especially valuable clues to Attitude.

HOTSPUR'S ANSWER

My liege, I did deny no prisoners.
But I remember, when the fight was done,
When I was dry with rage and extreme toil,
Breathless and faint, leaning upon my sword,
Came there a certain lord, neat, trimly dress'd,   5
Fresh as a bridegroom; and his chin new reap'd
Show'd like a stubble-land at harvest-home.
He was perfumed like a milliner;
And 'twixt his finger and his thumb he held
A pouncet-box, which ever and anon   10
He gave his nose and took't away again;
Who therewith angry, when it next came there,
Took it in snuff; and still he smil'd and talk'd;

And as the soldiers bore dead bodies by,
15   He call'd them untaught knaves, unmannerly,
To bring a slovenly unhandsome corse
Betwixt the wind and his nobility.
With many holiday and lady terms
He question'd me; amongst the rest, demanded
20   My prisoners in your Majesty's behalf.
          —William Shakespeare, *I Henry IV* (1598)

> Now, why does Hotspur not finish the sentence immediately after line 2? Why elaborate upon that theme for two more lines? And then, having described the lord in line 5—with perhaps line 6 thrown in for good measure—why does he not proceed immediately to line 19? What new impulse generates line 8? And having finished line 8, why does he go on and on about the pouncet-box, lines 9–13? Why not proceed directly to line 19? Notice the new tangent introduced in line 14. Do you see how each bitter recollection impels another, so that what started out to be a simple answer develops into a string of accusations? (More important to reading aloud, do you see that each interruption is generated by a fresh burst of energy and that the attitude becomes more and more intense as the speech proceeds?) The easy answer, "He does it for emphasis," misses most of what is going on.

In summary, then, Attitude is the relation between the speaker and the reality he is creating. To detect Attitude, we must observe carefully the details he includes, the details he emphasizes, the words he applies to those details, the details he omits, and the details which loom so large as to deflect the line of argument. Phrased as questions, this becomes, briefly:

What is the speaker's Attitude?
  Why use this word instead of an alternate?
  What has been omitted that we would expect to find?
  Why has this point been emphasized instead of another?
  Why interrupt the selection to insert this detail?

The search for Attitude is an excellent device for correcting misconceptions arising from an over-hasty search for Mood; the detection of Mood will, conversely, help to unify the swiftly changing Attitude. Attitude analysis may keep us from splitting hairs in a search for abstract Sense; but Sense alone is the clue to complicated syntax. Sense, Mood, and Attitude are all valuable aspects of meaning.

SOCIAL INTENT

Intent, in its broadest and simplest sense, is the purpose for which a piece was written. However, such a definition may plunge us deep into Freudian or Jungian analysis, or into aesthetic arguments about the relation between truth and beauty, or (since artists must eat) into an investigation of the cost-of-living index in the author's lifetime. So we had better restrict ourselves to the didactic and hortatory element in literature. Let us consider only Social Intent. And Social Intent we shall define as that which the writer wants his audience to do, within the realm of practical affairs, about the details he is presenting. Does he want us to rectify some injustice? Overthrow some tyranny? Become indignant over some situation? Feel sorry for some class of people? What does he want us to do?

Social Intent, then, will not be discernible in most literature. All lyrics and most short stories or novels or plays are their own excuse for being; they try chiefly to embody an experience which is valuable in and of itself. Only the most intransigent moralists and slogan-seekers will conclude that *Othello,* for example, is a warning against jealousy. On the other hand, in most essays and speeches, in all satire, and in all of what are called thesis plays or thesis novels, the writer seeks to draw our attention to a particular situation in the real world; often he tries to persuade us to change it. Usually he will try to make his message palatable by entertaining us liberally; in turn, we, as oral readers, must take care that the entertainment does not blind us to the import of the message.

The most difficult step in the analysis of Social Intent is to determine, in borderline cases, whether a significant amount of it is present. Even though we don't like to see a moral tacked on to what we read, such is our capacity for message-hunting and code-solving that even the most innocuous works are sometimes obliged to carry the familiar disclaimer, "All persons and events are fictitious, and any resemblance to actual persons or places is purely coincidental." In order to avoid the pitfalls of superficial reading, on the one side, and of finding a hidden cipher, on the other, we must be especially careful to temper our analysis with common sense.

Almost as important as the ability to find the clues is the capacity to judge their frequency and their strength. In other words, we must ask not only

"What is there?" but equally, "How much of it is there?" For example, we must gauge the number and the strength of the references to actual situations in the world outside the selection. Any murder story set in New York will probably contain references to actual places in New York, but we needn't suspect that the writer is trying to reform the police force. If the similarities between fact and fiction are numerous, however, and if, furthermore, the "factual details" play a large part in the plot, then we should become suspicious.

A useful critical weapon here is causation. Do the "factual details" seem to have *caused* a significant part of the action? Was the negligence of this "factual" police force responsible for the crime? Did this "factual" environment force the characters to act in this way? Another clue is the relevance to real life of the generalizations which are made directly or which can be inferred from the incidents. Are these generalizations emphasized? Do they apply systematically to a particular section of real life? Do we feel we have learned something concrete about a situation or character in real life?

Having determined the presence of a significant amount of Social Intent, we can usually decide what the intent is. Most of the time the clues are obvious; but at the risk of confusing the self-evident we shall briefly discuss a few of them. First, of course, are the stated opinions of the writer. These are found easily enough, in a speech or essay, by an analysis of emphasis: what points have been given most space; what points have been placed in positions of rhetorical strength, at the beginning and, especially, at the end; what points have been claimed to be most important; what points have been repeated or restated most often? In a novel or short story, we must study the places where the writer interrupts his narrative in order to make observations of his own. Here, in addition to the questions above, we must ask what points have been made when the suspense was highest.

Second, we must examine the opinions of the central character and those of other characters who have been shown to be both admirable and successful within the frame of the selection. Often the hero or heroine is the author's mouthpiece, but sometimes he will speak through the lips of an impartial observer or of a "wise man" to whom the other characters look for precept and example. Third, we gain valuable clues by analyzing the author's attitude toward the characters he creates: what epithets does he use to describe them; what is their relation to the obviously sympathetic characters—does a character line up with the "goods" or the "bads"; what extra details are given about the character's past life or present circumstance that tend to bias us one way or other? Fourth, we should apply a pragmatic test: what fate is assigned to each character—how does his philosophy work out in practice? Finally, perhaps, we should ask what the writer's audience can be reasonably expected to do about the situation or characters described.

But even after we have decided that Social Intent is present and have determined what the Social Intent is, we are faced with a further problem: who comprises the writer's audience? Does it consist of everybody in his generation; is it restricted to the contemporaries who read his works; or does it include posterity? The question is a vexing one, with implications for your whole theory of literature. Perhaps we can skirt most of the difficulties if we agree, for the present, that *you,* in your role as a responsible citizen, are the writer's sole audience. (Later on, we shall modify this arrangement.) For the present, then, your major question here will be: "How does the Social Intent apply to me and to the world I live in?"

Sometimes you can ignore the Social Intent as being no longer relevant. For example, modern research has pretty well established that Chaucer was satirizing a particular shipman in *The Canterbury Tales;* but you will appreciate the General Prologue, if at all, as a series of sly character sketches. On the other hand, you may find literary selections, written for another age and another place, which have a disconcertingly specific application to current affairs.

THE PEOPLE

The people is a beast of muddy brain,
 That knows not its own force, and therefore stands
 Loaded with wood and stone; the powerless hands
 Of a mere child guide it with bit and rein;
One kick would be enough to break the chain;   5
 But the beast fears, and what the child demands,
 It does; nor its own terror understands,
 Confused and stupified by bugbears vain.
Most wonderful! with its own hand it ties
 And gags itself—gives itself death and war   10
 For pence doled out by kings from its own store.
Its own are all things between earth and heaven;
 But this it knows not; and if one arise
 To tell the truth, it kills him unforgiven.

    —Tommaso Campanella (1622),
     trans. J. A. Symonds (1878)

In such cases you must be especially careful to use the common sense which we advocated earlier. Remember that for centuries crackpots have used the

Book of Revelation or the inscriptions on the pyramids as proof positive that the end of the world was at hand. But, having registered this warning, we must agree that if your total response—intellectual as well as emotional— shows you that the selection has a peculiarly modern application, then according to our present arrangement you should exploit it. Most of the time, of course, you will not be faced with such extremes; usually you will abstract from the Social Intent only that part which concerns you and your world— you will generalize the Social Intent. For example, the Civil War is far behind us, but the "Gettysburg Address" still touches pertinently, though generally, upon national problems. Since at present you are the authority, you alone can apply the tests. Is the passage directed at some of your actions or opinions? Is it directed at situations in which you, as a responsible citizen, should be interested? Does it convey information which you can use directly as a citizen? If so, the Social Intent is germane.

TONE

By Tone we mean the writer's adaptation to his audience, resulting from his attitude toward his audience, and his realization of their attitude toward him and toward the reality he is creating. If that sounds complicated, try to figure out for yourself the implications of the analogous phrase "tone of voice." Or consider how our definition differs from one of I. A. Richards': tone is "the perfect recognition of the writer's relation to the reader in view of what is being said and their joint feelings about it."[15]

Obviously, Tone will be greatly determined by Attitude and Intent, but it will not ordinarily consist of a simple sum of the two. For example, the writer's attitude toward his details may be one of fury; his intent may be to persuade us to crush the infamy, but his Tone need not be furious and incendiary: it may be coldly ironical; it may be ranting, expostulatory; it may be contemptuous of us for tolerating the abuse; it may seem to ignore us entirely; it may be facetious; or it may be one of a number of further possibilities that suggest themselves. Compare the Tone of such reformers as Edwin Markham, in "The Man with the Hoe"; Voltaire, in *Candide;* Daniel Webster, in "The Murder of Joseph White"; Aldous Huxley, in *Ape and Essence;* Shelley, in "Epipsychidion"; or Byron, in "The Vision of Judgment." Attitude and Social Intent will help you to detect Tone; but the chances are just as strong that Tone will help you to detect Attitude and Social Intent.

[15] *Op. cit.,* p. 207.

Implicit in our definition are two broad approaches to the investigation of Tone. One of them lies in the writer's apparent sense of proportion—in how he fits his subject into the accepted scheme of things. When Shelley writes "I fall upon the thorns of life! I bleed! I die!" we may have the uncomfortable suspicion that things are not really that bad. We may feel that he has lost perspective, that his Tone is shrill. We should ask, then, whether the writer exaggerates the importance of what he has to say. Does he promise us a tale that will freeze our young blood and make our two eyes like stars start from their spheres? Does he promise us "Things unattempted yet in Prose or Rhime . . ."? Such a writer has put himself on the spot, and if his material does not fulfill his promises, we will think his Tone pompous. On the other hand, does he fail to emphasize the exciting and unusual parts—does he write in a monotone? Does he attack indiscriminately—does he tilt at windmills? Does he labor hard to state the obvious—is his Tone pedantic? Does he turn everything into a joke, and are the jokes cheap ones? Does his reasonableness compel your respect, even when he makes points with which you disagree? In short, pose the same questions you would normally ask yourself about the way in which any stranger advanced his opinions. We assume that you will dismiss some selections as the work of crybabies or crackpots, accord others your grudging respect, and with still others feel comfortable or delighted.

A second approach to Tone lies in the way the writer treats his audience—in the pose he adopts toward us. Does he ignore us entirely? If so, is he simply unconscious of our presence, or is he thoroughly self-centered? Does he step out of the scene in order to address us directly? Does he load his work with digressions about himself and his opinions—is he a chatterbox? Is he coy with us—does he pretend that his opinions, simply because they are his, cannot have much weight? Does he nag us? Does he abuse us? Does he imply that his subject is too lofty for us—is he arrogant or condescending? Has he the grace to apologize when he states the obvious? Does he try to anticipate our reactions—can we find such clues as, "one might think . . .," "but the blow did not fall yet . . .," "unlike a careful man, he did not . . ." and so forth? Does he enjoy anticipating our reactions—does he tease us? As we stated earlier, for our present purposes you should consider yourself, as a responsible citizen, to be the writer's audience; hence your impression of the way he treats you will be the Tone.

The major question in the detection of Tone is probably this: "What kind of person is speaking?" And, as in everyday life, your strongest clue probably lies in your overall early impression. Because Tone is a quantitative as well as a qualitative thing, because it depends on the accumulation of emphases, we cannot easily give short examples. But if you compare the two selections below, you will doubtless find that your impressions of their Tones are quite clear, even though we have not discussed specific clues.

THE PORTRAIT OF MURDER

An aged man, without an enemy in the world, in his own house, and in his own bed, is made the victim of a butcherly murder, for mere pay. Truly, here is a new lesson for painters and poets. Whoever shall hereafter draw the portrait of murder, if he will show it as it has been exhibited, where such example was last to have been looked for, in the very bosom of our New England society, let him not give it the grim visage of Moloch, the brow knitted by revenge, the face black with settled hate, and the bloodshot eye emitting livid fires of malice. Let him draw, rather, a decorous, smooth-faced, bloodless demon; a picture in repose, rather than in action; not so much an example of human nature in its depravity, and in its paroxysms of crime, as an infernal being, a fiend, in the ordinary display and development of his character.

—Daniel Webster, "The Murder of Joseph White" (1830)

CATHERINE DEAD

I went into the room and stayed with Catherine until she died. She was unconscious all the time, and it did not take her very long to die.

Outside the room, in the hall, I spoke to the doctor, "Is there anything I can do tonight?"

"No. There is nothing to do. Can I take you to your hotel?"

"No, thank you. I am going to stay here a while."

"I know there is nothing to say. I cannot tell you—"

"No," I said. "There is nothing to say."

"Goodnight," he said. "I cannot take you to your hotel?"

"No, thank you."

"It was the only thing to do," he said. "The operation proved—"

"I do not want to talk about it," I said.

"I would like to take you to your hotel."

"No, thank you."

He went down the hall. I went to the door of the room.

"You can't come in now," one of the nurses said.

"Yes I can," I said.

"You can't come in yet."

"You get out," I said. "The other one too."

But after I had got them out and shut the door and turned off the light it wasn't any good. It was like saying good-by to a statue. After a while I went out and left the hospital and walked back to the hotel in the rain.[16]

—Ernest Hemingway, *A Farewell to Arms* (1929)

In trying to confirm your early impression, you may find this oversimplified formula useful for some selections: "Apply the techniques of Attitude analysis to the clues of Social Intent." We try to discover what the writer wants us to do (by searching for the clues to Social Intent) and then ask how he sets about getting us to do it (by discovering how he phrases the clues to his intent). Does he make his points brusquely, with no apology or modification? Does he qualify them out of existence? Does he state them directly; does he leave them chiefly to inference?

In selections in which there is no discernible or relevant Social Intent, you may find that the Tone is almost indistinguishable from the Mood. In such selections (and they comprise the vast majority of literature) your chief clues to Tone will be those which indicate that the speaker is aware of the Mood he is creating. Does he indicate that the Mood is fleeting or that he finds it unusual? Does he try to dissociate himself from the details that create the Mood? For example, if he fills his work with the arguments of a lot of angry characters, the Mood is likely to be one of anger; but his own sorrowful or disapproving reactions to those characters may be strong enough to create a Tone of sorrow or disapproval. Again, sometimes—as in the Hemingway selection above—the Mood seems to spring spontaneously from the details, and the speaker, separating himself from the details and hence from the Mood, carefully suppresses his own reactions; the Tone, then, is impersonal, and in our oral reading we must somehow indicate the impersonality while at the same time preserving the Mood.

Ultimately, then, our investigation of Tone concerns itself with this problem: "What evidence is there of a personality at work behind the selection, guiding and confirming our reactions to the details of the selection? Is that evidence strong enough to influence the way in which we must read the selection aloud?" Where Social Intent is discernible there will almost certainly be

---

[16] Reprinted by permission from *A Farewell to Arms* by Ernest Hemingway. Copyright, 1929, by Charles Scribner's Sons.

a relevant Tone. Even when there is no apparent Social Intent, there may be clues from which we can infer the speaker's sense of proportion or from which we can detect a personality who is clearly trying to communicate with us. But often—notably in plays, for example, or dramatic monologues—the personality of the writer is suppressed and can be discovered, if at all, only after an exhaustive scholarly study of the whole of his works. Obviously, in such cases, our own investigation of Tone will yield nothing, and we will make no attempt to suggest a Tone when we read the selection aloud.

Irony

Perhaps we should include a postscript upon irony, since it contributes greatly to the Tone of much of the greatest literature of all periods except, perhaps, the Romantic Age.[17] Irony—as opposed to dramatic irony, which we shall discuss in Chapter Six—is the contrast between apparent, or surface, meaning and the contextual meaning: the context is so arranged that the ironical statement has meanings different from—and usually contrary to—its ostensible meanings. Sarcasm is often ironic: "Oh sure! you're a real genius!" Note that the words here, on the surface, indicate high praise; but the context (here the "Oh sure!" plus probably the tone of voice and expression of face) indicates the opposite of praise. Understatement is often another form: "Well, the Korean Action wasn't exactly a picnic." The 1957 slang phrase, "Big deal!" is a good example of irony; so is the traffic cop's inevitable "Where's the fire, bud?"

Students who use irony effectively in conversation sometimes display a surprising inability to detect it in literature. Maybe some are careless, maybe some revere the printed word unduly, and perhaps still others think of art as exclusively "spiritual." Whatever the cause, the obvious advice is unfortunately a little too pat: "Be alert to the possibility that a given statement may not mean what it literally says." And so, even though it's a little like trying to explain a joke, let us consider a few clues you can watch for.

One of the devices of irony is to pretend to be coldly objective in situations which demand an expression of sympathy or of indignation. Sometimes this objectivity appears as a healthy curiosity, as in Swift's "Last week I saw a woman flayed, and you will hardly believe how it altered her appearance for the worse." Sometimes it pretends to miss the point. Sometimes it professes

---

[17] But see, for example, Cleanth Brooks, *The Well-Wrought Urn*, Reynal and Hitchcock, 1947 (also available in paperback: Harcourt, Brace, Harvest Books, HB-11), for persuasive analyses of the irony in Wordsworth, Keats, and Tennyson.

impersonally to call a spade a spade. Sometimes it naïvely oversimplifies. How many of these options can you detect in the following?

THE AUTO-DA-FÉ

The University of Coimbra had pronounced that the sight of a few people ceremoniously burned alive before a slow fire was an infallible prescription for preventing earthquakes; so when the earthquake had subsided after destroying three-quarters of Lisbon, the authorities of that country could find no surer means of avoiding total ruin than by giving the people a magnificent auto-da-fé.

They therefore seized a Basque, convicted of marrying his god-mother, and two Portuguese Jews who had refused to eat bacon with their chicken; and after dinner, Dr. Pangloss and his pupil Candide were arrested as well, one for speaking and the other for listening with an air of approval. Pangloss and Candide were led off separately and closeted in exceedingly cool rooms, where they suffered no inconvenience from the sun, and were brought out a week later to be dressed in sacrificial cassocks and paper mitres. The decorations on Candide's mitre and cassock were penitential in character, inverted flames and devils without tails or claws; but Pangloss's devils had tails and claws, and his flames were upright. They were then marched in procession, clothed in these robes, to hear a moving sermon followed by beautiful music in counterpoint. Candide was flogged in time with the anthem; the Basque and the two men who refused to eat bacon were burnt; and Pangloss was hanged, though that was not the usual practice on those occasions. The same day another earthquake occurred and caused tremendous havoc.[18]

—Voltaire, *Candide* (1758), trans. John Butt (1947)

Understatement is another device of irony—Mark Twain cabling from Europe that the reports of his death were grossly exaggerated. One clue that the writer is saying less than he means is undue intensification. Note that the prisons in *Candide* were "exceedingly" cool rooms, that the reports about Twain were "grossly" exaggerated. Of course, such intensives as "really," "very," "genuine," "exactly," "certainly," "absolutely," etc., are common enough, but when they appear un-

---

[18] Reproduced from Voltaire's *Candide,* translated by John Butt, and published by Penguin Books, Inc., 3300 Clipper Mill Road, Baltimore 11, Maryland.

necessarily, or when they begin to pile up, we should pay close attention. Notice the "altogether" in Hazlitt's remark, "I do not think altogether the worse of a book for having survived the author a generation or two." Another clue to understatement is undue restriction. Notice that Hazlitt adds the gratuitous "a generation or two"; note too the restriction—the unnecessary qualification—"I think" in Marvell's lines:

> The grave's a fine and private place,
> But none, I think, do there embrace.

A third clue to understatement is unexpected concession. Marvell concedes that the grave may be fine and private (an intensive?); Swift concedes that a "prodigious number of children . . . is, in the present deplorable state of the kingdom [another concession?], a very great additional grievance," before proposing that the rich landowners buy these children—and eat them.

Overstatement, as an ironic device, is perhaps less common than the others. But when the ironist does choose to overstate his case, he will generally toss in a mundane detail to bring us to earth with a jolt. Hence we should watch for the juxtaposition of dissimilarities. Here are two examples from "The Rape of the Lock":

> Sooner let earth, air, sea, to Chaos fall,
> Men, monkeys, lap-dogs, parrots, perish all!

> Here Britain's statesmen oft the fall foredoom
> Of foreign Tyrants and of Nymphs at home;
> Here thou, great Anna! whom three realms obey,
> Dost sometimes counsel take—and sometimes tea.

Just to be on the safe side, perhaps we should make a passing reference to one of the most obvious clues to satiric irony—the advocacy of extremes. Surely there are few students who will believe, for example, that in *A Modest Proposal* Swift is seriously advocating cannibalism as a solution to Ireland's population problems. For those very few, we suggest that you be as incredulous of an outrageous proposal in literature as you would if it occurred in conversation. When a writer makes a suggestion that violates your humanitarian principles, react as you would in ordinary life and ask "Is he kidding?"

Irony is, of course, one of the chief weapons of satire; but it is also used surprisingly often in lyrical poetry in order to keep the speaker, and us, from going overboard. To avoid the rather hysterical note that can turn up in intense passages—Shelley's "I pant, I sink, I tremble, I expire!"—poets often prefer to understate their case or to state it wryly. The great advantage of irony here—of even the irony, like Marvell's, that addresses a sweetheart in language appropriate to the football field—is that it helps its user to maintain perspective; it forces him to face the ridiculous side of even the most intensely serious experience and thus prevents him from confusing that experience with the whole of existence. And therefore, even when we are not reading satire, we must be alert enough to be surprised by incongruity, we must be sensitive to the Tone of irony.

THE MAJOR STEPS IN ANALYSIS

As we stated earlier, the five viewpoints from which we have chosen to examine the total unity are not mutually exclusive; they form many combinations and blend into each other so thoroughly that the same item may provide a clue to each of them. Accordingly, you should be suspicious of the procedure we outline below; certainly you should not feel obliged to follow it in all circumstances. If it doesn't work for you, modify it.

Nevertheless, the following steps, taken in roughly the order indicated, may yield you maximum results in a minimum of time.

1. Read the selection carefully and sympathetically. Since you are trying to form a general impression, do not linger over the tough spots and do not examine the details closely. Do not try to evaluate or decide whether this is good or bad or right or wrong; do not raise objections—not yet. Probably you will get better results if your initial reading is silent.

2. Decide tentatively upon the Mood. Immediately after your first reading, try to determine the feelings which have been evoked in you. If, during the reading, you were careful to refrain from raising objections or weighing merits, the feelings you now have are a pretty good indication of the Mood. Try to label the Mood—melancholy, anger, reverence, etc.—but don't spend much time searching for exactly the right word. At this stage you can settle for the sort of sentence that begins: "Well, it's sort of. . . ." Sometimes you will be wise to write that sentence down.

3. Decide tentatively upon the Tone. This may require a special reading, exactly like the first, but focused on the problem: What kind of person is writing? Sometimes the Tone is inseparable from Mood and Attitude, but if you do

find one, try to secure a rough label for it—indignation, resignation, accusation, etc. Again, you may have to settle for a somewhat vague sentence.

If the Tone seems to you to be ironic, proceed at once to an analysis of Attitude, since the Sense of an ironic statement may be totally misleading.

4. Determine the Sense. Reread the selection as often as necessary, paying special attention to the parts that appear complicated, vague, or questionable.
  a. Consult a dictionary of collegiate size or larger for the meanings of all words about which you are in the least uncertain.
  b. Paraphrase all the difficult sections, line by line. If the syntax is complicated, first attempt a grammatical analysis or itemize the details contained in the sentence. In extreme cases, sketch a map or diagram. If the selection is important, write out the paraphrase and check it against the original to insure that it accounts for every word; finally, read it carefully to check its logic.
  c. Write out a précis, whether or not the selection is difficult. Avoid using the words of the original and avoid reporting at second-hand.
  d. Test the accuracy of your précis by rereading the selection. Are all the important parts accounted for?

5. Analyze the selection carefully for Attitude. Study the word choice for evidence of slanting, bias, and try to decide upon the direction of slanting. Compare the wording of the original with the wording of your paraphrase or précis. Be especially alert to the connotations of the important words; keep asking, "Why use this word instead of _____?" Note the details that have been emphasized and those which have been omitted. Be especially suspicious of "unnecessary" repetition and of quick changes of subject.

If you suspect the Tone to be ironic, watch for evidences of inappropriate objectivity—pretending to miss the point, oversimplification, insistence upon calling a spade a spade; watch for clues to understatement—undue intensification, undue qualification, unexpected concession; watch for the juxtaposition of dissimilarities, the advocacy of extremes.

6. Determine the Social Intent, if any. Your analysis of Attitude will doubtless have revealed the presence of any significant amount of Social Intent; but a special rereading may be necessary. Examine the narrator's opinions, especially where they intrude into the main line of the action; examine the opinions of the author's spokesman, if there is one. Study the fate of any character whom you suspect to be a mouthpiece for, or a symbol of, a relevant code of opinion or behavior. Guard against the temptation to find veiled references to actual events; if you suspect that such references are intended, apply stringent tests of their validity and of their causal relationship to the outcome of the selection.

If the selection is ironic, you can often find the real social message disguised as a counterproposal which the writer advances and then rejects as absurd.

7. Fix upon the Mood. Reëxamine your early impression of Mood in the light of your investigation of Attitude. If there is any discrepancy between the two, check first to discover which "Mood" is more appropriate to the Sense, and then reëxamine the connotations of the most important words in an attempt to see a pattern. Read the selection aloud to determine whether the sounds fit the Mood.

8. Fix upon the Tone. Reëxamine your early hunch in the light of what you have discovered when analyzing Attitude and Social Intent. Apply the tools of Attitude analysis to the clues you discovered in your search for Social Intent. If no Social Intent emerges, look for evidence that the writer dissociates himself from the Mood. Weigh the writer's sense of proportion: how does he fit his subject into your world view? Examine the role he adopts toward you; watch especially for evidence of his awareness that communication is taking place. If none of these approaches yields a significant pattern, you may conclude that Tone is not a distinct aspect of this selection and has become submerged in Mood and Attitude.

At present your answers to many of these questions will necessarily be vague because so far we have been simply "adding up" all the details in an effort to get an overall impression. Our next major task in analysis, to be discussed in Chapters Six and Seven, will be to determine *how* the details have been put together. But there you will discover that how-it-is-said can usually be translated roughly into what-is-said. So, even after we have discussed Structure, there will be no additional steps in the procedure above—merely more clues to seek at each step.

EXERCISES AND ASSIGNMENTS

Paraphrase

1. Below are some familiar sayings which are commonly misinterpreted. Paraphrase the accepted interpretation. (As a hint, we have italicized the crux of the misunderstanding.) Paraphrase the common misinterpretation.

O Romeo, Romeo! *wherefore* art thou Romeo? (*Romeo and Juliet*)

The exception *proves* the rule. (Folk)

Feed a cold, *and* starve a fever. (*Note:* If you're not a medical student, try beginning with "If you. . . .)

God rest ye merry, gentlemen. (Christmas carol)

. . . down the naked *shingles* of the world. ("Dover Beach")

Sleep that knits up the ravell'd *sleave* of care. (*Macbeth*)

Strait is the gate. (Matthew 7)

O *Attic* shape! ("Grecian Urn")

2. A paraphrase is sometimes wordier than the original. Paraphrase these aphorisms as succinctly as clarity allows. Can you approach the brevity of the original?

There is properly no History; only Biography. (Emerson)

Who will watch the watchdog? (Latin tag)

Let the buyer beware. (Latin tag)

After us the deluge. (de Pompadour)

A stitch in time saves nine. (Folk)

3. Some of the following passages are very difficult; some are deceptively simple. Be prepared to offer an oral paraphrase of any line.

a.

SATAN'S DEFIANCE

(Satan . . . who, revolting from God, and drawing to his side many Legions of Angels, was by the command of God driven out of Heaven with all his Crew into the great Deep. . . . Here Satan with his Angels lying on the burning Lake, thunder struck and astonisht, after a certain space recovers, as from confusion . . . [and] comforts them with hope of yet regaining Heaven. . . .)

What though the field be lost?
All is not lost; the unconquerable Will,
And study of revenge, immortal hate,
And courage never to submit or yield:
5   And what is else not to be overcome?
That Glory never shall his wrath or might
Extort from me. To bow and sue for grace
With suppliant knee, and deifie his power
Who from the terrour of this Arm so late
10   Doubted his Empire, that were low indeed,
That were an ignominy and shame beneath
This downfall; since by Fate the strength of Gods
And this Empyreal substance cannot fail,
Since through experience of this great event
15   In Arms not worse, in foresight much advanc't,
We may with more successful hope resolve
To wage by force or guile eternal Warr,
Irreconcileable, to our grand Foe,

Who now triumphs, and in th' excess of joy
Sole reigning holds the Tyranny of Heav'n.   20
    —John Milton, *Paradise Lost,* I (1667)

b.

DECLARATION OF CAUSES

When, in the course of human events, it becomes necessary for one people to dissolve the political bands which have connected them with another, and to assume among the powers of the earth, the separate and equal station to which the Laws of Nature and of Nature's God entitle them, a decent respect to the opinions of mankind requires that they should declare the causes which impel them to the separation.

We hold these truths to be self-evident, that all men are created equal, that they are endowed by their Creator with certain unalienable rights, that among these are life, liberty and the pursuit of happiness. That to secure these rights, governments are instituted among men, deriving their just powers from the consent of the governed. That whenever any form of government becomes destructive of these ends, it is the right of the people to alter or to abolish it, and to institute new government, laying its foundation on such principles and organizing its powers in such form, as to them shall seem most likely to effect their safety and happiness. Prudence, indeed, will dictate that governments long established should not be changed for light and transient causes; and accordingly all experience hath shown, that mankind are more disposed to suffer, while evils are sufferable, than to right themselves by abolishing the forms to which they are accustomed. But when a long train of abuses and usurpations, pursuing invariably the same object, evinces a design to reduce them under absolute despotism, it is their right, it is their duty, to throw off such government, and to provide new guards for their future security.

            —Thomas Jefferson, *The Declaration of Independence* (1776)

c.

DEATH BE NOT PROUD

Death, be not proud, though some have callèd thee
Mighty and dreadfull, for, thou art not soe,
For, those, whom thou think'st, thou dost overthrow,
Die not, poore death, nor yet canst thou kill mee.
From rest and sleepe, which but thy pictures bee,   5
Much pleasure, then from thee, much more must flow,
And soonest our best men with thee doe goe,
Rest of their bones, and soules deliverie.

Thou art slave to Fate, Chance, kings, and desperate men.
And dost with poyson, warre, and sicknesse dwell,   10

And poppie, or charmes can make us sleepe as well,
And better than thy stroake; why swell'st thou then?
One short sleepe past, wee wake eternally,
And death shall be no more; death, thou shalt die.
                                    —John Donne (1633)

4. A paraphrase is not of much use unless it makes logical sense and unless it accounts for every major word in the original. Here are some paraphrases of lines 5-8 of "Death Be Not Proud" above. Where, specifically, does the error—if there is an error—occur? Where is the gap in logic? What words have been ignored?
   a. You can't tempt me to death with such bait as rest and sleep, or comfort for the bones and delivery of the soul. After all, the best people go first.
   b. When I am dead, I will enjoy then the pictures of rest and sleep. I'd prefer that the best men be allowed to go first to rest their bones and deliver up their souls.
   c. If rest and sleep, which are only imitations of you, give us much pleasure, then you will give us even more. (Another proof of your benignity is that) only the good die young, oh you who rest our bones and deliver our souls.
   d. (You cannot remove me) from my rest and sleep, which give me such pleasant pictures, unless you can promise me that even pleasanter pictures will flow from you. Let the best men go first (I prefer to stay here); so you take the rest of their bones and souls.
   e. Rest and sleep are only illusions by which you lure us into a pleasant state of false security. Even the best men are tricked, and think they'll rest their bones and deliver up their souls.
5. Paraphrase the last six lines of "Since There's No Help," p. 68. Do you find it valuable to itemize the details? Do you have to perform a grammatical analysis in order to find the referent of "his"? Who or what is dying?
6. Paraphrase lines 3-8 of Shelley's "Ozymandias," p. 101. What is stamped; whose is the hand; whose the heart? How do the passions yet survive—in the statue? In modern tyrants? In us? Does grammatical analysis help? Does itemization?
7. Paraphrase the Meredith sentence, p. 125. Does itemization help here?

ADDITIONAL EXERCISES

"A Glass of Beer," p. 76, first stanza. "The Patriot," p. 79, lines 21-22; last stanza. "Hotspur's Answer," p. 81, lines 18-20. "Love Not Me for Comely Grace," p. 36. "To His Coy Mistress," p. 99, lines 5-12, 37-44; "Westminster Bridge," p. 178, lines 9-10; "The Windhover," p. 275; "The Second Coming," p. 280, stanza 1; "God's Grandeur," p. 283, lines 1-4; "At the Round Earth's Imagined Corners," p. 280.

The Précis

1. Which of the following is the most satisfactory précis of "Satan's Defiance," p. 96? Even in the best one there is at least one serious misinterpretation; what is it?

a. What if we have lost the field? Will and I shall study about revenge and other things we cannot overcome. With bow and arrows we will defy their power; through lawsuits we will cast doubt upon his empire, and thus repay him for his low tricks. Experience shows that this imperial combination cannot fall. We shall overcome their guile and free the captured tyrant.

b. Even though victorious in battle, God shall never gain the glory of having forced me to surrender. To beg for pardon just because He has strong arms would be shameful. Since we are immortal, and since we have learned by experience, we may, with better hope of success, resolve to continue the struggle by warfare and subversion.

c. He says that even though he has lost a field he hasn't lost an empire. Even though Will is unconquerable and not to be overcome, he's not going to succeed in his extortion. He says he will pretend to bow down until he gets a chance to defy Will's power, and then the tyrant Will had better watch out.

d. God has defeated us once through His unconquerable will, and the fact that He cannot be overcome. It would be a shame to defy His strong arm so late, because Fate decrees that He and his empire cannot fail. But with foresight, we may attack the excesses of the Church, which is a tyrant.

2. In the following poem, the lover makes his plea as skillfully and carefully as if he were a lawyer arguing a case. Make a précis; then, if you have had public speaking experience, outline his argument. Which device is the more valuable to you?

To His Coy Mistress

Had we but world enough, and time,	
This coyness, lady, were no crime.	
We would sit down, and think which way	
To walk, and pass our long love's day.	
Thou by the Indian Ganges' side	5
Shouldst rubies find: I by the tide	
Of Humber would complain. I would	
Love you ten years before the Flood,	
And you should, if you please, refuse	
Till the conversion of the Jews.	10
My vegetable love should grow	
Vaster than empires, and more slow:	
An hundred years should go to praise	
Thine eyes, and on thy forehead gaze;	
Two hundred to adore each breast,	15
But thirty thousand to the rest;	
An age at least to every part,	
And the last age should show your heart.	
For, lady, you deserve this state,	
Nor would I love at lower rate.	20

But at my back I always hear
Time's wingèd chariot hurrying near,
And yonder all before us lie
Deserts of vast eternity.
25   Thy beauty shall no more be found,
Nor, in thy marble vault, shall sound
My echoing song; then worms shall try
That long-preserved virginity,
And your quaint honor turn to dust,
30   And into ashes all my lust.
The grave's a fine and private place,
But none, I think, do there embrace.

Now, therefore, while the youthful hue
Sits on thy skin like morning dew,
35   And while thy willing soul transpires
At every pore with instant fires,
Now let us sport us while we may,
And now, like amorous birds of prey,
Rather at once our time devour,
40   Than languish in his slow-chapped power.
Let us roll all our strength and all
Our sweetness into one ball,
And tear our pleasures with rough strife
Thorough the iron gates of life;
45   Thus, though we cannot make our sun
Stand still, yet we will make him run.
—Andrew Marvell (1681)

3. Prepare a précis of "Sailing to Byzantium," p. 44. Does that poem have as tight a logical structure as does "To His Coy Mistress"? As "I Hear an Army"? Does the presence of a central symbol preclude a logical organization?

4. Write out a two- or three-line précis of "All These Blessings," p. 66; check it for accuracy, and then file it away until you attempt to read this selection aloud. Does the précis help you to hold the passage together?

ADDITIONAL EXERCISES

"Medical Strategy," p. 65; "Studies," p. 57; "Style and the Man," p. 157; "I Am Born," p. 145; "An Important Omission," p. 158; "God's Grandeur," p. 283; "The Second Coming," p. 280; "The Express," p. 284; "Waterloo," p. 315; "Boulder Dam," p. 354.

Mood

1. What is the Mood of "The Evil Eye," p. 80? Hysteria? Triumph? Impatience? Contempt? Hatred? What? Why do you think so?

2. According to one textbook in the field, "Ozymandias," "conveys a tone of despair and desolation." Does "tone" mean what we have called Tone, or does it mean Mood? Do you agree that the Mood is one of "despair and desolation"? Cite evidence for your viewpoint. Cite evidence for that textbook's viewpoint.

OZYMANDIAS

I met a traveller from an antique land
Who said: "Two vast and trunkless legs of stone
Stand in the desert. Near them, on the sand,
Half sunk, a shattered visage lies, whose frown,
And wrinkled lip, and sneer of cold command,   5
Tell that its sculptor well those passions read
Which yet survive, stamped on these lifeless things,
The hand that mocked them, and the heart that fed:
And on the pedestal these words appear:
'My name is Ozymandias, king of kings: 10
Look on my works, ye Mighty, and despair!'
Nothing beside remains. Round the decay
Of that colossal wreck, boundless and bare
The lone and level sands stretch far away."
　　　　　　　　—Percy Bysshe Shelley (1818)

3. What is the Mood of the following selection? Why do you think so?

THE DEATH OF VICTORIA

When, two days previously, the news of the approaching end had been made public, astonished grief had swept over the country. It appeared as if some monstrous reversal of the course of nature was about to take place. The vast majority of her subjects had never known a time when Queen Victoria had not been reigning over them. She had become an indissoluble part of their whole scheme of things, and that they were about to lose her appeared a scarcely possible thought. She herself, as she lay blind and silent, seemed to those who watched her to be divested of all thinking—to have glided already, unawares, into oblivion. Yet, perhaps, in the secret chambers of consciousness, she had her thoughts, too. Perhaps her fading mind called up once more the shadows of the past to float before it, and retraced, for the last time, the vanished visions of that long history—passing back and back, through the cloud of years, to older and ever older memories—to the spring woods at Osborne, so full of primroses for Lord Beaconsfield—to Lord Palmerston's queer clothes and high demeanour, and Albert's face under the green lamp, and Albert's first stag at Balmoral, and Albert in his blue and silver uniform, and the Baron coming in through a doorway, and Lord M. dreaming at Windsor with the rooks cawing in the elm-trees, and the Archbishop of Canterbury on his knees in the dawn, and the old King's turkey-cock ejaculations, and Uncle Leopold's soft voice at Claremont, and Lehzen with the globes, and her mother's feathers sweeping down towards her, and a great old repeater-watch of her father's in its tortoiseshell case, and a yellow rug, and some friendly flounces of sprigged muslin, and the trees and the grass at Kensington.[19]

—Lytton Strachey, *Queen Victoria* (1921)

4. How does the Mood vary in the several translations of the simile from the *Iliad,* p. 153? In which translation is the Mood most appropriate to the Sense? Why do you think so?

5. Read "Bells for John Whiteside's Daughter," p. 103.

    a. What is the Mood? Why do you think so? Is the Mood shattered by the intrusion of any inappropriate details? If so, what are the details?

    b. After you have analyzed the Attitude (exercise 5 under Attitude), decide again upon the Mood. Does your answer differ from that in (a)? Can you account for the difference?

    c. After you have searched for evidences of irony in the poem (exercise 1 under Irony), decide upon the Mood again. Is there any difference in your answer now? Was Tone a better guide than Mood in this exercise? Was Attitude?

    d. Were all three steps necessary to give a full understanding of the poem?

ADDITIONAL EXERCISES

"Harry's Address at Harfleur," p. 175; "Westminster Bridge," p. 178; "The Runaway Slave," p. 215, paragraph 4; "Rose-Cheekt Laura, Come," p. 274; "Ariel's Song," p. 279; "Tears, Idle Tears," p. 281; "Moonlight and Music," p. 340; "Raleigh in the Tower," p. 355; "The Young King," p. 365.

Attitude

1. Your duties as a citizen in a democracy require that you be skilled in detecting bias, conscious or unconscious. You may as well start practicing here. On page 000 we cited an example of our bias; have you found others? Do we stack the cards? Do we distort fact? Read suspiciously from now on. (And if you find evidence of strong bias, please let us know!)

2. In "Education," p. 106, does Ruskin write with the accuracy he demands in his readers? Does he overstate? Does he slant? Why do you think so?

3. What is the attitude of the narrator in "Catherine Dead," p. 88? Why does he say "I do not," instead of "I don't"? What is the attitude of the doctor? Why does he refer so often to the hotel?

4. Is there a change of Attitude in "Since There's No Help," p. 68? Where does it occur? Is the change prepared for? How? What is the function of line 3?

---

[19] From *Queen Victoria* by Lytton Strachey, copyright, 1921, by Harcourt, Brace and Company, Inc.; renewed, 1949, by James Strachey. Reprinted by permission of the publisher.

5. In the following selection some mourners have gathered for a little girl's funeral. To introduce talk of geese into such a setting might shatter the Mood we conventionally expect and perhaps outrage the sentimentalist. But does such reference preclude a consistent Attitude? Do you find any places where the Attitude seems false? Where are they?

BELLS FOR JOHN WHITESIDE'S DAUGHTER
There was such speed in her little body,
And such lightness in her footfall,
It is no wonder her brown study
Astonishes us all.

Her wars were bruited in our high window.   5
We looked among orchard trees and beyond,
Where she took arms against her shadow,
Or harried unto the pond

The lazy geese, like a snow cloud
Dripping their snow on the green grass,   10
Tricking and stopping, sleepy and proud,
Who cried in goose, Alas,

For the tireless heart within the little
Lady with rod that made them rise
From their noon apple-dreams, and scuttle   15
Goose-fashion under the skies!

But now go the bells, and we are ready;
In one house we are sternly stopped
To say we are vexed at her brown study,
Lying so primly propped.[20]   20
            —John Crowe Ransom (1924)

6. As a counterpoise to exercise 5 above, is Attitude analysis a very useful approach to the following selection? Is Mood the dominant aspect here? Is Tone?

Peace, peace! he is not dead, he doth not sleep—
He hath awakened from the dream of life—
'Tis we, who, lost in stormy visions, keep
With phantoms an unprofitable strife,
And in mad trance, strike with our spirit's knife   5
Invulnerable nothings. *We* decay
Like corpses in a charnel; fear and grief

[20] Reprinted from *Selected Poems* by John Crowe Ransom, by permission of Alfred A. Knopf, Inc. Copyright 1924, 1945 by Alfred A. Knopf, Inc.

> Convulse us and consume us day by day,
> And cold hopes swarm like worms within our living clay.
> —Percy Bysshe Shelley, "Adonais" (1821)

7. In "Mending Wall," p. 222, what is the narrator's Attitude toward his neighbor? Cite evidence for your views.

ADDITIONAL EXERCISES

"For a Dead Lady," p. 262; "Satan's Defiance," p. 96; "Death Be Not Proud," p. 97; "Cloistered Virtue," p. 106; "Mock On, Mock On," p. 41; "The Meaning of Glory," p. 53; "Education," p. 106; "Why So Pale and Wan," p. 278; "When I Heard the Learned Astronomer," p. 283; "Claudius' Prayer," p. 359.

Social Intent

1. Even in this very short excerpt from a famous satire, you may be able to infer the Social Intent from the presence of one "irrelevant" clue. What is the clue? What is the Social Intent?[21] Is it any longer relevant?

> Shimei, whose youth did early promise bring
> Of zeal to God, and hatred to his king,
> Did wisely from expensive sins refrain,
> And never broke the Sabbath, but for gain.
> —John Dryden,
> "Absalom & Achitophel" (1681)

2. In the following passage, the aspect of Sense seems to predominate, but how many clues to Social Intent can you detect? List them.

EXPRESSION OF OPINION

... speaking generally, it is not, in constitutional countries, to be apprehended, that the government, whether completely responsible to the people or not, will often attempt to control the expression of opinion, except when in doing so it makes itself the organ of the general intoler-
5   ance of the public. Let us suppose, therefore, that the government is entirely at one with the people, and never thinks of exerting any power of coercion unless in agreement with what it conceives to be their voice. But I deny the right of the people to exercise such coercion, either by themselves or by their government. The power itself is illegitimate. The
10   best government has no more title to it than the worst. It is as noxious,

---

[21] Do you need as an additional clue the next two lines?

> Nor ever was he known an oath to vent,
> Or curse, unless against the government.

or more noxious, when exerted in accordance with public opinion, than when in opposition to it. If all mankind minus one were of one opinion, and only one person were of the contrary opinion, mankind would be no more justified in silencing that one person, than he, if he had the power, would be justified in silencing mankind. Were an opin- 15 ion a personal possession of no value except to the owner, if to be ob- structed in the enjoyment of it were simply a private injury, it would make some difference whether the injury was inflicted only on a few persons or on many. But the peculiar evil of silencing an expression of opinion is, that it is robbing the human race: posterity as well as the 20 existing generation; those who dissent from the opinion, still more than those who hold it. If the opinion is right, they are deprived of the op- portunity of exchanging error for truth: if wrong, they lose, what is al- most as great a benefit, the clearer perception and livelier impression of truth, produced by its collision with error. 25

—John Stuart Mill, *On Liberty* (1859)

3. What is the Social Intent behind "The Man with the Hoe," p. 186? In what stanza are the clues most frequent? What are the clues?
4. Is there a significant amount of relevant Social Intent in "Ozymandias," p. 101? If so, what is it? If not, why do you think not? (*Note:* In a class full of "ultimate authorities," you can expect little final agreement here, but your classmates' reason- ing may be enlightening.)
5. What is the Social Intent implicit in "Arms and the Boy," p. 183? Is it relevant to today?
6. What is the function of the two long paragraphs (lines 5–16 and 31–44) in "Mr. Polly's Decision," pp. 107–108? Are these reports of Mr. Polly's internal anguish? Are they stream-of-consciousness? Are they a plea for a type of morality? Why do you think so? Can they be all three at once?
7. What is the Social Intent, if any, in "The Early Church," p. 109? In "The Auto- da-fé," p. 91? In the Hellman passage on p. 318? In which of these three is the intent clearest? Why do you think so; which of the other aspects most influences your opinion?
8. What two institutions are attacked in "The Runaway Slave," p. 215? Which is the prime target? How do you know?

ADDITIONAL EXERCISES

"Mock On, Mock On," p. 41; "The World Is Too Much with Us," p. 62; "Decla- ration of Causes," p. 97; "The Proposal: II," p. 110; "An Important Omission," p. 158; "Mending Wall," p. 222; "When a Man Hath No Freedom," p. 277; "When I Heard the Learned Astronomer," p. 283; "Man and Gadgets," p. 296; "The Young King," p. 365.

Tone

1. We think the Tone of the "Adonais" excerpt, p. 103, is one of shrill expostulation, one clue being the restatement in line 1. Can you find others? Can you find clues that weaken our position? What *is* the Tone?
2. What is the Tone of "Mending Wall," p. 222? Account for the presence of such terms as "as it seems to me," "mischief," "a notion in his head," and "shade of trees." What other clues influenced your answer?
3. Arguing against the censorship of books prior to their publication, John Milton wrote the following passage. Is there any difference between its Tone and that of "Expression of Opinion," p. 104? Is there a similarity of Social Intent?

CLOISTERED VIRTUE

I cannot praise a fugitive and cloistered virtue unexercised and un-breathed, that never sallies out and sees her adversary, but slinks out of the race, where that immortal garland is to be run for, not without dust and heat. Assuredly we bring not innocence into the world, we bring impurity much rather; that which purifies us is trial, and trial is by what is contrary. That virtue therefore which is but a youngling in the contemplation of evil, and knows not the utmost that vice prom-ises to her followers, and rejects it, is but a blank virtue, not a pure; her whiteness is but an excremental whiteness. . . .

—*Areopagitica* (1644)

4. What is the Tone of the following? Do you detect any shrill insistence? Any con-descension? What else? Is the Tone appropriate to the Sense? Does it make the argument more, or less, authoritative and persuasive?

EDUCATION

And, therefore, first of all, I tell you, earnestly and authoritatively, (I *know* I am right in this,) you must get into the habit of looking in-tensely at words, and assuring yourself of their meaning, syllable by syllable—nay, letter by letter. For though it is only by reason of the opposition of letters in the function of signs, to sounds in the function of signs, that the study of books is called "literature", and that a man versed in it is called, by the consent of nations, a man of letters instead of a man of books, or of words, you may yet connect with that acci-dental nomenclature this real principle:—that you might read all the books in the British Museum (if you could live long enough), and re-main an utterly "illiterate" uneducated person; but that if you read ten pages of a good book, letter by letter,—that is to say, with real accu-racy,—you are for evermore in some measure an educated person. The entire difference between education and non-education (as regards the merely intellectual part of it), consists in this accuracy. A well-educated person may not know many languages,—may not be able to speak any but his own,—may have read very few books. But whatever language he

knows, he knows precisely; whatever word he pronounces, he pronounces rightly; above all, he is learned in the *peerage* of words; knows
the words of true descent and ancient blood, at a glance, from words of
modern canaille; remembers all their ancestry—their inter-marriages,
distantest relationships, and the extent to which they were admitted,
and offices they held, among the national noblesse of words, at any time,
and in any country. But an uneducated person may know by memory
any number of languages, and talk them all, and yet truly know not a
word of any,—not a word even of his own.

—John Ruskin, *Sesame and Lilies* (1863)

5. In "Ozymandias," p. 101, is there a significant difference between Mood and Tone,
such that an adequate oral reading would attempt to preserve both? If so, try to
label them.

6. We have suggested that one element of Tone is the way in which a message has
been fitted into your world view. If your world view were different, would you
detect a different Tone? Test this possibility by determining the Tone of "The
World Is Too Much with Us; Late and Soon," p. 62, and comparing your answer
with those of your classmates. Did you find a spectrum of opinion? Was world view
at the heart of the difference?

7. The following selection has been included here, rather than at some other point,
because we believe that the first half is more successful than the second. Further,
we believe that the difference is accountable chiefly by Tone. Do you agree that
there is a change in Tone? If so, try to label the two. Does another aspect become insistent in the second half? If so, what? Why do you think so?

MR. POLLY'S DECISION

"Old cadger! She hadn't no business to drag me into her quarrels.
[She] ought to go to the police and ask for help! Dragging me into a
quarrel that don't concern me.

"Wish I'd never set eyes on [her] rotten inn!"

The reality of the case arched over him like the vault of the sky, as   5
plain as the sweet blue heavens above and the wide spread of hill and
valley about him. Man comes into life to seek and find his sufficient
beauty, to serve it, to win and increase it, to fight for it, to face anything
and dare anything for it, counting death as nothing so long as the dying
eyes still turn to it. And fear, and dullness and indolence and appetite,   10
which indeed are no more than fear's three crippled brothers who make
ambushes and creep by night, are against him, to delay him, to hold him
off, to hamper and beguile and kill him in that quest. He had but to lift
his eyes to see all that, as much a part of his world as the driving clouds
and the bending grass, but he kept himself downcast, a grumbling, in-   15
glorious, dirty, fattish little tramp, full of dreads and quivering excuses.

"Why the hell was I ever born?" he said, with the truth almost win-
ning him.

20   What do you do when a dirty man who smells, gets you down and under in the dirt and dust with a knee below your diaphragm, and a large hairy hand squeezing your windpipe tighter and tighter in a quarrel that isn't, properly speaking, yours?

"If I had a chance against him—" protested Mr. Polly.

"It's no Good, you see," said Mr. Polly.

25   He stood up as though his decision was made, and was for an instant struck still by doubt.

There lay the road before him going this way to the east and that to the west.

Westward, one hour away now, was the Potwell Inn. Already things
30   might be happening there. . . .

Eastward was the wise man's course, a road dipping between hedges to a hop garden and a wood and presently no doubt reaching an inn, a picturesque church, perhaps, a village and fresh company. The wise man's course. Mr. Polly saw himself going along it, and tried to see
35   himself going along it with all the self-applause a wise man feels. But somehow it wouldn't come like that. The wise man fell short of happiness for all his wisdom. The wise man had a paunch and round shoulders and red ears and excuses. It was a pleasant road, and why the wise man should not go along it merry and singing, full of summer happi-
40   ness, was a miracle to Mr. Polly's mind. But, confound it! the fact remained the figure went slinking—slinking was the only word for it— and would not go otherwise than slinking. He turned his eyes westward as if for an explanation, and if the figure was no longer ignoble, the prospect was appalling.

45   "One kick in the stummick would settle a chap like me," said Mr. Polly.

"Oh, God!" cried Mr. Polly, and lifted his eyes to heaven, and said for the last time in that struggle, "It isn't my affair!"

And so saying, he turned his face towards the Potwell Inn.

50   He went back, neither halting nor hastening in his pace after this last decision, but with a mind feverishly busy.

"If I get killed I get killed, and if he gets killed I get hung. Don't seem just somehow."[22]

—H. G. Wells, *The History of Mr. Polly* (1909)

ADDITIONAL EXERCISES

"Slander," p. 31; "Mock On, Mock On," p. 41; "Studies," p. 57; "Style and the Man," p. 157; "I Am Born," p. 145; "On First Looking into Chapman's Homer," p. 197; "Invictus," p. 187; "The Runaway Slave," p. 215; "The Illumination," p. 224.

[22] From *The History of Mr. Polly,* by H. G. Wells. Reprinted by permission of the executors of the H. G. Wells estate, and of Dodd, Mead & Company. Copyright 1909, 1937, by H. G. Wells.

Irony

1. Examine the ironical devices in "To His Coy Mistress," p. 99. What is the chief device in lines 1–20? Are there others? What Mood (or, if you prefer, Tone) is established in these lines? What device is implicit in the bird-of-prey image, lines 38–40? In the soccer-football image, lines 41–44? Does the irony help to harmonize the Mood with the Sense? Or does it destroy the Mood?

2. Read "Romance," p. 189, and tentatively determine the Mood. Does the ironic last paragraph destroy the Mood, or does it prevent the Mood from becoming sentimental?

3. In the following, note how the highfalutin terms give the effect of conspicuous tact: "so advantageous an offer," "the doubtful and imperfect faith of modern ages," "has not been found agreeable to experience," etc. Find more examples of elaborate circumlocution. Are you reminded of the maxim, "Chivalry is the subtlest form of contempt"? What other ironic devices can you locate?

THE EARLY CHURCH

When the promise of eternal happiness was proposed to mankind on condition of adopting the faith, and of observing the precepts of the gospel, it is no wonder that so advantageous an offer should have been accepted by great numbers of every religion, of every rank, and of every province in the Roman empire. The ancient Christians were animated by a contempt for their present existence, and by a just confidence of immortality, of which the doubtful and imperfect faith of modern ages cannot give us any adequate notion. In the primitive church the influence of truth was very powerfully strengthened by an opinion, which, however it may deserve respect for its usefulness and antiquity, has not been found agreeable to experience. It was universally believed that the end of the world and the kingdom of heaven were at hand. The near approach of this wonderful event had been predicted by the apostles; the tradition of it was preserved by their earliest disciples, and those who understood in their literal sense the discourses of Christ himself were obliged to expect the second and glorious coming of the Son of Man in the clouds, before that generation was totally extinguished, which had beheld his humble condition upon earth, and which might still be witness of the calamities of the Jews under Vespasian or Hadrian. The revolution of seventeen centuries has instructed us not to press too closely the mysterious language of prophecy and revelation; but as long as, for wise purposes, this error was permitted to subsist in the church, it was productive of the most salutary effects on the faith and practice of Christians, who lived in the awful expectation of that moment when the globe itself, and all the various race of mankind, should tremble before the appearance of their divine Judge.

—Edward Gibbon, *The Decline and Fall of the Roman Empire* (1776)

4. In "Bells for John Whiteside's Daughter," p. 103, what is the function of such terms as "brown study," "astonishes," "wars were bruited," "cried in goose," "vexed," "primly propped"? Can you find other ironic terms? Would the Mood be more intense, or the Tone more sincere, if these mundane details were omitted? Is her death more painful because she seems so much alive?

5. Continue the above analysis in "For a Dead Lady," p. 262. Note there the intrusive rhymes, and the resulting echo of gaiety. Would her death seem a greater loss if a more "spiritual" Tone had been attempted?

6. Read the poems listed in Additional Exercises below. In your opinion, is irony destructive of loftier Moods?

7. In the following passage neither the author nor his representatives appear; is there a clearly discernible Tone? What devices are used?

THE PROPOSAL: II[23]

GWENDOLEN: Married, Mr. Worthing?

JACK (*astounded*):   Well . . . surely. You know that I love you, and you led me to believe, Miss Fairfax, that you were not absolutely indifferent to me.

GWENDOLEN: I adore you. But you haven't proposed to me yet. Nothing has been said at all about marriage. The subject has not even been touched on.

JACK: Well . . . may I propose to you now?

GWENDOLEN: I think it would be an admirable opportunity. And to spare you any possible disappointment, Mr. Worthing, I think it only fair to tell you quite frankly beforehand that I am fully determined to accept you.

JACK: Gwendolen!

GWENDOLEN: Yes, Mr. Worthing, what have got to say to me?

JACK: You know what I have got to say to you.

GWENDOLEN: Yes, but you don't say it.

JACK: Gwendolen, will you marry me? (*Goes on his knees*)

GWENDOLEN: Of course I will, darling. How long you have been about it! I am afraid you have had very little experience in how to propose.

JACK: My own one, I have never loved anyone in the world but you.

GWENDOLEN: Yes, but men often propose for practice. I know my brother Gerald does. All my girl-friends tell me so. What wonderfully blue eyes you have . . . ! They are quite, quite blue. I hope you will always look at me just like that, especially when there are other people present.

---

[23] If a longer reading is desired, "The Proposal: I," p. 364, which in the original immediately precedes this excerpt, may be added.

(*Enter Lady Bracknell*)

LADY BRACKNELL: Mr. Worthing! Rise, sir, from this semi-recumbent posture. It is most indecorous.

GWENDOLEN: I am engaged to Mr. Worthing, mamma. (*They rise together*)

LADY BRACKNELL: Pardon me, you are not engaged to anyone. When you do become engaged to some one, I, or your father, should his health permit him, will inform you of the fact. An engagement should come on a young girl as a surprise, pleasant or unpleasant, as the case may be. It is hardly a matter that she should be allowed to arrange for herself.

—Oscar Wilde, *The Importance of Being Earnest* (1895)

8. Compare the Tone of "Arms and the Boy," p. 183, with that of the excerpt from "What Is a Boy?" p. 43. Are they equally appropriate to their Sense? What is the chief ironic device of the former? Are there others?

ADDITIONAL EXERCISES

Prose: "The Proposal: I," p. 364; "Medical Strategy," p. 65; "An Important Omission," p. 158; "The Meaning of Glory," p. 53; "The Runaway Slave," p. 215.

Poems: "Love Not Me for Comely Grace," p. 36; "There Is a Garden," p. 42; "Since There's No Help," p. 68; "The Major-General's Song," p. 252; "When a Man Hath No Freedom," p. 277; "Why So Pale and Wan," p. 278; "The Social Structure of Early Massachusetts," p. 285; "Because I Could Not Stop for Death," p. 281.

TO EMBODY UNDERSTANDING
IN EXPRESSION

The Bare Essentials: Clear Expression

SO FAR, we have been immediately concerned with what is on the page and your adequate response to it. In short, we have tried to lay foundations for effectively *studying* a text, pointing out, however, that reading aloud is a necessary part of effective study. Now we must get on more particularly to the oral part of the business—turning the text into properly expressive, and therefore impressive, speech.

One thing must be made crystal clear before we go a paragraph further: *language does not exist in print.* John B. Carroll puts it well when he defines language as "a structured system of arbitrary vocal sounds and sequences of sounds which is used, or can be used, in interpersonal communication by an aggregation of human beings, and which rather exhaustively catalogs the things, events, and processes in the human environment."[1] A text is a *printed representation* of a *segment* of language. *The Oxford English Dictionary* is no more the English language than the best geographical globe in the world is the earth itself. Each is a representation or *map.* Just as there are many geographical maps, of many kinds, so there are many language texts. The fundamental structure of each must be understood; if you are to read a map correctly you must understand its relation to its territory. For instance, a Mercator projection will accurately represent cardinal directions: each place on the map will show its north, south, east, west relationship to every other place, but if you expect it to show relative areas of countries, you will erroneously conclude that Alaska has almost as many square miles as all the rest of the states put together instead of only one-fifth as many. A good copy of any text will give the words in their proper order, one after another; but if you assume the spaces between the printed words represent spaces between spoken words, your reading will be wretched. Therefore, let's consider briefly the relationship of text to the oral reading of it.

[1] *The Study of Language,* Harvard, 1955.

Speech Sounds into Words

Look at this page, which is a map of the information we are trying to convey. You recognize words which are composed of letters. Since the letters are
the smallest units on this page, let's start with them. What are they? Letters
of our alphabet—absolutely silent. What do they represent? Sounds? Maybe.
But what sounds?

Say the sound you think of when you see the letter *s*. Say it again and listen
carefully to it. Now say the following sentence:

> Bryce was measuring sugar.

Note that only once as you *said* that sentence did you use the sound that you
ascribed to the letter *s*, and then you used it for the letter *c* in Bryce. The letter *s* appears three times in the written sentence, but when you spoke the sentence you gave it three different sounds and not one was the sound you thought
of for the letter *s*. Listen to the three different sounds of *th* as you say the following sentence:

> Thomas is older than Theodore.

And what about the sounds of *c* in

> Carry the cello to the cellar.

And the sounds of *ai* in

> He said he laid plaid in the aisle.

And what about the single so-called long *ā* sound represented by three different
spellings in this one:

> The doctor hunted in vain for Mrs. Vane's vein.

What sounds do the letters *ough* represent in the following?

> Although he coughed with the hiccoughs, he ploughed through the
> rough.

Letters are units of spelling. They may or may not represent sound, and when they do, there is not always constant correspondence between them and the sounds they represent. We have to see the letters clustered into "words" before we can ascribe proper sound to them.

Words into Ideas

In writing and printing each word stands by itself with a neat blank space on each side of it. When we speak, however, there is no such corresponding time interval between words—we string words together into word clusters. We make no more space between some words than we do between the syllables of an important polysyllabic word. We write or see on a page "I'm going to town," but we say "I'mgoingtotown," stringing all four words together into one cluster of uninterrupted sounds. We see the sentence, "He is absolutely wrong," and if we are very emphatic we may say "Heisabsolute lywrong," taking more time between the third and fourth syllables of "absolutely" than between any two of the words.

We must determine the basis for clustering words into uninterrupted strings of sound. Following is a column of word clusters. The plus signs are junctures which indicate that the words in each cluster are joined together. Now read the column aloud so that each line (word cluster) is a continuous string of sound with no silences at the plus marks; inhale *after* each line so as to insure a definite silence between each two word clusters.

> Marley + was + dead + to
> begin + with + there
> is + no + doubt + what
> ever | about + that + the
> register + of + his
> burial + was
> signed + by + the
> clergyman + the + clerk + the
> undertaker + and + the + chief
> mourner + Scrooge
> signed + it + and + Scrooge's
> name + was + good + upon
> 'Change + for + anything
> he + chose + to + put
> his + hand + to

It did not make very much sense, did it?

Now read aloud the next column in the same way, being sure to take a breath after each line.

> Marley
> was + dead
> to + begin + with
> There + is + no + doubt + whatever + about + that
> The + register + of + his + burial
> was + signed + by + the + clergyman
> the + clerk
> the + undertaker
> and + the + chief + mourner
> Scrooge + signed + it
> And + Scrooge's + name
> was + good + upon + 'Change
> for + anything + he + chose + to + put + his + hand + to

That made sense. Each line was a cluster of words comprising an *idea,* a psychological entity, essential to the whole meaning; each one was a continuous flow of speech sound and each was separated from its neighbors by silences. If silences do not come at the right places—between ideas—intended meaning is not achieved, as you saw in reading the first column.

The idea, then, is the unit of speech; it is found in a word or a cluster of words which constitutes a psychological entity. None of the word clusters in the first column makes a psychological unit. Look at "Marley was dead to." The "to" simply does not belong. The first possible psychological entity (idea) is "Marley." You can *think* "Marley." "Was dead" is a possible idea, "was dead to" is not. "Marley was dead" is possible and so is "to begin with." The two can be combined into "Marley was dead to begin with" but "Marley was dead to begin" is not, and so on.

So your first oral task is to translate the text (the language map) into speech (the real language). To do this you must cluster the words into the proper speech units (ideas) and utter each unit as a single sequence of articulate sound. Until this is firmly grasped, we cannot go on.

Look again at the units in the second column. Note that ideas may be composed of one or a number of words. Read aloud the following sentence, clustering the words as indicated by the underlining brackets.

\In order to prevent misunderstanding,/ \please note/ \that the ordinal numbers,/ \are first,/ \second,/ \third,/ \fourth,/ \and so on,/ \while the cardinal numbers/ \are one,/ \two,/ \three,/ \four,/ \and so forth./

Of the fourteen idea units in that sentence, six contain only one word each, three contain two words each, two contain three, two contain four, and one contains five. This shows clearly that the numbers of words in idea units may vary greatly and are determined by sense.

Read the following unpunctuated sentences, making sure that you have clustered the words into proper idea units, and note how many idea units are in each sentence.

What a silly thing to do

Never before have I been so embarrassed

He said one two three go

Run you sluggard step on it

To think beforehand is to save time later

Her sails from heaven received no motion
Her keel was steady in the ocean

Were you tempted to read the first line of the foregoing couplet

\Her sails from heaven/ \received no motion?/

What sense does "Her sails from heaven" make?

And the Lord God said It is not good that the man
should be alone I will make him an help meet for him

Did you read the words "help meet" as if they were a synonym for "help-mate"? If you did, you made the sentence ungrammatical. Thus read, it has a redundant indirect object in the two "him's."

Under "help meet" *The American College Dictionary* has the following: "n. helpmate. (erroneously from Gen. 2:18, 30 'an help meet for him')."

Look up the word "meet" right now, before you go on to the next paragraph.

How much richer is the passage when the words are clustered correctly:

\And the Lord God/ \said/ \It is not good/ \for the man to be alone/
\I will make him an help/ \meet/ \for him/

Read the following sentences aloud, clustering the words so that they will make the most satisfactory sense: (How many word clusters in each?)

How far from heaven is a lying tongue

I shall go when I have had enough and not a moment before

He can't or won't understand why I have refused

Hence home you idle creatures get you home
—William Shakespeare, *Julius Caesar* (1623)

He had however in the contemplation of what he was falling into anxiety about what he might be losing
—George Meredith, *The Egoist* (1879)

Yet by your gracious patience
I will a round unvarnished tale deliver
Of my whole course of love what drugs what charms
What conjuration and what mighty magic
For such proceeding I am charged withal
I won his daughter
—William Shakespeare, *Othello* (1622)

Thus saith the Lord God Let it suffice you O princes of Israel remove violence and spoil and execute judgment and justice take away your exactions from my people saith the Lord God
—Ezekiel

They heard and were abashed and up they sprung
Upon the wing as when men wont to watch
On duty sleeping found by whom they dread
Rouse and bestir themselves ere well awake
—John Milton, *Paradise Lost* (1667)

What difficulties did you have in getting the sense? Stick with them until you get it. Did grammatical analysis help you? For instance, what is the object of "had" in the Meredith sentence and what part of speech is "spoil" in the passage from Ezekiel?

WORD CLUSTERS AND PUNCTUATION.   Punctuate correctly each of the eight sentences quoted. Now read them aloud again, just as you did when you finally got the sense. In clear oral reading of those sentences, how many times were you silent at spots where you had not put punctuation marks? It is evident that good reading calls for many more silences than there are punctuation marks in the script. But does the opposite hold true—is there ever a punctuation mark at a spot where you should *not* be silent? Look at the third sentence; it may be correctly punctuated as follows:

> He can't, or won't, understand why I have refused.

Note that you do not have to break at the second comma to make perfectly good sense.

> I told him that, in spite of his feelings, or, indeed, in spite of his wife's feelings, he would do it.

If you have been erroneously taught "to pause at commas," you will read that sentence poorly. If you happened to *say* that sentence spontaneously in conversation, you would cluster the words as follows:

> \I told him/ \that in spite of his feelings/
> \or indeed in spite of his wife's feelings/ \he would do it./

Note: There are two commas where there are no silences—one after "that" and one after "or," and it is quite likely that in spontaneous speech there would be no silence after "indeed."

Would you put a silence at the comma after "but" in the following?

> I'll tell you—but, never mind, it isn't worth it.

If you will make a verbatim transcript of good speech, punctuate it correctly, and also mark all the silences with vertical lines, you will discover three interesting things about punctuation and silences, or vocal breaks:

1. There are many breaks where there are no punctuation marks.
2. There are many breaks where there are punctuation marks.
3. And most interesting: there are frequent marks where there are no breaks!

Moral: Treat punctuation for what it is—a visual aid for clarity. We cannot be too emphatic about this. Punctuation is strictly for the eye, not for the ear.[2] It was invented because, since there is much more to word relationship in language than mere word order, maps of language (printed texts), at least maps of *our* language, require marks to help indicate some of that further relationship. So we have the , ; : . ?, etc., each with its varying visual significance. Even the exclamation point is a sign for the eye.

We are here concerned, then, with punctuation only as it helps you to see grammatical relationships necessary for understanding. Having arrived at understanding, turn it into language—that is, speak the words in the proper oral, and therefore audible, relationships. Do not carry punctuation beyond its function and ruin your reading by trying to limit silences to punctuation marks, or to turn every mark into a silence.

We hope it is now clear to you that the first and basically important word relationship in language is the clustering of words into the proper idea sound units with appropriate silences between the units.

Ideas into Thoughts

Now let us look at ideas (word clusters) as they are combined into thoughts (sequences of word clusters). Here we are concerned broadly with the "sentence" as a composite of ideas. Short simple sentences may seem to give little trouble, but how about long sentences containing many ideas? A reader's listeners rarely have a script to follow. How are you going to make clear each idea as part of the overall thought unit?

Read the following sentence aloud so that it will positively answer the question, "What were you doing on the morning of April First, 1946?"

> On the morning of April First, 1946, I was sitting at my table eating my breakfast.

How would your questioner know that the sentence you have just read is your complete answer to his question? Well, he might guess it by the fact that you

---

[2] *The American College Dictionary* defines punctuation: "The practice, art, or system of inserting *marks* or *points* in *writing* or *printing* in order to make the meaning clear; the punctuation of *written* or *printed* matter with commas, semicolons, periods, etc." (The italics are ours.)

stopped after "breakfast" and did not go on. But his surest cue would be in the way you said "breakfast," with a falling vocal inflection which suggested finality.

Now answer the same question with the following sentence:

> On the morning of April First, 1946, I was sitting at my table eating my breakfast, wondering what fool capers my colleagues would try to play on me.

If you said "breakfast" with the same finality that you did in the first sentence, your reading was misleading. How did you make it perfectly evident in your second reply that you had not finished your thought at "breakfast"? The first thing you did, of course, was to have in mind the whole thought—that you were doing a complex thing: eating breakfast and wondering about April Fool. You made your thought evident by finishing the word "breakfast" with a rising vocal intonation, and your listeners knew you had not finished until they heard the falling finality on "play on me." The tune for "play on me" in the second reply is almost exactly like the tune for "breakfast" in the first reply. Note how the falling terminal ending indicates finality of thought, whereas the rising terminal ending suggests there is more to come.

Now, try answering the question still a third time, with

> On the morning of April First, 1946, I was sitting at my table eating my breakfast, wondering what fool capers my colleagues would try to play on me, and was considering how I might be on my guard against them.

Did you say it so that it was completely clear that you had not finished your reply either at the word "breakfast" or at the word "me," and that you *had* finished at the word "them"? If you did, you accomplished that clarity with your rising terminal endings on "breakfast" and "me" and a falling intonation on "them."

This is vital! Let's recapitulate.

As words are held together in sound clusters to convey ideas, ideas are combined into thoughts by appropriate vocal symbols which we have called terminal endings. A terminal ending is the direction that pitch is taking as a word cluster is concluded. This direction is of the greatest importance to sense, since by it listeners can tell whether an idea is an interior or concluding part of a thought. The terminal ending which indicates completeness or finality of a thought is a vocal inflection falling toward the lower level of your pitch range. Obversely, the terminal ending which shows there is something to follow, either explicitly in words or (NB!) *by implication,* is a rising (or possibly a level) vocal inflection. Test this on the two sentences answering the question, "What were you doing on the morning of April First, 1946?" Let us continue the exercise. Answer the question with each of the following sentences so that listeners will know you have not finished answering before the end of the sentence and that you *have* finished at the end:

1. On the morning of April First, 1946, I was sitting at my table eating my breakfast, wondering what fool capers my colleagues would try to play on me, and was considering how I might be on my guard against them, when Andrew Sharp threw open the door and shouted that the sea in the bay had withdrawn beyond the breakwater.

2. On the morning of April First, 1946, I was sitting at my table eating my breakfast, wondering what fool capers my colleagues would try to play on me, and was wondering how I might be on my guard against them, when Andrew Sharp threw open the door and shouted that the sea in the bay had withdrawn beyond the breakwater, leaving thousands of fish flopping among the rocks.

3. On the morning of April First, 1946, I was sitting at my table eating my breakfast, wondering what fool capers my colleagues would try to play on me, and was considering how I might be on my guard against them, when Andrew Sharp threw open the door and shouted that the sea in the bay had withdrawn beyond the breakwater, leaving thousands of fish flopping among the rocks, and before I could obey my impulse to tell him to go lay an egg, there was a terrific roar of surf and crash of splintering timber.

4. On the morning of April First, 1946, I was sitting at my table eating my breakfast, wondering what fool capers my colleagues would try to play on me, and was considering how I might be on my guard against them, when Andrew Sharp threw open the door and shouted that the sea in the bay had withdrawn beyond the breakwater, leaving thousands of fish flopping among the rocks, and before I could obey my impulse to tell him to go lay an egg, there was a terrific roar of surf and crash of splintering timber; the entire house was heaved from its foundations as if it had been a cork.

"April Fool"

5. On the morning of April First, 1946, I was sitting at my table eating my breakfast, wondering what fool capers my colleagues would try to play on me, and was considering how I might be

on my guard against them, when Andrew Sharp threw open the door and shouted that the sea in the bay had withdrawn beyond the breakwater, leaving thousands of fish flopping among the rocks, and before I could obey my impulse to tell him to go lay an egg, there was a terrific roar of surf and crash of splintering timber; the entire house was heaved from its foundations as if it had been a cork, and I found myself battling for my life in swirling, debris-laden water, the April Fool of a cosmic jest.

Did you manage to read each sentence so that the word which, by its falling terminal ending, clearly concluded the preceding sentence, just as clearly indicated by a rising terminal ending, that there was more to follow?

Why should an author write so long a sentence? In this case he could have made a dozen sentences of it. Had he done so, however, he would not have achieved the impact of the single sentence. To get its impact, you, as reader, must perceive all the ideas (word clusters) as parts of one *sequence* of ideas; reading it aloud, you must hold all the ideas together in a single sequence in order to convey the impact. Your listeners are able to discern the sequence by hearing the vocal terminal endings on the ideas.

So we see that in English, the pitch terminal endings—that is, the directions that intonation is taking as word clusters end—are symbols of sense. They should be counted as much parts of the structure of English as vowels and consonants. If you change the vowel between *b* and *d* as in from "bad" [bæd] to "bed" [bɛd], that sound change has changed the *sense*. Changing the terminal ending on the words "I shall" from falling to rising also changes the sense. When you say the first, you indicate the thought is ended; nothing more belongs to that thought. What do you indicate when you say the second? Whatever it is, you either invite a reply or imply some further notion to be added.

In order to show the fusion of the processes of clustering words into ideas and of combining ideas into thoughts, let us probe the following sentence:

He was not well able to employ his mind on its customary topic, being, like the dome of a bell, a man of so pervading a ring within himself concerning himself, that the recollection of a doubtful speech or unpleasant circumstance touching himself closely, deranged his inward peace; and as dubious and unpleasant things will often occur, he had great need of a worshipper, and was often compelled to appeal to her for signs of antidotal idolatry.

—George Meredith, *The Egoist* (1879)

Suppose we break it into the smallest idea units possible. Do you agree that each word cluster in the following columns is as small as it can be and still represent a *relevant* idea?

He	touching himself
was not well able	closely
to employ	deranged
his mind	his inward peace
on its customary topic	and as dubious
being	and unpleasant things
like the dome	will often occur
of a bell	he
a man	had great need
of so pervading a ring	of a worshipper
within himself	and was often compelled
concerning himself	to appeal
that the recollection	to her
of a doubtful speech	for signs
or unpleasant circumstance	of antidotal idolatry

Certainly, any further division will reduce relevancy. Don't you feel, however, that sense has already been distorted by too minute division? For instance, you can think "he"—especially if you have already read what goes before about Sir Willoughby Patterne. Maybe you can think "was not well able" without much frustration, although you certainly want to get on to *what* "he" was not able, as soon as possible. "To employ" in this context is definitely unsatisfactory; "to employ his mind" makes a much more relevant and therefore satisfying idea unit. Dropping down a couple of units, how much more satisfactory is "like the dome of a bell" than "like the dome—of a bell?" Note the increase in relevancy if we cluster the words as follows:

He was not well able to employ his mind
on its customary topic
being
like the dome of a bell
a man
of so pervading a ring within himself
concerning himself
that the recollection of a doubtful speech
or unpleasant circumstance

touching himself closely
deranged his inward peace
and as dubious and unpleasant things
will often occur
he had great need of a worshipper
and was often compelled to appeal to her
for signs of antidotal idolatry

Putting idea units into a column this way clearly indicates a break between each two. However, surely there are at least hints of breaks within some of the units, suggestive of the previous listing. And are not the breaks between the clusters of very different lengths? Is not the break between "his mind" and "on its" shorter than that between "topic" and "being"? The breaks between "occur" and "he had," and "worshipper" and "and was," are both longer than the one between "to her" and "for signs." Breaks keep the ideas clearly distinct; *length* of breaks shows the *closeness* or remoteness between ideas. "On its customary topic" is much more closely related to "to employ his mind" than to "being," and so on.

In order to make a map to indicate all this, let us try the following system: + to link words together into idea clusters and to indicate no break or silence whatsoever between words so linked; − to suggest "hints of breaks" within word clusters; ⌐_____/ to mark word clusters between which there are unquestionable breaks of varying length; and ↗, →, ↘ to show terminal endings. Does the following visual arrangement help? NB: An important caution must be sounded here: remember that the terminal ending marks indicate only direction of pitch; they do not indicate at what pitch the inflection starts or at what pitch it ends.

He + was + not + well + able − to + employ + his + mind − on + its +
customary + topic ↗ being ↗ like + the + dome + of + a + bell ↗
a + man − of + so + pervading + a + ring − within + himself ↗
concerning + himself ↗
that + the + recollection − of + a + doubtful + speech ↗
or + unpleasant + circumstance ↗ touching + himself − closely ↗
deranged − his + inward + peace ↘
and + as + dubious + and + unpleasant + things ↗
will + often + occur ↗
he + had + a + great + need + of + a + worshipper →
and + was + often + compelled − to + appeal + to + her ↗
for + signs − of + antidotal + idolatry ↘

Such marking is only a means to a vocal end, as extensive fingering on a piano score is a visual aid to early practice.

Read the foregoing again and again until you can make it sound like spontaneous speech, being sure to maintain the sequence. Note that we have suggested two falling terminal endings. As you listen to yourself and others say the sequence, do you detect any difference in the falling endings on "peace" and "idolatry"? If you are maintaining the integrity of the sequence, the ending on "idolatry" is nearer the bottom of your pitch range than the one on "peace." This leads us to consider the significance of pitch level in idea sequence.

Imagine your normal voice range for speech—this does not mean your entire vocal register, but the pitch range you use for speaking—to be divided into four segments:

4. High; used sometimes for special emphasis and under emotional stress.
3. Range above habitual pitch.
2. Usual range; one most frequently used.
1. Range just below usual to lowest speech level.

We have numbered the segments from lowest to highest to keep the numbers analogous with the direction of pitch.

If we could say Meredith's sentence to you according to our markings, you would hear that the ending of "idolatry" is down in segment 1, and because of its lowness you would know "idolatry" is the end of the sequence. "Peace" ends in 2. The falling inflection indicates a partial completeness, but it does not go low enough to suggest complete finality of Meredith's complex thought.

This illustrates that pitch level of terminal endings is also *significant:* that a falling terminal ending in one pitch segment will give a different meaning from a falling terminal ending in another segment. In visual schematic arrangement, then, a terminal ending marked ↘2 indicates partial completeness, and one marked ↘1 would tell the thought is completed.

Even at the risk of exaggeration, try to read the following stanza from Gray's "Elegy" with the terminal endings suggested:

> Perhaps ↗3 in this neglected spot ↗2 is laid ↗2
>   Some heart ↗3 once pregnant with celestial fire ↘2
> Hands ↗2 that the rod of empire ↗3 might have swayed →2
>   Or waked to ecstasy ↗2 the living lyre ↘1

Having got the "feel" of the sequence, say it from memory.

When we first used the word *sentence* in connection with idea sequence, we put it in quotation marks because written sentences and idea sequences do not always coincide. A period, though it may point the end of a sentence does not necessarily mark the full completion of a thought. Note another stanza from the "Elegy":

> The boast of heraldry, the pomp of power,
>   And all that beauty, all that wealth e'er gave,
> Awaits alike the inevitable hour.
>   The paths of glory lead but to the grave.

Write a tight, one-sentence précis of that stanza. Do not the whole four lines merge as a single thought, a single sequence of ideas? Although the stanza is printed in two declarative sentences, the last one (fourth line) is the summarizing clincher of the first one which ends with "hour," and "hour" should be read therefore so that listeners are prepared for the clincher. Finish "hour" with →2 or ↘2 and save ↘1 for "grave."

Do not let a period fool you. Of the four periods in the following passage, only one should coincide with the terminal ending ↘1. Why?

> I clutched the balustrade to steady me in my terror. I felt my eyes would burst their sockets as I strove to pierce the blackness of the great stair-well. Strain as I might, I could hear no sound from the death I knew to be relentlessly waiting somewhere beneath me. Only the soft, slow, implacable tock-tock-tock of the ancient clock far below penetrated that velvet void, to be answered by the surging rhythm of my own blood pounding in my ears.

RELATIVE VALUES OF IDEAS.   Sometimes the ideas in a sequence are about equal in psychological value, as in these sentences:

> The shipment included food, clothing, tools, and medicines.

> We must rise early, finish breakfast by five-thirty, have the camp dismantled by six, and be at the foot of the glacier by sun-up.

> We believe in being honest, true, chaste, benevolent, virtuous, and in doing good to all men.

> To express satisfaction the Casterbridge market-man added to his utterance a broadening of the cheeks, a crevicing of the eyes, a throwing back of the shoulders, which was intelligible from the other end of the street.
> —Thomas Hardy, *The Mayor of Casterbridge* (1886)

As you say these aloud, you show the equal value of the ideas by using essentially the same intonation terminal ending ↗ for each of the idea units except the concluding one, ↘, which shows the end of the sequence. Note that psychological parity of word clusters does not require equality in number of words. "And in doing good to all men" is basically equivalent to each of the preceding idea units. In the next excerpt note how the single word ideas, "seditious," "cruel," etc., are coördinate with multiple word ideas.

> We declare thee to be a condemner of God even in his sacraments, a prevaricator of divine law, of sacred doctrine and of ecclesiastical sanction, seditious, cruel, apostate, schismatic, having committed a thousand errors against religion, and by all these tokens rashly guilty towards God and Holy Church.
>
> —Trial of Joan of Arc (1431)

Read the following sentence aloud a number of times and listen carefully to your intonation. Be sure you read it so that it is clear as a sequence.

> Two men suddenly found themselves kneeling together in the High Road over a wisp of a grocer's boy.

We are going to enlarge this sequence. Remember the passage about the tidal wave? This time, we shall make the enlargement by interpolation as well as addition. Put in the interpolations without changing the terminal endings preceding the interpolations. For example, make "Two men" in the following sequence sound just the same as it did when you read the sentence above. Again be sure you read the sentence as a single sequence of ideas.

> Two men, coming from opposite ends of the town, suddenly found themselves kneeling together in the High Road over a wisp of a grocer's boy.

"Coming from opposite ends of the town" is not coördinate with, but modifies and is subordinate to "Two men." You must make this differential clear to your listeners. Did you do it? Did you say the words of the main clause with the same terminal endings as you did when you read it before the interpolation was added? And did you read the interpolation on a little lower pitch level than the main clause, and give "town" a rising terminal ending, so that "suddenly" began where "Two men" left off?

Now we shall increase the sequence again by adding a modifier to "boy." This time you must change the terminal ending on "boy" so as to include the modifying addition in the sequence.

> Two men, coming from opposite ends of the town, suddenly found themselves kneeling together in the High Road over a wisp of a grocer's boy who had been struck down by a passing lorry.

The further additions we shall make will all be interpolations. Carefully retain the terminal endings of the preceding sequence as you read the next one:

> Two men, coming from opposite ends of the town, one from the great Manor, the other from a nameless tenement, suddenly found themselves kneeling together in the High Road over a wisp of a grocer's boy, who, as he tried to round the corner with his cart, had been struck down by a passing lorry.

To read the last one, start "Two men" on a pitch two or three notes higher than when you read the first main clause by itself. This will give you a wider range for making the subordinations clear.

THE GROCER'S BOY

> **Two men, coming from the opposite ends of town, one from the great Manor, the pride of all the countryside, the other from a nameless tenement hidden in a labyrinth of squalid streets, suddenly found themselves kneeling together in the High Road over a wisp of a grocer's boy—unknown to either of them—who, as he tried to round the corner with his cart, which was much too heavy for him, had been struck down by a passing lorry.**

Did you manage it without having a completely final terminal ending until you got to "lorry"? Did you make the main thought stand out so that listeners would hear "Two men suddenly found themselves kneeling together in the High Road over a wisp of a grocer's boy" as the main thought, and catch the relative values of all the subordinate ideas? How many degrees of subordination are there?

Here is the first part of the sentence which the Bishop of Beauvais read at Joan of Arc's trial. It presents a nice problem in oral reading skill: in clustering words into idea units, in maintaining them in a thought sequence, and in showing relative values of ideas:

We judges, having Christ before our eyes and also the honour of the true faith, in order that our judgment may proceed from the Lord himself, do say and decree that thou hast been a liar, an inventor of revelations and apparitions said to be divine; a deceiver, pernicious, presumptuous, light of faith, rash, superstitious, a soothsayer, a blasphemer against God and his saints.

Length of Silences

On page 127 we mentioned that the amount of silence between two word clusters helps to show the remoteness or closeness of those ideas to each other. Beyond that, there is an interdependence between and among the silences themselves. To illustrate: turn back to page 118 to the "Marley" selection. If you make a break after "Marley" you must shorten the break after "dead." If you make "Marley was dead" a word cluster, you must lengthen the break after "dead."

CENTERING ATTENTION

The Core and Meaning

In every meaningful utterance of words there is a central idea which is the core of the meaning. It is audibly indicated to listeners by emphasis. In effective, spontaneous speech, speech which academic sterility has not dulled, this emphasis is automatically achieved. That is, the speaker's intent is sufficient stimulus to induce in him the physiological acoustical behavior which produces the emphasis. Reading aloud, however, is not spontaneous speech, and therefore the reader—having got the sense—must deliberately supply the necessary emphasis. Emphasis is a complex business. Its essence is change in manner of utterance; this change may entail difference in loudness, difference in pitch, difference in rate, difference in vocal timber. Usually, although by no means invariably, it is achieved by increasing the loudness, raising the pitch, and slowing the rate.

Let's take the sentence, "She will be here next week." Read it aloud so it will convey the following meanings:

1. Whoever else may or may not come, you can depend on it SHE will be here next week.
2. She WILL be here next week, come hell or high water.
3. She cannot possibly be there next week, because she is going to be HERE.

4. She cannot get here today or tomorrow, and I am not sure what day she will arrive, but she will be here sometime next WEEK.

5. She will not be here this week, but she will be here NEXT week.

In each case you conveyed the important or central idea by giving special emphasis to a different word, and the word emphasized in a given sequence was louder, higher in pitch, and took a little longer to say than any other word in the sentence. Repeat aloud the numbered sentences and note how your emphasis of the core words changes the loudness, pitch, and rate of all the other words.

Since core words must be emphasized, and since emphasis indicates the important idea, errors in emphasis will lead to errors in understanding, even as failure to understand will result in false, and therefore misleading, emphasis. Recall the case of "help meet" on page 119.

Macbeth, mulling over his planned murder of Macduff, says to himself,

> If it were done when 'tis done, then 'twere well
> It were done quickly.

What does he mean? What a load of meaning the first "done" carries! It says in effect, "completely finished, without any ill effects afterward." The first "done" is by all odds the most important word in the first seven; it is the core word and therefore must be read with the greatest emphasis. Here meaningful emphasis may or may not require a higher pitch, depending on subtlety of intent; it does call for *change* in pitch and marked increase in stress and time for utterance.

Read the lines so that they clearly mean, "If killing the king *ended* the business completely, resulting in no evil consequences, then it would be a good thing to kill him at once and with dispatch."

Of the fourteen words of Macbeth's speech, only two are really emphatic, and the first is more emphatic than the second.

Pick out the core word in each of the following statements by Abraham Lincoln:

> There is no grievance that is a fit object of redress by mob law.

> I believe this government cannot endure permanently half slave and half free.

> Calling a tail a leg don't make it a leg.

> In giving freedom to the slave we assure freedom to the free.

Do you agree that the most emphatic words are "no," "permanently," "make," and "assure"? If you do not, analyze the statements again very carefully. Had Lincoln omitted the word "permanently" in the second statement, which would be the emphatic word?

Among the other words there are varying degrees of stress depending on their relative importance to each other. These are likely to be pretty well managed if the central idea is grasped. Getting the central idea from the printed text and making it audibly clear is the very essence of oral reading skill.

In a first reading one often misses the core word because its importance is not revealed until later in the text. Here is the first part of an idea sequence. Read it aloud.

> It is possible to know about Christ so well

Where did you put your strongest emphasis? Now read the whole sequence through silently and then read it aloud:

> It is possible to know about Christ so well that, satisfied with that, we never come to know him; possible to haunt the holy place, and bustle about its precincts, yet catch no view of the Holy One.
> —*The Interpreter's Bible* (1952)

Unless you have a large eye span which will comprehendingly take in all the words up to the semicolon, you are not likely to emphasize "about," because you cannot know that it is the most important word in the first line until you have reached the semicolon.[3]

The quotation from *The Interpreter's Bible* illustrates the role of contrast in pointing up core words. This is easily clear in such simple sentences as

> If you spend your time doing this, you cannot do that.

> Will you come quietly, or must we use force?

> You take the high road and I'll take the low road.

But how often have you heard the parable of the Prodigal Son read and yet have never caught the contrast between "kid" and "fatted calf" because the reader

---

[3] Note that the break between "well" and "that" where there is no comma, is greater than the break between "that" and "satisfied" where there is a comma. Read aloud the preceding sentence and listen to your clustering of words, your maintaining of sequence, and your emphasis on the important ideas.

failed to see that "kid" is a core word and therefore failed to give it proper emphasis? You remember the story: the wayward son has returned after squandering his inheritance and his father kills for him a "fatted calf." The brother, who has not transgressed, complains to his father, and in his complaint says, ". . . and yet thou never gavest me a kid, . . ." Almost invariably those words are read with the greatest emphasis on "me," "thou never gavest ME a kid," which false emphasis clearly implies that his father HAS given the prodigal brother a kid, and that is not true. What the complainer is saying in effect is this: "You have never given me so much as a MEASLY YOUNG GOAT, but this wastrel brother comes along and for him you kill a FATTED CALF!" Quite a difference between a kid and a calf. There is a double contrast in the complaint, first between "me" and "him," and the more emphatic contrast between "kid" and "fatted calf." Read the brother's whole speech making "kid" and "fatted calf" properly emphatic.

> Lo, these many years do I serve thee, neither transgressed I at any time thy commandment: and yet thou never gavest me a KID, that I might make merry with my friends: but as soon as this thy son was come, which hath devoured thy living with harlots, thou hast killed for him the FATTED CALF.

Note the contrast in the father's reply:

> Son, thou art ever with me, and all that I have is thine. It was meet that we should make merry, and be glad: for this thy brother was dead, and is alive again; and was lost, and is found.

Study the following carefully; locate the core words; and then read it so that it will sound like meaningful, spontaneous speech.

THE STUDY OF OTHELLO

A convenient starting point for the study of *Othello* is the idea of a contradiction between appearances and reality. It is an idea that pervades *Twelfth Night.* "Nothing that is so is so." The whole story of the twins enforces the idea: "I am ready to distrust mine eyes/ And wrangle with my reason. . . . There's something in't/ That is deceivable." In *Othello* Iago seems honest and isn't. Othello does not seem jealous but is; Desdemona is given a double twist. She seems chaste and is; but Othello doesn't think so; his opinion is that, though she seems chaste, she isn't; his discovery is that, though in Iago's accounts she seemed unchaste, she is actually chaste. "Men should be what they seem."[4]

—Eric Bentley, *The Play: A Critical Anthology* (1951)

In the light of what has been said in this chapter, state the oral reading problems which the foregoing excerpt presents.

Reducing Stress

When one is conscientiously working to improve his oral reading skill, and is therefore desirous of not missing any meaning, he tends to give strong emphasis to too many words. Take any sentence of ten or a dozen words and yell each word on the same fairly high pitch, maintaining a uniform rate of utterance. In so doing you use a great deal of energy: you increase stress; you make a lot of noise, but where is the central idea, the core word? There is really no emphasis in the sense that we have been using the word. It is like driving over a "corduroy road" at high speed. The bumps come in such rapidly even succession that the road is almost smoothed out. However, if you ride over a road whose bumps are unevenly and more infrequently spaced, you have an *emphatic* ride. Effective emphasis is achieved only in relation to lesser emphasis. The Empire State Building is emphatic in the New York skyline, with the Chrysler Building, Radio City, etc., still strong but lesser points of emphasis. If all the buildings perceivable as part of the skyline were of uniform height, even though they were the height of the Empire State, the skyline would lose its breathtaking "emphasis." The relatively little buildings are absolutely essential to our perceiving the "meaning" of the New York skyline.

In English, reduction of stress is an integral part of language structure. Making the central idea clear calls for emphasizing the word (or maybe phrase) which in proper relationship to other words carries the important idea. In order to achieve proper relationship, some words must be touched very lightly. That is, they will be given relatively little stress, are likely to be said in lower pitch, and will be said more rapidly—indeed, they may actually be greatly shortened as "and" in "bread 'n' butter," or the first "that" in "I think th't that one will do." If you say both "that's" exactly alike, the central idea is missed. Proper reading calls for emphasis of the second "that," and marked reduction of stress on the first "that." This requires an actual difference in pronunciation of the words "that," just as "and" in the first example becomes quite correctly "n." Proper

---

[4] Reprinted by permission from *The Play: A Critical Anthology*, by Eric Bentley, p. 372. Copyright, 1951, by Prentice-Hall, Inc., Englewood Cliffs, N.J.

reduction of emphasis, then—or, as it is commonly called, unstressing—is not a negative thing; it is a positive decreasing of the magnitude of utterance—a reduction of the totality of stress, pitch, and length of utterance. It is an absolute essential in utterances comprising a sequence of ideas. The most frequent failures properly to reduce emphasis occur in overemphasizing articles ("a" and "the"), conjunctions, and prepositions. Warning: this is not to say that an article, conjunction, or preposition is never a core word. Ordinarily the article "a" is touched lightly and quickly and is not more than a vowel murmur. "An" hardly ever rhymes with "man," it sounds more like the last syllable of "human." "The" is rarely pronounced like "thee"; if followed by a word beginning with a vowel, it rhymes with the first syllable of "meander"—providing you say it fast. "And" sounds like the last syllable of "husband," or it may become just "nd" or even "n." You see, reducing emphasis is not only a matter of reducing stress. Oftener than not, it also means not only speeding up, but cutting short, frequently to the point of actual truncation.

Read the following, paying special attention to reducing emphasis on the words in small print. Do not worry about emphasizing the words in large print; focus attention on touching the small print lightly. Moreover, give to the apostrophes quick, nondescript vowel murmurs; that is, very slight vowel sounds that cannot be definitely distinguished as u, e, i, o, u, etc., as in "James 'nd John," "tit f 'r tat," etc.

Hamlet to the Ghost

ANGELS 'nd MINISTERS 'v GRACE DEFEND 's!
Be thou ' spirit 'v HEALTH 'r goblin DAMNED,
Bring w'th thee AIRS fr'm HEAVEN 'r BLASTS fr'm HELL,
Be thy intents WICKED 'r CHARITABLE,
Thou comst in sucha QUESTIONABLE SHAPE,
Th't I will SPEAK t' THEE.[5]

—William Shakespeare, *Hamlet* (1600)

Your first attempt was probably stilted. Try it a number of times. Does not the deliberate reduction of emphasis of the small print make the words in large print more emphatic? Now pick out the core words which will give the central ideas; emphasize them and keep the small print lightly stressed. Say the passage without looking at it, as if you were replying to the question, "You know what you should do; why don't you do it?"

As a final illustration of the importance of getting and emphasizing the central

---

[5] The orthographical liberties here are in the interest of orthoepy!

idea or core word, and of avoiding too many strong stresses, let us take a speech which nearly every high school student has read, even if, surprisingly, he has not had to learn it—Lincoln's "Gettysburg Address." We have put into capital letters the words which we consider to be emphatic—note how few there are. Following the text we discuss our emphases, line by line.

GETTYSBURG ADDRESS

1   Four score and seven years ago our fathers brought forth upon
2   this continent, a NEW NATION, conceived in LIBERTY, and dedicated
3   to the proposition that ALL men are created EQUAL.
4   Now we are engaged in a great CIVIL WAR, testing whether that
5   nation or ANY nation so conceived and so dedicated, can LONG en-
6   dure. We are met on a great BATTLE-FIELD of that war. We have
7   come to DEDICATE a portion of that field, as a final resting place for
8   those who here GAVE their LIVES that that nation might LIVE. It is
9   altogether FITTING and PROPER that we should do this.
10 But in a LARGER sense we CANNOT dedicate—we cannot CONSE-
11 CRATE—we cannot HALLOW—this ground. The brave men, LIVING
12 and DEAD, who struggled here, have consecrated it, FAR ABOVE our
13 poor power to add or detract. The world will little NOTE, nor long
14 REMEMBER what we say here, but it can never FORGET what they DID
15 here. It is for US the LIVING, rather, to be dedicated here to the
16 UNFINISHED work which they who fought here have THUS FAR SO
17 nobly advanced. It is rather for US to be here dedicated to the great
18 task remaining before US—that from these honored DEAD WE take
19 INCREASED devotion to that cause for which they gave the LAST FULL
20 MEASURE of devotion—that WE here HIGHLY RESOLVE that these
21 DEAD shall NOT have died in VAIN; that this NATION, under God,
22 shall have a NEW birth of freedom—and that GOVERNMENT of the
23 people, BY the PEOPLE, FOR the PEOPLE, SHALL NOT PERISH from
24 the earth.

> 1–3—Eighty-seven years ago our fathers established in this land a NEW NATION which they had conceived in LIBERTY and which they dedicated to the principle that ALL men were created EQUAL.

> The first six words merely remind the audience of the number of years since the nation's founding; they state a temporal fact. Strong emphasis on "fathers" tends to suggest that the fathers

did the job in contradistinction to someone else. "Brought forth upon this continent" merely introduces the spatial fact. The first really emphatic words are NEW NATION.

NEW and NATION are emphatic: the NATION,[6] a thing of magnitude, uniting the peoples of thirteen separate colonies. Why not NATION without NEW? It was not just ANOTHER nation. Its newness lay not merely in the recency of its establishment but in its spiritual structure. Its dedication to the proposition of EQUALITY for ALL men was NEW among the nations of the earth.

4-5—Now after eighty-seven years, we are INTERNALLY at WAR, to PROVE whether that nation, or indeed for that matter, whether ANY nation, conceived and dedicated as this nation was, can endure for LONG.

"That nation" is not emphatic because it is an echo of "NEW NATION." The nation has endured for eighty-seven years but is now threatened with destruction. We are fighting to test whether it can endure for LONG.

6—Today we have come together on a great BATTLE-FIELD of the war. "War" is not emphatic—mere echo; "great" is merely an intensifier.

7-8 — We have come here to DEDICATE part of this battle-field, as a permanent burial ground for the men who GAVE their LIVES—ALL they had to GIVE—in order that the nation we have been talking about, might LIVE.

Emphasizing "portion" introduces an irrelevant distinction. "DEDICATE" indicates the purpose of the gathering. "Final resting place" can be made adequately impressive without strong emphasis; moreover, under the circumstances, the ground would not be dedicated for any other purpose. Emphasizing "GAVE" calls to mind the voluntary nature of the sacrifice and Lincoln is going to call upon the living for voluntary support. "LIVES": What of more value could they have given? "That nation": echo. Note the two "that's" in line 8. Neither is emphatic but the second requires more stress and time than the first. They are very differently pronounced :"th't that." "LIVE" is emphatic because the whole purpose of the sacrifice was that the nation might "LIVE."

8-9—It is completely APPROPRIATE and RIGHT that we should dedicate this battle-field as a permanent burial ground.

---

[6] "A body of people associated with a particular territory who are sufficiently conscious of their unity to seek or to possess a government peculiarly their own" (*The American College Dictionary*).

10–11 — But looking at things very BROADLY, that is, in a LARGER sense, it is IMPOSSIBLE for us to dedicate this ground.

"Dedicate" is echo. "CANNOT" is a new, contrasting, and therefor very emphatic element.

We CANNOT dedicate it, nor can we CONSECRATE it, nor can we HALLOW it.

"Consecrate" and "hallow" climactically build on "dedicate." The second and third "cannots" are important but echoing negations.

11–12 — The brave men, ALL of them—the LIVING as WELL as the DEAD, who struggled here, have consecrated it FAR ABOVE our little abilities one way or another.

"Brave men," "struggled," "consecrated" are important but are not emphatic.

12–14 — The world will pay little ATTENTION and it will not REMEMBER for very long what we say today on this battle-field.

"Little" and "long" are descriptive modifiers. The basic sense can be conveyed without them: "The world will neither NOTE nor REMEMBER what we say here."

Oftener than not, readers make "say" emphatic. This is not only unwarranted anticipation of the contrast to be made in a moment but such emphasis implies that the world may note and remember something else that we may do here. If "say" is emphasized, then "we" must be also.

But the world can never FORGET what they DID here.

"FORGET": very emphatic contrast to "REMEMBER." "DID": contrast to "say."

15–17 — Therefore, it is for US, who are ALIVE, to be dedicated to the UNFINISHED work which they, UP to THIS POINT, so nobly advanced.

"US" here is not mere echo; it is emphatic repetition. Lincoln still had a war to win. That job faced the living. There is a climactic power in the repetitive emphasis of "US"—"US"—"US" and also of "WE"—"WE" in lines 17 and 19. "Dedicated" is echo. "Great task" is the echoed projection of "unfinished work."

"UNFINISHED" is not merely descriptive; it is emphatically definitive. "THUS FAR": remember, the war was by no means over. Those who fought at Gettysburg had nobly advanced the fight TO THAT POINT; the LIVING had the responsibility to carry on from there.

17–19 — The thing that remains for US is that from these honored DEAD WE take INCREASED devotion—

"Honored" is descriptive. Making "DEAD" emphatic keeps before us the dedicative purpose of the occasion. "WE": again the insistence upon the responsibility of all present. "INCREASED" is definitive; that the audience had SOME devotion is clearly assumed, else they would not have been there. That devotion must be INCREASED.

19–20 — to that cause for which these dead gave ALL they HAD—the LAST FULL MEASURE—of devotion.

"Devotion" here is mere echo. "WE": again the emphatic call to personal responsibility. Emphatic "DEAD" maintains the poignancy of the occasion.

21–22—In order that with God's help this NATION shall have a new beginning in freedom.

"NATION" is emphatic. It was preservation of the NATION that Lincoln was fighting for. "God": fervent, but beware an emphasis which implies a false alternative. Neither "birth" nor "freedom" are emphatic. The nation had a birth of freedom four score and seven years previously. Now the NATION needs a NEW birth of freedom to the end:

23–24 — that the GOVERNMENT of the nation, operated by the PEOPLE in behalf of THEMSELVES, should NEVER PERISH.

Nearly always the concluding clause is read with these emphases: "OF the people, BY the people, FOR the people." We think this is injudicious reading, possibly induced by slavish observance of an all too fallible "rule," and certainly perpetuated by shallow habit.

It is true that frequently in a series of phrases where each differs from another by but a single word, the unique words may require emphasis. For example:

We wondered whether we should go OVER the fence, UNDER the fence, THROUGH the fence, or AROUND the fence.

Here, the prepositions are clearly core words. But is this case comparable with "of the people, by the people, for the people," in our context?

We are striving to give the nation a NEW birth. The

nation cannot endure without GOVERNMENT. If there be GOVERNMENT, ipso facto, the people (who comprise the nation) are the governed ("of"). No one other than the people are the governed. As surely as there are governed ("of"), there are governors ("by") and beneficiaries of government ("for"). In our nation, the GOVERNMENT of the people shall be run BY WHOM? The PEOPLE. FOR WHOSE BENEFIT? The PEOPLE'S. How long shall this GOVERNMENT of the people, by the PEOPLE and for the benefit of THEMSELVES endure? It must NEVER PERISH!

How often, oh how often, has this speech been lacerated by orators flaunting their orotunds. It has fared even worse in the mouths of tortured students, goaded on by teachers who themselves could not read it very well because they had never really tried to get the sense. They took without question that which had been handed to them by their teachers. There is no substitute for judicious digging.

By way of summary suggestion the following should be used to center attention properly :

1. Locate the key words—the words which indispensably carry the greatest burden of sense for the whole selection. Emphasize these words.

2. Find the core words in each meaningful utterance. Emphasize these words.

3. Look for contrasts in the text; the words carrying the burden of contrast will be core words, and therefore should be emphasized. However, beware of an emphasis which suggests a contrast incompatible with the text.

4. Look for words which introduce new elements into the sense. They will be core words.

5. Avoid emphasizing words whose sense merely echoes that of previous words. Repetition of a word may be an echo, in which case, the repetition will not be emphatic. For example,

Three of them were going; ONE of the three was a novice.

The second "three" is an echo of the first. (Why is "one" emphatic?)

Repetition of a word may be a means of emphasis:

Three were there. I said THREE and I MEANT three.

The second "three" is emphatic. The third "three" is not emphatic if "meant" is intended as the core word in the last phrase. However, the third "three" can be properly more emphatic even than the second. This entails a lessening of emphasis on "meant." Why?

6. Beware the temptation to emphasize articles, prepositions, and conjunctions. Very rarely in good speech will "a" be emphasized to the point where it rhymes with "say," as it correctly may in

> I said A book, not THE book.

Oftener than not, the indefinite article is a mere vocal murmur. One frequently hears

> It is the only thing TO do.

We think the emphasis on "to" cannot be justified.

7. Check all grammatical modifiers to determine whether they are more or less important than the words they modify. That is, are they emphatically definitive or merely descriptive? In the following sentences, the modifier "brown" is clearly more important than "hand" in the first, and less important in the second:

> Hans and Rastus reached out to me as I passed; I took the brown hand first.

> He shook the brown hand of his son.

> Sense is the criterion for determining emphasis.

EXERCISES AND ASSIGNMENTS

Words into Ideas

1. Note carefully the difference in sense in each pair of the following sentences, and then read them so that other class members, listening, will unequivocally get the sense. Note the differences in emphasis!

    John said Jim is crazy.
    "John," said Jim, "is crazy."

    Barking dogs do not bite.
    Barking, dogs do not bite.

    If you can meet me at the station I shall be there at two o'clock.
    If you can, meet me at the station; I shall be there at two o'clock.

What do you mean? You will sell the house and include the car?
What? Do you mean you will sell the house and include the car?

We shall receive shoes and clothes which have had little wear.
We shall receive shoes, and clothes which have had little wear.

The plans which John drew up should be abandoned.
The plans, which John drew up, should be abandoned.

Do you know how to play the piano?
Do you know, "How to Play the Piano?"

He has to make another speech in Honolulu.
He has to make another speech, in Honolulu.

Will you telephone Dan?
Will you telephone, Dan?

George listened while I talked.
George listened, while I talked.

He has a bright red tie.
He has a bright, red tie.

I asked for milk, and bread, and butter.
I asked for milk, and bread and butter.

2. Study and read aloud carefully the following excerpts. Do you sound as if you were reading?

THE SINS OF THE FATHER

Yes, truly; for, look you, the sins of the father are to be laid upon the children: therefore, I promise you, I fear you. I was always plain with you, and so now I speak my agitation of the matter: therefore be o' good cheer; for, truly, I think you are damned. There is but one hope in it that can do you any good; and that is but a kind of bastard hope neither.

— William Shakespeare, *Merchant of Venice* (1596)

Note the pauses without commas, and, more important, the commas without pauses in that excerpt.

TO KNOW WHAT TO DO

If to do were as easy as to know what were good to do, chapels had been churches, and poor men's cottages princes' palaces. It is a good divine that follows his own instructions: I can easier teach twenty what were good to be done, than be one of the twenty to follow mine own teaching. The brain may devise laws for the blood; but a hot temper leaps o'er a cold decree. Such a hare is madness the youth, to skip o'er the meshes of good counsel the cripple. But this reasoning is not in the fashion to choose me a husband.

— William Shakespeare, *Merchant of Venice* (1596)

Paris at Evening

It was the evening hour, but daylight was long now and Paris more than ever penetrating. The scent of flowers was in the streets, he had the whiff of violets perpetually in his nose; and he had attached himself to sounds and suggestions, vibrations of the air, human and dramatic, he imagined, as they were not in other places, that came out for him more and more as the mild afternoons deepened—a far-off hum, a sharp, near click on the asphalt, a voice calling, replying, somewhere, and as full of tone as an actor's in a play.

—Henry James, *The Ambassadors* (1903)

Maybes

So far as man stands for anything and is productive or originative at all, his entire vital function may be said to deal with maybes. Not a victory is gained, not a deed of faithfulness or courage is done, except upon a maybe; not a service, not a sally of generosity, not a scientific exploration or experiment or textbook, that may not be a mistake. It is only by risking our persons from one hour to another that we live at all.

—William James, *The Will to Believe* (1897)

Creativity

Where creativity is blocked or thwarted, our very capacity to become fully human is endangered: so much so that the affirmation of life may take the form of negative creativity—that is, senseless violence and destruction, as has indeed happened on a large scale in our own day.

—Lewis Mumford, *The Role of the Creative
Art in Contemporary Society* (1958)

Also, go back to "Slander," p. 32; "The Portrait of Murder," p. 88; and "The Auto-da-fé," p. 91, and see how much you can improve your former reading of them by careful attention to putting words into ideas.

3. Take plenty of time to read the following, making sure you have clustered the words properly into ideas.

I Am Born

On the fifth day of November, 1718, which to the era fixed on (in the previous chapter), was as near nine calendar months as any husband could in reason have expected,—was I, Tristram Shandy, Gentleman, brought forth into this scurvy and disastrous world of ours.—I wish I had been born in the moon, or in any of the planets, (except Jupiter or Saturn, because I never could bear cold weather) for it could not well have fared worse with me in any of them (though I will not answer for Venus) than it has in this vile, dirty planet of ours,—which, o' my conscience, with reverence be it spoken, I take to be made up of the shreds and clippings of the rest;—not but the planet is well enough, provided a man could be born in it to a great title or to a great estate; or could anyhow contrive to be called up to public charges, and employments of dignity or power;—but that is not my case;—and therefore every man will speak of the fair as his own market has gone in it;—for which cause I affirm it over again to be one of the vilest worlds that ever was made;—for I can truly say, that from the first hour I drew my breath in it, to this, that I can now scarce draw it at all, for an asthma I got in skating against the wind in Flanders;—I have been the continual sport of what the world calls Fortune; and though I will not wrong her by saying, She has ever made me feel the weight of any great or signal evil;—yet with all the good temper in the world, I affirm it of her, that in every stage of my life, and at every turn and corner where she could fairly get at me, the ungracious duchess has pelted me with a set of as pitiful misadventures and cross accidents as ever small Hero sustained.

—Laurence Sterne, *Tristram Shandy* (1759)

4. Make the following sound like thoughtful but spontaneous conversation. Work on this until you can say it without the book.

Seidman's Success

So it came out all right. I made a success. People are coming now from all over to my Style shows, even from Australia I get fine write-ups in the papers. I am invited to be president of the Garment Manufacturers Association. Nowadays I walk into the bank, nobody looks like they wished they would be somewhere else. I got valuable opinions about conditions, politics, labor relations. Now that I don't need it, I could have all the credit I want, at special rates. I don't blame them, you understand. This is the way business is. But I'll tell you something, I'm wondering sometimes what is it all about. There is a certain satisfaction, I suppose, to make a success, to have an idea, fight it out, prove you are right with it. But doesn't last, the satisfaction. In a funny way, it's only the struggle lasts. The memory. I'm still reaching for the aspirin in my desk. I'm still getting up sometimes the middle of night, sweating, I'm afraid, I don't know of what. And in the shop, so it's on a bigger scale now but it's still the same business, the same problems, the same aggravations. If I want to go away for a while, I still got to worry what's going to be while I'm gone. Or maybe I don't have to worry. But I worry. You know what I mean?

My son? Well, this is a question. I couldn't answer you in one word. I had for him other ambitions than to be a dress manufacturer. You know, a lawyer, a doctor, something in the professions. But three years in the army, away from home, it changes a boy. You couldn't expect he should come back the same as when he went away. So there's problems. I'll tell you the truth, we had with him a few months after he got back from Korea, I thought I would lose my mind. It's anyway a touchy situation with the children nowadays. Like there would be a revolution, not only in politics, but the whole family relationship. But parents are still parents. They're sitting with their worries. How many years it's been going on now, one thing after another—Hitler, the war, communism, Korea, the atomic bomb—and then what you're reading every day in the papers, what's going on with the young generation, hot rods, cold propositions, gambling, dope, stealing, killing—honestly, sometimes your mind, it's too much to take in, you would think the world is turning into a Dante's Inferno altogether.

I suppose in my young days it was the same thing, different names only. Hijacking, low-lifing, bootlegging—there's always some kind of problems like this. But who had time to notice? I came over to this country, I was thirteen years old, right away I had to make a living. Not next week. Next day, if I wanted to eat. So I had a job in a grocery in the morning, in the afternoon delivering for a florist and three times a week, in the evening, pin boy in a bowling alley. The rest of the time I had for myself, except when I would go to night school. You know what was my biggest problem those days? How to save up six cents for a malted once a week, Saturday night. And maybe how to sit on the bench in night school so the teacher she shouldn't know I'm catching up a little sleep while she's reading to us.

We had in the neighborhood, I remember, bums too. I'll tell you the truth, I would maybe have liked to be one myself. But the first thing, my mother wouldn't let me. She was a plain woman, she had for the children plain ambitions. A lawyer, doctor, violinist, yes. A bum, no. In the second place, it's a very tough career, you know, to be a successful bum, and I didn't have the gist for it. Maybe just to be a regular bum, yes, but to work myself up to be a politician, a Tammany boss, maybe even the mayor, for this you got to have the right stuff. Nowadays it's different. It's no future for a bum. A kid steals an automobile, right away they rush him to a psychiatrist. They don't figure this is maybe a boy who's got a real talent for being a crook, he's practicing on automobiles, gradually he could work himself up, someday maybe steal a bus or a streetcar or maybe even a whole traction company. Then with the money, he could start up a big foundation, with a staff of psychologists who are making research about what to do with the problem of juvenile delinquency.[7]

—Elick Moll, *Seidman and Son* (1956)

5. Put the words of the following selection carefully into ideas. Underline word clusters as we did on pages 119–121. Compare your markings with those of your classmates.

PREACHING
"And he came into all the country about Jordan, preaching the baptism of repentance for the remission of sins."—St. Luke.

Consider the significance of that one word preaching. John the Bap-

---

[7] Reprinted with permission from Elick Moll, *Seidman and Son,* G. P. Putnam's Sons, 1956.

tist was a preacher, and that is all that he was. The baptism which he performed for those who were moved by what he said was the consequence of his preaching, and thus can be considered as bound up with it in one unity. Besides his preaching there is no record of anything that he did. His whole ministry was in the power of the spoken word.

Now and then someone arises with the shallow and weak suggestion that we need a moratorium on preaching. For the wrong kind of preaching—the preaching which is careless or halfhearted or conventional—we need not only a moratorium but a morgue. But to say that for preaching in its great full meaning there should be a moratorium is to express only the dull defeatism produced in those who have never discovered what preaching at its best can be. The power of the spoken word when the Spirit of God breathes in it is limitless. Remember John Wesley and George Whitefield bringing their vast awakening to multitudes of souls in eighteenth-century England. Remember what Dwight L. Moody did a century later to light new fires of consecration in many men and women, among whom was Sir Wilfred Grenfell. Remember what Phillips Brooks brought to Boston, and what other preachers later than he have given to their own communities. Consider also how, in the twentieth century, newspapers and books and particularly the radio have immeasurably extended the possible influence of the man who has something vital to say. Whether for good or for evil, the spoken word heard by the ears of listeners immediately present or transmitted in the press or over the radio has proved in the twentieth century to be a gigantic force in shaping the history of our earth. Remember, on the one hand, Hitler, on the other hand, Winston Churchill. If in the light of these facts any Christian preacher disparages his opportunity, it is only a sorry disparagement of himself. Never has there been a time when the pulpit and the word which goes out from it could represent a more thrilling opportunity for the man who may be a spokesman of the truth of God.[8]

—*The Interpreter's Bible*, Vol. 8 (1952)

Ideas into Thoughts

1. Here are some interesting idea sequences. Read them so as to make the unity of each perfectly clear.

INTERNATIONAL OBLIGATIONS

I have sought this opportunity to address you because I thought that I owed it to you, as the council associated with me in the final determination of our international obligations, to disclose to you, without reserve, the thought and purpose that have been taking form in my mind in regard to the duty of our government in those days to come when it will

---

[8] By Walter Russell Bowie in *The Interpreter's Bible*, Vol. 8. Copyright 1952 by Pierce and Smith. By permission of Abingdon Press.

be necessary to lay afresh and upon a new plan the foundations of peace among the nations.

—Woodrow Wilson, address to the U.S. Senate, January 22, 1917

NATIONAL POLICY

I am proposing, as it were, that the nations should with one accord adopt the doctrine of President Monroe as the doctrine of the World: that no nation should seek to extend its policy over any other nation or people, but that every people should be left free to determine its own policy, its own way of development, unhindered, unthreatened, un-afraid, the little along with the great and powerful.

—Woodrow Wilson, address to the U. S. Senate, January 22, 1917

CONSENT OF THE GOVERNED

I am proposing government by the consent of the governed; that free-dom of the seas which in international conference after conference rep-resentatives of the United States have urged with the eloquence of those who are the convinced disciples of liberty; and that moderation of arma-ments which makes of armies and navies a power for order merely, not an instrument of aggression or of selfish violence.

—Woodrow Wilson, address to the U. S. Senate, January 22, 1917

Note: What are the direct objects of the verb "am proposing"?

SERIOUS OBSTACLES

Although Oliver was assisted by a sort of ground-plan, made out and transmitted by Joseph Tomlins, whose former employment in Dr. Rochecliffe's service had made him fully acquainted with the place, it was found imperfect; and, moreover, the most serious obstacles to their progress occurred in the shape of strong doors, party-walls, and iron grates—so that the party blundered on in the dark, uncertain whether they were not going farther from, rather than approaching, the extrem-ity of the labyrinth.

—Walter Scott, *Woodstock* (1826)

LAMENT

She weeps bitterly by night,
   with her tears upon her cheeks;
She has no comforter
   out of all her lovers;
All her friends have betrayed her;
   they have become her enemies.

Judah has been carried into exile,
   to suffer tribulations and hard servitude;

She has to live among the nations,
  she can find no home;
Her pursuers have all overtaken her
  in the midst of her troubles.
                —The Bible, Lamentations

2. Locate the main thought in each of the following and then add to it, thus enlarging
the sequence, the subordinate ideas, as you did with the passage on page 131.

THE REAPERS

And as afield the reapers cut a swathe
Down through the middle of a rich man's corn,
And on each side are squares of standing corn,
And in the midst a stubble, short and bare—
So on each side were squares of men, with spears
Bristling, and in the midst, the open sand.
                —Matthew Arnold,
            "Sohrab and Rustum" (1853)

THE STRICKEN WHALE

As when the stricken whale, that from the tub has reeled out hundreds of fathoms of rope; as, after deep sounding, he floats up again, and shows the slackened curling line buoyantly rising and spiralling towards the air; so now, Starbuck saw long coils of the umbilical cord of Madame Leviathan, by which the young cub seemed still tethered to its dam.
                —Herman Melville, *Moby Dick* (1851)

PEDDLARS FROM CABOOL

But as a troop of peddlars, from Cabool,
Cross underneath the Indian Caucasus,
That vast sky-neighboring mountain of milk snow;
Crossing so high, that, as they mount, they pass
Long flocks of traveling birds dead on the snow,
Choked by the air, and scarce can they themselves
Slake their parched throats with sugared mulberries—
In single file they move, and stop their breath,
For fear they should dislodge the o'er hanging snows—
So the pale Persians held their breath with fear.
            —Matthew Arnold, "Sohrab and Rustum" (1853)

RUSTUM EYES THE DRUDGE

As some rich woman, on a winter's morn,
Eyes through her silken curtains the poor drudge
Who with numb blackened fingers makes her fire—
At cock-crow, on a starlit winter's morn,

When the frost flowers the whitened window panes—
And wonders how she lives, and what the thoughts
Of that poor drudge may be; so Rustum eyed
The unknown adventurous youth, who from afar
Came seeking Rustum, and defying forth
All the most valiant chiefs; long he perused
His spirited air, and wondered who he was.
    —Matthew Arnold, "Sohrab and Rustum" (1853)

3. How many complete thoughts (idea sequences) are there in the following selection
by Montaigne? Practice reading it aloud.

THAT THE INTENTION IS JUDGE OF OUR ACTIONS

Death, they say, releases us from all our obligations. I know of some
who have taken this saying in a different sense. Henry the Seventh, King
of England, made an agreement with Don Philip, son of the Emperor
Maximilian, or, to place him more honourably, father of the Emperor
Charles the Fifth, whereby the said Philip was to deliver into his hands
the Duke of Suffolk of the White Rose, his enemy, who had fled and
withdrawn into the Low Countries, Henry promising to make no attempt on the life of the said Duke; when he came to die, however, he
commanded his son in his will to put him to death immediately after
his own decease.

More recently, in the tragedy which the Duke of Alva presented to us
at Brussels in the persons of the Counts Horn and Egmont, there was
an abundance of remarkable incidents; among others, that Count Egmont, on whose word and assurance the said Count Horn had surren-
dered to the Duke of Alva, very earnestly prayed that he might be the
first to die, to the end that his death might release him from the obliga-
tion he was under to the said Count Horn.

To me it seems that death did not acquit the former of his given word,
and that the latter was discharged from it, even without dying. We cannot be bound beyond our strength and means, for this reason, that effect
and performance are not in our power, for nothing is really in our
power except the will; on this are necessarily founded and established
all the rules of the duty of man. Therefore Count Egmont, deeming his
soul and will to be indebted to his promise, though it was not in his
power to redeem it, was without doubt absolved from his duty, even if
he had survived Count Horn.

But the King of England, intentionally failing to keep his word, is not
to be excused for having delayed the performance of his disloyal action
until after his death; any more than was the mason in Herodotus, who,
having loyally kept during his lifetime the secret of the treasures of his
master the King of Egypt, revealed it at his death to his children.

I have known several in my time who, convicted by their conscience
of withholding others' property, arranged to satisfy it by their last will

and after their decease. But their act avails them naught, either by fixing a term for so urgent a matter or by trying to redeem an injury at so little cost to their feelings and their purse. They owe something of what is really their own. And the more burdensome and inconvenient the restitution, the more just and meritorious is the satisfaction. Penitence demands a burden.

They do still worse who reserve for their last will the declaration of some spiteful intention against a neighbour after having concealed it during life; thereby manifesting little regard for their own honour, since they irritate the offended against their memory, and less for their conscience, not having been able, even out of respect to death itself, to let their ill-will die down, but extending the life of their hatred beyond their own. Unjust judges, who defer judgement to a time when the case is beyond their jurisdiction!

I shall see to it, if I can, that my death discovers nothing that my life has not first declared [and that openly].

—Montaigne, *Essays* (1595)

4. Pay particular attention to terminal endings in reading the next selection.

THE LORD CHANCELLOR

LONDON.   Michaelmas Term lately over, and the Lord Chancellor sitting in Lincoln's Inn Hall. Implacable November weather. As much mud in the streets, as if the waters had but newly retired from the face of the earth, and it would not be wonderful to meet a Megalosaurus, forty feet long or so, waddling like an elephantine lizard up Holborn Hill. Smoke lowering down from chimney-pots, making a soft black drizzle, with flakes of soot in it as big as full-grown snowflakes—gone into mourning, one might imagine, for the death of the sun. Dogs, undistinguishable in mire. Horses scarcely better; splashed to their very blinkers. Foot passengers, jostling one another's umbrellas, in a general infection of ill-temper, and losing their foothold at street-corners, where tens of thousands of other foot passengers have been slipping and sliding since the day broke (if this day ever broke), adding new deposits to the crust upon crust of mud, sticking at those points tenaciously to the pavement, and accumulating at compound interest.

Fog everywhere. Fog up the river, where it flows among green aits and meadows; fog down the river, where it rolls defiled among the tiers of shipping, and the water-side pollutions of a great (and dirty) city. Fog on the Essex marshes, fog on the Kentish heights. Fog creeping into the cabooses of collierbrigs; fog lying out on the yards, and hovering in the rigging of great ships; fog drooping on the gunwales of barges and small boats. Fog in the eyes and throats of ancient Greenwich pensioners, wheezing by the firesides of their wards; fog in the stem and bowl of the afternoon pipe of the wrathful skipper, down in his close cabin; fog cruelly pinching the toes and fingers of his shivering little 'prentice boy on deck. Chance people on the bridges peeping over the parapets into a nether sky of fog, with fog all round them, as if they were up in a balloon, and hanging in the misty clouds.

Gas looming through the fog in divers places in the streets, much as the sun may, from the spongy fields, be seen to loom by husbandman and ploughboy. Most of the shops lighted two hours before their time—as the gas seems to know, for it has a haggard and unwilling look.

The raw afternoon is rawest, and the dense fog is densest, and the muddy streets are muddiest, near that leaden-headed old obstruction, appropriate ornament for the threshold of a leaden-headed old corporation: Temple Bar. And hard by Temple Bar, in Lincoln's Inn Hall, at the very heart of the fog, sits the Lord High Chancellor in his High Court of Chancery.

—Charles Dickens, *Bleak House* (1853)

Idea Sequences and Relative Value of Ideas

1. In order to give you practice in making perfectly clear sequences and main and subordinate values within sequences, here are eleven different translations of a passage from Book III of Homer's *Iliad:*

When the veteran Menelaus saw him striding towards him in front of the crowd, he was as happy as a hungry lion when he finds the great carcass of an antlered stag or wild goat and devours it greedily in spite of all the efforts of the sturdy huntsmen and the nimble hounds to drive him off. Thus Menelaus rejoiced when his eye fell on Prince Paris, for he thought his chance had come of paying out the man who had wronged him. He leapt down at once from his chariot to the ground with all his arms.[9]

—E. V. Rieu (1950)

Him, Menelaus, loved of Mars, beheld
Advancing with large strides before the rest;
And as a hungry lion who has made
A prey of some large beast—a hornèd stag
Or mountain goat—rejoices, and with speed
Devours it, though swift hounds and sturdy youths
Press on his flank, so Menelaus felt
Great joy when Paris, of the god-like form,
Appeared in sight, for now he thought to wreak
His vengeance on the guilty one, and straight
Sprang from his car to earth with all his arms.

—William Cullen Bryant (1870)

---

[9] Reproduced from Homer's *Iliad.* Translated by E. V. Rieu, and published by Penguin Books, Inc., 3300 Clipper Mill Road, Baltimore 11, Maryland.

Whom when the man, wrong'd most
Of all the Greekes, so gloriously saw stalke before the host,
As when a lion is rejoyc't (with hunger halfe forlorne)
That finds some sweet prey (as a Hart, whose grace lies in his horne,
Or Sylvane Goate) which he devours, though never so pursu'd
With dogs and men, so Sparta's king exulted when he view'd
The faire-fac'd Paris so exposed to his so thirsted wreake—
Whereof his good cause made him sure. The Grecian front did breake
And forth he rusht, at all parts arm'd, leapt from his chariot
And royally prepar'd for charge.

—George Chapman (1611)

    As thus, with glorious air and proud disdain,
    He boldly stalk'd, the foremost on the plain,
    Him Menelaus, loved of Mars, espies,
    With heart elated, and with joyful eyes:
    So joys a lion, if the branching deer
    Or mountain goat, his bulky prize, appear;
    Eager he seizes and devours the slain,
    Press'd by bold youths and baying dogs in vain.
    Thus fond of vengeance, with a furious bound,
    In clanging arms he leaps upon the ground
    From his high chariot:

—Alexander Pope (1720)

Forthwith, when Menelaüs, belovèd of Ares, espied him
Marching with long strides, proudly parading in front of the army,
Like as a lion is glad when he lights by chance on a carcass
Huge of a branch-horned stag or a horned wild goat in a forest—
He in his ravenous hunger devoureth amain, no matter
Even though many fleet hounds and young men lusty beset him:
Thus Menelaüs rejoiced, when before him he saw Alexander
Godlike under his eyes; for he vowed in his heart to avenge him
There on the sinner, and leaped full-armored down from his chariot.[10]

—William B. Smith and Walter Miller (1944)

Now as soon as Menelaos the warlike caught sight of him
making his way with long strides out in front of the army,
he was glad, like a lion who comes on a mighty carcass,
in his hunger chancing upon the body of a horned stag
or wild goat; who eats it eagerly, although against him
are hastening the hounds in their speed and the stalwart young men:
thus Menelaos was happy finding godlike Alexandros

---

[10] Reprinted by permission from William B. Smith and Walter Miller (trans.), Homer's *Iliad,* Book III, copyright, 1944, by The Macmillan Company, p. 57.

there in front of his eyes, and thinking to punish the robber,
straightway in all his armour he sprang to the ground from his chariot.[11]

—Richmond Lattimore (1951)

When, therefore, Menelaus, dear to Ares, caught sight of him advancing with long strides before the host, then, as a lion is glad when he
chances on some great carcass, finding in his hunger a horned stag or
a wild goat, for he greedily devours it although swift dogs and lusty
huntsmen drive upon him, so was Menelaus glad when his eyes beheld the godlike Alexander, for he thought he should punish the wrong-
doer. Promptly he jumped with his weapons from his chariot to the
ground.[12]

—Alston H. Chase and William G. Perry, Jr. (1950)

But when Menelaus, dear to Ares, was ware of him as he came forth
before the throng with long strides, then even as a lion is glad when he
lighteth on a great carcase, having found a horned stag or a wild goat
when he is hungry; for greedily doth he devour it, even though swift
dogs and lusty youths set upon him: even so was Menelaus glad when
his eyes beheld godlike Alexander; for he thought that he had gotten
vengeance on the sinner. And forthwith he leapt in his armour from his
chariot to the ground.[13]

—A. T. Murray (1924)

Him when the warlike Meneläus saw
With haughty strides advancing from the crowd;
As when a lion, hunger-pinch'd, espies
Some mighty beast of chase, or antler'd stag,
Or mountain goat, and with exulting spring
Strikes down his prey, and on the carcase feeds,
Unscar'd by baying hounds and eager youths:
So Meneläus saw with fierce delight
The godlike Paris; for he deem'd that now
His vengeance was at hand; and from his car,
Arm'd as he was, he leap'd upon the plain.[14]

—Edward, Earl of Derby (1910)

But when the warlike Menelaus saw him
As with great strides he passed before the throng,

[11] Reprinted by permission of The University of Chicago Press, p. 100. Copyright 1951 by University of Chicago.

[12] Reprinted by permission from Alston H. Chase and William G. Perry, Jr. (trans.), Homer's *Iliad,* Book III, copyright, 1950, by Little Brown & Company, p. 46.

[13] Reprinted by permission from A. T. Murray (trans.), Homer's *Iliad,* Book III, Harvard University Press, Loeb Classical Library, p. 119.

[14] Reprinted by permission from Earl of Derby (trans.), Homer's *Iliad,* Book III, copyright, 1910, by E. P. Dutton & Co., Inc. (Everyman's Library), p. 43.

> Glad as a lion when he has chanced on some
> Great carcase, antlered stag or jungle-goat,
> Which he has found when famished, and devours
> With relish, though stout youths and hunting dogs
> Attempt to drive him off; so glad at heart
> Was Menelaus when his eyes beheld
> The godlike Alexander, for he thought
> To have got his vengeance on the adulterer;
> And instantly he leapt in armour clad
> Down from his car to earth.[15]
>   —Sir William Marris (1934)

But when Menelaos dear to Ares marked him coming in the forefront of the multitude with long strides, then even as a lion is glad when he lighteth upon a great carcase, a horned stag, or a wild goat that he hath found, being an hungered; and so he devoureth it amain, even though the fleet hounds and lusty youths set upon him; even thus was Menelaos glad when his eyes beheld godlike Alexandros; for he thought to take vengeance upon the sinner. So straightway he leapt in his armour from his chariot to the ground.

—Andrew Lang, Walter Leaf, and Ernest Myers (1883)

Aren't the differences interesting? On the bases of these differences what valid conclusions can you draw about sequence and relative values of ideas?

Centering Attention

1. Study the following for central idea. After you feel sure you have done a good job, justify your reading as we did with the Gettysburg speech. If you are unusually keen as well as very diligent, each one will give you several hours concentrated study and practice.

IF IT WERE DONE

> If it were done when 'tis done, then t'were well
> It were done quickly. If th' assassination
> Could trammel up the consequence, and catch,
> With his surcease, success; that but this blow
> Might be the be-all and the end-all here,
> But here, upon this bank and shoal of time,
> We'ld jump the life to come. But in these cases
> We still have judgement here; that we but teach
> Bloody instructions, which being taught return
> To plague th' inventor. This even-handed justice

---

[15] Reprinted by permission from William Marris (trans.), Homer's *Iliad,* Book III, Oxford University Press, 1934, p. 54.

Commends th' ingredients of our poisoned chalice
To our own lips. He's here in double trust:
First, as I am his kinsman and his subject,
Strong both against the deed; then, as his host,
Who should against his murtherer shut the door,
Not bear the knife myself. Besides, this Duncan
Hath borne his faculties so meek, hath been
So clear in his great office, that his virtues
Will plead like angels trumpet-tongued against
The deep damnation of his taking-off;
And pity, like a naked new-born babe,
Striding the blast, or heaven's cherubin horsed
Upon the sightless couriers of the air,
Shall blow the horrid deed in every eye,
That tears shall drown the wind. I have no spur
To prick the sides of my intent, but only
Vaulting ambition, which o'erleaps itself
And falls on th' other.

—William Shakespeare, *Macbeth* (1606?)

STYLE AND THE MAN

According to the well-known saying, "The style is the man," complex
or simple, in his individuality, his plenary sense of what he really has to
say, his sense of the world; all cautions regarding style arising out of so
many natural scruples as to the medium through which alone he can ex-
pose that inward sense of things, the purity of this medium, its laws or
tricks of refraction: nothing is to be left there which might give convey-
ance to any matter save that. Style in all its varieties, reserved or opulent,
terse, abundant, musical, stimulant, academic, so long as each is really
characteristic or expressive, finds thus its justification, the sumptuous
good taste of Cicero being as truly the man himself, and not another,
justified, yet insured inalienably to him, thereby, as would have been
his portrait by Raffaelle, in full consular splendour, on his ivory chair.

A relegation, you may say perhaps,—a relegation of style to the subjectivity, the mere caprice, of the individual, which must soon trans-
form it into mannerism. Not so! since there is, under the conditions
supposed, for those elements of the man, for every lineament of the
vision within, the one word, the one acceptable word, recognisable by
the sensitive, by others "who have intelligence" in the matter, as absolutely as ever anything can be in the evanescent and delicate region of
human language. The style, the manner, would be the man, not in his
unreasoned and really uncharacteristic caprices, involuntary or affected,
but in absolutely sincere apprehension of what is most real to him.

—Walter Pater, *An Essay on Style* (c. 1890)

AN IMPORTANT OMISSION

Perhaps the critics may accuse me of a defect in my following system of polite conversation; that there is one great ornament of discourse, whereof I have not produced a single example; which indeed I purposely omitted, for some reasons that I shall immediately offer; and, if those reasons will not satisfy the male part of my gentle readers, the defect may be applied in some manner by an appendix to the second edition; which appendix shall be printed by itself, and sold for sixpence, stitched, and with a marble cover, that my readers may have no occasion to complain of being defrauded.

The defect I mean is, my not having inserted into the body of my book all the oaths now most in fashion for embellishing discourse, especially since it could give no offence to the clergy, who are seldom or never admitted to these polite assemblies. And it must be allowed, that oaths well chosen are not only very useful expletives to matter, but great ornaments of style.

What I shall here offer in my own defense upon this important article, will, I hope, be some extenuation of my fault.

First, I reasoned with myself, that a just collection of oaths, repeated as often as the fashion requires, must have enlarged this volume at least double the bulk, whereby it would not only double the charge, but likewise make the volume less commodious for pocket carriage.

Secondly, I have been assured by some judicious friends, that themselves have known certain ladies to take offence (whether seriously or not) at too great a profusion of cursing and swearing, even when that kind of ornament was not improperly introduced, which I confess, did startle me not a little, having never observed the like in the compass of my own several acquaintance, at least for twenty years past. However, I was forced to submit to wiser judgments than my own.

—Jonathan Swift, Introduction to *A Complete Collection
of Genteel and Ingenious Conversation* (c. 1738)

2. In the light of your study and practice thus far, read aloud the following: "All These Blessings," page 66; "The House of Usher," page 72; "The Portrait of Murder," page 88; "The Death of Victoria," page 101.

3. The following selections will give you opportunity to practice all you have learned in this chapter.

CONSIDER SLEEP

Do but consider what an excellent thing sleep is: it is so estimable a jewel, that, if a tyrant would give his crown for an hour's slumber, it cannot be bought; of so beautiful a shape is it, that though a man lie with an Empress, her heart cannot beat quiet till he leaves her embracements to be at rest with the other; yea, so greatly indebted are we to this kinsman of death, that we owe the better tributary, half of our life to him; and there is good cause why we should do so; for sleep is that golden chain that ties health and our bodies together. Who complains of want? of wounds? of cares? of great men's oppressions? of captivity whilst he sleepeth? Beggars in their beds take as much pleasure as kings; can we therefore surfeit on this delicate Ambrosia? Can we drink too much of that whereof to taste too little tumbles us into a churchyard, and to use it but indifferently throws us into Bedlam? No, No, look upon Endymion, the moon's minion, who slept three score and fifteen years, and was not a hair the worse for it.

—Thomas Dekker, *The Gull's Horn Book* (1609)

THE RURAL WALK

For I have loved the rural walk through lanes
Of grassy swarth, close cropped by nibbling sheep,
And skirted thick with intertexture firm
Of thorny boughs; have loved the rural walk
O'er hills, through valleys, and by rivers' brink,
E'er since, a truant boy, I passed my bounds
To enjoy a ramble on the banks of Thames:
And still remember, nor without regret,
Of hours that sorrow since has much endeared,
How oft, my slice of pocket-store consumed,
Still hungering, penniless, and far from home,
I fed on scarlet hips and stony haws,
Or blushing crabs, or berries that emboss
The bramble, black as jet, or sloes austere.
Hard fare! but such as boyish appetite
Disdains not, nor the palate, undepraved
By culinary arts, unsavory deems.
No sofa then awaited my return;
Nor sofa then I needed. Youth repairs
His wasted spirits quickly, by long toil
Incurring short fatigue; and though our years,
As life declines, speed rapidly away,
And not a year but pilfers, as he goes,
Some youthful grace that age would gladly keep,
A tooth or auburn lock, and by degrees
Their length and color from the locks they spare;
The elastic spring of an unwearied foot
That mounts the style with ease or leaps the fence;
That play of lungs, inhaling and again
Respiring freely the fresh air, that makes
Swift pace or steep ascent no toil to me,
Mine have not pilfered yet; nor yet impaired
My relish of fair prospect; scenes that soothed
Or charmed me young, no longer young, I find
Still soothing, and of power to charm me still.

—William Cowper, "The Task" (1784)

LINCOLN'S INN AT NIGHT

It is night in Lincoln's Inn—perplexed and troublous valley of the shadow of the law, where suitors generally find but little day—and fat candles are snuffed out in offices, and clerks have rattled down the crazy wooden stairs, and dispersed. The bell that rings at nine o'clock has ceased its doleful clangor about nothing; the gates are shut; and the night-porter, a solemn warder with a mighty power of sleep, keeps guard in his lodge. From tiers of stair-case windows, clogged lamps like the eyes of Equity, bleared Argus with fathomless pocket for every eye and an eye upon it, dimly blink at the stars. In dirty upper casements, here and there, hazy little patches of candle-light reveal where some wise draughtsman and conveyancer yet toils for the entanglement of real estate in meshes of sheepskin, in the average ratio of about a dozen of sheep to an acre of land. Over which bee-like industry, these benefactors of their species linger yet, though office hours be past: that they may give, for every day, some good account at last.

—Charles Dickens, *Bleak House* (1853)

MR. KROOK'S OBSTINACY

Some of these authorities (of course the wisest) hold with indignation that the deceased had no business to die in the alleged manner; and being reminded by other authorities of a certain inquiry into the evidence for such deaths, reprinted in the sixth volume of the Philosophical Transactions; and also of a book not quite unknown, on English Medical Jurisprudence; and likewise of the Italian case of the Countess Cornelia Baudi as set forth in detail by one Bianchini, prebendary of Verona, who wrote a scholarly work or so, and was occasionally heard of in his time as having gleams of reason in him; and also of the testimony of Messrs Foderé and Mere, two pestilent Frenchmen who would investigate the subject; and further, of the corroborative testimony of Monsieur Le Cat, a rather celebrated French surgeon once upon a time, who had the unpoliteness to live in a house where such a case occurred, and even to write an account of it;—still they regard the late Mr. Krook's obstinacy, in going out of the world by any such byway, as wholly unjustifiable and personally offensive.

—Charles Dickens, *Bleak House* (1853)

THE BAR OF ENGLAND

The bar of England is scattered over the face of the earth. How England gets on through four long summer months without its bar—which is its acknowledged refuge in adversity, and its only legitimate triumph in prosperity—is beside the question; assuredly that shield and buckler of Britannia are not in present wear. The learned gentleman who is always so tremendously indignant at the unprecedented outrage committed on the feelings of his client by the opposite party, that he never seems likely to recover it, is doing infinitely better than might be expected, in Switzerland. The learned gentleman who does the withering business, and who blights all opponents with his gloomy sarcasm, is as merry as a grig at a French watering-place. The learned gentleman who weeps by the pint on the smallest provocation, has not shed a tear these six weeks. The very learned gentleman who has cooled the natural heat of his gingery complexion in pools and fountains of law, until he has become great in knotty arguments for Term-time, when he poses the drowsy Bench with legal "chaff," inexplicable to the uninitiated and to most of the initiated too, is roaming, with a characteristic delight in aridity and dust, about Constantinople. Other dispersed fragments of the same great Palladium are to be found on the canals of Venice, at the second cataract of the Nile, in the baths of Germany, and sprinkled on the sea-sand all over the English coast. Scarcely one is to be encountered in the deserted region of Chancery Lane. If such a lonely member of the bar do flit across the waste, and come upon a prowling suitor who is unable to leave off haunting the scenes of his anxiety, they frighten one another, and retreat into opposite shades.

—Charles Dickens, *Bleak House* (1853)

THE CHURCH SERVICE

As the bell was yet ringing and the great people were not yet come, I had leisure to glance over the church, which smelt as earthly as a grave, and to think what a shady, ancient, solemn little church it was. The windows, heavily shaded by trees, admitted a subdued light that made the faces around me pale, and darkened the old brasses in the pavement, and the time and damp-worn monuments, and rendered the sunshine in the little porch, where a monotonous ringer was working at the bell, inestimably bright. But a stir in that direction, a gathering of reverential awe in the rustic faces, and a blandly ferocious assumption on the part of Mr. Boythorn of being resolutely unconscious of somebody's existence, forewarned me that the great people were come, and that the service was going to begin.

—Charles Dickens, *Bleak House* (1853)

FAST-FISH AND LOOSE-FISH

The allusion to the waifs and waif-poles in the last chapter but one, necessitates some account of the laws and regulations of the whale fishery, of which the waif may be deemed the grand symbol and badge.

It frequently happens that when several ships are cruising in company, a whale may be struck by one vessel, then escape, and be finally killed and captured by another vessel; and herein are indirectly comprised many minor contingencies, all partaking of this one grand feature. For example,—after a weary and perilous chase and capture of a whale, the body may get loose from the ship by reason of a violent storm; and drifting far away to leeward, be retaken by a second whaler, who, in a calm, snugly tows it alongside, without risk of life or line. Thus the most vexatious and violent disputes would often arise between the fishermen, were there not some written or unwritten, universal, undisputed law applicable to all cases.

Perhaps the only formal whaling code authorized by legislative enactment, was that of Holland. It was decreed by the States-General in A.D. 1695. But though no other nation has ever had any written whaling law, yet the American fishermen have been their own legislators and lawyers in this matter. They have provided a system which for terse comprehensiveness surpasses Justinian's Pandects and the By-Laws of the Chinese Society for the Suppression of Meddling with Other People's Business. Yes; these laws might be engraven on a Queen Anne's farthing, or the barb of a harpoon, and worn round the neck, so small are they.

I. A Fast-Fish belongs to the party fast to it.

II. A Loose-Fish is fair game for anybody who can soonest catch it.

But what plays the mischief with this masterly code is the admirable brevity of it, which necessitates a vast volume of commentaries to expound it.

First: What is a Fast-Fish? Alive or dead a fish is technically fast, when it is connected with an occupied ship or boat, by any medium at all controllable by the occupant or occupants,—a mast, an oar, a nine-inch cable, a telegraph wire, or a strand of cobweb, it is all the same. Likewise a fish is technically fast when it bears a waif, or any other recognized symbol of possession; so long as the party waifing it plainly evince their ability at any time to take it alongside, as well as their intention so to do.

These are scientific commentaries; but the commentaries of the whalemen themselves sometimes consist in hard words and harder knocks—the Coke-upon-Littleton of the fist. True, among the more upright and honorable whalemen allowances are always made for peculiar cases, where it would be an outrageous moral injustice for one party to claim possession of a whale previously chased or killed by another party. But others are by no means so scrupulous.

Some fifty years ago there was a curious case of whaletrover litigated in England, wherein the plaintiffs set forth that after a hard chase of a whale in the Northern seas; and when indeed they (the plaintiffs) had succeeded in harpooning the fish; they were at last, through peril of their lives, obliged to forsake not only their lines, but their boat itself. Ultimately the defendants (the crew of another ship) came up with the whale, struck, killed, seized, and finally appropriated it before the very eyes of the plaintiffs. And when those defendants were remonstrated with, their captain snapped his fingers in the plaintiffs' teeth, and assured them that by way of doxology to the deed he had done, he would now retain their line, harpoons, and boat, which had remained attached to the whale at the time of the seizure. Wherefore the plaintiffs now sued for the recovery of the value of their whale, line, harpoons, and boat.

Mr. Erskine was counsel for the defendants; Lord Ellenborough was the judge. In the course of the defence, the witty Erskine went on to illustrate his position, by alluding to a recent crim. con. case, wherein a gentleman, after in vain trying to bridle his wife's viciousness, had at last abandoned her upon the seas of life; but in the course of years, repenting of that step, he instituted an action to recover possession of her. Erskine was on the other side; and he then supported it by saying, that though the gentleman had originally harpooned the lady, and had once had her fast, and only by reason of the great stress of her plunging viciousness, had at last abandoned her; yet abandon her he did, so that she became a loose-fish; and therefore when a subsequent gentleman reharpooned her, the lady then became that subsequent gentleman's property, along with whatever harpoon might have been found sticking in her.

Now in the present case Erskine contended that the examples of the whale and the lady were reciprocally illustrative of each other.

These pleadings, and the counter pleadings, being duly heard, the very learned judge in set terms decided, to wit,—That as for the boat, he awarded it to the plaintiffs, because they had merely abandoned it to save their lives; but that with regard to the controverted whale, harpoons, and line, they belonged to the defendants; the whale, because it was a Loose-Fish at the time of the final capture; and the harpoons and line because when the fish made off with them, it (the fish) acquired a property in those articles; and hence anybody who afterwards took the fish had a right to them. Now the plaintiffs afterwards took the fish; ergo, the aforesaid articles were theirs.

A common man looking at this decision of the very learned judge, might possibly object to it. But ploughed up to the primary rock of the matter, the two great principles laid down in the twin whaling laws previously quoted, and applied and elucidated by Lord Ellenborough in the above cited case; these two laws touching Fast-Fish and Loose-Fish, I say, will, on reflection, be found the fundamentals of all human jurisprudence; for notwithstanding its complicated tracery of sculpture, the Temple of the Law, like the Temple of the Philistines, has but two props to stand on.

Is it not a saying in every one's mouth, Possession is half of the law: that is, regardless of how the thing came into possession? But often possession is the whole of the law. What are the sinews and souls of Russian serfs and Republican slaves but Fast-Fish, whereof possession is the whole of the law? What to the rapacious landlord is the widow's last mite but a Fast-Fish? What is yonder undetected villain's marble mansion with a door-plate for a waif; what is that but a Fast-Fish? What is the ruinous discount which Mordecai, the broker, gets from poor Woebegone, the bankrupt, on a loan to keep Woebegone's family from starvation; what is the ruinous discount but a Fast-Fish? What is the Archbishop of Savesoul's income of £100,000 seized from the scant bread and cheese of hundreds of thousands of broken-backed laborers (all sure of heaven without any of Savesoul's help), what is that globular 100,000 but a Fast-Fish? What are the Duke of Dunder's hereditary towns and hamlets but Fast-Fish? What to that redoubted harpooner, John Bull, is poor Ireland, but a Fast-Fish? What to that apostolic lancer, Brother Jonathan, is Texas but a Fast-Fish? And concerning all these, is not Possession the whole of the law?

But if the doctrine of Fast-Fish be pretty generally applicable, the kindred doctrine of Loose-Fish is still more widely so. That is internationally and universally applicable.

What was America in 1492 but a Loose-Fish, in which Columbus struck the Spanish standard by way of waifing it for his royal master and mistress? What was Poland to the Czar? What Greece to the Turk? What India to England? What at last will Mexico be to the United States? All Loose-Fish.

What are the Rights of Man and the Liberties of the World but Loose-Fish? What all men's minds and opinions but Loose-Fish? What is the principle of religious belief in them but a Loose-Fish? What to the ostentatious smuggling verbalists are the thoughts of thinkers but Loose-Fish? What is the great globe itself but a Loose-Fish? And what are you, reader, but a Loose-Fish and a Fast-Fish, too?

—Herman Melville, *Moby Dick* (1851)

ADDITIONAL EXERCISES

Prose: "The Meaning of Glory," p. 53; "Studies," p. 57; "The Portrait of Murder," p. 88; "Declaration of Causes," p. 97; "Education," p. 106; "The Early Church," p. 109; "Expression of Opinion," p. 104.

Poems: "Sailing to Byzantium," p. 44; "Since There's No Help," p. 68; "A Glass of Beer," p. 76; "Hotspur's Answer," p. 81; "Satan's Defiance," p. 96; "Death Be Not Proud," p. 97; "Bells for John Whiteside's Daughter," p. 103.

The Bare Essentials: Vivid Expression

IF THE PREVIOUS chapter was at all successful, you can now read aloud in such a way that the important units are prominent and their grammatical relations easy to grasp. But you have doubtless found—in your classmates' readings if not in your own—that even the mastery of these important steps is not enough to insure clarity. You may have noticed, for example, that it is hard to know when the subject has been changed; or who are the sympathetic characters; or whether information is being presented to surprise you, anger you, or teach you. In short, the reader frequently is removing from the words all vestige of personality. Undoubtedly you criticized such readings as "dull," "monotonous," "impersonal"; but we want to draw your attention particularly to the fact that they are also hard to follow. They are *not* clear.

The reason for this insistence is that the chapter headings may confuse you. "Clear Expression" versus "Vivid Expression"—it sounds like step 1 and step 2, does it not? And when we make the generalization that this chapter will treat of "emotional" details as opposed to the "intellectual" details of Chapter Four, you may fall victim to a very unfortunate dichotomy: you may conclude that a reader's task is to render the Sense as determined by the selection, and then to add on a thick layer of "emotion"—as determined, perhaps, by whatever tricks he has in his repertory. Even a superficial study of Chapter Three, though, should have been enough to show that Sense, Mood, Attitude, Social Intent, Tone, or any other aspect we choose to find, is nevertheless only an *aspect* of the whole and that every aspect will depend upon every other aspect. But just to be doubly safe, let us restate the principle in terms of Chapter Four: a reading will not be clear if it presents only the Sense, because this Sense has, after all, been imposed by a human organism; and if, in the presentation of this Sense, there is no indication of its impact upon a credible human being who behaves in an intelligible

165

way given his peculiar circumstances, then we will be dissatisfied—perhaps even mystified. The reading will not "make sense."

And so, even though we call this chapter "Vivid Expression," and even though we shall be talking about "emotive values" and so on, you must avoid the inference that we are trying to make your reading merely interesting—or worse, that we are trying to chrome-plate it. We shall be trying rather to make it more satisfying, more credible, more human.

EMOTIVE VALUES

Having insisted that this chapter is really a continuation of the previous one, we can now turn to its special task: the projection of "emotive values." We are keeping the nomenclature vague here, partly because precision would involve endless hairsplitting. For example, many psychologists are dissatisfied with the distinctions they draw between "emotions" and "feelings," and so we would be wise to avoid both. Furthermore we wish to make our chapters as self-contained as possible, so that your teacher can discuss them in the order best suited to your class; otherwise we might, for example, use the terms of Chapter Three, and say rather glibly that our concern is to project the Mood, the Tone, and the subjective component of Attitude. Instead we shall use the wastebasket term "emotive values," in the hope that it can suggest two important components of good reading.

The first of these components is the human reaction to phenomena. In Chapter Two we said that such human reaction provides the connotative part of meaning; in Chapter Three we suggested that the person who apparently organized the material will leave clues from which we can infer his Attitude toward what he is talking about, his Mood or overall emotional set, the Tone he is adopting toward us, and his Social Intent. To this we must add the bare fact—and trace its implications in Chapter Eleven—that you as a reader, and we as audience, presumably have some human reactions too. Hence when you present, say, a shocking detail, we expect you to seem shocked, or perhaps we expect you to seem sorry—or glad—you have shocked us; in any case, we expect some credible reaction *on your part* to the shocking detail. And so we must discuss the projecting of a credible human reaction—whether this is a conventional reaction (in the sense that most of us share a common reaction to cockroaches), or the narrator's reaction, or a character's reaction, or a character's pretended reaction, or the reaction of you the reader, or the reaction you expect of us, the audience.

The second component is the realization of sensuous detail—the making-real of what you read, the presentation of word symbols in such a way that they convey immediately to our senses some of the qualities of the objects for which they stand. When you read about stones, we may want to feel the hardness of those stones, or their coldness or dryness. Obviously, the "hardness" or "coldness" of your voice and manner will not duplicate the hardness or coldness of the stones you are describing; and yet, through the use of appropriate "color" of voice and manner, you can paint a word picture that will affect us in much the same way the real objects would. Even if you have not heard them, you have surely heard of readers and storytellers who "can make you see everything that happens." This realization—this making-real—of sensuous detail is different from the human reaction to that detail; but both are included in our term "emotive values," and most of the techniques for the projection of one may be used for the projection of the other.

This chapter then, is concerned with the projection of emotive values—roughly, with "getting an emotion across to the audience" and with "making the scene come alive." We shall describe eight techniques with which you can experiment. Some of them can be used during the actual performance if necessary; others are obviously restricted to rehearsal.

TWO PRINCIPLES: FOCUS, AND ABANDON

There are two general principles which, if applied, will increase the likelihood of success in following any of the procedures to be described. Accordingly, we shall discuss them first; then we shall distinguish between direct and indirect techniques; and after that we shall describe each technique in detail.

Focus

Although it is entirely possible to feel a general melancholy, or to be angry at nothing in particular, such moods tend sooner or later to become directed at something specific. We find something to be mad or sad about. This particularization, this directing of an emotion at something, we shall call *focus*.

We might have avoided this issue entirely if we had chosen to discuss "attitude" instead of "emotion." Attitudes are by definition always focused; indeed, some authorities hold that the internal set and the object to which it is directed are merely aspects of a single process. We could use such an emphasis in this section, where we want to insist that you will get far better results with the techniques discussed below if you aim at expressing not an emotion in general but a particular emotion: not anger, for example, but anger directed at the details which elicit it.

One easily discernible result of a lack of focus, of an attempt to express an emotion in general, is flabbiness at the ends of thought groups. Listen to your class-mates' readings. In some of them you will almost certainly detect this pattern: strong and seemingly appropriate emotion at the beginning of a unit (a sentence, say, or a poetic line), and then an increasing vagueness, until the end of the unit is merely "interesting"—if not downright impersonal. It is as if he started coasting halfway through the unit. Often there is a dying fall to the voice, and some-times volume fades out as well. Once you have noticed this pattern in others' readings, you will want to avoid it in your own. The best way of doing so is to concentrate intently upon the details in the selection that are supposed to be pro-ducing the emotional response. Put tersely: *what* are you steamed up *about?* Put even more tersely: focus!

Abandon

Few if any of the techniques of expression will work if you experiment timidly or half-heartedly. The main purpose of rehearsal, especially early rehearsal, is to free ourselves of our previous limitations, to explore as thoroughly as we can the new possibilities that suggest themselves, to rouse ourselves to the point where we are open to inspiration. If we deliberately limit ourselves to what we would *normally* do we may as well not rehearse. Indeed, we ought not to rehearse, for we will only destroy the last remnant of spontaneity. Even in performance we must not mistake inhibition for control. If we insist upon crouching within our everyday personality we will give little to—and get less from—an audience. At best our listeners will consider us distant and forbidding; at worst they will sus-pect we are the whispering dead.

What we need is the concept symbolized by the French word *abandon:* the idea of letting go, of lack of restraint, almost of indulgence. There is a hint of it in our English "abandon ship" or "abandon hope"; and insofar as it suggests the re-nunciation of something—specifically of our everyday way of doing things—we can manage without the French term. But abandoning hope may seem passive; the *abandon* we mean is dynamic. Perhaps this analogy is sufficiently close: if your path is blocked by a stream, and you have the choice of remaining where you are or of leaping across the stream, you know that you have to do one or the other; any attempt at compromise—conscious or not—will probably land you in midstream. Similarly in rehearsal: you can remain where you are, and learn noth-ing; or you can shoot the works, and explore what may be completely new territory. But any attempt to compromise, to do things by halves, will almost certainly fail.

In a sense our comparison is misleading. It may suggest that if you do not use *abandon* you will make a fool of yourself and that if you do use it you will escape the danger. Unfortunately the reverse is nearer the truth. By sticking in your normal rut you may give a wretched reading, but it probably won't be silly; by throwing yourself wholeheartedly into the practice, you may get new and thrilling results—but you may also look and feel a fool. This is one of the unavoidable hazards of a class in oral interpretation: you have to do much of your practicing in public, and your classmates may react as if you'd gone crazy. But don't worry: their turn comes next.

And in the longer view there is also reason for comfort: nobody expects you to continue a ridiculous display for very long. You are merely urged to overdo in order to "do" at all. Once you can "do" it, once you have learned to project emotive values, it will be a simple matter for you or your teacher to tone the reading down. But if you underplay you are simply deferring the unavoidable. It is usually easier to damp a fire than it is to ignite one; so do not be afraid to overdo at first. Drop your inhibitions whenever you practice, even in class; throw yourself wholeheartedly into the job, and save restraint for the later rehearsals and the actual performance.

This advice is especially pertinent to the communicating of emotion; if you're not going to go the limit you may as well skip to the next chapter.

DIRECT AND INDIRECT APPROACHES

The chief reason for separating the following procedures into two categories is that such a distinction may show you how they work. Since we run the risk of your labeling one group "mechanical" or "physical" and the other "natural" or "psychological," and then rejecting a whole group on the basis of your reaction to a label, we hasten to say that as soon as you understand how a given technique is supposed to work, you are free to forget its category.

The direct techniques require comparatively superficial adjustments in the reader's neuromuscular system; they work on the audience without necessarily involving the reader very deeply. The danger in relying upon them exclusively is that your reading may seem cold and insincere. On the other hand, if you reject them you may find yourself filled with torrents of passion and communicate not a drop. You know from your introductory psychology textbook that research into the social detection of emotion has yielded surprisingly conflicting results, that an audience is more likely to identify correctly, from a snapshot or motion picture of facial expression alone, an emotion that has been posed by an actor than one which was "actually being experienced" by someone not an actor.[1] Under the stress of emotion we can easily freeze into one of three or four habitual expressions and thus completely fail to communicate.

The indirect approach attempts to elicit within you, the reader, the emotive responses you seek to induce in your audience. In a sense you "live the part," you "think the matter through." The disadvantages of this approach we have mentioned above, but there is a very positive advantage: it avoids the artificiality, the hamming, that too easily results from the direct approach. If the indirect techniques work at all, they seem sincere.[2]

The most sensible course is to test each technique thoroughly. You will almost certainly find that some techniques work better for your classmates than for you and that some techniques work better at certain times—or on certain selections—than do others. So try all of them; try them in various combinations; try them on various kinds of selection; and *then* adopt the four or five that work best for you.

THE DIRECT APPROACH

Providing Conventional Clues

In any society there are accepted ways of indicating various emotions. In an American story, for example, the remark "His eyes widened" would probably be enough to suggest that someone was surprised; in a classical Chinese story the same expression would indicate anger. In our culture clapping the hands shows approval; in other cultures it can indicate derision. As oral readers we can capitalize upon the fact that nearly all members of our society use the same signs in order to indicate their reactions.

We merely analyze our friends' facial and bodily and vocal expressions and determine which clues enable us most easily to interpret their feelings; then we project those clues to an audience when we are reading.

Let us take a concrete example: How do we know when a person is angry? How does he act? Well, he may grit his teeth, he may tense his lips, clench

---

[1] The experiments of Carney Landis during the 1920's provide gritty food for those who hold that a "real" emotion is easily detected. See *Journal of Comparative Psychology,* 4 (1924), 447–507, or *Journal of General Psychology,* 2 (1929), 59–72.

[2] Probably the standard work on the vexed question of whether an actor need live his part is still William Archer's *Masks or Faces?* It is now available in paperback: Dramabooks Series, #D4.

his fists, frown, stick out his chin, plant his feet firmly and swing one shoulder back, breathe deeply and quickly, spit out the plosive consonants (*p, b, t, d, k, g*) and hiss the fricatives (*f, v, th, s, z, sh, h*). What clues have we omitted?

Now, for the purpose of illustration, let us assume the following selection demands an angry reading:

> Bowed by the weight of centuries he leans
> Upon his hoe, and gazes on the ground,
> The emptiness of ages in his face,
> And on his back the burden of the world.
> Who made him dead to rapture and despair—
> A thing that grieves not and that never hopes,
> Stolid and stunned, a brother to the ox?
> Who loosened and let down this brutal jaw?
> Whose was the hand that slanted back this brow?
> Whose breath blew out the light within this brain?
> —Edwin Markham,
> "The Man with the Hoe" (1899)

Stand up and look angry. Supply all the physical clues suggested above, plus any others that you have thought of. Bang the table or stamp your foot. Try spitting out the first four lines, with the muscles of lips and jaw tight with resentment. Explode sharply the *b*'s in "bowed," "back," and "burden"; the *g*'s in "gazes" and "ground"; the *pt* in "emptiness" and the *ck* in "back." In the fifth line, hoot out "who," snarl "made," "rap-," "-air." Hiss the *s* and spit the *t* in "stolid" and "stunned"; open your throat to the point of nausea on the *o* in "stolid" and especially in "ox." Do the last three lines in similar fashion.

Now take a breather, and then go through the selection again, seizing upon all the sounds in stressed words that are capable of being sneered or hissed or spat or resentfully prolonged.

Do the exercise again, continuing to exploit the sounds, but also concentrating upon the facts which evoke this anger. Focus upon the details of the indictment.

Do it yet again, focusing, and exploiting sounds, but also tensing your entire body. Glower accusingly, pull back your fist and shoulder in readiness to hit out at these tyrants, point accusingly if you wish, grip the floor with your feet, tense the muscles behind your knees. Any results? (And by the way, are you beginning to *feel* angry? See below, "Appropriate Physical Behavior," page 174.)

This is a pretty arbitrary exercise. We chose anger chiefly for ease of illustration. What emotion do *you* find in this selection? List what you consider the conventional clues to that emotion, and then supply them to another reading of the passage.

Perhaps you have seen that what sounds like a cold-blooded technique is really an exhausting physical task, demanding a great deal of participation from every point in your body. If you remember to use your whole body, you will avoid the greatest danger of this technique—degeneration into a pack of stereotyped stage tricks. The student who conveys puzzlement by scratching his jaw should not wonder that we find him unconvincing. He is taking too many shortcuts: he is not using his whole body; he is not even using his eyes, to see how people *really* look puzzled. Abandon is perhaps more necessary in this technique than anywhere else.

Tone Copying

Try to think of a short sentence which you might use to secure the same result as that attempted by the selection you practiced above, "Bowed by the weight of centuries" etc. The sentence might be "Look at that! Just look at that!" Or "What a shocking mess!" Or maybe "What is the meaning of this?" Or perhaps even "#%!!*#%&!!!" (Note that we are *not* looking for an abstract statement of theme!) Try thundering out your sentence as convincingly as you can. Now, using the words of an especially difficult part of the original selection, copy the tone you used when thundering your own sentence.

Tone Copying, then, is the process of choosing from your own everyday vocabulary a phrase or sentence which you might use to secure results similar to those attempted by the selection you are studying, saying the model phrase or sentence in the way you would normally employ it in the appropriate circumstances, and then transferring the resultant tone of voice to the language of the original passage.

If that definition seems complicated, let us try another example:

> Out of the night that covers me,
> Black as the Pit from pole to pole,
> *I thank whatever gods may be*
> *For my unconquerable soul.*

How would you try for the same effect in your own words? Would you say "I can lick any man in the house!" Or "Just step outside and say that!" Or "Sure! I'm proud of myself! I'm plenty proud of myself!" Find a sentence that seems most appropriate and most natural to you, one on which you can most easily use *abandon*. Say it as convincingly as you can. Now, read the italicized words in the passage, using the same tone.

Try it again, supplementing your Tone Copying with Conventional Clues.

Note that the phrase you use as a standard will not necesarily be a paraphrase of the selection, though sometimes the words of the original need be changed only slightly:

> And Joseph also went up from Galilee, out of the city of Nazareth, into Judea, unto the city of David, which is called Bethlehem, (because he was of the house and lineage of David), . . .
>
> —Luke 2:4

> And Joseph as well went out from Michigan, out of the city of Lansing, into Oregon, unto the city of Roses, which is called Portland, (because he was of a clan and family in Portland), . . .

Usually, however, you will find that the more colloquial your standard is, and the farther removed from the original, the better the results. The hardest part of the technique, perhaps, is to find the appropriate sentence in your workaday vocabulary. We shall touch on this problem more fully on page 179, when we discuss Sense Recall; but, to get started, be assured that the really important point is that *you* see the resemblance, however strained it may seem to others.

Tone Copying is valuable chiefly for very short passages, especially for the one or two sentences that "never seem to come out right." It may make longer excerpts seem unvaried, unless you split them up into short units, or use Tone Copying chiefly as a way of getting the Mood started.

A Method That Will Not Work: Tonal Trial and Error

Maybe you have noticed our omission of a technique that all beginners try sooner or later: the technique of saying a sentence over and over in different ways until "you find the right one." For example, a student will try "Since There's No Help" on a rising inflection, then on a descending, then on a high pitch, then in a gruff voice, etc., etc., etc.

When applied by an expert who seeks to choose between *what he has already established* to be equally valid readings, the technique may be a valuable one—*if* the alternative readings have been faithfully polished, and *if* he knows exactly what he is seeking, and *if* he has a tape recorder and a good ear.

But used by a beginner, in the initial stages of practice, the method is almost sure to fail. Try saying a familiar word—like "wash," or even your own name—thirty or forty times in deliberate succession; chances are you will find that the word has lost all meaning, and has become a foreign and somewhat absurd jumble of sound. You can be fairly sure of similar results if you try it on a passage charged with meaning.

Avoid tonal trial and error; the odds against success are staggeringly high.

Studying Models

Analyzing, and perhaps even imitating, a good oral reading is obviously the least flexible of the techniques we have discussed and should doubtless be saved as a last resort. Nevertheless, it *is* a last resort; many a student who has despaired of a selection—and sometimes despaired of the whole art of oral reading—has been helped by listening to his teacher, or to a talented classmate, or to a recording of an acknowledged artist.

The chief danger of this technique is that it may produce a slavish imitation, a carbon copy. But a few simple precautions will obviate the danger. First, listen to a variety of good readings of a given selection if possible. Try to obtain the same effects that your models do, without using their particular turns of style. Remember that few mimics are successful even on the night club circuit; don't try to mimic. And finally, try to distinguish between the model's reading and the model's reputation: obviously movie fame is hardly tantamount to reading excellence; but remember as well that an author is not to be revered as the possessor of THE true interpretation, nor dismissed because he is not a professional reader.

A little research in the recordings department of your library, or periodic consultation of *The Long Player, Schwann's,*[3] or some other such catalog available at your record dealer's, will reveal the surprising number of readings which have been recorded. Study lots of models, and don't be awed by any of them.

THE INDIRECT APPROACH

Performing the Appropriate Physical Behavior

This is one of the most important of all the techniques and is probably the most versatile in combining with the others. It consists of deliberately setting

---

[3] *The Long Player: A Comprehensive Catalog of Classical Longplay Records,* published monthly by Long Player Publications, Box 346, New York 19, N.Y.; *Schwann Long Playing Record Catalog,* published monthly by W. Schwann, 137 Newbury Street, Boston 16, Mass.

your muscles into the position they involuntarily take when you actually feel the relevant emotion. In one sense it is very similar to the technique of providing conventional clues, although in that technique you try to reproduce the behavior you have noticed in others. Its operation, however, is entirely different, and so we do not hesitate to call it a separate technique.

When you were spitting and gritting your way through the first verse of "The Man with the Hoe," on page 171, perhaps you noticed that you were becoming really angry. Certainly you have seen children *work themselves into* a tantrum. And you know that if you deliberately slouch, let your arms and shoulders hang loosely, gaze vacantly at the ground, relax your throat and jaw, draw down the corners of your mouth, and walk very slowly, you will soon find yourself melancholy; furthermore, you will probably think of something to be melancholy about! These common observations can be used to aid the reader or actor. A colleague of ours, unable to get a student to give an adequate portrayal of an arrogant enemy officer in a wartime propaganda play, sent the student out to watch some mynah birds, though maybe sparrows would have done as well. A verbal report was not enough; the student was to *show* how the birds behaved. Our colleague reports that after the student had acted like the mynahs for a while, he grew so arrogant that the rest of the cast had to cut him down to size!

All of these phenomena can be explained by the James-Lange theory of the nature of emotion, a theory which no longer commands as widespread support among psychologists as it once did, but is probably still sound enough, and certainly functional enough, for us to accept tentatively. James and Lange held that emotion is simply an awareness, a set, induced by a physical change in the body and the identification of that change with some similar change in past experience. We find ourselves running away; the last time we ran away we were afraid, and *therefore* we feel afraid. And however sweeping that explanation may seem, at the level on which we shall apply it the theory works.

Recall in minute detail what you did when feeling some particular emotion. What happened to your hands, your arms, your shoulders, jaw, mouth, eyebrows —to every observable part of your body? Now, deliberately make those parts of your body perform those actions, focus upon a situation that merits the emotive response you are after, and see if you don't begin to feel that emotion.

Here is a Shakespearean character, Henry V, putting the technique to military use. Perform the actions as you read the lines:

HARRY'S ADDRESS AT HARFLEUR
Once more unto the breach, dear friends, once more,
Or close the wall up with our English dead.

> In peace there's nothing so becomes a man
> As modest stillness and humility;
> But when the blast of war blows in our ears,
> Then imitate the action of the tiger;
> Stiffen the sinews, summon up the blood,
> Disguise fair nature with hard-favor'd rage;
> Then lend the eye a terrible aspect;
> Let it pry through the portage[4] of the head
> Like the brass cannon; let the brow o'erwhelm it
> As fearfully as doth a gallèd rock
> O'erhang and jutty his confounded base,
> Swill'd with the wild and wasteful ocean.
> Now set the teeth and stretch the nostril wide,
> Hold hard the breath, and bend up every spirit
> To his full height. On, on, you noblest English,
> . . . The game's afoot!
> Follow your spirit, and upon this charge
> Cry, "God for Harry! England and Saint George!"
> —*Henry V* (1599)

Do you feel like licking your weight in wildcats? If not, do the speech again.

You may find, as we have, that performing the appropriate physical behavior is the most versatile of all the techniques. If it does not seem to be giving you the results it should, check to make sure that you are indeed using your whole body. Get your forearms off the lectern; make sure your fingers, toes, and knees are contributing to the totality. Next, intensify your focus upon the details in the text. And lastly increase the *abandon*. If, after this double-check, you still don't feel the emotion, you are an inhibited soul indeed!

Interpolation and Extrapolation

This technique consists of inserting your own observations, your own translations, your own editorial comments, and especially your own transitional material, right into the body of the text, and saying them as part of the text in early rehearsals. Later you say these interpolations only to yourself, while reading the text aloud. Chances are that by the time of actual performance you can omit them entirely; but if you retain them you will of course say them only to yourself.

---

[4] Portage = port-hole.

The technique helps to solve a number of problems. In one way it turns you into a cheerleader, cheering yourself on. This is valuable whenever you find your enthusiasm waning or your focus diffusing. It keeps line ends from becoming flabby. It allows you to insert material for Tone Copying right into the text. And perhaps equally important, it encourages you to state the transitions aloud, so that you are forced to proceed smoothly from one attitude to another, thus unifying the selection.

Material may be added at any point in the text. In the following quotation, substitute your own expressions for the sample interpolations and extrapolations we have enclosed within parentheses:

(Well! if that's the way you want it, and) Since there's no help, (fine with me!), come, let us kiss and part (and good riddance too!). Nay, (none of that stuff), I have done, (finished!), you get no more of me. (Not a chance!) And I am glad, yea, (I mean it! I'm not fooling! I'm) glad with all my heart, (do you hear me?) that thus so (doggoned) freely I myself can free . . .

If the selection is unrecognizable in this form, turn to page 68 and interpolate freely throughout. You may need even more interpolations than supplied above, but you will probably manage with fewer.

Here is another exercise, designed to put some life into a process that is pretty dull in most readings—the announcement of title. Instead of mumbling that you are gonnareadtheman-withthehoe, try this, or something similar:

(Look here! I've got something I want to read to you! It's a real shocker, and I think it's important! It's called . . .) "The Man with the Hoe"!

Change the wording until it is natural to you, and conveys the attitude you wish us to adopt toward the selection. Now say it with zest. Try it again. Now try saying the extrapolated material *silently,* and only the actual title aloud. Practice the silent extrapolation and the overt announcement of title until it conveys a convincing attitude.

As we have indicated, material may be added at any point in the text. The main thing is to use these insertions freely and spontaneously during early rehearsals and to repeat the essential ones silently during the later ones. If you find that silent interpolations help you during the actual performance, by all means use them; as we shall note later, the audience will accept these pauses—if you are really working.

Sense Recall

Sense Recall helps you to experience again some emotion you have felt in the past; it helps you to relive some incident that elicited a response similar to the one demanded by the text. At the very least it can be used to "get into the mood" for reading; and at best, by capitalizing upon your own experience, it can conjure up an emotion that is sincere and intense.

Sense Recall consists of recalling the details of an incident which elicited from you an emotive response similar to the one which you seek to induce in the audience. Notice that you try to recall the *details* of the incident; you do not try to recapture the emotion directly. This is because emotion is a change, not a state; hence there is no *thing* to recapture. You can test this easily enough by trying—right now—to feel as you felt last Christmas. Does anything happen, other than that you get a faraway look on your face? But try to recall the details—the position of the tree, the color of that special gift, the clothes you wore, the people who were there and what they said—and you have a good chance of recapturing the incident, and the emotion with it.

LINES COMPOSED UPON WESTMINSTER BRIDGE, SEPTEMBER 3, 1802

Earth has not anything to show more fair:
Dull would he be of soul who could pass by
A sight so touching in its majesty:
This City now doth, like a garment, wear
5   The beauty of the morning; silent, bare,
Ships, towers, domes, theatres, and temples lie
Open unto the fields, and to the sky;
All bright and glittering in the smokeless air.
Never did sun more beautifully steep
10   In his first splendor, valley, rock, or hill;
Ne'er saw I, never felt, a calm so deep!
The river glideth of his own sweet will:
Dear God! the very houses seem asleep;
And all that mighty heart is lying still!
—William Wordsworth

Other techniques may not help much here. There isn't much vivid detail for you to visualize; Tone copying may help you to get started, and can get you past the initially ambiguous "steep" in line 9, but may accomplish little else; conventional clues and appropriate behavior may seem a little formless here; and interpolation may result merely in a series of "Gee!" and "Gosh!" (However, as a sporting proposition, you might try to see how far those techniques will take you into this poem.)

Now, when was the last time you saw a scene so peaceful that it left you awed and a little breathless? If it wasn't a scene, what was it? How did you feel on that occasion, you wonder. But the Sense Recall technique demands that you ask instead, What happened? What did you do? Who was with you? What did they wear? What time of day was it? What did so-and-so say, and what did you reply? As you grope for precise answers to these and similar questions, the details of your experience come back afresh, bringing the emotion with them.

When you have the emotion back, read the selection, reinforcing this technique with all the others you have learned.

Notice that the suggestions above have said nothing about remembering bridges or rivers or smokeless air; instead we counseled you merely to recall a peace that had left you awed. So perhaps at this point we might follow a tangent, and answer a question which may have arisen: "What incident can I use?" A similar question, "What phrase can I use?" occurred during our discussion of Tone Copying.

The answer is, use any vivid accessible experience (or phrase) which seems to you to have some relevance to the selection you are studying. Sometimes the most unlikely materials provide the most help. For example, few of us have had the experience of murdering our wives—indeed, most of us kill no one at all, to speak of. But we can still draw upon our experience in order to read Othello's "Out strumpet! Weep'st thou for him to my face?" As Richard Boleslavsky points out, we need only to recapture the cold rage with which we crushed a mosquito on our arm; "the rest is the work of magnification, imagination, and belief." [5] The ability to see a resemblance between killing a mosquito and killing Desdemona, like the ability to see resemblances in general, is a function of imagination—or of intelligence, if you like. It probably can't be taught, but if you lacked it completely you would never have finished grammar school. Since you are now safely in college, we can assume that you have it; what you need now is to realize its limitless possibilities.

[5] *Acting: The First Six Lessons,* Theatre Arts, Inc., 1933, p. 44.

Allow your imagination to range freely over your experience, and be prepared to use, if necessary, the most tenuous of resemblances. What matters, again, is that the experience is available, that it is vivid, and that *you* see its relevance to the problem at hand.

Identification

Identification, the "Magic If," is a technique similar to Sense Recall. It consists simply of asking yourself, "What would I try to do if this were actually happening to me?" Note that this question, too, has nothing to do with feelings or moods or mental states. *"What* would I *do?"* Not *"How* would I *feel?"*

Make your answer as specific and detailed as possible. Analyze the probable results of your action upon the other characters: what will they do in turn, and then what will you do? Reinforce the analysis with appropriate physical movement; try to visualize the other characters (as in imaging, discussed in the following section). Feel free to supplement this technique with any of the others.

> Turn back to "Mr. Polly's Decision," page 107, and try to project yourself into Mr. Polly. What would you do if you were he?—ask yourself this at every point in the episode. Now try the technique on something that does not at first glance lend itself so directly to such exploitation: "The World Is Too Much With Us; Late and Soon," on page 62. What would you do if you were in this man's position? Perhaps you would begin by flailing your arms and shouting "Let me out of here!" (Very well, do so!) Then you might state your objection. And what would we do? We might look skeptical. And what would you do? You would try to explain your stand:

> > . . . late and soon,
> > Getting and spending, we lay waste our powers:
> > Little we see in nature that is ours;
> > We have given our hearts away, a sordid boon!

> And then, when we said, "Oh, come, now! It isn't that serious!", what would you do? You might try to give us some examples:

> > This sea that bares her bosom to the moon;
> > The winds that will be howling at all hours,
> > And are up-gathered now like sleeping flowers;
> > For this, for everything, we are out of tune;
> > It moves us not.

> And when we looked tolerant, you might begin to bluster:

> Great God! I'd rather be
> A pagan suckled in a creed outworn

et cetera.

Obviously identification is a promising technique for short stories and dramas in which there are characters with whom we can identify. We chose to illustrate the second selection above, rather than the first, in order to demonstrate the applicability of the technique to lyrics as well. Any lyric represents the reaction of a person to a situation (and in this sense, many literary critics claim that all lyrical poetry is dramatic); so you can use the technique for a surprisingly vast body of literature.

The method is subject to abuse, of course. It may result in daydreaming; worse, it may allow the egotist free rein to project his own reactions willy-nilly upon a selection. But a moment's thought will reveal that the technique is merely a starting point. Once you have realize what *you* would do when

> Loveliest of trees, the cherry now
> Is hung with bloom along the bough

you proceed to modify that action till it accords with those described or implied by the speaker in the lyric, who happens to be someone twenty years old and very conscious of death. Focus, then, is especially important when using the technique of identification.

Imaging

The technique of imaging works so well for some people that they can rely upon it entirely; indeed, they seem astonished that anyone should need any other technique. "All you have to do," they say, "is to close your eyes and you can *see* the scene unfolding before you!" Unfortunately, psychologists discovered long ago that people vary widely in their capacity for sensation when external stimuli are absent—their ability to "see in their mind's eye." Some people are much better at hearing "with their mind's ear"; others have intense tactile imagery—in imagination they can touch things. No doubt you know already the kind of imaging facility you have. If not, and if you are curious, try to concentrate intently upon the idea of rain. Do you see imaginary rain falling? Do you hear it? Smell it? Feel it running down your back?

If you are lucky enough to have this gift, you can easily exploit it in reading, particularly in presenting sensuous detail. You simply conjure up images (whether of sight, or hearing, or smell, or taste, or touch) whenever you encounter a descriptive passage. The only secret is: take your time! Especially in beginning exercises, pause long enough to allow the words to conjure an image before you say the words. Don't let yourself be rushed.

I WANDERED LONELY AS A CLOUD

I wandered lonely as a cloud
That floats on high o'er vales and hills,
When all at once I saw a crowd,
A host, of golden daffodils,
Beside the lake, beneath the trees,
Fluttering and dancing in the breeze.

Continuous as the stars that shine
And twinkle on the Milky Way,
They stretched in never-ending line
Along the margin of a bay;
Ten thousand saw I at a glance,
Tossing their heads in sprightly dance.

The waves beside them danced, but they
Outdid the sparkling waves in glee—
A poet could not but be gay,
In such a jocund company.
I gazed—and gazed—but little thought
What wealth the show to me had brought.

For oft, when on my couch I lie
In vacant or in pensive mood,
They flash upon that inward eye
Which is the bliss of solitude,
And then my heart with pleasure fills,
And dances with the daffodils.
                    —William Wordsworth (1807)

Once you have realized how valuable an asset your imaging power can be, you will be more alert to maintain a good supply of available images—by remaining more alert, more aware of the sensations impinging upon you everywhere.[6]

---

[6] For an enthusiastic account of the value of sight images, see Sara Lowrey and Gertrude E. Johnson, *Interpretative Reading: Techniques and Selections,* rev. ed., Appleton-Century-Crofts, 1953, pp. 30–34.

For those who do not ordinarily see or hear vivid mental images (and this includes the majority of us) there are still some possibilities. In the first place, you may be responding habitually to elements in your psyche that you don't happen to consider as imagery. Images exist for all the senses, and there are more senses than the traditional five. Consider, for example, the motor sense. Can you imagine yourself skating, so that you almost feel your legs moving and your shoulder dipping as you round a curve? Try it (and reinforce with the technique of Appropriate Physical Behavior). Or again, you may be localizing your senses too narrowly; do you think of touch as residing mainly in your fingers? There are sense organs all over the body. "Ticklish spots" often provide vivid images. Imagine a hairy caterpillar, or a cockroach, crawling across your shoulder blades, or up the calf of your leg. Any results? Can you use these "ticklish spots" to help you communicate unpleasant or loathsome details? Do not forget the back of your tongue: try to imagine something greasy trickling down your throat. (Whether this is taste or touch we need not decide; the point is, can you use this device in the projection of nausea?) In short, don't give up until you have discarded all the senses you can reach: sight, hearing, smell, taste, touch (including warmth, cold, pain, pressure), kinesthesia (where one part of the body is in relation to another part), motion, balance, etc.

Try to exploit some of this "extra" imaging in this selection:

ARMS AND THE BOY
Let the boy try along this bayonet-blade
How cold steel is, and keen with hunger of blood;
Blue with all malice, like a madman's flash;
And thinly drawn with famishing for flesh.

Lend him to stroke these blind, blunt bullet-heads
Which long to nuzzle in the heart of lads,
Or give him cartridges of fine zinc teeth,
Sharp with the sharpness of grief and death.

For his teeth seem for laughing round an apple.
There lurk no claws behind his fingers supple;
And god will grow no talons at his heels,
Nor antlers through the thickness of his curls.[7]
—Wilfred Owen (1918)

Second, reflect that very few adults experience images as vivid as the actual objects. You can get results from fairly weak images, especially if you supplement the technique with others.

If all else fails, remember that even the intense imager can give more accurate descriptions of an object through intellectual analysis than through imaging. You can safely conclude Sense Recall is a more than adequate substitute for Imaging if your imaging power is weak.

FOR FUTURE REFERENCE

So far in this chapter we have been advocating what must seem to be an extreme position. We have urged *abandon* upon you; and you may well feel that this leads to ham acting, to tearing a passion to tatters. Again, you may object that some of the techniques don't feel natural. And if you have genuinely attempted to induce within yourself the bodily tensions necessary in, say, the technique of appropriate physical behavior, you may claim that it ties you in knots. Surely, you object, the experienced actor or reader doesn't work so hard—he simply wouldn't have the stamina to play a long run. So this may be a good time to allay a few misgivings.

The "natural" objection need not detain us long. A moment's reflection will show that you stopped being completely "natural" the moment you were first laid in your crib; you learned to lie horizontally instead of on your head, and almost every action you have performed since then has similarly had to be learned. To object to a new behavior on the grounds that it is not customary to you is to suggest that you have nothing more to learn. A more reasonable objection, and one that probably comes closer to your real feelings, is that what we are trying to teach you isn't worth learning. And here, of course, you may be right. But the only fair way of settling the matter would be for you to give it an honest trial, and *then* to reject it if it doesn't work.

The case against *abandon* is much stronger. Later on, in actual performance before an audience, you would be well advised to forego abandon and employ considerable restraint. Not only will you avoid emotionalism, not only will you maintain aesthetic distance,[8] but, by keeping some power in reserve and not revealing your entire strength, you may persuade an audience that you have more than you actually possess. The process is similar to a bluff in poker. But as you may know to your cost, a bluff won't work unless you can show some strength. And the purpose of abandon in early rehearsals and in the early stages of your training is to enable you to acquire that strength. We certainly do not

[8] See pages 388–390.

approve of tearing a passion to tatters, but our experience has been that most students have to shred it a little in order to grasp it at all.

"Tying yourself in knots" is, like abandon, useful in the early stages of training. You must control—and often overcontrol—your large muscles in order to gain a sort of generalized control over your finer muscles. A baby tenses his whole body in order to bring his fists into contact with an object he is trying to grasp; later he learns to use only his whole hand; still later he learns to refine the action to one of thumb and forefinger; perhaps eventually he will so control his fine muscles that he can operate a surgeon's probe. As you gain a finer control over your communicative apparatus you will begin to take similar "shortcuts"; you will find that tying yourself completely in knots is no longer necessary, that your tensions are subtler and more efficient, and therefore you can secure maximum results with a minimum of effort. But this ideal requires years of training, and in the meantime you would be wise to avoid shortcuts, and to get the results in any way you can.

Perhaps these reassurances will encourage you to tackle the following exercises with all the energy of which you are capable. Get results, however clumsily; and then we can worry about precision and control.

EXERCISES AND ASSIGNMENTS

Clarity Versus Vividness

1. Listen critically to classmates whom you consider to be good readers, and note especially passages that leave you puzzled. Was your mystification due chiefly to faulty emphasis or phrasing; or was it rather that the reader's attitude was not shifting as rapidly as was his material? Do you begin to see how your teacher can swoop so unerringly upon the sections which the reader does not understand?
2. Reread the discussion of irony in Chapter Three, especially the exercises on pages 109–111. Irony assigns emotive values inappropriate to the details which ostensibly elicit them; notice the great care taken—the number of verbal clues provided—to indicate that such misassignment is deliberate. (Concentrate especially upon any pieces which puzzled you at first.) At this stage, can you suggest any vocal or visual clues that a reader could provide which would be comparable to the verbal clues supplied by the ironist? Do the more "abandoned" of your classmates suggest any such clues?

Emotive Values

1. Try to restate our concept "emotive values" in the terms used in Chapter Three.
2. Would "Attitude and Image" be a clearer title for this chapter than "Vivid Expression"? Why? Could we then eliminate the section on "focus"? On *"abandon"?*

Technique of Expression

Although it is an interesting speculative exercise to determine in advance which technique will probably work best for each of the following selections, we think it healthier for you to experiment; indeed, we suggest that you try as many of the techniques, and combinations of techniques, as possible. Hence we have not tried to group the following selections.

1. Practice again each of the illustrative selections contained in this chapter, but this time try to use as many of the techniques of expression as you can. Do you get better results now, with a combination of techniques, than in your earlier attempts, when you were trying to use each technique in isolation?

2. Here is the complete poem from which our first selection was culled. Before attempting to read it entire, be sure to determine whether the Attitude and Tone change from stanza to stanza.

THE MAN WITH THE HOE
(*Written after seeing Millet's world-famous painting*)

Bowed by the weight of centuries he leans
Upon his hoe and gazes on the ground,
The emptiness of ages in his face,
And on his back the burden of the world.
5   Who made him dead to rapture and despair,
A thing that grieves not and that never hopes,
Stolid and stunned, a brother to the ox?
Who loosened and let down this brutal jaw?
Whose was the hand that slanted back this brow?
10   Whose breath blew out the light within this brain?

Is this the Thing the Lord God made and gave
To have dominion over sea and land;
To trace the stars and search the heavens for power;
To feel the passion of Eternity?
15   Is this the Dream He dreamed who shaped the suns
And pillared the blue firmament with light?
Down all the stretch of Hell to its last gulf
There is no shape more terrible than this—
More tongued with censure of the world's blind greed—
20   More filled with signs and portents for the soul—
More fraught with menace to the universe.

What gulfs between him and the seraphim!
Slave of the wheel of labor, what to him
Are Plato and the swing of Pleiades?
25   What the long reaches of the peaks of song,

The rift of dawn, the reddening of the rose?
Through this dread shape the suffering ages look;
Time's tragedy is in that aching stoop;
Through this dread shape humanity betrayed,
Plundered, profaned, and disinherited,   30
Cries protest to the Judges of the World,
A protest that is also prophecy.

O masters, lords and rulers in all lands,
Is this the handiwork you give to God,
This monstrous thing distorted and soul-quenched?   35
How will you ever straighten up this shape;
Touch it again with immortality;
Give back the upward looking and the light;
Rebuild in it the music and the dream;
Make right the immemorial infamies,   40
Perfidious wrongs, immedicable woes?

O masters, lords and rulers in all lands,
How will the Future reckon with this Man?
How answer his brute question in that hour
When whirlwinds of rebellion shake the world?   45
How will it be with kingdoms and with kings—
With those who shaped him to the thing he is—
When this dumb Terror shall reply to God,
After the silence of the centuries?
                                        —Edwin Markham (1899)

3. What technique would you suggest to a classmate who read line 7, above with a
   rising inflection (i.e., with a rise in pitch at the end)? Why?

4. Here is the complete poem from which our second example was chosen. Decide
   upon the Tone, and rehearse until you can convey it to the class.

                           INVICTUS
           Out of the night that covers me,
           Black as the Pit from pole to pole,
           I thank whatever gods may be
           For my unconquerable soul.

           In the fell clutch of circumstance
           I have not winced nor cried aloud.
           Under the bludgeonings of chance
           My head is bloody, but unbowed.

           Beyond this place of wrath and tears
           Looms but the horror of the shade,

And yet the menace of the years
Finds, and shall find me, unafraid.

It matters not how strait the gate,
How charged with punishments the scroll,
I am the master of my fate:
I am the captain of my soul.
—William Henley (1875)

5. The poem above forms an interesting exercise in the analysis of Tone: some critics detect in it a tone of manly independence, others defiance, and others shrill over-compensation. Try to read it convincingly in each of these three ways.

6.

THE FIRST ROUND

In the first round every one thought it was all over. After making play a short time, [Hickman] the Gasman flew at his adversary like a tiger, striking five blows in as many seconds, three first, and then following him as he staggered back, two more, right and left, and down he fell, a mighty ruin. There was a shout, and I said, "There is no standing this." Neate seemed like a lifeless lump of flesh and bone, round which the Gasman's blows played with the rapidity of electricity or lightning, and you imagined he would only be lifted up to be knocked down again. It was as if Hickman held a sword or a fire in that right hand of his, and directed it against an unarmed body. They met again, and Neate seemed, not cowed, but particularly cautious. I saw his teeth clenched together and his brows knit close against the sun. He held out both his arms at full length straight before him, like two sledge hammers, and raised his left an inch or two higher. The Gasman could not get over this guard— they struck mutually and fell, but without advantage on either side.
—William Hazlitt, *The Fight* (1822)

7.

THE FALL OF HICKMAN

Hickman generally stood with his back to me; but in the scuffle, he had changed positions, and Neate just then made a tremendous lunge at him, and hit him full in the face. It was doubtful whether he would fall backwards or forwards; he hung suspended for a minute or two, and then fell back, throwing his hands in the air, and with his face lifted up to the sky. I never saw anything more terrific than his aspect just before he fell. All traces of life, of natural expression, were gone from him. His face was like a human skull, a death's head spouting blood. The eyes were filled with blood, the nose streamed with blood, the mouth gaped blood. He was not like an actual man, but like a preternatural, spectral appearance, or like one of the figures in Dante's *Inferno.* Yet he fought on after this for several rounds, still striking the first desperate blow, and Neate standing on the defensive, and using the same cautious guard to the last, as if he still had all his work to do; and it was not till the Gas-man was so stunned in the seventeenth or eighteenth round, that his senses forsook him, and he could not come to time, that the battle was declared over.

— William Hazlitt, *The Fight* (1822)

8. The transitions in "Studies," page 57, are unusually abrupt. Does the technique of interpolation improve your reading of that selection?
9. Demonstrate how the context which surrounds the sensuous detail in the following selections changes your reading of that detail.

a.

ROMANCE

The girl and Mr. Polly did not meet on every one of those ten days; one was Sunday and she could not come, and on the eighth the school reassembled and she made vague excuses. All their meetings amounted to this, that she sat on the wall, more or less in bounds as she expressed it, and let Mr. Polly fall in love with her and try to express it below. She sat in a state of irresponsible exaltation, watching him and at intervals prodding a vivisecting point of encouragement into him—with that strange passive cruelty which is natural and proper in her sex and age.

And Mr. Polly fell in love, as though the world had given way beneath him and he had dropped through into another, into a world of luminous clouds and of desolate hopeless wildernesses of desiring and of wild valleys of unreasonable ecstacies, a world whose infinite miseries were finer and in some inexplicable way sweeter than the purest gold of the daily life, whose joys—they were indeed but the merest remote glimpses of joy—were brighter than a dying martyr's vision of heaven. Her smiling face looked down upon him out of the heaven, her careless pose was the living body of life. It was senseless, it was utterly foolish, but all that was best and richest in Mr. Polly's nature broke like a wave and foamed up at the girl's feet, and died, and never touched her. And she sat on the wall and marvelled at him and was amused, and once, suddenly moved and wrung by his pleading, she bent down rather shamefacedly and gave him a freckled, tennis-blistered little paw to kiss. And she looked into his eyes and suddenly felt a perplexity, a curious swimming of the mind that made her recoil and stiffen, and wonder afterwards and dream. . . .

And then with some dim instinct of self-protection she went and told her three best friends, great students of character all, of this remarkable phenomenon she had discovered on the other side of the wall.[9]

—H. G. Wells, *The History of Mr. Polly* (1909)

[9] From *The History of Mr. Polly,* by H. G. Wells. Reprinted by permission of the executors of the H. G. Wells estate, and of Dodd, Mead & Company. Copyright 1909, 1937, by H. G. Wells.

b.

MEMORIES

TYRONE: She's still moving around. God knows when she'll go to sleep.

EDMUND: For Christ's sake, Papa, forget it! *(He reaches out and pours a drink. Tyrone starts to protest, then gives it up. Edmund drinks. He puts down the glass. His expression changes. When he speaks it is as if he were deliberately giving way to drunkenness and seeking to hide behind a maudlin manner.)*   Yes, she moves above and beyond us, a ghost haunting the past, and here we sit pretending to forget but straining our ears listening for the slightest sound, hearing the fog drip from the eaves like the uneven tick of a rundown, crazy clock—or like the dreary tears of a trollop spattering in a puddle of stale beer on a honky-tonk table top! *(He laughs with maudlin appreciation)*   Not so bad, that last, eh? Original, not Baudelaire. Give me credit! *(Then, with alcoholic talkativeness)*   You've just told me some high spots in your memories. Want to hear mine? They're all connected with the sea. Here's one. When I was on the Squarehead square rigger, bound for Buenos Aires. Full moon in the Trades. The old hooker driving fourteen knots. I lay on the bowsprit, facing astern, with the water foaming into spume under me, the masts with every sail white in the moonlight, towering high above me. I became drunk with the beauty and singing rhythm of it, and for a moment I lost myself—actually lost my life. I was set free! I dissolved in the sea, became white sails and flying spray, became beauty and rhythm, became moonlight and the ship and the high dim-starred sky! I belonged, without past or future, within peace and unity and a wild joy, within something greater than my own life, or the life of Man, to Life itself! To God, if you want to put it that way. Then another time, on the American Line, when I was lookout on the crow's nest in the dawn watch. A calm sea, that time. Only a lazy ground swell and a slow drowsy roll of the ship. The passengers asleep and none of the crew in sight. No sound of man. Black smoke pouring from the funnels behind and beneath me. Dreaming, not keeping lookout, feeling alone, and above, and apart, watching the dawn creep like a painted dream over the sky and sea which slept together. Then the moment of ecstatic freedom came. The peace, the end of the quest, the last harbor, the joy of belonging to a fulfillment beyond men's lousy, pitiful, greedy fears and hopes and dreams! And several other times in my life, when I was swimming far out, or lying alone on a beach, I have had the same experience. Became the sun, the hot sand, green seaweed anchored to a rock, swaying in the tide. Like a saint's vision of beatitude. Like the veil of things as they seem drawn back by an unseen hand. For a second you see—and seeing the secret, are the secret. For a second there is meaning! Then the hand lets the veil fall and you are alone, lost in the fog again, and you stumble on toward nowhere, for no good reason! *(He grins wryly)* It was a great mistake, my being born a man, I would have been much more successful as a sea gull or a fish. As it is, I will always be a stranger who never feels at home, who does not really want and is not really wanted, who can never belong, who must always be a little in love with death![10]

—Eugene O'Neill, *Long Day's Journey into Night* (1956)

10. The illustrations and exercise materials in Chapter Three provide particularly good practice here. It might be wise to avoid the ironic selections at first, and to concentrate upon such as these: "The World Is Too Much with Us," p. 62; "Since There's No Help," p. 68; "The House of Usher," p. 72; "I Hear an Army," p. 73; "The Patriot," p. 78; "The Evil Eye," p. 80; "Hotspur's Answer," p. 81; "The People," p. 85; "The Portrait of Murder," p. 88, and, of course, the exercises, pp. 96–108.

11. For the student who has rationalized his inhibitions into a philosophy of restraint we offer this little test: read to the class either "Catherine Dead," p. 88, or "The Auto-da-Fé," p. 91; if the class agrees that beneath an apparent impersonality you have conveyed the hopelessness and the pain of the first, or the slashing savagery of the second, we would concede that you have progressed beyond the need for *abandon,* and refer you to Chapter Nine. But if the class claims your reading is cold, you had better go back to the easier exercises above and use some *abandon.*

ADDITIONAL EXERCISES

"Love Not Me for Comely Grace," p. 36; "Mock On, Mock On," p. 41; "The Meaning of Glory," p. 53; "Rose-Cheekt Laura Come," p. 274; "The Windhover," p. 275; "Why So Pale and Wan," p. 278; "The Dragoons' Chorus," p. 279; "The Second Coming," p. 280; "At The Round Earth's Imagined Corners," p. 280; "Tears, Idle Tears," p. 281; "When I Heard the Learned Astronomer," p. 283; "God's Grandeur," p. 283; "The Express," p. 284.

The prose selections in "To Reveal Feeling," pp. 317–319.

---

[10] Reprinted by permission of Yale University Press.

TOWARD DEEPER UNDERSTANDING

Between and Around the Lines

IN THIS CHAPTER we shall wrestle with the problem of structure—how the material has been put together. In one sense we shall be merely continuing our earlier research, and much of what we discover will be readily translatable into Sense, Attitude, Tone, etc. However, attention will now be focused, not on "What does this add up to?", but on "How does this fit?" Reverting to an analogy used in Chapter Three: we may look at a person's head from any of thousands of viewpoints and see a unique aspect from each, even though the same element—the nose, say—may appear in a number of different aspects; but we will be unable to re-create that head in clay until we see how that nose fits into the aspects we have observed—until we have examined bone structure, musculature, and skin texture. In other words, we must now discover how the elements have been assembled into the aspects we looked at in Chapter Three. By studying the *how* instead of the *what* we may discover more of the *what*, because, as we pointed out in Chapter Three, how a thing is said—even in requesting a cup of coffee—will often be interpreted as part of the thing said. In a sense, therefore, this chapter will seek nothing more than new clues to Sense and Attitude and Mood and the rest.

But in another sense the analysis of structure is a venture entirely new. In asking how a passage has been put together, we uncover a host of new problems, most of them directly related to timing and emphasis and phrasing. Unless you know why paragraph 6 belongs in your story—what task it performs—you won't know how to emphasize it; unless you see why Little Red Riding Hood needs a mother (when Goldilocks does not), you will not know, from the two or three speeches assigned her, what kind of character you must establish, or whether indeed you can omit her speeches entirely; and unless you see that paragraph 13 in a certain story attempts to make us relax, so that we shall be the more startled

by paragraph 14, you may rush through it boisterously and glibly—and completely miss the contrast. These three examples might, of course, be considered
problems of Sense, Attitude, and perhaps Mood, respectively—and certainly the
insights they provide should strengthen the grasp of those three; but because
structure—the way in which a passage has been built—offers a direct clue to the
way it should be rebuilt aloud, the analysis of structure has a value all of its own.

We thus have two reasons for examining structure: first, to find further clues
to Sense, Mood, Attitude, Social Intent, and Tone;[1] and second, for help in planning the structure of our oral version.

MEANING IS A FUNCTION OF STRUCTURE

The second reason above is so clearly and directly applicable to oral reading
that it may obscure the first. Unless you have been warned you may search for
contrasts in character, let us say, for the purpose of plotting a vocal contrast, and
so scoring points for VARIETY!!!—never once asking yourself whether that contrast has shown anything about the characters' attitudes, or has affected the
mood, or contributes to the social intent. In a temporal art—an art that unfolds
in time—structure can too easily be considered a matter of timing; it can be
simplified into what-happens-next; and though not onomatopoietic perhaps,
your readings may turn into tone poems, dealing only in sound effects.

Accordingly, we must reëmphasize the fact that what-is-said and how-it-is-
said are twin aspects of the same process; indeed, how-it-is-said is often easily
translatable into what-is-said. In analysis, when you examine the relation between fact 13 and facts 22–27, you may discover an additional fact that has been
left to inference—and that implied fact may well prove more important than
anything stated explicitly. To cite a famous example: in *Hamlet* I, v, though the
ghost is at first constantly interrupted by Hamlet, after revealing the identity of
his murderer he is allowed to speak fifty lines without any interjections at all;
Hamlet's silence, in this context, is more revealing than anything he might put
into words.

In this section, then, we shall try to unearth some meanings in structure, some
clues that you might otherwise miss. First we shall examine the word order in
a sonnet in search of additional sense. Then we shall turn to narrative in an effort
to show how each of the components—the *who, where, what, how*—can shed
light on all of the others.

---

[1] Having reminded you of these aspects, we now abandon the capitalization. The practice served well
enough in Chapter Three, in which we discussed the total effect; but here, where we discuss fragments,
there seems something unduly enormous in a reference to the Attitude of one of the characters or to the
Mood of a scenic description.

Structure and Sense

Let us undertake an analysis of a poem with which you are familiar, Keats' "On First Looking into Chapman's Homer," in an attempt to discover additional meanings. We shall ignore sound and rhythm and standard sonnet form, examining only word order. Further, we shall concentrate upon the most "literal" and "concrete" of the aspects of meaning—the sense; we shall look for meanings that can be spelled out. (But en route we shall try to show how the connotations interlock within a well-constructed work, so that everything reinforces something else.) And to demonstrate the importance of inference in analysis, we shall postulate a fairly bright student who doesn't even know that "realms of gold" refers to literature, but who is determined to make sense of it. Here is how he might proceed:

ON FIRST LOOKING INTO CHAPMAN'S HOMER	
Much have I travell'd in the realms of gold,	1
And many goodly states and kingdoms seen;	2
Round many western islands have I been	3
Which bards in fealty to Apollo hold.	4
Oft of one wide expanse had I been told	5
That deep-brow'd Homer ruled as his demesne;	6
Yet did I never breathe its pure serene	7
Till I heard Chapman speak out loud and bold:	8
Then felt I like some watcher of the skies	9
When a new planet swims into his ken;	10
Or like stout Cortez when with eagle eyes	11
He star'd at the Pacific—and with all his men	12
Look'd at each other with a wild surmise—	13
Silent, upon a peak in Darien.	14

— John Keats (1816)

Minimum First Impression: The speaker seems to be a traveler; he has been to the realms of gold (wherever they are), has seen some fine kingdoms (unidentified), and has gone round many western islands. Then he heard a man named Chapman speak boldly, and felt like an astronomer or like Cortez. Somebody is on a peak; or maybe that's an old spelling of "peek" and refers to "looking into" as in the title.

Establishing Major Denotations: Better look up bards, fealty, etc. Perhaps serene—can you breathe some serene? Realms? He says *the* realms; better try realms of gold. If western islands were a definite place they'd be capitalized, but better not take chances.[2] Homer, Chapman, Darien. Apollo was a Greek god; surely I can skip him.

Well, Chapman was a Renaissance poet who translated Homer into English; Homer, a Greek poet, composed the greatest of epics, the *Iliad* and the *Odyssey*. One is about the siege of Troy, and the other about the wanderings of Ulysses. Any connection between wanderings and this traveler? Cortez conquered Mexico; no reference to his seeing the Pacific, which was discovered by Balboa. Darien is a province in E. Panama, or a gulf, or the Isthmus of Panama; if it has peaks it can't be a gulf.

Précis: I've been to many places (including the Realms of Gold?) and to some islands ruled by poets subject to Apollo. I'd heard of a place ruled by Homer, but had never breathed its serene (air? or experienced its serenity?) until I heard Chapman speaking boldly (or read his bold translation?). When I did (hear him? or visit Homer?) I felt like an astronomer discovering a new planet or like Cortez standing on a mountain in Panama (East Panama?) and looking at the Pacific.

Preliminary Analysis of Title: Clear but clumsy. Why not "To Homer" or at most "To Chapman's Homer"? "Looking into" sounds like skimming; if it were "studying" there'd be a closer connection to "watcher" (9) "star'd" (12) or "look'd" (13). Not making much headway; better move on.

Inferring a Crucial Meaning: Why *the* realms? They're connected with states and kingdoms (2), but the first "and" is ambiguous: does he see the kingdoms while in the realms, or does the "and" mean "and also"? But a realm *is* a kingdom; furthermore, it's old-fashioned and a state is modern; if they were inside a realm they'd be estates, not states. "And" (2) must mean "and also." Or else "realms" is being used loosely.

Bards (4) were antique poets—myths and legends and so on. And they got islands from a legendary god. Are those islands real ones? Why Apollo, anyway? Better look him up after all. Aha! god of youth, poetry, the intellect, healing, and later of the sun. Poetry again. Realms associated with islands ruled by poets appointed by the god of poetry; wonder if this is all metaphoric. Realm of letters, perhaps.

First Implication from Structure: But bards aren't Greek: long beards and Welshmen and Druids and minstrel boys.[3] Medieval? Demesne (6), fealty (4) and realms (1) are medieval;

[2] Our hypothetical student will find neither realms of gold or western islands in the dictionary. But if he consults a large dictionary, and fails to find them, he has gained some definite though negative information. If he relies on a pocket dictionary he has not ruled out the possibility that they are standard words which have been omitted to save space. Moral: use a large dictionary.

[3] Note the wild and shapeless associations throughout. This free association is excellent in the early stages; the time for caution comes later, when you test the associations for closeness of fit.

goodly (2) is Robin Hood talk. But how do Homer and Apollo fit into the Middle Ages? Classical mythology didn't get revived till the Renaissance. Renaissance translator! Chapman! Now, what about the rest of the medieval terms . . . there aren't any more. After Chapman is mentioned, the classical and medieval references disappear, and we switch to science. This is almost too neat! I'd better go back to make sure.[4]

Chapman, then, seems to clinch the medieval and classical references—or maybe I should say, fuse them; and that's what happened historically.

Second Implication from Structure: Once we're in the Renaissance we discover planets. Well, why not? Galileo, Copernicus, Newton—all sorts of discoveries. Voyages of discovery—new worlds. Columbus, Cartier, Drake, Balboa. The Pacific was discovered then. New worlds, discovery: it ties up neatly enough, except for Cortez.

Third Implication from Structure: Do these voyages of discovery tie up with traveling (1–4)? Yes; except for lines 9–10, which turn us into astronomers, we travel throughout the poem. True, the planet is swimming (10) but we don't go up —or is it down?—to meet it. Why the sudden switch up into the air—or into the sea (9–10)? We were on—well, sort of *flat* space: realms, states, kingdoms, islands, wide expanse, deep-brow'd . . . why deep-browed? Why not broad-browed or wide-browed? Deep (6), swims (10), Pacific (12), peak (14)— a pattern begins to form. Homer—or it is Apollo, god of the sun—brings height and depth to the flat medieval world; space becomes vertical, or at any rate, three-dimensional. Isn't that what happened historically?

The Connotations Interlock: All those references to looking and staring and watching. Discovery? Apollo as god of the intellect? And then there's Apollo as god of the sun: gold (1), skies (9), planets (10), eagle (11). It all fits; it all fits in two or three ways. Except that Balboa, not Cortez, discovered the Pacific.[5]

Another thing: why do things fuse when he *hears* Chapman? No space there—even "looking into" is better. The title is pretty good after all. But why *hear* Chapman, especially when he's merely speaking "loud and bold"? "Loud and bold"—

---

[4] To avoid repetition, we omit this going back. Analyze the first eight lines for references to the Middle Ages. Are there any in the last six? "Ken"?

[5] We must confess to very slender ideas about this matter. From all we can recall of Cortez, he was too busy plundering the Aztecs to stand silent anywhere. The name is a mistake, but to us it isn't a disturbing one. Cortez fits well enough into the context "new worlds"—indeed, since he exerted a stronger influence upon the New World than did Balboa, perhaps he is the better choice. Historically he was close enough to the Pacific that our sense is not outraged. Perhaps the hidden pun in his name reinforces the courage-adventure theme. All of which, we admit, is pretty tenuous.

sounds like padding. It occurs at a pivotal point too. It was just about the only line I understood at first, and now I want to change it![6]

Well, it was a tough fight, but it got our hypothetical ignoramus to the point of criticizing Keats! He has not yet noticed the constellations, but he has found these themes:

> *Discovery Motif:* first looking into, travell'd, seen, been [to], been told, heard, watcher, ken, Cortez-Balboa, eyes, star'd, look'd, surmise, Apollo-intellect.
> *Medieval Motif:* realms, goodly, kingdoms, western islands [?], bards, fealty, ruled, demesne.
> *Classical Motif:* Apollo, Homer, western islands [?].
> *Horizontal Space Motif:* travell'd, realms, states, kingdoms, western, islands, wide, expanse, demesne, Pacific.
> *Vertical Space Motif:* looking into, deep-brow'd, breathe, skies, planet, swims, eagle, Pacific, upon, peak.
> *Sun Motif:* gold, western, Apollo, skies, planet.
> *Value Motif:* gold, goodly, demesne, pure, serene, new.
> *Poetry Motif:* bards, Apollo, Homer, Chapman.

Doubtless you can find others. Further, you can see how closely related these themes are, how the connotations interlock in many different ways.

Further, our student found that the structure of this sonnet (and he analyzed word order only, not rhythm or rhyme) contributed meanings which were not inferable from the words themselves. Even disregarding the more tenuous aspects, such as mood or tone, he discovered information on the bare level of sense, information which might be set forth somewhat like this:

> My experience paralleled that of Western Europe: a Renaissance translation from classical antiquity gave height and depth to my two-dimensional medieval culture, and led me to new discoveries within the world and outside it.

In this poem, structure can be translated into content.

Before leaving this subject, we should meet an obvious objection: "This is all very ingenious, but do these authors really expect me to get all that into

---

[6] Our student doesn't see the implication of rebellion in "speak out," and so doesn't connect it to the theme of ruling—realms, kingdoms, fealty, ruled, demesne. The latter disappear with the mention of Chapman. Hence he misses the implication of intellectual freedom. Can you trace that history here?

my oral reading?" No, we don't. We don't expect anyone now living to do so. But wouldn't it be marvelous if somebody could? If we could develop artists who can read as well as Keats could write? Just as Chaucer and Surrey and Dryden and Wordsworth and Pound gave direction to the haphazard experiments of their contemporaries, so perhaps you or one of your classmates can give direction to ours, and out of the tradition thus founded great artists will soon emerge.

Far less idealistically, we suspect that even the beginner can communicate something of what we have just discussed. You can suggest some of the excitement of discovery, if not the discovery motif; you can suggest the deepening of knowledge, if not the spatial fusion; perhaps you can suggest some of the difference between medieval and Renaissance world view. At very least, you will try to show that the tone changes somewhere around line 8. In short, if you see new meanings there's a chance that you'll try to communicate them, whereas if you don't see them, there's not much chance at all.

Structure and the Other Aspects

We shall now examine some of the components of narrative, which is usually more complicated than such other forms of discourse as description, exposition, or argumentation;[7] but the components described are not nearly so important to structural analysis as are the relations among them. We might have selected Aristotle's "beginning, middle, and end," or the standard plot ingredients, "presuppositions, complications, and resolution," but the components we have chosen are *who, where, what, how*—or *character, setting, action, means*.[8] When examining them it would be helpful if you could apply some equivalent of a basic trick of night vision, looking a little to the left or right of the object you are trying to see, because we are interested not in what is in a narrative, but in how it hangs together.

In well-constructed narrative every component will condition the others. The moment we choose a hero, a *who*, for our story, we automatically exclude a wide

[7] For excellent discussions of these other forms, albeit from the writer's rather than the reader's viewpoint, see: Cleanth Brooks and Robert Penn Warren, *Modern Rhetoric*, 2nd ed., Harcourt, Brace, 1958, part 2; Monroe C. Beardsley, *Thinking Straight*, 2nd ed., Prentice-Hall, 1956, chap. 1.

[8] This is a heavily diluted version of the "pentad" used so provocatively in Kenneth Burke, *A Grammar of Motives*, Prentice-Hall, 1945. Beginners are advised that even the appendix of that work, which applies most clearly to literary criticism, is extremely subtle and that they will find more of immediate value in Burke's *Philosophy of Literary Form*, Louisiana State University Press, 1941; (in paperback, K-51 in the Vintage Series). For a simple application of that pentad, though perhaps more complex than ours, see Don Geiger, "A 'Dramatic' Approach to Interpretative Analysis," *Quarterly Journal of Speech*, 38 (April, 1952), 189–194.

range of otherwise promising courses of action—*what's*—because those actions would be inappropriate to the hero we have chosen. And if our setting, our *where,* is a rodeo, we will probably have to forego as our means, our *how,* a brilliant oral reading of "Patterns." Every component has to fit; indeed, sometimes one will merge into the others: in Hardy's novels, for instance, the setting becomes less a *where* than a *who,* and in *Tristan und Isolde* the drinking of the potion is as much *what* as *how.* And so we should expect every component to shed some light on the others; we might, for example, get some clues to character by examining means.

Much of character can, of course, be discovered with the techniques of attitude analysis, such as those mentioned in Chapter Three: note the details he mentions and those he suppresses; seek the connotations of the words he applies to those details, and observe the details with which he couples them; determine why he emphasizes this point instead of that; scrutinize all interruptions and abrupt switches of subject. You can also find clues in what other characters say of him—after having made due allowance for *their* attitudes. But frequently you can find additional clues in the setting. What kind of character belongs in such a setting? What kind of character will be produced by such a setting? Always look closely at any scenic description that precedes the entrance of—or especially the introduction of—a character; in economical writing, you may be confident that that "scenic description" has been placed at that point in order to clarify much more than setting. (We discuss the process under "Symbolic Transfer," page 209.) Similarly, we can infer much of the setting from an examination of the characters who people it. "Verona: a public place" may not mean much until we see the Montagues and Capulets fighting.

The relation of character to action is fertile grounds for analysis. Anyone can see that what a character does is relevant to an analysis of that character; but there can be considerable confusion over the relevance of what *is done to him.* Some students can use *hamartia,* the fatal flaw, to explain—and explain away—almost anything: "it was Othello's anger that led him to tragic error; it was Juliet's grief that caused the fatal blunder in that tragedy."[9] But other students, especially the very youthful, ignore a character's fate entirely unless they can see a "moral." Even in real life, which is often disordered indeed, a person's fate may shed some light on his character; what kind of person could get into such a mess, we may ask. Our point may be morbid, but it is not moralistic, and in your more sardonic moments you may test its corollary by predicting the fate of your classmates! (A complex assignment, with none of the simple I-told-you-so smugness about it; nevertheless, some fates will seem incongru-

[9] Cornelius C. Cunningham, *Making Words Come Alive,* Brown, 1951, p. 120.

ous: where you might see many a heart attack or traffic fatality, you see few executions, and few if any axe murders.) So, in analyzing literature, be wary of abstracting a pat moral from *what happens to* a character, or of finding in it his one fatal flaw; on the other hand, order implies a sort of poetic justice; in literature—obscurely and indirectly perhaps—everyone deserves what he gets. That she may be forced to marry Paris is a revelation of Juliet's character as well as of her father's; and unless we see it so we may not fully appreciate her intense speech beginning "Farewell! God knows when we shall meet again" (IV, iii), in which she expresses her fear of the vault; nor will we comprehend her relation to the Nurse.

The relevance of character and action to means is usually clear enough : the hero resourcefully thinks of a plan, the heroine jealously suspects Another Woman, a Capulet rushes a Juliet into marriage. These and a hundred other switches are indications of character and action as much as of means. But sometimes the means can contribute clues far subtler than any so far discussed. Minor characters especially are often sketched quickly and appear too infrequently to produce a clear impression; then the major clues may lie in the *how's* and *why's* of the action—specifically in the *function* performed by such a character.

A familiar example is Red Riding Hood's mother: in the story she does little more than pack some cookies and warn her daughter away from strangers. Are these facts important? After all, Goldilocks doesn't need a mother at all. But Goldilocks' action was at very least a gross abuse of hospitality; she more than deserved what happened to her. Red Riding Hood's action arose out of generosity—she was friendly and polite to a stranger. If the story is to have form—"make sense"—the audience must realize that friendliness and politeness are not always virtues; and unless that moral is to be stated directly, someone must be fashioned to deliver it. A wise old owl would do, perhaps—except that since the warning is ungenerous a symbol of generosity is needed—and lest we miss the point, she shall be engaged in generous pursuits, making cookies for a sick old grandma.

Far more complex is Tybalt in *Romeo and Juliet*. Here the clues are contradictory: Mercutio describes him as one of those "antic lisping affecting fantasticadoes" (II, iv) "that fights by the book of arithmetic" (III, i); and yet his impatience to slay Benvolio (I, i) and Romeo (I, v) suggest an extremely hot temper. Let us examine the part he must play in the action: Romeo must be removed to a distance and kept there; he can't be imprisoned or kidnapped because he must return for the resolution. He shall be banished; therefore he must commit a crime; as hero he must enlist our sympathies, and so the crime must be justifiable. He avenges the death of a friend (and perhaps Mercutio must be removed before he eclipses the hero); the revenge must be unpremeditated and therefore immediate; for maximum impact the event should occur when things look rosiest—when the imminence of the marriage, and Romeo's attitude toward the Capulets, promise to bring peace to the warring families. Somehow Romeo must be forced to the action, and he must not have time to plan.

We see, then, that however we credit Mercutio's description of him, Tybalt cannot be bloodless. Furthermore, if Romeo is not to be pardoned for avenging the Prince's kinsman, Tybalt must not be clearly a brawler. We must search for other clues, of course, but insofar as he is a means to the action, like everyone but Laurence he must contribute to the general *haste*. "The fiery Tybalt" must have in him something of old Capulet.

Even such simple examples require fairly complex reasoning; nevertheless, a very valuable clue to character—sometimes, as in a "thesis" novel or play, the major clue—may be obtained by asking: Why is this character needed; what function does he fill? Similar investigations might be conducted into the minor pieces of action. Why is that action needed? What does it contribute to the whole?

Since each component of narration, then, may provide clues to another component, it is therefore an oversimplification to assume that setting, for example, determines the mood, or that attitude is detected chiefly through the analysis of character, or that sense resides largely in the action. Any component of narration—or of exposition, description, and argument—may contribute clues to any of the aspects: sense, mood, attitude, tone, and intent.

WHY BRING IT UP NOW?

Our emphasis now shifts from structure-as-meaning to structure-as-temporal-sequence; henceforth the immediate application of the thory will lie in the area of phrasing, emphasis, and vivid expression. But as we have said again and again, the structure of the written work will rarely correspond to the structure of the oral—the translation is almost never one-to-one; therefore you should relate to Chapters Two and Three whatever insights you gain.

Why Bring It Up Now? is probably the most important single question you can bring to structure. You should ask it and its variants again and again. Why is the description of the hot-dog stand given here instead of on page 57? Why do we meet the wedding guest before we hear from the ancient mariner, or return to the wedding feast at the end? Why not begin and end with the mariner's tale? Why do we meet the ghost and Claudius and Gertrude before we meet Hamlet? Indeed, why do we not see the murder? Why does our story begin *in medias res* and recount most of its events in flashback? The specific form of the question will depend of course on the work being studied, but always it aims to discover why a particular unit—a detail, a description, a comment, an episode—was inserted at one particular point instead of at another. Why is this unit placed here? Why bring it up now?

The following sections contain some probable answers. You will readily see that some categories overlap others; but we are more interested in the utility of the divisions than in their logical neatness. Think of them as directions in which to look, rather than airtight compartments. Reflect that economy in writing demands that every detail serve two or three functions at once.

Establishing Presuppositions

Obviously, unless we understand the original situation we will not follow the complications that arise out of it: unless we know that the farmhouse is mortgaged we will fail to see why Sally is afraid of the landlord. To many beginning readers the establishing of presuppositions is less a problem of analysis than of adequate expression; you may have noticed that some of your classmates use too little projection at the beginning, and you are well into the thick of the action before you discover what their story is all about.

The major analytical problem arises in works whose presuppositions are scattered. In "The Patriot," page 78, for example, not until lines 20 or 22 do we learn that the narrator is en route to his execution. Instead of creating a completely superfluous manservant and maid to discuss the previous history of the major characters, any competent modern dramatist will insure that such anterior information seems to spring spontaneously from the action; this ordinarily means that the clues are widely scattered. Even in so short an example as this, you can see the process at work:

SMALL AUNT CECILY

JACK: . . . I simply want my cigarette case back.

ALGERON: Yes, but this isn't your cigarette case. This cigarette case is a present from someone of the name of Cecily, and you said you didn't know anyone of that name.

JACK: Well, if you want to know, Cecily happens to be my aunt.

ALGERNON: Your aunt!

JACK: Yes. Charming old lady she is, too. Lives at Tunbridge Wells. Just give it back to me, Algy.

ALGERNON (*retreating to back of sofa*):   But why does she call herself little Cecily if she is your aunt and lives at Tunbridge Wells? (*Reading*)   "From little Cecily with her fondest love."

JACK: My dear fellow, what on earth is there in that? Some aunts are tall, some aunts are not tall. That is a matter that surely an aunt may be allowed to decide for herself. . . . For Heaven's sake give me back my cigarette case. (*Follows Algernon round the room*)

ALGERNON: Yes. But why does your aunt call you her uncle? "From little Cecily, with her fondest love to her dear Uncle Jack." There is no objection, I admit, to an aunt being a small aunt, but why an aunt, no matter what her size may be, should call her own nephew her uncle, I can't quite make out. Besides, your name isn't Jack at all; it is Ernest.

JACK: It isn't Ernest; it's Jack.

ALGERNON: You have always told me it was Ernest. I have introduced you to everyone as Ernest. You answer to the name of Ernest. You look as if your name was Ernest. You are the most earnest looking person I ever saw in my life. It is perfectly absurd your saying your name isn't Ernest. It's on your cards. Here is one of them. "Mr. Ernest Worthing, B 4, The Albany." . . .

JACK: Well, my name is Ernest in town and Jack in the country, and the cigarette case was given to me in the country.

ALGERNON: Yes, but that does not account for the fact that your small Aunt Cecily, who lives at Tunbridge Wells, calls you her dear uncle. Come, old boy, you had much better have the thing out at once. . . .

JACK: Well, produce my cigarette case first.

ALGERNON: Here it is. Now produce your explanation, and pray make it improbable.

—Oscar Wilde, *The Importance of Being Earnest* (1895)

Two facts vital to the play are presented: Jack has assumed the name of Ernest; he bears an avuncular relationship to someone called Cecily. Omitted from this excerpt are references to the formidability of Lady Bracknell and to Algy's invention of Bunbury, both of which loom large in the rest of the drama; but even after these other presuppositions have been suppressed, notice how widely the clues are spread. The information is parceled out in small units: "someone by the name of Cecily" becomes "little Cecily" before we finally learn that she considers Jack her uncle; further discussion of Cecily's identity is interrupted by the information that Jack is posing as Ernest, and only after that presupposition has been thoroughly established do we return to the previous subject. Notice too that Wilde exploits the comic possibilities of repetition in order to hammer home his two essential facts; other authors will not give you as much help in projecting information to your audience. Finally, notice that at the end of the excerpt, Wilde has prepared for yet a fuller explanation of Cecily's identity, which duly follows the excerpt above.

Because the clues may be widespread and the situation complex, you may have to draw up a full Statement of Presuppositions, a short essay of two or three paragraphs describing the preëxistent situation and documenting your sources by line number. Then, during rehearsal, you will be more likely to project the relevant lines clearly.

Reinforcement

We have just seen a spectacular use of the simplest forms of reinforcement —repetition and restatement, which were discussed in Chapter Three; here we shall concentrate upon subtler forms. Note, however, that just as the answer "It's repeated because it's important" begged the question in Chapter Three, so the answer "It's repeated for reinforcement" is rarely adequate to the question here. Why bring it up *now?* Why not do the reinforcing earlier or later?

In the Wilde excerpt above the reinforcement is designed to establish two presuppositions. One of them, that Jack is not really named Ernest, must be firmly established before the next major scene (which, called "The Proposal: I," is reprinted on page 364) in order to exploit its comic possibilities. The other presupposition, the existence of Cecily, develops into the subplot—the romance between Algernon and Cecily; in placing it here rather than later, Wilde doubtless reinforces our interest in Jack's proposal, by a form of symbolic transfer. Given Jack's reluctance to discuss Cecily, we are allowed to question his honesty or his fidelity—and so suspense is built.

Reinforcement, then, is only part of the answer; the rest must be found in the other sections below.

THE SUBPLOT.   A device used often, especially in drama, to reinforce the major action: the actions and desires of the major characters are duplicated in smaller compass by those of less important characters. Consider *King Lear:*

> Lear gives his kingdom to his two older daughters, disinherit-ing the worthy youngest. Gloucester banishes his worthy younger son. Lear's two older daughters cast their father out homeless; Gloucester's older son betrays his father and con-dones the latter's blinding. Lear journeys in search of his loyal youngest daughter in the company of a faithful noble and a fool; Gloucester seeks his faithful younger son, guided by that (noble) son disguised as a madman. Gloucester discovers his error the sooner, but both men are harrowed by their children's ingratitude, and both defy a universe believed to be hostile and pitiless. Both are shattered when right is finally restored.

The parallels are rarely so close; Act II of Lillian Hellman's *Watch on the Rhine* has a subplot whose relevance is far harder to detect:

> Toward the end of the act, Sara encourages her husband to re-turn to his duty in Germany, even though she knows that his mission will lead to his certain death. She does not mention their children and fights hard against facing the implications of her husband's ill health. Earlier in the act, Marthe separates from her husband, admitting in public that she loves another man. She helps that man to avoid announcing that he loves her; she refuses an invitation to remain where she could fight his domineering mother; and at the moment of decision she mentions neither his weakness nor her loneliness.
>
> Perhaps even this simple but slanted summary does not hint strongly enough at the parallel: both women decide upon a course of action whose consequences they believe will be pain-ful: the men they love will be killed, one literally and the other metaphorically. Neither woman uses the weapons readily avail-able to her; each chooses instead to allow her man to do what he feels he ought.

A reader, then, has first the problem of detecting subplots; in a novel by Aldous Huxley there may be six or seven. Sometimes fully as difficult is the detection of parallel incidents and parallel speeches; few authors will quote themselves verbatim. Juxtaposed as they are here, the following scenes are obviously similar; it is a harder task to locate them when they are separated by about thirty pages or half an hour's playing time.

—We live, as I hope you know, Mr. Worthing, in an age of ideals, . . . and my ideal has always been to love some one of the name of Ernest. There is something in that name that inspires absolute confidence. The moment Algernon first mentioned to me that he had a friend called Ernest, I knew I was destined to love you. . . .

—But you don't really mean to say that you couldn't love me if my name wasn't Ernest? . . . I must say I think there are lots of other much nicer names. I think, Jack, for instance, a charming name.

—Jack? . . . Jack is a notorious domesticity for John! And I pity any woman who is married to a man called John. . . .

—Gwendolen, I must get christened at once—I mean we must get married at once.

—You must not laugh at me, darling, but it had always been a girlish dream of mine to love some one whose name was Ernest. There is something in that name that seems to inspire absolute confidence. I pity any poor married woman whose husband is not called Ernest.

—But, my dear child, do you mean to say you could not love me if I had some other name?

—But what name?

—Oh, any name you like—Algernon, for instance.

—But I don't like the name of Algernon.

—Well, my own dear, sweet, loving little darling, I really can't see why you should object to the name of Algernon. It is not at all a bad name. . . . Cecily, if my name was Algy, couldn't you love me?

—I might respect you, Ernest, I might admire your character, but I fear I should not be able to give you my undivided attention.

—Ahem! Cecily! Your Rector here . . . I must see him at once on a most important christening—I mean, on most important business.

The technical implications of all this to reading aloud should be clear enough. The audience must recognize the similarities immediately; somehow you must establish in the first scene a pattern sufficiently strong and sufficiently unique that you can echo yourself in the second—a task that calls for considerable audible and visible subtlety.

SYMBOLIC TRANSFER.   The slowest student in a freshman composition class knows that any description of heartbreak or loneliness should include the words, "Outside a cold gray rain was falling." During the more hysterical periods in our history the principle of guilt by association has attained quasi-legality. Both are manifestations of our tendency to transfer our feelings about one thing to something that happens to be near it. The process is at work when words take on the connotations of the contexts in which they occur; it sustains metaphor. Here we are concerned with its use as a structural device: many an apparently irrelevant description, many an ostensible tangent, will have been inserted in order to reinforce—or perhaps even to modify—our attitude to what follows.

In Ivan Bunin's "The Gentleman from San Francisco," as the protagonist is breathing his last, there occurs this passage:

> . . . one could distinctly hear the ticking of the clock in the lobby, where a lonely parrot babbled something in its expressionless manner, stirring in its cage, and trying to fall asleep with its paw clutching the upper perch in a most absurd manner. The Gentleman from San Francisco lay stretched in a cheap iron bed, under coarse woolen blankets. . . . His blue, already lifeless face grew gradually cold; the hoarse, rattling noise which came from his mouth, lighted by the glimmer of the golden fillings, gradually weakened. . . .

> The symbolism of a clock within a context of death is easy enough, but how did a parrot get into the scene? To ask such a question is almost to discover the answer. Babbling, expressionless, trying to fall asleep—all these apply to the stertorous Gentleman; so does the implicit mindlessness, and the discomfort if not the absurdity of his position. At the very least, the description of the parrot prepares us for a similar description of the Gentleman, even if we do not automatically transfer the description ourselves.

> Even in the bald summary of *King Lear* on page 208, you could see the bitter propriety of placing the mistaken old men, whose worlds had turned topsy-turvy, in the company of fool and madman. You may even have noticed the poetic justice of blinding a man who refused to "see."

Since you will meet Symbolic Transfer again and again in the exercises at the end of this chapter, we shall illustrate it no further for the present. Be suspicious of any tangent; ask yourself whether it gives emotional coloring to that which precedes or follows—whether there is an incomplete simile, an implicit appeal to the principle "Birds of a feather flock together," a half-stated analogy.

ITERATIVE IMAGERY.   If you look closely at some selections you will notice that many symbols, images, metaphors, and "irrelevant details" spring from one rather limited field of experience. In the analysis of Keats' "On First Looking into Chapman's Homer," for example, we detected an unusually large number of references to learning. We called these the Discovery motif, but do not insist on that label; the point is simply that the references gained cumulative force through frequent iteration or repetition. Such a cluster of images can provide valuable insight into the subtler forms of literary meaning; we see *Macbeth* more clearly after a Caroline Spurgeon has shown us that the dominant image there— established by repetition after repetition—is one of borrowed robes; *Hamlet* is filled with references to disease, *Othello* with images of "animals in action, prey-ing upon one another."[10] Indeed, such iterative imagery may too easily suggest the Freudian slip and the word-association test—certainly it leads some contem-porary criticism into psychoanalysis.

Without pressing curiosity or ingenuity so far, we can nevertheless gain con-siderable information about the sense of a work—to say nothing of attitude and tone—by noting the recurrence of images. Much can be gained through the mere clerical process of adding them up, with no attempt to weigh the vividness of each; chances are, however, that you will get best results by keeping a rough score, because in that way you allow yourself to react to the prominence of the details.

The application of this method to oral reading may be immediate. Marvell's "To His Coy Mistress" (1681) contains at least two brilliant epigrams:

> But at my back I always hear   21
> Time's winged chariot hurrying near,

> The grave's a fine and private place,   31
> But none, I think, do there embrace.

Which is more important? Which demands the greater em-phasis? Part of the answer may be found by turning to page 99 and analyzing the references to time and hurrying, and to death

---

[10] Caroline Spurgeon, "Leading Motives in the Imagery of Shakespeare's Tragedies," in Anne Bradby, *Shakespearean Criticism 1919–1935,* London, 1936, pp. 18–61. An expanded form of the thesis forms part 2 of Spurgeon's *Shakespeare's Imagery: and What It Tells Us,* Cambridge, 1935 (available in paperback as Beacon BP53). Part 1, however, attempts to infer Shakespeare's character; it concludes that he was handy to have around the house.

and embracing. Does time, or death, dominate the poem? Or does the emphasis shift at some point between these two epigrams, so that they become equally important? Get out your computer and go to work.

Iterative imagery may be seen clearly in the exercises at the end of this chapter, especially in Jessamyn West's "The Illumination." By noting recurrent references to some phase of experience you may discover some of the subtlest clues to structure.

Contrast

Since contrast is one of the basic principles of organization, the term may be too inclusive to be useful. As an answer to the question "Why bring it up now?" it is only a little more definite than "for structure." Accordingly we shall turn to some of the structural tasks which contrast may perform.

FOCUS.   We can see an object more clearly when we place it against a contrasting background; the edges stand out more sharply, the object ceases to be a blur and becomes limited or defined. Similarly we can make our explanations clearer through the use of "negative definition": "By liberty I do not mean . . . and I do not mean . . .; I mean. . . ." Placing something into opposition with something else helps us to see where one leaves off and the other begins.

A character in a story may appear to be a typical social climber; by introducing or describing another "irrelevant," social climber, the author may show us that the first one is unique. Cordelia's first speeches to Lear are pretty abrupt and sanctimonious, but they would be insufferably rude if we had not first encountered the cloying flatteries of Goneril and Regan; whatever her faults, we decide, Cordelia is honest. In Frost's "Mending Wall," the tolerance of the narrator takes on sharper focus when it is juxtaposed with the attitude that "Good fences make good neighbors."

An apparently irrelevant or unnecessary detail or character or episode may have been inserted in order to limit the range of speculation—in other words, to sharpen the focus.

MAGNIFICATION OR DIMINUTION.   The moon seems largest near the horizon, where it can be contrasted with hills and trees; later against the whole of the sky, it seems to have shrunk. Hamlet's muddy-mettled hesitation appears greater to him when he contrasts it with the activity of the First Player and of Fortinbras. The third little pig seems wise above the ordinary, simply because we have already seen the foolishness of his two brothers. And Lucy, you remember, was "fair as a star when only *one*/Is shining in the sky."

A detail of character or incident may be inserted in order to provide a standard by which we can judge the rest. In this connection note that contrast may build suspense: often in fiction there are three attempts to surmount an obstacle; two failures not only magnify the final triumph, but they keep us on edge. As an oral reader, you would be well advised to exploit the opportunities that such a triad provides.

THE CALM BEFORE THE STORM.   The device suggested by this phrase is common enough to deserve special attention. Even in the frivolous "The Proposal: II," pages 110–111, you may recall there is a short period of lyrical calm before Lady Bracknell explodes upon the scene; Gwendolen becomes almost tender.

> What wonderfully blue eyes you have, Ernest! They are quite, quite blue. I hope you will always look at me just like that, especially when there are other people present.

Since the last few words are merely a reworking of a gag that has been used three or four minutes earlier, they will elicit a mild chuckle at best; everything is quiet —before all Bracknell breaks loose! We need hardly mention that the calm after the storm is as frequent as the calm before; note the change which is rung "forlorn" in "Ode to a Nightingale." Shakespeare is full of lyrical pauses and comic interludes; they precede or follow almost any period of tension. Indeed, the technique is so basic to timing that often your chief problem is to remember to exploit it during rehearsal.

Notice, too, that the device is used to trick us into settling back secure: Jack's proposal is successful; all is settled; and then comes Lady Bracknell. The principle reaches deep in our psyche; even today, with Nemesis long since dead and *hubris* an old superstition, we "knock wood," are mildly unsettled by great success. And so, as a reader, you touch a near-universal chord when you show in your manner that things are too rosy to last.

Look for, and exploit, details and episodes that have been inserted to induce a false sense of security, and adjust your timing so that the lyrical pauses, the comic interludes, and other such "breathers" allow us to gather our strength.

Suspense

To most beginning readers the building of suspense is more a problem of delivery than of analysis. With the help of Chapter Five much of that problem is solved if you reflect upon the wisdom of the language: suspense is not something that is done, it is not accomplished, it is not meant; it is *built*. Suspense is built out of details and incidents, and if there are not enough details inherent in the plot, we should expect an author to go out and fetch some. In other words, we should not be surprised to find a little padding.

Nor should we as audience be surprised to detect some padding in your reading. You are not allowed to interject words, of course, but you certainly can prolong them; you can insert pauses, you can tease us. And as long as neither you nor the author is obvious or coy we enjoy the teasing. So, have fun with suspense. Prolong the agony.

Foreshadowing

Suspense and surprise are so common to modern popular fiction that it is easy to forget another basis of literature: recognition. The audiences for whom Shakespeare and Sophocles and Aeschylus wrote knew all the stories beforehand; yet out of them there grew a literature more imposing than anything built on surprise. Indeed, even the most ingenious detective story will disappoint us if we are thoroughly surprised by the ending; in an honest job of writing, Inspector Whosis never produces a totally unforeseen clue on the last page. The *deus ex machina*—the rabbit out of the hat—was rarely used by Euripedes, whatever you may have learned to the contrary. Literature, by the very fact of its organization, is never completely surprising; even in detective fiction the author takes great care to "plant" the clue that his hero will finally discover.

We can almost lay down a rule: whenever there is a real surprise in literature, you can go back and find the clues that foretold its coming. Another rule: the shorter or more intense the work, the nearer to the beginning are the clues. In Drayton's sonnet "Since There's No Help," page 68, where fourteen lines must accommodate the thesis "I want to go I don't want to go," we suspected that the blustering in the first line was overdone and that the "glad, yea, glad" of line 3 was overargued. *Hamlet,* with a five-hour playing time, begins with a sentry's receiving, instead of issuing, a challenge; to the alert reader the very first line indicates that the time is out of joint, if not that something is rotten in the state of Denmark.

Sometimes the foreshadowing takes the form of calm-before-the-storm, and then there are many references to the idyllic state of affairs; in "The Runaway Slave," next page, notice Huck's inordinate delight in having written the letter. Ordinarily the shadows of the future are somewhat more defined; the moment the earlier, and wrong, decision is reached, Huck ceases to refer to "nigger," and begins to talk of "Jim." In a superbly constructed work like *Oedipus Rex* every temporary "solution" reveals the seeds of its own destruction.

In presenting such foreshadowing the oral reader must not nudge his audience too sharply; fortunately, in a well-written work, the early clues will often pose as something else—negative definition, insistent exposition, restatement, or minor modification.

Red Herring

Except in classical and Elizabethan tragedy, foreshadowing is usually flecked with will-o'-the-wisp: some clues will have been inserted to mislead us, so that our delight in arriving at the correct solution will be the more intense. As a reader you must be alert to such false starts, because you may wish to tease your audience with them; but, like the author, you must avoid giving them such prominence that they arouse an expectation which you will not satisfy. This note is simply a restatement, within the context of surprise and suspense, of what we said earlier about focus and magnification-diminution.

Dramatic Irony

Irony, as we described it in Chapter Three, occurs when a context is so manipulated that a term means roughly the opposite of what it ostensibly says. Dramatic Irony occurs when the context is so manipulated that an action has results precisely the opposite of those intended, or that our interpretation of a situation is completely different from—and usually the opposite of—that of one of the characters. The most common form of the first variety is a sort of poetic justice, whereby someone falls into the trap he has set for another; but often an action that was designed to save becomes the cause of destruction. You can find examples in your newspaper: the traffic commissioner gets a ticket for speeding, something is stolen from the police station, someone trips over a first aid kit, or a fire engine smashes an ambulance. The second variety of irony supplies the audience with information withheld from a character; we know the true situation and are amused or appalled to watch the character operate upon the basis of his incomplete data. For a simple example, watch someone playing pin-the-tail-on-the-donkey. Often the two forms will fuse, as in the following:

The Runaway Slave

(1)   It made me shiver. And I about made up my mind to pray, and see if I couldn't try to quit being the kind of a boy I was and be better. So I kneeled down. But the words wouldn't come. Why wouldn't they? It warn't no use to try and hide it from Him. Nor

from *me,* neither. I knowed very well why they wouldn't come. It was because my heart warn't right; it was because I warn't square; it was because I was playing double. I was letting *on* to give up sin, but away inside of me I was holding on to the biggest one of all. I was trying to make my mouth *say* I would do the right thing and the clean thing, and go and write to that nigger's owner and tell where he was; but deep down in me I knowed it was a lie, and He knowed it. You can't pray a lie—I found that out.

(2)   So I was full of trouble, full as I could be; and didn't know what to do. At last I had an idea; and I says, I'll go and write the letter—and *then* see if I can pray. Why, it was astonishing, the way I felt as light as a feather right straight off, and my troubles all gone. So I got a piece of paper and a pencil, all glad and excited, and set down and wrote:

(3)   Miss Watson, your runaway nigger Jim is down here two mile below Pikesville, and Mr. Phelps has got him and he will give him up for the reward if you send.

Huck Finn.

(4)   I felt good and all washed clean of sin for the first time I had ever felt so in my life, and I knowed I could pray now. But I didn't do it straight off, but laid the paper down and set there thinking—thinking how good it was all this happened so, and how near I come to being lost and going to hell. And went on thinking. And got to thinking over our trip down the river; and I see Jim before me all the time: in the day and in the night-time, sometimes moonlight, sometimes storms, and we a-floating along, talking and singing and laughing. But somehow I couldn't seem to strike no places to harden me against him, but only the other kind. I'd see him standing my watch on top of his'n, 'stead of calling me, so I could go on sleeping; and see him how glad he was when I come back out of the fog; and when I come to him again in the swamp, up there where the feud was; and such-like times; and would always call me honey, and pet me, and do everything he could think of for me, and how good he always was; and at last I struck the time I saved him by telling the men we had smallpox aboard, and he was so grateful, and said I was the best friend old Jim ever had in the world, and the *only* one he's got now; and then I happened to look around and see that paper.

(5)   It was a close place. I took it up, and held it in my hand. I

was a-trembling, because I'd got to decide, forever, betwixt two things, and I knowed it. I studied a minute, sort of holding my breath, and then says to myself:

(6)   "All right, then I'll *go* to hell"—and tore it up.

(7)   It was awful thoughts and awful words, but they was said. And I let them stay said; and never thought no more about reforming. I shoved the whole thing out of my head, and said I would take up wickedness again, which was in my line, being brung up to it, and the other warn't. And for a starter I would go to work and steal Jim out of slavery again; and if I could think up anything worse, I would do that, too; because as long as I was in, and in for good, I might as well go the whole hog.

—Mark Twain, *The Adventures of Huckleberry Finn* (1884)

We, who know the "true" morality, are amused and touched by Huck's belief that his second decision is immoral. We are perhaps shocked to find that a God of all mankind is expected to condone the enslavement of a part of mankind and that a God of Love is expected to punish an act of brotherly love. The writing is so skillful that the effect seems to spring automatically out of the facts of the case; but actually two fundamental religious and social questions are discussed: Is slavery wrong? (Remember that slavery was clearly "right" for over 4000 years.) What is the nature of God? (Reflect that even in contemporary Christianity both the God of Love and the God of Justice can find theological champions.) The passage is superbly constructed, and merits our closest attention.

Notice first of all that the padding, the "lyrical pause" in (1) and (2) gives us a chance to catch up, and to think the matter over. More important, we are encouraged to think it over, and to do so for ourselves; the vagueness and the naïveté of the language are obviously inadequate to the discussion of a sophisticated problem: "see if I couldn't try to quit being the kind of a boy I was"—the muddled grammar, the verbosity, and the vagueness of the charge force us to "find the meaning" ourselves; "my heart warn't right," "I warn't square," "I was playing double"—the naïveté here, like that of "the right thing and the clean thing," encourages us to substitute our own more sophisticated concepts. What is the effect of restatement that does not really restate? Inarticulateness? Muddled thinking? Sheer love of words? Emotionalism? All of these and perhaps more? What would be the result if the following were substituted for the respective quotations above: "try to stop lying and stealing"; "I didn't mean what I said," "I was lying to God Hisself,"

"I was mighty mixed up"; and "obey the law" (or even "do what folks expect")? What else might have been done to hold our opinions in abeyance and force us to accept Huck's thinking?

Notice the ironic device of pretending to miss the point. Huck does not see the problem we see: should a runaway slave be returned to his owner? Huck has the answer to that one—it's easy; *his* problem is far more important: why can't I pray? What would be the effect if the restatements of the obvious, the clichés, and the signs of overwriting were removed? Would we begin to take Huck's problem more, or less, seriously? And then what would happen to the real problem?

Why is there so little concrete, and human, detail in (1) and (2) and so much in (4)? Is there any connection with the fact, mentioned earlier, that the impersonal "nigger" shifts into the personal "Jim"? What would happen if (1) contained references to "Miss Watson"? To "poor old Miss Watson" or even to "poor old Miss Watson back home who never had but one nigger to help her with things and he run away"?

Why are the two basic questions never separated? When Huck has a societal problem in (1) and (2) (after all, Miss Watson *was* old, and she had presumably paid for Jim) he turns it into a religious one. And instead of testing his solution to the religious problem, he switches to the social. Why is (7) essential? What might happen if Huck's decision were allowed to remain societal?

By way of review, why bring it up now? Why mention "reward" in (3), near the end of (3). Why not mention it in (1) or (7)? Similarly, why does the mention of Jim's gratitude occur late in (4), rather than early? Why the ambiguous "how good it was all this happened so" in (4)? Is a transition necessary at all? Why is "in the day and in the night-time . . . talking and singing and laughing" (4) placed where it is? Does the false start increase the effectiveness of this excerpt? Would (1) through (3) be better omitted? Why the stalling in (5) or why insert (5) at all? Why are the thought groups in (5) so short? What does the defiance in the last sentence of (7) tell us about Huck's character? About his present certainty? Does it provide an effective ending for the excerpt? How so?

Although we have not discussed this yet, try to compare the rhythm—especially the length of the thought groups—of (1) and (4). Can you account for the difference?

As we have said, the two forms of dramatic irony are frequently mixed, but so long as you remain alert to both possibilities there is no need to keep them distinct in your mind. Indeed, you may find it more convenient, as do many critics, to consider dramatic irony merely another form of irony itself. Probably the most powerful example of it in all literature is Sophocles' *Oedipus Rex;* do not graduate from college without having read it.

SOME PROCEDURAL HINTS

We have insisted that meaning is a function of structure and that structural analysis is largely a matter of asking again and again, Why bring this up now? We have discussed a number of probable reasons for inserting a unit at one point rather than at another and have advised you to look for more than one explanation of the presence of most details. This might well conclude the present chapter, but for those of you who prefer "systematic" procedure, we offer a number of useful tips. The steps need not necessarily be taken in the order given; your own experience will readily suggest modifications.

Find the Motivational Units

Since a motivational unit is simply a section in which something happens, the verb "find" may be a little misleading. Basically, you merely break the selection up into manageable chunks in order to concentrate upon one part at a time. If your divisions are completely arbitrary you will miss some valuable clues to structure—and to emphasis and timing—because you will not be able to find adequate answers to the question: What does this section accomplish? Instead we suggest you "find" the units—in other words, secure a provisional answer to the important question, What is accomplished first? Next? Or, to oversimplify: What happens first? Next?

> Turn back to "The Runaway Slave," page 215. What happens first? Well, the answer might be "Huck tries to pray"; our first motivational unit, then, would comprise the first three sentences. What happens next? "Huck fails"—and our next unit is sentence 4. What happens next? "Huck wonders why he can't pray"—sentences 5–13. And so on.
>
> However, we seem to be chopping a simple incident so fine that we shall soon be lost in a crowd of units. Perhaps we should aim for larger ones. What happens first? "Huck decides to write the letter"—our first unit is paragraph (1) and the first two sentences of (2). What happens next? "Huck writes the letter"—last sentence of (2) and all of (3). But what about the third sen-

tence of (2): "Why it was astonishing . . . my troubles all gone"? Does it belong in our first unit or our second?

Such a question is not a problem of definition or of procedure; it is a question of structure, and of timing and the expression of attitude; hence it is an important question. One of the values of "finding" motivational units is that the process engenders such questions.

Notice that the sentence is closely connected with the previous one. Should we include it in our first unit? Or should we consider the second and third sentences of (2) to be a separate unit? Or does our first unit really end with the first sentence of (2); so that the second unit begins "At last I had an idea . . ."?

Each of these options seems to us defensible. The final answer depends upon how you can best make things hang together—and that must be tested in rehearsal.

Motivational units, then, are often provisional. One of the major values of searching for them is that the search forces you to analyze connections you might otherwise take for granted, to group details into some defensible structure. And it forces you to become especially sensitive to changes of attitude.

Having discovered some principles of coherence which group the details into a defensible unit, you have probably answered the question, What does this unit accomplish? But pose the question a second time, just to make sure. The answer, a clear statement of the motivation of the unit, will focus your analysis of mood and tone and attitude and clarify the relation of that unit to the next.

Analyze Each Unit

Look first of all for sources of conflict. You have decided upon the motivation of the unit; what is it that obstructs the accomplishment of that goal? Some units, especially those of description, will not contain any conflict; but in the majority you will detect a character, or a principle, or perhaps even simple inertia, which acts in opposition to the main motivation.

If there are any characters in the unit, decide upon the part each plays in accomplishing the purpose of the unit. What does each want at this point? What is each trying to accomplish?

Justify the inclusion of all the details, chiefly through the use of the key question: Why bring it up now?

Trace the Rise and Fall of Tension

The analysis of attitude should reveal a rise in tension, a climax, within practically every unit. If you are working with large units, do not be surprised to discover more than one peak of intensity within some of them. Probably what you have done is to combine several units in one, a matter of minor importance unless you discover that the point of highest intensity is at the beginning of the unit; when that happens you had better question the validity of your divisions. Ordinarily, as we have hinted, the peak of intensity will be close to the end of the unit, with perhaps one or two lesser peaks preceding.

Attitude analysis will also have revealed that some units are more intense than are others. Ordinarily the highest peak will be near the end.

During this part of your analysis, you should see clearly the "padding" for suspense, the lyrical pauses, the interludes, and the other "unnecessary delays" discussed earlier.

Look for Balance

In a beginning course we cannot go deeply into the matter of balance. However, your analysis of structure will have revealed details—or characters, incidents, units—which have the same weight, the same importance, as do other details. They are of approximately the same length or the same intensity; more frequently the products of their length "multiplied" by intensity are approximately equal. They seem to cancel out.

The first four lines of "Since There's No Help," page 68, are of approximately the same importance as the next four lines; and the two together—i.e., the first eight lines—are balanced by the last six. Algernon and Cecily balance Jack and Gwendolen; and the four of them, plus two or three supernumeraries, manage to make up the sum of Lady Bracknell.

Broadly speaking, the solution balances the problem—remember that in your oral presentation. Generally the longer you stretch the suspense (which is a form of imbalance), the more intense must be the climax. The purpose of determining the other balance systems by analysis is to prevent giving some episode or character more weight than its counterweight. Hamlet must not be clearly stronger than Claudius or the play becomes pointless; similarly, for the time during which they are counterpoised, Laertes must be Hamlet's approximate equal (when the poisoned tip of his sword is added) or the duel becomes one-sided. The point here is that in things dynamic, balance can never be constant; just as in walking we shift our weight from foot to foot and thus maintain an overall distribution, so in literature the equilibrium is constantly disturbed and redressed, as a character is balanced now by this opponent and now by that, and an episode now poises against another and then combines with it in order to balance a third. If you can manage, in this course, to detect the major balance systems within a selection, you need not let the others worry you much.

Insure That Everything Fits

This is the final check and will ordinarily be made toward the end of rehearsal. Pay particular attention to the sections that never seem to "come out right" when you read them aloud. First of all, are you sure you understand their literal sense? Is the attitude clear? Then concentrate on structure. Why does the section belong? How does it fit into everything else? Why bring it up now?

EXERCISES AND ASSIGNMENTS

1. Analyze the structure of this poem:

MENDING WALL

	Something there is that doesn't love a wall,	a
	That sends the frozen-ground-swell under it,	
	And spills the upper boulders in the sun;	
	And makes gaps even two can pass abreast.	
5	The work of hunters is another thing:	b
	I have come after them and made repair	
	Where they have left not one stone on a stone,	
	But they would have the rabbit out of hiding,	
	To please the yelping dogs. The gaps I mean,	c
10	No one has seen them made or heard them made,	
	But at spring mending-time we find them there.	d
	I let my neighbor know beyond the hill;	
	And on a day we meet to walk the line	
	And set the wall between us once again.	
15	We keep the wall between us as we go.	e
	To each the boulders that have fallen to each.	f
	And some are loaves and some so nearly balls	
	We have to use a spell to make them balance:	
	"Stay where you are until our backs are turned!"	
20	We wear our fingers rough with handling them.	g
	Oh, just another kind of outdoor game,	h
	One on a side. It comes to little more:	
	There where it is we do not need the wall:	
	He is all pine and I am apple orchard.	
25	My apple trees will never get across	
	And eat the cones under his pines, I tell him.	
	He only says, "Good fences make good neighbors."	i
	Spring is the mischief in me, and I wonder	j
	If I could put a notion in his head:	
30	*"Why* do they make good neighbors? Isn't it	k
	Where there are cows? But here there are no cows.	

Before I built a wall I'd ask to know
What I was walling in or walling out,
And to whom I was like to give offense.

l   Something there is that doesn't love a wall,   35
That wants it down." I could say "Elves" to him,

m   But it's not elves exactly, and I'd rather
He said it for himself. I see him there,
Bringing a stone grasped firmly by the top
In each hand, like an old-stone savage armed.   40
He moves in darkness, as it seems to me,
Not of woods only and the shade of trees.
He will not go behind his father's saying,
And he likes having thought of it so well
He says again, "Good fences make good neighbors."[11]   45
                     —Robert Frost (1914)

a. We have divided this poem into defensible motivational units; how do you agree
with these divisions? Would you preserve the distinction between *e* and *f, j* and
k? Would you start a new one at line 44? Would you begin *m* at line 36? How
would you divide the poem?

b. Do any of the narrative components in this poem shed light on any other?
   1) Here we see one character through the eyes of another; what allowance must
      we make for the narrator's bias? How are lines 21–22, 41 germane to this
      problem? Can you find others? What implications does the problem have
      for tone?
   2) Here are some clues to setting: lines 2, 3, 5–9, 17, 24, 31. Can you find
      others? In what ways does setting clarify character?
   3) How does the action provide clues to character?
   4) Besides lines 13–16, what are the clues to means? How important are they?
      How has this question shed further light upon sense, mood, attitude, tone,
      or intent?

c. Do lines 5–9 perform any function other than negative definition or focus? Are
   they related to lines 21–22? To lines 25–26, 31–32, 40? Are they related to
   lines 1 and 35? Return to this question after you have answered questions d–5–b
   and i.

d. Justify the diction of line 24.
   1) Why not "his" and "mine"?
   2) Why not "I am all pine and he is apple-orchard"?
   3) Do lines 25–26 provide the answer to the preceding question, or is there a
      greater symbolism at work?
   4) Why not "and I am fields of grain"?

[11] From *Complete Poems of Robert Frost*. Copyright, 1930, 1949, by Henry Holt & Co., Inc. By permission
of the publishers.

5) Why is he all pine?
   a) Do you find an answer in line 26 or in lines 41–42? Anywhere else?
   b) Why are the boulders in line 17 not jagged? Would that not reinforce line 20? Why not "And some are rough as pine-cones, but so round"?

e. Justify the inclusion of lines 18–19, 36–37.

f. On page 48 we wondered about the inversion in line 1, repeated in line 35; does that analysis now appear sound? How important is the inversion?

g. Why are they mending a wall instead of building one?

h. What is the relevance of line 15? Why does it echo line 14?

i. Is there any dramatic irony in the poem? Is theirs an act of construction?

j. Line 1 is repeated in line 35, and line 27 in line 45. Why does the neighbor have the last word?

2. The structure of this short story will repay careful analysis. Although classroom time may be too limited to read the entire story aloud, you may wish to read parts of it. Accordingly we have numbered the excerpts which are reasonably self-contained and provide valuable practice, indicating the end of each by an asterisk.

The Illumination

a   1. It was a May morning, early. The morning of a piece meal flicker-light day. It was the time of the return of shadows. The time once again when there was sun enough and leaf enough to give some variety to the monotony of a wall or strip of land.

b   The old man sat on his side of the bed putting his foot into a white wool sock. He gazed at the sunlight coming through the east windows, like water tinged with a little squeezed juice from a red geranium, he decided. He had a head full of quizzical ideas about himself and the world—at the minute his foot was busy feeling its way into the sock, and his eye with watching the sun set the water pitcher on the floor. There it was on the gray rag carpet.

"Appears to be a big-eared animal," he said, figuring it out finally.

c   His wife, who had the May morning in her veins but was giving no thought to it, gartered her stockings neatly with the soft pieces of rolled red silk she used. She was a Quaker and didn't hold with distracting the eye of man with violent colors. But under three skirts, knee-high, and visible only to God, she didn't reckon it mattered. And she knew it was there.

d   "Thee's choosing a poor time to be fanciful, Jess," she said. "I can feel all the steps I got to take before night jolting my spine right now. Kitchen to dining room. Dining room to kitchen." She got up from her side of the bed and walked to the middle of the room, where she gave a little bounce.

"Tickled?" her husband asked.

"Gratified," she said, without studying about it. "Praising God in his glory. It'll be a convenience. Beautiful at night. Shining through the trees, too. To say nothing of the novelty."

"It was my idea," the old man reminded her.   e

"Thee was the vessel. The Lord filled thee."

Jess was used to that. Eliza had given God the credit for all he'd ever done, but she was a fine woman and a Quaker preacher.

She had on all but her dress now. It was hard to say what was plump-   e1
ness and what was starch. There was plenty of both. "Stir thy stumps,   e2
Jess," she said, "twenty people for supper—thirty, maybe, and thee shilly-shallying in thy shirt-tail at six in the morning."

Jess smiled on her fondly. The best training for a woman, he figured, was to put her early in the pulpit. It didn't cut down any on her flow of talk, but it bettered it, and relieved the pressure.* A pity none of his daughters had had pulpit learnings. He pulled his nightshirt over his head. There was more warmth under it than outside.

"I got more heat than the sun," he said.

2.   Eliza didn't encourage him to talk. He watched her, her plump fingers flying in and out of her still black hair. Like birds at dusk. That was his own thought of them. The pleasing thoughts God let him have! So long as he had a head and shoulders to lodge it, he would never be bereft. He was jolted from daylight to dark with pleasing ideas. Whether God was the fount of all he could not say, but for their having he was grateful.

Eliza, looking in her mirrow, saw him naked behind her. She took an eye off her plaiting.

"At thy age," she said through her hairpins.

The old man came to life. "I ain't never been this age before," he complained. "Thee seems never hard put for what's becoming to thy years." He meant it. Whatever she did was becoming, waking or sleeping. A child in her arms or tanning its behind, she had a face of love and beauty. What could a man ask further—with that face opposite him for forty years and ideas popping in his mind like firecrackers? He buttoned his shirt meditatively.

Eliza's face got pink. She'd never learned to take a compliment—and she'd had two a day for forty years. They made her feel uneasy—as if she weren't taken for granted like sun and moon. "Don't put on thy good shirt, now," she said sharply. "Save it till evening—there's a mort of work to be done—unless thee plans to sit in the parlor saving thy strength for the Illumination."

The old man slowly pulled off the fresh shirt. "The Illumination," he said. "So that's what thee calls it? Sounds Biblical. The Annunciation. The Transfiguration. The Illumination. Sounds as if the Lord himself had a hand in it."

Eliza bridled. "Thee'd be a sorry piece—saying He hadn't.* But what," she asked reasonably, "would thee call it, Jess Millhouse? Thee's rigged up a gas plant in the cellar—we light the jets tonight and ask in the neighbors. That's the Illumination. Does thee feel marble cake, coconut drops, floating island, and French custard ice cream will be a sufficiency as dessert, Jess?"

"Scanty pickings," he said. "Scanty pickings. No pie."

Eliza's black eyes searched her husband's face anxiously until she saw his Adam's apple fluttering.

"Pie's kind of commonplace," she said.

The bedroom door opened without a knock. In the doorway stood a figure half-way between all known stopping places. A face too sharp-cut for a Negro—too dark for anything else—too much mustache for a woman, too much bosom for a man.

"Preacher," she intoned, "gravy's gobbling up the skillet, morning's gobbling up the day, pretty soon the daylight's going far away." Then she waited.

"That's pretty, Emanuela," said Eliza. "One of thy best. We'll be right down."

Emanuela walked away limber-legged, satisfaction oiling her knee-hinges.

"There's nothing about that woman I like," said Jess. "Calls thee 'preacher.' Always rhyming. No answer unless she can rhyme it."

Eliza was leaving the room, her Bible for breakfast Scripture reading in her hand. "After twenty years, Jess, thee might be reconciled."

"I'm still sane," the old man said. "Though after twenty years it's a wonder."

Eliza was going light-foot down the stairs. "Thee get thy sanity down to the breakfast table," she called back. "Feed it some ham and gravy. Don't get stuck up there preening thyself on it."

3.   The old man stood fully dressed but not descending. It was his morning's pleasure to stand thus at the day's rim as over a pool of water before plunging in. There was no telling what the day might hold—what vexations seize him belowstairs. Or what joys. He stood now, uncommitted to either, his own man, as silent and at peace as the clapper in a ropeless bell. Silent—silent. Here now at six o'clock in the morning with the pink light on the gray carpet, and the bed not yet made up, shutting out the night, he, Jess Millhouse, sixty-two years old, stood committed as yet to nothing but the unraveling of his own soul.

"Taste eternity," he said aloud, "on a May morning in a white clapboard house on the banks of the Muscatatuck. How to taste it—there's so much of it and none you want to waste."

Gratingly his strong finger stroked his long Irish upper lip—his eyes sharply focused on something beyond the chamber's edge. Then he walked slowly to the secretary which stood between the two south windows and took down Janney's *Life of William Penn*. With the stub pencil he always carried in his shirt pocket he wrote quickly. "Eternity," the soft blunt pencil set firmly down, "is experienced in life by sampling as many of the elements as is possible."

Around the sentences went quotation marks and under them the words, "From the writings of Dr. Samuel Johnson." The old man's books were filled with sentences of his own with other men's names under them. He was not a wasteful man, he was pious and he was Irish. The good thoughts God gave him he would save. He kept his stub pencil handy to write them down. But say he wrote them himself—he was too bashful for that—it would plague him to death to have it thought he set himself up to be a John Greenleaf or Henry Wadsworth. So his books were filled with wisdom from Charles Lamb and John Milton and John Woolman. When once in a while he had a thought he was convinced was true, but maybe not one a writer'd like to own, he labeled it "Anon."

"Sample as much as possible," he said to himself, put back the book, shut the secretary, and descended to the day that lay belowstairs, waiting.*

4.   Mattie bent over the hearth in the sitting room, turkey brush in hand, brushing up the night-before's ashes. She was bent, but not brushing.

"Well, daughter," said Jess.

"Good morning, Pa," the girl said soberly, not lifting her eyes to peer beyond the blinkers of her black frizzed bangs.

"Thee's like a witch, with thy broom—bent double and ready to fly."

"A witch," Mattie said, standing bolt upright and staring her father sadly in the eye. Then tears rolled out of her own gray eyes and down to the corners of her crooked mouth.

"Hoity-toity!" her father sighed. There was scarcely a word safe to say to fifteen-year-olds. They took exception to Holy Writ itself. Thinking to take her mind off the witch business, if that was what upset her, he said, "Thee have a fever blister on thy lip, Mattie."

Then Mattie sobbed, threw down the wing brush, cried, "Oh, Pa," and ran to the kitchen.

Now I'm in the day and fairly launched, Jess thought, and walked into the kitchen.

There Mattie sat at the breakfast table, her head in her arms, and Eliza faced him, her black eyes crackling. "A pretty way to start a day of celebration with twitting thy daughter about her looks."

"Twitting!" Jess said aghast. He wouldn't twit a shooting enemy about his looks. There was nothing so personal as looks.

"Call her first a witch—then take notice of a blemish that's plaguing her."

A witch—old, bent, ugly. A fever blister—a blemish big as a mountain and visible miles off and akin to leprosy in repulsiveness. I got to retravel so many miles to get back to fifteen, he thought, and even that don't turn the trick for I ain't female.

He sat down to the table. "Ever hear the word bewitching, Mattie?" he asked. Mattie raised her sorrowing head. "Bewitching. Like a witch. I don't know about now—but when I was a young blade, there was nothing a man could say in way of praise beyond that. Bewitching. Thy mother was bewitching. Don't thee ever read poetry, Mattie? Bee-stung lips? A fev—a fullness such as thine is highly regarded."

Mattie's sniffs were drying up. Eliza's eyes had given over blazing. The four of them, Jess and Eliza, Mattie and Emanuela sat at the breakfast table. The hired man had eaten earlier.

"Let us return thanks," said Jess, and the four heads bowed in silent prayer.

Jess meditated on God but asked for nothing. Eliza talked with her Father of gifts and wants alike. Emanuela floated wordless before a blazing throne. Mattie prayed, "Take away my fever blister, take away my fever blister." Then being of a reasonable and conciliatory nature, "or if Thee'd rather just make it invisible. Thee has the power, O Lord," she reminded Him.

"Make it invisible for the Illumination."*

The other three heads lifted while Mattie's was still bowed. Eliza said, "Help thyself to the gravy, Mattie."

Prayer was a solace, but there were twenty—thirty people coming for supper, and solace didn't chew like bread.

Mattie raised her head and looked about the table. No one was paying any attention to her fever blister. Perhaps it was already invisible. She helped herself to ham and gravy and soda biscuits, eating with lifted lip.

5.   Eliza planned her day like a general: terrain to be covered, redans thrown up, posts held. She gave out the commissions: "Emanuela, thee's not to set foot outside the kitchen today. Thee's to take care of the cooking. The chickens and ham should go on now. Those hens are all muscle. I'll make the floating island myself, and the corn pudding."

Emanuela drew a long breath to show speech was welling up. "Preacher, while your back is turned none of the vittles will be burned."

The old man swallowed heavily.

"Emanuela, it's time thee's learned
Prose is nothing to be spurned."

"Jess, Jess," Eliza chided. This was no day to get a rhyming hoedown started between those two. It could go on till candle-lighting time with Jess the winner, Emanuela sulking in her room, and Eliza with the work to do.

"Mattie," she said, "thee's to redd up the bedrooms, get fresh flowers, dust, set tables, and be at all times near at hand. No dallying down by the branch."

"Yes, Ma," said Mattie.

"Jess, thee set this down on paper."

"Otherwise," Jess said, "it might slip my mind slick as a whistle."

"Bring up from the springhouse dill pickles, the sour cream jar, the apple butter, and all yesterday's milk. Bring up from the icehouse enough ice for the freezing. Go out to the south wood lot and see if there's dogwood blooming there we could use as table flowers. Take a bucket of hot water and see that all signs of thy ducks is off the back steps. Go out—"

"Whoa there!" said Jess. "Whoa there! When that's done I'll come back for further orders."*

They darted like needles through the morning—they wove the bright May morning into a fabric strong enough to support a party. Eliza and Emanuela filled in the groundwork sturdy and firm while Mattie and Jess feather-stitched around the edges. Mattie sang while she dusted, not clearly, because of her sore lip:

> I am a stranger here within a foreign land.
> My home is far away, upon a coral strand.

She believes it, Jess thought, listening to her loud and sorrowing voice. She ain't used to Indiana yet. Life's a shock to the young. Shock to have an old man for a father instead of an angel. Shock to eat ham gravy instead of honey dewdrops. And to like ham gravy. That's the worst shock of all. Find yourself fitting into this sorry world.

Mattie came down the back steps, walking carefully so's not to disturb the flowers she was carrying. "Look, Pa," she cried. "Isn't it beautiful?"

Jess didn't care for it much. The old gravy bowl, mounded high as a lump of raising bread with white bridal wreath in the center, had red geraniums running in a scarlet circle round the outer edge.

"I just got to find something blue," Mattie said. "One big blue flower or four little ones would do it. To go right in the center of the white. Then look what I've got, Pa. Red, white, and blue."

Jess saw it otherwise. Blue eye with red rim. Bad case of pinkeye's what it'll look like, he thought, but said nothing.

Red, white, and blue. If he'd been of a suitable age how'd his Quaker principles've stood up during the war? Had he been in his prime could he have held out against fighting for what he believed in? Union and the slaves free? The Lord didn't ask me to make that decision. But it goes against the grain now to have to take these things, things I most believe in, from men I never laid eyes on. He watched a cloud shadow pass over the pail of cooling water at his feet.

6.   Eliza came down the steps bouncing. "Cold water'll never do the trick," she said.

"Time was," Jess answered, "when thee'd of been too fine-haired to direct me in dousing duck manure off the back steps."

She nodded her head, remembering that girl.

"Was we better then, Jess?" she asked. "When we's young? When we couldn't bear nought but flowers and sweet words? Couldn't bear to have a mouse die—let alone a bird? Thought hens unladylike for laying eggs? Now I say clean off the duck dung like 'draw up a chair.' And none of this world's beauties break my heart anymore—no, nor words, any more, Jess, like once I cried for 'As for man, his days are as grass: as a flower of the field so he flourisheth.' Is it gaining or losing, Jess?"

She hoisted her gray chambray skirts so the old man's final swishing would not spatter them.

"Both, both," he said, leaning on his broom. This was a way he seldom saw Eliza. Ordinarily she fit snug and without questioning into one of her two worlds, this world of work, the next of love.

"Both," he repeated. "The thing being to taste each in its turn."

Eliza shook her head. "I don't know."

The shadows of morning had shortened. Fingers of light came through the leafing maple on to her kitchen-warmed face. Enoch's voice came up from the west forty in the kind of guttural horse talk he used in plowing. Mattie walked by not seeing them, intent on her red, white, and blue. Emanuela clanged like a forge in the kitchen. Far off, on a farm out of sight, a dog barked as if to someone returning after long absence.

"The mind," said Eliza, puzzled, to her husband, "the live mind can hardly take in the idea of death."

"No need," Jess said. "No need. It ain't in nature."

"We ought to prepare."

"This is preparing," he answered, lifting his face to the sky.*

Mattie was finished with her work. She went from room to room, leaning in their doorways, seeing their perfection and seeing Mattie, stepping under the gaslights tonight, fair as the Illumination itself. She stepped across a threshold to tauten a coverlet or pick up a fallen petal, and stepped back, to watch the room silent in its waiting.

She had not looked in a glass at her fever blister since morning. She trusted the Lord and felt it to be invisible.

Eliza said, "I've got to have a body bath." She hadn't planned on it. Not on getting that hot. She washed in a corner of the kitchen while Emanuela kept her eyes modestly on the cast-iron kettles.

The day's light flowed over the edge of the western hills. Mud daubers left the road puddles with their last loads for home. The Muscatatuck moved like steel under the light-drained sky. The curtains in the parlor lifted a little in the wind off the river.

Eliza was getting panicky—the way she always did before a doings—fearful maybe the knives had been left off the table, or the salt out of the gravy.

Jess went upstairs to get into his Sunday shirt.

"Don't thee leave thy dirty shirt on the floor," Eliza called after him.

He put it in the closet, and as he stood in his undershirt and work pants the thought came to him: Better see if the gas plant's working. Sixty years of living had convinced him that something wry and sardonic had a hand in the world's management, something that arranged for invitations to be sent out to Illuminations and then put a stop to the gas supply. It didn't make the old man bitter—it made him alert. When he was bested he listened for that far-off laugh—when things went without a hitch, he laughed himself.

He went downstairs silent as shadow in the shadowy house. In the parlor he turned the jet, heard the gas whisper like a snake, set his match to it, saw its tongue of flame.

7.   Eliza crackled in, sweet with soap and sunlight. This was the hour when she always feared no one would come to the party.

"Jess," she whispered, "what if no one comes? What'll we do with all the food? I've been casting up in my mind what to do with the food."

"Thee never remembers from one time to the next, does thee?" Jess asked patiently. "Surreys'll be turning off the pike in ten minutes."

"Then why's thee standing here in thy underwear? Ten minutes and the house'll be full of people and thee in thy underwear." She pushed him toward the stairs. "It's enough to rile a saint. Hustle into thy clothes."

The old man hustled.

By the time the threads of his silk tie were catching on his rough fingers, he heard, as he had said they would, the wheels of the first surrey become silent as they turned off the pike's gravel on to the soft dust of the Maple Grove drive.

He lingered at the stairhead before descending. The balloon of party preparations which had swollen to vast proportions now burst belowstairs.

People can't be that glad to see each other, he thought. They's taken aback to feel so little joyful and talk loud to hide it. Half the evening passes before it's natural to them.

"Jess, Jess," came Eliza's voice. "It's time for the lighting. We're waiting for thee to set the match to them."

He walked downstairs slowly. A party for him was like a thunderstorm—a fine sight to see, and music to the ears, but nothing to be caught plumb in the heart of.

"Howdy, Jess, howdy."

"Think it's safe, does thee?"

"Cost a mint of money, I reckon."

"The Illumination, eh? Well, light up."

Jess set matches to the jets, and parlor and sitting room, dining room and parlor-bedroom were light-struck as flowers at midday, clear and shining and orderly as petals beneath the yellow lights. The faces turned upward as if to a marvel—and it was a marvel, here in the backwoods a house lit with something flowing up through pipes from the cellar. No lamps to be washed and filled, no coal oil splashing over the cornmeal and sugar on trips home from town.

"The Illumination," Mattie whispered marveling,* yellow lights in her gray eyes as she looked upward.

They were all there: the Copes and the Armstrongs, the Coffins and Naylors and Hadleys. Quakers who dressed plain and Quakers who didn't. Methodists from the Rush Branch neighborhood. Talking naturally now beneath the artificial lights, and drifting more often past the dining room, where the cold foods were already set out on the table.

In the kitchen was the crisis of dishing up, but it was over in a minute: chicken with dumplings like yellow clouds floating on top, coleslaw in green and white glacier drifts, and mashed potatoes like cloud and snow together were carried in by Emanuela.

Eliza stood in the doorway, untying her apron. "Friends," she said, "supper is ready."

They were twenty-eight at table. Young and old. Oldsters for whom food had a meaning, and young 'uns—and inbetween, those whose hearts had not yet fed, and who could eat on bread or stone, so little were they centered in swallowing, so much in seeing, searching.

Eliza was the minister at table, but it was a man's place to return grace. Grace was silent, except on occasions like this—with Methodists present who liked to hear what people were saying to God.

Jess shut his eyes. "Father, for food and friends we thank Thee. Amen." It was over before the youngest had started to peek.

After supper there was a little lull. The men talked crops while the women cleared dishes and had some final bites under the excuse of not letting anything waste.

This was a Quaker home and play-party prancing would never shake its floors—but the songs could be sung even if the feet couldn't be lifted.

As Jess walked outside, "Skip to My Lou," was being sung in the parlor and he thought he could hear Mattie's eager, asking voice above the others. He walked up to the little rise they called the pasture knoll where he could see the house, have a look at the fireworks from a sheltered spot.

From the pasture knoll the house was a shell of light. The night was mild and from the raised windows light fell out in golden bars across the dark earth. Jess nodded his head, approving—for man whose time on earth is so short it was a brave job, this installing gaslights and eating chicken dumplings like children of eternity. Considering man's lot nobody could berate him, if he chose to molder in some dark corner, thinking on the sorry upshot of it all. Taste all, he thought, taste all.

As he leaned on the fence that separated pasture from orchard, he heard someone come up the orchard side of the knoll, heard the fence creak as it was leaned against.

"Well, Mr. Millhouse," said a thin-grasshopper voice, "I see you're pouring it out tonight."

"Pouring it out?" Jess asked. Thinking he meant the lights, but, knowing Old Eli Whitcomb, not sure.

"The money," Eli said, "the money," and he moved nearer so that his smell, like leaves wet with the first fall rains, was stronger in the May night than anything spring could muster.

"A lot of money going down the drainpipe, there. Food and lights nobody needs. Don't it irk you?"

8.   The old coot ain't ashamed of being a miser, Jess thought. No need my being ashamed for him. For the first time in his life he spoke to the man he knew his forty-year neighbor to be: said farewell to makeshifts and politeness and plunged right in to that hard core where Eli lived.

"Money," he said. "Thee prizes it above all else?"

"No," said old Eli Whitcomb, "not money. Anything you can get your hands on. Anything you can count or weigh or measure. There's nothing else to rely on. Looky," he said, and beat out his words on Jess's arm with a finger as light as a withered flower stalk. "What's the main idea behind this world? A wasting away—a wasting away. Trees rotting. Ground carried off by the rivers. The sun getting less hot. Iron rusting. I run counter to that. I put a stop to it. God don't care. Wreckage is His nature. It ain't mine. I save. Piles of everything. Boxes, papers, I get old papers from as far as Kokomo. Nails, money too. I save all. Me alone. Against the drift. The rest of you letting it run down the spout."

Jess turned to the old fellow he couldn't see. "I never figured it in that light."

"Of course you didn't. If you had there'd be none of that."

He pointed to the house. "Devouring, gnawing away. I got to get home," he said abruptly. "A little of a sight like that is as much as I can stomach. Clean against reason. Farewell, Jess Millhouse. You got it in you to've been a credit to the world if things'd taken another drift."

He went away in the May night with the sound of leaf brushing against leaf.

"Eli," Jess called after him, "Eli, is thee happy?"

"Not in sight of that," he said, and Jess knew he was looking at the house, "but against I get home, see what one man's done by way of putting a check to the wasting away of the world, I reckon I will be."

Jess leaned back against the fence arms stretched along the top rails. "Well, well," he said.

Here where the woods had been so thick a star could be seen only if a leaf was lifted by the wind, here where the Indians had trod silent-foot, here he, Jess Millhouse, the Quaker, stood under the open sky regarding his farm land, his house, his family.

He turned and looked in the direction Old Eli had gone. "That's another way if I don't misdoubt."

He walked into the house and up the back stairs to his and Eliza's chamber. He lit a lamp and took down the book he'd written in that morning, and under his morning's writing he set down, "One or many —it don't matter. Eternity's how deep you go."

Not a finished way of saying it, he thought, but for the first time he signed his own name. "Eternity's the depth you go. Jess Millhouse."*

He closed the book and replaced it, turned the light low and walked down the front stairs. Oldsters were sitting at ease, talking and listening while the young people were singing:

> Oh, when I'm gone, don't you, don't you grieve,
> Oh, when I'm gone, don't you, don't you grieve after me.

Mattie came to the bottom stair and looked up at him.
"Where's thee been, Pa?"
"Outside to see the lights—from outside."
"How's it look from outside, Pa?"
"Like an oversize lightning bug."
"I just love Illuminations. Don't thee, Pa?"
"Well," said Jess, "they's much to be said for them." Then he joined the young folks in their singing:

> Oh, when I'm gone, don't you, don't you grieve after me.[12]

—Jessamyn West (1943)

a. We have divided the first major section into small motivational units. Do you agree with our divisions? Study the unit marked *e;* would you break it further, and begin *f* where we marked *e1* and *g* at *e2?* Do you find larger units more useful—something of the size of excerpts 1, 2, 3, etc.? Divide the rest of the story into motivational units of convenient size.

b. Analyze the excerpts marked 1, 2, 3, and so on; are any of them self-contained? What threads are "left dangling" in each? Do these threads become tied elsewhere? In what way do you find another key to structure here?

c. Notice the symbolism in the story.
   1) Why does the story concern the installation of gas light? Why not running water, or central heating?
   2) Why is Eliza a Quaker preacher; why is she not an agnostic?
   3) Why are we told about Mattie's fever blister and the steps she takes to re-remove it?
   4) Why are we told about the Methodists?
   5) Why does Jess object to Emanuela's rhyming; does that detail not show him to be less tolerant than we had thought?

6) Why is the Illumination related explicitly to God? Why is this done so early (excerpt 2)?

7) Why does Jess sign his name to the last entry?

8) Justify both words in the title.

d. Analyze Jess's character. Be prepared to cite lines as evidence for your views.

e. What does Eliza's character tell us about Jess?

1) Why is she a Quaker; why not Roman Catholic or Methodist or Jewish?

2) Does she contrast sufficiently with Jess?

   a) Why are we told about the red garters?

   b) What is the significance of her remark about Jess's nudity?

   c) Of what significance is her defense of Emanuela and of Mattie?

   d) Again, why are we told about the Methodists?

   e) Cite clues which do point to a contrast with Jess.

f. What are the functions of the "lyrical pause" in excerpt 6?

g. Analyze the descriptions of the weather. Which ones influence the episodes they precede?

h. Is there any dramatic irony in the story?

i. What function does Eli Whitcomb perform?

1) Why is he not introduced earlier? Why not after excerpt 6?

2) Why is he not at the party? Why are his views not allowed to split the guests into factions? Why does he meet Jess alone?

3) Why does he have to be a miser? Could not Jess's illumination be elicited as well by a ne'er-do-well?

4) How does he conceive of his relation to God? Why are we told?

j. Do you see any balance in this cast of characters? How do each of them—Eli, Mattie, Emanuela, Eliza and Jess—see reality?

k. What songs are sung in the story? Why these? Is each appropriate to the point at which it is mentioned?

3. Analyze the structure of this excerpt from *Watch on the Rhine:*

YOU'LL COME BACK

Fanny Farrelly	*63, strong-willed Washington society woman.*
David Farrelly	*39, her son, a successful lawyer.*
Sara Müller	*42, David's sister, married to Kurt, home after 20 years in Europe.*
Kurt Müller	*47, Sara's German husband, a leader in the anti-Nazi underground.*
Teck de Brancovis	*45, a Roumanian count, a "refugee."*
Marthe de Brancovis	

Scene: living room of the old Farrelly mansion, outside Washington, late spring, 1940. Kurt has been called out to the phone.

[SARA: It is the first birthday party my children have ever known. Does that surprise you?

TECK: You are a very generous woman, Madame Fanny. Did you also give my wife her sapphire bracelet?]

DAVID: No. I gave Marthe the bracelet. And I understand that it is not any business of yours.

FANNY: Really, David—

TECK: Did you tell him that, Marthe?

MARTHE: Yes.

TECK: I shall not forgive you for that. *(To David)*   It is a statement which no man likes to hear from another man. You understand that? *(Playfully)*   That is the type of thing about which we used to play at duels in Europe.

DAVID *(coming toward him):*   We are not so musical comedy here. And you are not in Europe.

TECK: Even if I were, I would not suggest any such action. I would have reasons for not wishing it.

DAVID: It would be well for you not to suggest *any* action. And the reason for *that* is you might get hurt.

TECK *(slowly):*   That would not be my reason. *(To Marthe)*   Your affair has gone far enough—

MARTHE *(sharply):*   It is not an affair—

TECK: I do not care what it is. The time has come to leave here. Go upstairs and pack your things. . . . Go on, Marthe.

MARTHE *(to David):*   I am not going with him. I told you that.

DAVID: I don't want you to go with him.

FANNY *(carefully):*   Really, David, aren't you interfering in all this a good deal—

DAVID *(carefully):*   Yes, Mama. I am.

TECK *(to Marthe):*   When you are speaking to me, please say what you have to say to me.

MARTHE: You are trying to frighten me. But you are not going to frighten me any more. I will say it to you: I am not going with you. I am never going with you again.

TECK *(softly):*   If you do not fully mean what you say, or if you might change your mind, you are talking unwisely, Marthe.

MARTHE: I know that. . . . You can't make me go, can you, Teck?

TECK: No, I can't make you.

MARTHE: Then there's no sense talking about it.

TECK: Are you in love with him?

MARTHE: Yes.

FANNY *(sharply):*   Marthe! What is all this?

MARTHE *(sharply):*   I'll tell *you* about it in a minute.

DAVID: You don't have to explain anything to anybody.

TECK: Is he in love with you?

MARTHE: I don't think so. You won't believe it, because you can't believe anything that hasn't got tricks to it, but David hasn't much to do with this. I told you I would leave some day, and I remember where I said it—and why I said it.

TECK: I also remember. But I did not believe you. I have not had much to offer you these last years. But if now we had some money and could go back—

MARTHE: No. I don't like you, Teck. I never have.

TECK: And I have always known it.

FANNY: I think your lack of affection should be discussed with more privacy.

MARTHE: There is nothing to discuss. . . . And I am going. There is nothing you can do. I would like you to believe that now.

TECK: Very well, Marthe. I think I made a mistake. I should not have brought you here. I believe you now.

MARTHE *(to David):*   I'll move into Washington, and—

DAVID: Yes, later. But I'd like you to stay here for awhile, with us, if you wouldn't mind.

FANNY: It's very interesting that I am not being consulted about this. I have nothing against you, Marthe. I am sorry for you, but I don't think—

MARTHE: Thank you, David. But I'd rather move in now. *(To Fanny)* But, perhaps, I have something against you. Do you remember my wedding? . . . Do you remember how pleased Mama was with herself? Brilliant Mama, handsome Mama—everybody thought so, didn't they? A seventeen-year-old daughter, marrying a pretty good title, about to secure herself in a world that Mama liked. She didn't ask me what I liked. And the one time I tried to tell her, she frightened me— Maybe I've always been frightened. All my life.

TECK: Of course.

MARTHE: I remember Mama's face at the wedding—it was *her* wedding, really, not mine.

FANNY *(sharply):*   You are very hard on your mother.

MARTHE: 1925. No, I'm not hard on her. I only tell the truth. She wanted a life for me, I suppose. It just wasn't the life I wanted for myself. And that's what you have tried to do. With your children. In another way. Only Sara got away. And that made you angry—until so many years went by that you forgot.

FANNY: I usually don't mind people saying anything they think, but I find that—

MARTHE: I don't care what you mind or don't mind. I'm in love with your son—

FANNY *(very sharply):*   That's unfortunate—

MARTHE: And I'm sick of watching you try to make him into his father. I don't think you even know you do it any more and I don't think he knows it any more either. And that's what's most dangerous about it.

FANNY *(very angrily):*   I don't know what you are talking about.

DAVID: I think you do. *(Smiles)*   You shouldn't mind hearing the truth—and neither should I.

FANNY *(worried, sharply):*   David! What does all this nonsense mean? I—

MARTHE: Look. That pretty world Mama got me into was a tough world, see? I'm used to trouble. So don't try to interfere with me, because I won't let you. *(To David)*   Let's just have a good time. *(To Teck)*   You will also be going today? . . . Then let us make sure we go in different directions, and do not meet again. Goodbye, Teck.

TECK: Goodbye, Marthe. You will not believe me, but I tried my best, and I am now most sorry to lose you.

MARTHE: Yes. I believe you. *(She moves out.)*

FANNY: Well, a great many things have been said in the last few minutes. [David, have someone pack for Count de Brancovis.]

TECK: Do not bother. *(Kurt comes in. . . . He does not look at Sara. Teck watches him.)*   It will not take me very long.

SARA: What is it, Kurt?

KURT: It is nothing of importance, darling—*(He looks quickly at Teck, who is leaving very slowly.)*

SARA: Don't tell me it's nothing. I know the way you look when—

KURT *(sharply):*   I said it was of no importance. I must get to California for a few weeks. That is all.

TECK *(turning back):*   It is in the afternoon newspaper, Herr Müller. I was waiting for the proper moment to call it to your attention. "Zurich, Switzerland: The Zurich papers today reprinted a despatch from the *Berliner Tageblatt*—on the capture of Colonel Max Freidank. Freidank is said to be the chief of the anti-Nazi Underground Movement. Colonel Freidank has long been an almost legendary figure. . . . He was a World War officer and a distinguished physicist before the advent of Hitler." That is all.

SARA: Max!

KURT: Be still, Sara.

TECK: They told me of it at the [German] Embassy last night. They also told me that with him they had taken a man who called himself Ebber, and a man who called himself Triste. They could not find a man called Gotter. I shall be a lonely man without Marthe. I am also a very poor one. I should like to have ten thousand dollars before I go.

DAVID *(carefully):*   You will make no loans in this house.

TECK: I was not speaking of a loan.

FANNY: God made you not only a scoundrel but a fool. That is a dangerous combination.

DAVID *(leaping toward Teck):*   Damn you, you—

KURT: Leave him alone. . . . *David! Leave him alone!*

DAVID: Keep out of it! I'm beginning to see what Marthe meant. Blackmailing with your wife— You—

KURT (*very sharply*):   He is not speaking of his wife. Or you. He means me. Is that correct?

TECK: Good. It was necessary for me to hear you say it. . . .

DAVID: What is all this about? What the hell are you talking about?

TECK (*sharply for the first time*):   Be still. (*To Kurt*)   At your convenience. Your hands are shaking, Herr Müller.

KURT: My hands were broken. [By the Nazis.] They are bad when I have fear.

TECK: I am sorry. I can understand that. It is not pleasant. . . . You should get yourself a smaller gun, Herr Müller. That pistol you have been carrying is big and awkward. . . . It is a German army Luger? . . . Keep it in your pocket, Herr Müller. You will have no need to use it. And in any case, I am not afraid of it. You understand that?

KURT: I understand that you are not a man of fears. That is strange to me, because I am a man who has so many fears.

TECK: Are you? That is most interesting. (*He laughs, and goes out.*)

DAVID (*softly*):   What is this about, Kurt?

KURT: He knows who I am and what I do and what I carry with me. . . .

FANNY: I don't understand.

KURT: I am going to tell you: I am a German outlaw. I work with many others in an illegal organization. [Against the Nazis.] I have so worked for seven years. I am on what is called a desired list. But I did not know that I was worth ten thousand dollars. My price has risen.

DAVID: And what do you carry with you?

KURT: Twenty-three thousand dollars. It has been gathered from the pennies and nickels of the poor who do not like Fascism, and who believe in the work we do. I came here to bring Sara home and to get the money. I had hopes to rest here awhile, and then—

SARA: And I had hopes someone else would take it back and you would stay here with us— Max is not dead?

KURT: No. The left side of his face is dead. It was a good face.

SARA: It was a very good face. He and Kurt—in the old days—(*To Kurt*)   After so many years. If Max got caught, then nobody's got a chance. Nobody. (*She suddenly sits down.*)

DAVID: [De Brancovis] wants to sell what he knows to you? Is that right?

KURT: Yes.

FANNY: Wasn't it careless of you to leave twenty-three thousand dollars lying around to be seen?

KURT: No, it was not careless of me. It is in a locked brief-case. I have thus carried money for many years. There seemed no safer place than Sara's home. It was careless of you to have in your house a man who opens baggage and blackmails.

DAVID (*sharply*):   Yes. It was very careless.

FANNY: But [if] you knew he'd seen it—

KURT: Yes, I knew it the first day we were here. What was I to do about it? He is not a man who steals. This is a safer method. I knew it would come some other way. I have been waiting to see what the way would be. That is all I could do.

DAVID *(to Fanny):*   What's the difference? It's been done. *(To Kurt)*   If he wants to sell you, he must have another buyer. Who?

KURT: The Embassy. Von Seitz, I think.

DAVID: . . . But you're here. You're in this country. They can't do any-thing to you. They wouldn't be crazy enough to try it. Is your pass-port all right?

KURT: Not quite.

FANNY: Why not? Why isn't it?

KURT *(wearily, as if bored):*   Because people like me are not given visas with such ease. And I was in a hurry to bring my wife and my children to safety. [Five of us—] *(Sharply)*   Madame Fanny, you must come to understand it is no longer the world you once knew.

DAVID: It doesn't matter. You're a political refugee. We don't turn back people like you. People who are in danger. You will give me your passport and tomorrow morning I'll see [a friend of mine.] Tell de Brancovis to go to hell. There's not a damn thing he or anybody else can do.

SARA: You don't understand, David.

DAVID: There's a great deal I don't understand. But there's nothing to worry about.

SARA: Not much to worry about as long as Kurt is in this house.

[DAVID: You mean that if this swine talks you'll be—

SARA *(very softly):*   Caught and killed. Of course. If they're lucky enough to get killed quickly. You should have seen Kurt's hands in 1935.]

KURT: The Count has made the guess that—

SARA: That you will go back to get Ebber and Triste and Max. Is that right, Kurt? Is that right?

KURT: Yes darling. I will try. They were taken to Sonnenburg. Guards can be bribed— It has been done once before at Sonnenburg. We will try for it again. I must go back, Sara. I must start.

SARA: Of course you must go back. I was trying to think it wouldn't come. But—Kurt's got to go back. He's got to go home. He's got to buy them out. He'll do it, too. You'll see. . . . It's hard enough to get back. Very hard. But if they knew he was coming—They want Kurt bad. Almost as much as they wanted Max— And then there are hun-dreds of others, too—*(She goes to Kurt, trying to speak without crying.)* Don't be scared, darling. You'll get back. You'll see. You've done it before—you'll do it again. Don't be scared. You'll get Max out all right. *(Gasps)*   And then you'll do his work, won't you? That's good. That's fine. You'll do a good job, the way you've always done. *(She is crying very hard. To Fanny.)*   Kurt doesn't feel well. He was

wounded and he gets tired—*(To Kurt)* You don't feel well, do you?
... Don't be scared, darling. You'll get home. Don't worry, you'll get
home. Yes, you will.

(The curtain falls)[13]

—Lillian Hellman, *Watch on the Rhine* (1941)

a. Do you agree with our analysis, on page 208, of the relation between the plot
and subplot? Cite lines which corroborate it; those which weaken it.
b. Notice the bracketed interpolations, which we have taken from other parts of
the play. What additional information do they provide? Do they spoil the
structure? Should they have been omitted?
c. Does Marthe know of the blackmail scheme? Are there direct clues, or must
you infer an answer from what you know of her character?
   1) Is Marthe really in love with David?
      a) What do you infer from her willingness to announce her love to a room-
      ful of people?
      b) Why does she not keep silent and allow David to answer Teck's ques-
      tion, "Is he in love with you?"?
      c) From what you know of women's wiles, do you think she could have
      forced David to confess a love for her? How? Could this be done within
      five speeches?
      d) What do you infer from her willingness to move out and leave David
      to her chief rival?
      e) Does the rather unflattering picture she draws of David on page 237
      suggest that she loves him?
   2) Why did Marthe marry Teck?
      a) Does her explanation on page 237 square with the other facts?
      b) David is a lawyer, but she asks Teck whether she can be forced to re-
      main with him. What do you infer from this?
      c) What do you infer from Teck's line "I have not had much to offer you
      these last years"? Why did she stay with him?

    3) What trait does she ascribe most often to herself? Is her picture of herself realistic?

        a) What do you infer from the repetition in her speech on page 236, beginning "You are trying to frighten me"? From that in the speech beginning "There is nothing to discuss"?

        b) What do you infer about her from "I'm used to trouble," on page 238?

        c) Do her actions reveal her to be as frightened as she claims?

    4) Trace the rise and fall of tension in her speeches about her mother and her wedding. What do we learn from "She wanted a life for me, I suppose"? Is she very hard on her mother, as Fanny claims? And what does that reveal about her character?

  d. Is David going to marry Marthe? Are there any direct clues, or must you infer the answer from his character?

    1) Is Marthe's analysis of his relationship with Fanny substantially correct?

    2) Twice he offers to hit Teck; what do you infer from that?

    3) Is there any evidence that his character is changing?

  e. Why is Teck a European? Could he not as well be from Chicago?

  f. Why is Fanny kept onstage, when she could so easily have decided to oversee the children upstairs? If we heard only secondhand reports about her, would she not seem stronger and more domineering than if we saw her? Or is that her function?

  g. What two characters contribute most directly to the social intent?

  h. Is Kurt ever going to return from Germany? Build the case for and against, citing the lines as evidence.

  i. Compare the case in (h) with that which Sara offers in her last speech. Does she think he is ever going to come back?

  j. What things are accomplished by the exchange between Teck and Kurt about the trembling of Kurt's hands, page 239?

  k. What things are accomplished by David's assumption that the blackmail is directed against him, page 238?

  l. In the next act, Kurt murders Teck. What clues have been planted in this scene to render such murder inevitable?

ADDITIONAL EXERCISES

"The Meaning of Glory," p. 53; "Death Be Not Proud," p. 97; "Ozymandias," p. 101; "Bells for John Whiteside's Daughter," p. 103; "Mr. Polly's Decision," p. 107; "Pray Employ Major Namby," p. 320; "Boulder Dam," p. 354; "Raleigh in the Tower," p. 355; "Death at Jamestown," p. 357; "The Young King," p. 365; "The Proposal: I and II," p. 364 and 110.

What About Poetry?

ONE REASON FOR deferring a discussion of poetry to this point was our strong hunch that in the meantime you would have learned some of the rudiments through the process of trial and error. The problems posed by poetry are infinite in their complexity—two thousand years of argument find the chief ones still unsolved—but from the beginner's viewpoint the difficulty lies in applying the "rules" presented in Chapters Three to Five. The sentence you just read may have seemed a little tinkling, but you got over it smoothly enough; now, notice what happens when you encounter it in this form:

> The problems posed by poetry
> Are infinite in their complexity—
> Two thousand years of argument
> Find the chief ones still unsolved—
> But from the beginner's viewpoint
> The difficulty lies
> In applying the "rules" presented
> In Chapters Three to Five.

Problems, problems. First of all, notice, you stop worrying about the sense, attitude, or tone; you focus your chief efforts upon making it scan—should it be "poetree" and "complexitee" and "argue-meant"? Then, when you do get the swing of it, when you discover that there are three beats to a line, you find that the swing is all-important. Phrasing becomes dictated not by ideas but by line ends; the last three lines, which were smooth enough as "prose" become three short spurts of "poetry." Similarly, emphasis is dictated not by the importance of the word's contribution to the meaning, but by its position in the line—"their" in line 2 and "from" in line 5 become as important as anything in the "poem." And the projection of sense or attitude disappears in impersonal singsong.

This is the first stage, and a few students never get beyond it. But by now you have doubtless learned another trick. After listening for a couple of weeks to classmates chanting

> I WAN-dered LONE-ly.   AS a CLOUD.
> That FLOATS on HIGH.   O'er VALES and HILLS.
> When ALL at ONCE.   I SAW a CROWD.
> A HOST of GOLD-en.   DAF-fo-DILS.

you decided that this would never do, and, in your efforts to make the sense clear, you started to read poetry as if it were prose. If you managed simultaneously to convey some of the emotive values, you have already attained the bare minimum. You are already doing what some teachers advise you to do—read poetry as if it were prose; so, even if this chapter does not alter your reading one jot, you have licked one of the main problems and are probably doing a competent job.

But there is a third stage in the evolution of the usual reader, and one not overly hard to reach. After all, poetry's structure is different from that of prose, and a good reading (not necessarily an excellent one, or a magnificent one, but simply a good one) will preserve a large part of that structure. The singsong reader preserves the meter; the prosy reader preserves the message; the good reader preserves meter *and* message—and sound. He preserves the rhythm. If your sense of rhythm is sharp enough to make you even barely acceptable as a dancer or singer, you have no reason to believe you have a tin ear—and you can look forward confidently to becoming a good reader of poetry.

In attempting to reach the essentials of a complex subject, and to reveal some simple solutions to a number of specific problems, this chapter cuts a wide swath through the laws of prosody. We shall discuss rhythm as the result of three forces: meter, sound, and message. We shall discuss each of these forces, explaining the difficulties they commonly present to beginners. We shall then indicate some frequent exceptions to the principles contained in the other sections.

RHYTHM

There is a wide difference between rhythm and meter as we use the terms. Rhythm is the overall pattern formed by the fusion of three smaller patterns—meter, message, and sound.

Meter is the mechanical pattern of stresses or emphases. Chapter Four explained that some words—mainly nouns, verbs, adjectives, and adverbs—usually demand more emphasis in the average sentence than other words, and conventional pronunciation places more emphasis upon one or two of the syllables in a polysyllable than upon the rest of the syllables. Meter is easy to write; anyone can fit such emphases into a pattern.

But there are patterns within a message as well. Word order need not form as rigid a pattern as metrical beats, but nevertheless there are principles in English which predetermine what a writer can say. Ordinarily we expect the order subject-verb-object, and in some messages we pretty well insist on it: "Mary sees her father" admits of only one common variation. Ordinarily we expect an adjective to precede the noun it modifies and a preposition to begin its phrase; rhetorically we expect first things first, and we expect that the most important element will come either first or last. Points of equal importance will not take widely dissimilar construction; double negatives are hard to follow; and so on. Out of these principles—out of the way the language works—the message will develop its own beats. These beats may not be patterned, though, as you will notice, readability-wise hodgepodged polysyllabic concatenations of governmentese are not entirely effective, partly because they lack a pattern of beats.

There are patterns of sound, some of which seem almost as mechanical as meter. We say clickety-clack, not clack-clickety or clackety-click; we say flimflam, not flamflim; pishtush, seesaw, mishmash. Why does breakfast food not say "pop, crackle, snap"? What system of classification accounts for the fact that the widely dissimilar flags of the United Kingdom, France, and the United States are "red white and blue"—never blue red and white or white blue and red? We need not at this point consider assonance—"brown cow"—or alliteration—"sing a song of sixpence"—in order to demonstrate that we expect sound to be patterned at least enough to render pronunciation easy.

When these three patterns—meter, message, and sound—are superimposed, the result may be chaos, because the patterns have canceled each other out; or it may be a new pattern, richer and subtler and more interesting than any of its component patterns. Each of the three subpatterns will at times reinforce the others, at times pull independently, and at times combine, now with one and now with the other, in order to pull the third. It is this resultant over-pattern, formed of the interplay among the others, that we have called rhythm.

When we read poetry effectively we attend not only to the three semimechanical subpatterns, each of which may yield its own surprises, but also to the overall system which is formed by the temporary clashes and alliances among the subpatterns. The singsong reader finds only a meter—let us say it is iambic *dedum dedum dedum*; the prosy reader finds a message that refers to, say, spilled ink; but the reader who is alert to all three subpatterns sees a great difference between

> A bit of it is dripping.
>
> Two pools of blue form slowly.

The meters are identical and within our context the messages are almost alike; but rhythmically they are far apart. The singsong reader and the prosy reader miss too much of what is going on.

Furthermore, they have unnecessary difficulty in finding the very subpattern they seek. In the second example above, the word "form" may spoil the meter for singsong, and the first message is incomplete until we have inferred "quickly." Sometimes one subpattern provides clues to the others. Moreover, because the subpatterns must interweave, each may become somewhat modified, and so become less perfectly a pattern. Such imperfections, which may shatter the poem for singsong or prosiness, are a source of joy to good readers; since each subpattern obeys its own laws it resists modification, and out of this resistance there springs the tension which is part of the magic of poetry.

We have said enough perhaps to suggest that rhythm is to be traced in the interrelationship of meter, message, and sound. The following sections deal with each component separately, but we must take care to avoid the implication that any of them are of paramount importance. The important thing is the interplay. Accordingly we shall swing rapidly from one to the other, headings notwithstanding, in order to show how each subpattern affects, and is affected by, both of the others.

METER

Meter is, as we said, the mechanical pattern of word stress in a poem—the system built by arranging syllables in series of light and heavy emphases. You decide whether there are two light beats for every heavy beat, or only one; then you decide whether the light beats belong in front of the heavy beat or behind it; and lo, you have discovered the meter. To make the task easier, by preventing one part of the pattern from blurring into the next, you should probably divide the poetic line into *feet*. Provisionally we can define a foot as a unit containing *one* heavy beat, plus one or two light ones perhaps.

The Common Meters

Fortunately, the beginner need consider only four or five metrical possibilities—a person thoroughly frightened of meter can probably get by with only two! By far the greatest number of poems in English—no two of which, remember, have identical *rhythms*—are based upon one of the following meters.

IAMBIC. One unemphasized syllable and one emphasized.

> We keep | the wall | between | us as | we go |
>
> When I | have fears | that I | may cease | to be |
>
> They al-|so serve | who on-|ly stand | and wait |

An iamb is called a *rising* or ascending foot, because it "builds up" to the important part. Apparently it is peculiarly amenable to English; it is the most popular of our meters and can lend itself to an astonishingly wide variety of rhythmical effects.

ANAPESTIC. Two unemphasized syllables and then an emphasized one.

> But our love | it was strong-|er by far | than the love |
>
> In my youth,| Father Wil-|liam replied | to his son |
>
> And his co-|horts were gleam-|ing in pur-|ple and gold |

An anapest is also a *rising* foot. It has a rushing, if not galloping effect, and is much used in light verse. Frequently anapestic feet are inserted into iambic lines.

TROCHAIC. One emphasized syllable and one unemphasized.

> Jumping | from the | chair she | sat in |
>
> By the | shores of | Gitche | Gumee |
>
> Comrades,| leave me | here a | little,| while as | yet 'tis | early | morn |

A trochee is a *falling* or descending foot, because it "moves down" from the important part. The trochee and the iamb are the two basic feet in English; the others may be considered modifications or substitutions.

DACTYLIC. One emphasized syllable and two unemphasized.

This is the | forest pri-|meval, the | murmuring | pines and the | hemlocks |

Touch her not | scornfully;|| Think of her | mournfully |

We that had | loved him so,| followed him,| honored him |

A dactyl is a *falling* foot. In English it sometimes seems to be rearing back-wards. It is less common than the three previous.

SPONDAIC AND DOUBLE SPONDAIC.   The spondee has two emphasized sylla-bles; the true spondee is so rare in English that beginners will find the term less useful than the concept of the hovering accent, to be discussed later. The double spondee has a single emphasized syllable—double because it must be twice as conspicuous as the spondee in order to preserve the time.

Break,| break,| break |

For auld | lang | syne |

And no | birds | sing | [1]

The term "double spondee" may be less useful than "incomplete foot."

Few poems use any one meter exclusively; as we shall see later, the message pattern will introduce all sorts of interesting irregularities into the basic met-rical pattern.

While we are reminding you of terms you have encountered before, we might mention some other labels which you doubtless met at the same time as those above, and with which you may have confused them. Remember the terms ap-plied to *line length?* A one-foot line is called *monometer;* two-foot is *dimeter;* three is *trimeter;* four, *tetrameter;* five, *pentameter;* six, *hexameter;* and seven, *hep-tameter.* Tetrameter, pentameter, and trimeter are by far the most common; hep-tameter lines, and those with more than seven feet, tend in English to break into two or three shorter lines.

How to Scan

Some students know the names of the common meters—and of several un-common ones—but have never quite learned how to scan. This section is for such students.

---

[1] Since we have chosen, where possible, completely regular examples, from familiar poems in which these are the predominant meters, perhaps you will find the titles useful. Respectively: Frost, "Mending Wall," Keats, "When I Have Fears," Milton, "On His Blindness"; Poe, "Annabel Lee," Carroll, "You Are Old, Father William," Byron, "The Destruction of Sennacherib"; Hunt, "Jenny Kissed Me," Longfellow, "Hia-watha," Tennyson, "Locksley Hall"; Longfellow, "Evangeline," Hood, "The Bridge of Sighs," Browning, "The Lost Leader." The double spondees are from Tennyson, Burns, and from Keats' "La Belle Dame Sans Merci."

First of all, you can avoid confusion by refusing to scan isolated lines. Since the whole point of scansion is the discovery
of a basic pattern, always choose enough consecutive lines to
allow that pattern to emerge. Four consecutive lines is probably a minimum, and you would be wise to hold in reserve
another four from a different part of the poem.

The next step is to tick off the accented syllables of the words
you would normally stress in a prose reading. The mark (′)
is as good as any. Then indicate with a mark like (˘) the
words you definitely would not stress. Use the same mark for
the unaccented syllables of the important words. Put no mark
on any syllable that you are unsure of.

> I wandered lonely as a cloud
> That floats on high o'er vales and hills,
> When all at once I saw a crowd,
> A host, of golden daffodils

That first line is a mess, but the other three can show you
whether there are usually two "unstresses" between the heavy
beats, or only one. Extend that pattern provisionally throughout. If there are any spots where it simply will not fit—because there are too many or too few "unstresses"—skip that
section, and pick up the pattern where it seems to reappear.

> I wandered lonely as a cloud
> That floats on high o'er vales and hills,
> When all at once I saw a crowd,
> A host, of golden daffodils

We changed the marking on "o'er" and "-dils"; the only uneven spot remaining is "-ly as a" and that problem is solved
easily enough by stressing "as." Until we discuss substituted
and inverted feet, later in this chapter, you may have to skip
over the parts that do not fit into the pattern because they
have too many or too few "unstresses." Now provisionally
mark off the thought groups and the idea units.

> I wandered | lonely | as | a cloud|
> That floats | on high | o'er vales | and hills, |
> When all at once | I saw | a crowd, |
> A host, | of golden | daffodils |

The first line may be trochaic, but the second is obviously iambic. Analyze the third and fourth; which pattern requires fewer adjustments? Now extend the pattern throughout.

I wan-|dered lone-|ly as | a cloud |
That floats | on high | o'er vales | and hills, |
When all | at once | I saw | a crowd, |
A host, | of gold-|en daf-|fodils |

The lines have turned out to be regular iambic tetrameter; but at this point you should be able to arrange into feet any sections you skipped because they did not conform. For example, by the time you have identified the anapestic structure of "Annabel Lee," the leftover feet become obvious:

It was man-|y and man-|y a year | ago
In a king-|dom by the sea
That a maid-|en there lived | whom you may know
By the name | of An-|nabel Lee |

So far we have made no attempt to classify the irregularities that commonly occur; but you should still be able to detect most of them. Scan these lines:

Beauty is but a flower,
Which wrinkles will devour,
Brightness falls from the air,
Queens have died young and fair,
Dust hath clos'd Helen's eye.
I am sick, I must die:
Lord, have mercy on us.

The detection of such irregularities is the major justification of scansion.

Meter and Message

Scansion is boring work, and insofar as focusing attention upon the mechanical pattern can encourage singsong, it may be dangerous. But we believe its usefulness outweighs its disadvantages.

The major purpose, as we said, is the detection of irregularities. Much of the rest of this chapter is devoted to an explanation of the variations which can occur, but simple scansion will get you started. Further, the meter can provide clues to meaning—clues which the message neglects, or indeed seems to contradict. Whatever you think of the meter in the rest of this poem, in these two lines it tells us as much as the message:

> 'Twas the night before Christmas, when all through the house,
> Not a creature was stirring, not even a mouse.

Nothing stirring indeed! Housman, Hardy, and many other poets use a simple jigging meter as an ironic counterpoint to their message.

Among its narrowly practical advantages, meter is one way—sometimes the only way—of discovering the pronunciation of proper names. No doubt you pronounce "Don Juan," quite properly, as "don wan" or "don hwan"; but what *is* the name of Byron's hero?

> Had stopp'd this Canto, and Don Juan's breath.

> 'Twixt her and Juan interposed the crew.

> I leave Don Juan for the present, safe—

And if meter is not enough, try rhyme:

> I want a hero: an uncommon want,
> When every year and month sends forth a new one,
> Till, after cloying the gazettes with cant,
> The age discovers he is not the true one:
> Of such as these I should not care to vaunt,
> I'll therefore take our ancient friend Don Juan—
> We all have seen him, in the pantomime,
> Sent to the devil somewhat ere his time.

Obviously, meter will not solve all such problems, because poets often substitute feet, but it should at least make you suspicious. When you encounter lines like these in Pope and Swift,

> Awake! my St. John! leave all meaner things

> And St. John's self (great Dryden's friends before)

> Remote from St. John, Pope, and Gay

> St. John, as well as Pulteney, knows

> St. John himself will scarce forbear

you will know enough to reach for your dictionary.

Last, but hardly least, meter is fun. Some poetry and much light verse depend for their effect *primarily* upon the bounce of the meter. To subordinate meter to message in such poems is to miss the point. You would be far wiser to exploit the meter to the utmost.

THE MAJOR-GENERAL'S SONG

I am the very model of a modern Major-General,
I've information vegetable, animal, and mineral,
I know the kings of England, and I quote the fights historical,
From Marathon to Waterloo, in order categorical;
I'm very well acquainted too with matters mathematical,
I understand equations, both the simple and quadratical,
About binomial theorem I'm teeming with a lot o' news—
With many cheerful facts about the square of the hypotenuse.

I'm very good at integral and differential calculus,
I know the scientific names of beings animalculous;
In short, in matters vegetable, animal, and mineral,
I am the very model of a modern Major-General.

I know our mythic history, King Arthur's and Sir Caradoc's,
I answer hard acrostics, I've a pretty taste for paradox,
I quote in elegaics all the crimes of Heliogabalus,
In conics I can floor peculiarities parabolous.
I can tell undoubted Raphaels from Gerard Dows and Zoffanies,
I know the croaking chorus from the *Frogs* of Aristophanes,
Then I can hum a fugue of which I've heard the music's din afore,
And whistle all the airs from that infernal nonsense *Pinafore*.
Then I can write a washing bill in Babylonic cuneiform,
And tell you every detail of Caractacus's uniform;
In short, in matters vegetable, animal, and mineral,
I am the very model of a modern Major-General.

In fact, when I know what is meant by "mamelon" and "ravelin,"
When I can tell at sight a chassepôt rifle from a javelin,
When such affairs as sorties and surprises I'm more wary at,
And when I know precisely what is meant by "commissariat",
When I have learned what progress has been made in modern gunnery,
When I know more of tactics than a novice in a nunnery:

In short, when I've a smattering of elemental strategy,
You'll say a better Major-General has never *sat* a gee—

For my military knowledge, though I'm plucky and adventury,
Has only been brought down to the beginning of the century;
But still in matters vegetable, animal, and mineral,
I am the very model of a modern Major-General.

—W. S. Gilbert, *The Pirates of Penzance* (1880)

> In this classic piece of foolery, by all means pronounce "vege-table" as if it were "vege-tabbel," and make "General" clearly a trisyllable. Would you gallop through this as fast as you could? Well, why not? And what will you do with the outrageous rhymes? Listen to a D'Oyly Carte recording of this song; notice such horseplay as "lot o' news . . . hmmm . . . lot o' news . . . I have it! With many cheerful facts," etc.; do you think it is overdone?
>
> Such comic verse may not only be tongue-twisting; it may require some visible comedy as well. No doubt you have read "The Walrus and the Carpenter" at one time or other; have you ever experimented with a "double-take"? How about this?

[expansive]	The sun was shining on the sea,
	Shining with all his might,
[proudly]	He did his very best to make
	The billows smooth and bright—
	[vastly pleased]
[double-take]	And this was odd, [puzzled? pained?]
	because it was
[wide-eyed innocence]	The middle of the night,

> And how quickly do the Oysters catch on, before they say "But not on us!"?

Light verse, then, may require something close to singsong in order to exploit the meter; and the problem of accommodating the message to the meter is at least as complex as the problem that worries you—the accommodation of meter to message. Sometimes wild mispronunciations must be justified by some visible indication of attitude; at other times you must avoid all suggestion of characterization, and communicate only your own delight at the outrageous. These are matters of audible and visible subtlety, and we mention them here only to emphasize our belief that effective exploitation of meter is not as easy as your experience with singsong might indicate.

SOUND

The sound of some words seems so well adapted to their sense, and some poetic lines require movements of the tongue and lips that seem so "right" and so inevitable, that philosophers and critics have made repeated attempts to discover intrinsic meaning in isolated sounds. So far their efforts have been unsuccessful, and we must assume that there are no intrinsically meaningful or beautiful sounds. Hence it is difficult to discuss *euphony* systematically and concretely. You know from experience that in the proper context of meaning, some combinations of sounds are pleasing and some are not; we can go little further than that. However, some combinations of sounds are more difficult to articulate than others; and, *where meaning permits,* some sounds will take longer to form than will others. Remembering constantly that the message will almost certainly affect the way we deliver—and even receive—vocal sounds, we can hazard some useful if limited generalizations.

Sound and Meter

Meter, remember, is simply the pattern of light stress and heavy stress; metrically every light stress is identical to every other light stress, and there are no shades of emphasis to distinguish one heavy stress from another. Light or heavy, and no middle ground. But in spoken language there are infinite gradations of emphasis; by controlling sound, we can stretch or contract a syllable. Let us take a simple meter, and progressively "fill it with sound."

Ă bóy | ĭs cóm-|ĭng ín | Thĕ bóy | ĭs cóm-|ĭng ín |

Thĭs bóy | ĭs cóm-|ĭng ín| Thĭs yóuth | ĭs cóm-|ĭng ín |

Thĭs yóuth | cŏmes ín | thĕ hóuse | Thĭs yóuth | cŏmes thróugh | thĕ crówd |

We still have an iambic line, but the rhythm has been slowed considerably. If we continue, we can blur the distinction between heavy and light stress:

Thĭs yóuth | thrùsts thròugh | thăt crówd |

In the second foot, if not in the first, the emphasis is now equally divided between the two syllables; we have a *hovering* accent. Let us continue.

This youth | thrusts through | that throng |

This youth | thrusts through | those throngs |

We have hovering accents in the last two feet, and probably in all three; the meter has almost completely disappeared. (If this were part of a poem, we would have to reëstablish the meter strongly within the next couple of lines.) Now, how did we get the effect? We changed the message and loaded it with fairly important words; perhaps more important here, we used longer sounds, and packed in so many tongue-twisters that the line has been greatly slowed down. Even if message exerted no effect on meter—and it always does—differences in length of sounds and combinations of sounds would make a pure unvaried meter extremely unlikely—unless two or three sounds were repeated over and over.

QUANTITY. The quantity of a sound or of a combination of sounds is the amount of time needed to produce it. Like meter, quantity cannot be divorced from message. But message permitting, vowels made with the tongue tensed or the jaw dropped have longer quantities than those made with lax tongue or jaw neutral: compare the vowels in "bead" and "shooed" with those in "bid" and "should"; those in "bad," "ask," "dog," with those in "bed," "hut." Message again permitting, diphthongs, such as those in "high," "boy," "cow," and "cheer," "air," "car," "pore," "sure," are longer than pure vowels. Generally the plosive consonants—*p, b, t, d, k, g*—are shorter than the rest. Usually voiced consonants have longer quantities than voiceless or "whispered": compare *b, d, g, v, th* (as in "then"), *z, zh* (as in "azure"), *j, m, n, ng,* with *p, t, k, f, th* (as in "thin"), *s, sh, ch,* and *h.* Finally, a vowel followed by a voiced consonant will usually be longer than if followed by a voiceless one, and it will be still longer if followed by no consonant at all; compare "bee," "bead," "beat," or "go," "goad," "goat." We need not attempt to establish a precise scale of quantity, even if such were possible; however, the principles we have listed should focus your attention upon duration of sound.

Do parts of this poem speed up, or are the quantities fairly constant?

JABBERWOCKY

'Twas brillig, and the slithy toves
Did gyre and gimble in the wabe:
All mimsy were the borogoves,
And the mome raths outgrabe.

"Beware the Jabberwock, my son!
The jaws that bite, the claws that catch!
Beware the Jubjub bird, and shun
The frumious Bandersnatch!"

He took his vorpal sword in hand;
Long time the manxome foe he sought—
So rested he by the Tumtum tree,
And stood awhile in thought.

And, as in uffish thought he stood,
The Jabberwock, with eyes of flame,
Came whiffling through the tulgey wood,
And burbled as it came!

One, two! One, two! And through and through
The vorpal blade went snicker-snack!
He left it dead, and with its head
He went galumphing back.

"And hast thou slain the Jabberwock?
Come to my arms, my beamish boy!
Oh frabjous day! Callooh, Callay!"
He chortled in his joy.

'Twas brillig, and the slithy toves
Did gyre and gimble in the wabe:
All mimsy were the borogoves,
And the mome raths outgrabe.

—Lewis Carroll,
Through the Looking Glass (1872)

Notice that even here the message is helping to determine the quantities.

CLUSTERING.   One of the stunts used on page 254 in order to pack a line with sound was to fill it so full of *th*'s that it became a tongue-twister. Tongue-twisters are fairly common in poetry, although rarely so obvious as in our line, or these from early Tennyson:

> The callow throstle lispeth,
> The slumbrous wave outwelleth,
> The babbling runnel crispeth,
> The hollow grot replieth,
> Where Claribel low-lieth.

Ordinarily a poet proceeds more subtly; but by crowding together a number of sounds which the tongue cannot navigate quickly, he can force us to slow down, thus stretching out his line. Usually such clusters will consist of consonants which lack an intervening vowel.

> When Ajax strives some rock's vast weight to throw
>   ks strvz s m r ks v st w   t t thr

> Now at the last gasp of Love's latest breath
>   t th   st g sp v l   vz l   st br

> And first one universal shriek there rush'd
>   d f st w n y   sl shr k th r r sht

You may have noticed that a particularly good way of forcing a pause—and causing an accent to hover, perhaps—is to begin a word with the same sound as that which concluded the previous word. It occurs in the lines above, and in the Tennyson excerpt; here it is again, in Pope:

> And ten low words oft creep in one dull line
>   d t   w w   l l

There are ways, then, of speeding up or slowing down part of a line; and you should remain alert to such changes of pace. Notice sound especially in lines that carry a change of subject or of attitude.

Sound Forms Patterns

Much of what we say here may be as familiar to you as were the common meters of English; but it is important that you refresh your memory of the ways in which sound is frequently patterned. If you do not remember what to look for you probably will not see it; and if you do not see it we probably will not hear it.

ALLITERATION.   Usually the term alliteration is restricted to the repetition of initial "consonant" [2] sounds; but to avoid introducing such extra terms as hidden alliteration, attenuation, acrostic scrambling and so forth, we shall apply the word "alliteration" to all of them. Alliteration, then, is the repetition, within consecutive or nearly consecutive words, of similar consonant sounds; hence you can consider the voiced or voiceless variant of a sound to be part of its alliterative potential, and you might notice that *sh* will probably reinforce an *s* alliteration.

The most obvious effect of alliteration is simple reinforcement; if the sound seems to echo the sense, then repeating it should heighten the effect.

> From the *d*epth of the *d*reamy *d*ecline of the *d*awn through a
>   *n*otable *n*imbus of *n*ebulous *n*oonshine

> And the *s*ilken, *s*ad, un*c*ertain ru*st*ling of ea*ch* purple curtain

> Thou, from who*s*e un*s*een pre*s*en*c*e the leave*s* dead
> Are drive*n*, like gho*s*ts from a*n* e*n*cha*n*ter fleeing

> O *W*estern *w*ind, *wh*en *w*ilt tho*u* blo*w*

> The *m*oan of doves in i*mm*e*m*orial e*lm*s
> And *m*ur*m*uring of innu*m*erable bee*s*

But probably alliteration is even more useful as a binder; it holds things together, holds lines together. Students who do not miss a single dreary-weary internal rhyme in the rest of "The Raven" will fail to notice that in the second example above, "uncertain" rhymes with "curtain"; the *s* alliteration pulls them past an otherwise inevitable caesural break.

Pope often uses alliteration to strengthen his ironic linkings. Here are the contents of a lady's dressing table:

> Puffs, powders, patches, Bibles, billet-doux

Or here again:

> And s*l*eep*l*ess *l*overs, just at t*w*el*v*e, a*w*ake

> Not *l*ouder shrieks to pitying *H*eaven are cast
> When *h*usbands, or when *l*ap-dogs breathe their *l*ast

---

[2] Since the terms "consonants" and "vowels" are frequently used in referring to letters of the alphabet, we use the expression "consonant sounds" to call attention to the fact that alliteration (and hereafter assonance) are matters of sound and not of spelling. For example: *c*arry *ch*emicals to the *k*indergarten is alliterative; *c*an he *c*ite *Ch*arles is not.

Not ty*r*a*n*ts fie*r*ce that u*n*repe*n*ting die,
Not Cy*n*thia whe*n* her ma*n*teau's pi*nn*ed aw*r*y
E'e*r* felt such *r*age, *r*ese*n*tment, a*n*d despai*r*

Perhaps you begin to see that the alliteration of a single sound, especially an initial sound, is a fairly obvious device that can probably be exploited openly by the oral reader; but the more complex patterns of alliteration require not only considerable tact in their presentation, but considerable alertness for their detection. Trace the *w, s,* and *k* alliteration in this poem:

UPON JULIA'S CLOTHES
Whenas in silks my Julia goes,
Then, then, methinks, how sweetly flows
That liquefaction of her clothes.
Next, when I cast mine eyes, and see
That brave vibration, each way free—
O, how that glittering taketh me!
—Robert Herrick (1648)

In what crucial word are these three alliterative patterns united? (As a strong hint, remember that *q* has a *w* sound in it.) Note how Keats uses a complicated sound play to link three words:

What leaf-fringed legend haunts about thy shape

Having forced a hovering accent in the second foot, so that "fringed" and "legend" become equally important, he ties "leaf-fringed legend" with this pattern: *l n j d, l j n d.* Recalling an earlier discussion, notice how he slows the line down; anticipating a later discussion, you might wonder why he should have slowed it.

ASSONANCE. Assonance is the repetition of vowel sounds. The term is also applied to a sort of incomplete rhyme which we shall discuss in the next section. Like alliteration, assonance is used for reinforcement of an effect and for binding units together.

Here is a passage from Swinburne, who if anything was overly conscious of sound patterns:

Before the be*gi*nning of years	i		
There came to the making of man	ay	ay	a
Time, with a *gi*ft of tears;	i		

Grief, with a glass that ran;	a	a	
Pleasure, with pain for leaven;	e	ay	e
Summer, with flowers that fell;	e		
Remembrance fallen from heaven,	e	e	
And madness risen from hell;	a	i	e
Strength without hands to smite;	e	i	a
Love that endures for a breath;	e?	e	
Night, the shadow of light,	a		
And life, the shadow of death.	a	e	

5

10

    This message is not easily held together; not only does it deal in abstractions, but it forms no more than a recipe, a list—a very loose kind of organization. Notice that antithesis is used to couple the items, and that the antithetic lines, which might tend to break into couplets, are usually placed so that they do *not* coincide with the rhyme scheme. These precautions help to keep the stanza from breaking into isolated lines or couplets. But perhaps the chief unifying devices are alliteration and assonance. There is a tendency, perhaps reinforced by the rushing anapests and the shortness of the lines, for the stanza to break into three quatrains—four-line stanzas; the danger is especially strong after line 8, which concludes an antithesis, and which has, after all, added up an even half-dozen ingredients! Notice the great care taken in line 9 to repeat the sounds of line 8, and in line 10 perhaps to repeat the sounds of line 7. Only the patterns of assonance are indicated; to what extent are the patterns of alliteration similar? What happens at the other danger point —line 5? Why are comparatively few precautions taken there? Do you feel a gap between lines 4 and 5, and if so, does it force a gap between lines 8 and 9? In short, does the stanza hold together for you?

    Assonance, perhaps more subtly than alliteration, can strengthen sound-effects and bind units together.

    CONSONANCE.   Consonance, a relatively new term in criticism, refers to the shifting of vowel sound within a pattern of consonants: tit for tat, snicker-snack, singsong. If you like, it is consonantal rhyme, in which consonant pattern is duplicated with the vowel changed; you might consider it a complex form of alliteration.

        The *owl* for *all* his feathers was a-co*ld*

        . . . in *faery lands forlorn*

> The *hu*ngry judges *soo*n the *se*ntence *sig*n,
> And wretches *ha*ng that jurymen may dine

In the third example, notice that in addition to the soon-sen-sign and the hung-hang series, there is an involved alliteration in "udges-etches" which could be considered consonance. Notice too that consonance can bind terms so closely that you become aware not so much of their similarity as of their difference, just as when you see identical twins you turn your attention to distinguishing between them.

RHYME.   Rhyme consists of the duplication of the last stressed vowel and all consonant sounds which follow it; in English rhyme the consonants which precede should differ. If the stressed vowels are similar but not identical, we have *slant rhyme;* if the vowels look alike but are pronounced differently, we have *eye rhyme.* Let us review quickly:

> rhyme—heard, word; hearing, cheering; faded, they did
> slant rhyme—heard, weird; hearing, daring; faded, she did
> eye rhyme—heard, beard; hearing, bearing; fade, façade
> assonance—heard, swirl; hearing, nearly; faded, making
> consonance—heard, hard; hearing, her wrong; faded, fetid.

Rhyme can clinch things together so tightly as to divide them off from everything else. A danger in writing or reading couplets—two consecutive lines that rhyme—is that anticipation may be satisfied too quickly; matters seem concluded in the second line, and there is little impetus to go on to the third.[3] Because rhyme can bind so tightly, some rather intricate rhyme patterns—*rhyme schemes*—have been developed. The more common ones are listed here.

Rhyme scheme is conventionally indicated by letters, *a* representing the first rhyme, *b* the second, *c* the third, and so on, and *x* represents an unrhymed terminal ending.

> Are those her ribs through which the Sun   x
> Did peer, as through a grate?   a
> And is that Woman all her crew?   b
> Is that a Death? and are there two?   b
> Is Death that woman's mate?   a

Couplet, a a b b c c d d, etc. Iambic pentameter couplets, called *heroic* couplets, were used extensively in the seventeenth and eighteenth centuries.

---

[3] But the couplets in Browning's "My Last Duchess" are so skillfully managed that many people think the poem is unrhymed. In the arts, any generalization is at best only broadly true.

Tercet, a a a b b b c c c d d d, etc. Such tercets or triplets are seldom used for an entire poem, as on page 259; they are more likely to be encountered singly, to vary another rhythm scheme, as on page 267. Where tercets do organize a poem, they usually take the form of *terza rima:* a b a, b c b, c d c, etc.

Quatrain is a four-line stanza that takes a number of forms, of which the most common, perhaps, is a b a b, c d c d, etc.; frequent too is a b b a, c d d c, etc. The *ballad* stanza—in which the odd-numbered lines are iambic tetrameter and the even-numbered iambic trimeter—can take any of the forms above, but more usually runs: x a x a, x b x b, x c x c, etc.

Rhyme royal has seven lines of iambic pentameter: a b a b b c c.

Ottava rima, much used by the Romantics, is a rhyme scheme having eight lines of iambic pentameter: a b a b a b c c. See page 251.

Sonnet, as you know, has fourteen lines of iambic pentameter. The Italian sonnet usually presents the "problem" or the situation in the first eight lines, the *octave*—a b b a a b b a—and the "solution" or conclusion in the last six lines, the *sestet*—c d e d d e, or perhaps c d c d c d, or again c d e d c e, or one of a number of other variations. The *Shakespearean* sonnet ordinarily develops the situation in three quatrains—a b a b, c d c d, e f e f—and presents a conclusion in a final couplet—g g.

Blank verse. Many of the greatest long poems in the language are written in blank verse—unrhymed iambic pentameter.

You probably should learn these rhyme schemes, simply because an educated audience will know them and will expect you to reveal in your reading the way in which these conventional forms have been handled.

Rhyme forms. When the accented rhymed syllable is the final one, it is called a masculine rhyme—behead, dead, praise, delays; but when the accented rhymed syllable is followed by an unstressed (rhymed) syllable, it is called a feminine rhyme—beheaded, dreaded, praising, blazing. Ordinarily a masculine rhyme seems more abrupt and final, and therefore more emphatic; feminine rhymes blur the ending with a sort of afterthought, and therefore can provide smoother transitions into the next line. Compound rhymes, which duplicate three or four syllables, usually draw attention to themselves and away from the message; hence they can be used for comic effect—"lot o' news, hypotenuse"; "American, I swear I can." Ordinarily you will exploit any unusual rhymes. But the following poem indicates they can sometimes provide a very subtle irony.

FOR A DEAD LADY

No more with overflowing light
Shall fill the eyes that now are faded,

Nor shall another's fringe with night
Their woman-hidden world as they did.
No more shall quiver down the days
The flowing wonder of her ways,
Whereof no language may requite
The shifting and the many-shaded.

The grace, divine, definitive,
Clings only as a faint forestalling;
The laugh that love could not forgive
Is hushed, and answers to no calling;
The forehead and the little ears
Have gone where Saturn keeps the years;
The breast where roses could not live
Has done with rising and with falling.

The beauty, shattered by the laws
That have creation in their keeping,
No longer trembles at applause,
Or over children that are sleeping;
And we who delve in beauty's lore
Know all that we have known before
Of what inexorable cause
Makes Time so vicious in his reaping.[4]
   —Edward Arlington Robinson
      (1910)

How does the faintly humorous effect of the ingenious rhymes help to make the narrator, and by implication the lady, more human?

Lastly, rhyme can occur within a line as well as at the end; such internal rhyme usually rhymes the end word with one at the middle. Since this process is likely to split the line in half, the effect may be lilting or boisterous.

Sound Should Be Exploited

Some students are so afraid of singsong that they try to pretend that the sound patterns do not exist, and some textbooks advise you not to emphasize

[4] Reprinted with the permission of Charles Scribner's Sons from *The Town Down the River* by Edwin Arlington Robinson, copyright 1910 Charles Scribner's Sons; renewal copyright 1938 Ruth Nivison.

a rhyme word if you can avoid it. We too have repeatedly warned you against reading sound effects. Nevertheless, though we deplore the mooing and moaning of poetry, we think that the sound is part of the poem—sometimes the major part—and that to minimize it in reading is at least as mistaken as to exaggerate it. Have fun with the sound patterns; that is doubtless what they are there for.

All of which does not solve many problems. But beyond a few very general principles, there is no one solution possible, for in art *degree* is all-important. Where a compound rhyme or a consonance strikes you as funny or ingenious, you should certainly communicate that reaction to the audience. Indeed, if a slant rhyme or an eye rhyme strikes you as outrageous, you might even increase the outrage by pronouncing it as an exact rhyme. You may have to consider your own preferences and those of your audience before you can decide.

> Here lay poor Fletcher's half-eat scenes, and here
> The frippery of crucified Molière

We would pronounce "eat" as "et" in order to preserve the assonance; but we would not preserve the rhyme—many modern Americans try hard to preserve foreign pronunciations of foreign words, and we would have to nudge them too strongly in order to show that the mistake was deliberate.

> I'll tell you who they were, this female pair,
> Lest they should seem princesses in disguise;
> Besides, I hate all mystery, and that air
> Of clap-trap, which your recent poets prize;
> And so, in short, the girls they really were
> They shall appear before your curious eyes,
> Mistress and maid; the first was only daughter
> Of an old man, who lived upon the water.

To rhyme this necessitates pronouncing "were" in two different ways within five lines; but why not? We would not rhyme the following lines, which did rhyme in 1714:

> Here thou, great Anna! whom three realms obey,
> Dost sometimes counsel take—and sometimes tea

—because "tay" may connote too quickly the comic Irishman, and so violate the precise filigree of "The Rape of the Lock." About the only conclusions you could safely draw from this is that your own comic sense is probably your best guide and that consistency is not greatly to be prized.

If the poem is not comic you will have to be even more careful in exploiting sound. Fortunately most rhyme words are important both to meter and to message, so that unless you deliberately avoid them, their emphasis will almost take care of itself. Run-on lines, which pose a special problem, are discussed in the next section. In general, do not draw strong attention to non comic rhymes by altering your pronunciation to accommodate them, though tastes differ about pronouncing "wind" as "wined." You should be alert, however, to assonance, alliteration, and consonance; where message and meter permit a choice between two almost equally acceptable readings, make your decision on the basis of sound.

MESSAGE

Once you have broken the habit of unvaried singsong, the poetic message itself should present no unique problems. However, since beginners often encounter two difficulties which we have discussed in other chapters, a few broad reminders may be in order. One difficulty arises out of the diction and syntax of some poetry. Since poets are expected to compress their messages, they are allowed some latitude in grammar and word order; do not be surprised to encounter inversions, "dangling" clauses, or loose sentence structure. Prepare your précis with more than usual care, use paraphrase freely, and remember that some of the ambiguity is almost certainly deliberate. In reading the poem aloud you will have to exercise special control over group sequence. Remember that such forms as "hath," "doth," "wert," "wast," "thee," "ere," "art," etc., are to be treated like their modern equivalents—which is to say that generally they are unstressed. Take special care of "doth": nine times out of ten it should be "d'th," the apostrophe representing merely a vowel murmur.

The other problem arises out of the intensity of poetry. Beginners can worry so much about structure that they neglect attitude and tone. Or they are bewildered when an innocent little poem kindles to white heat within five or six lines. We hope you are now disabused of the notion that poetry contents itself with numbering the streaks of the tulip; poetry is as exalted and as vicious, as wise and as ornery as mankind itself. But you may not have grasped the implications of the fact that most of the poems you read will be short ones: if a poem has fourteen lines in which to make its effect, it has no time to waste; the bomb is already ticking when you announce the title.

Message and Meter

This subject was introduced on page 254, when we "filled a line with sound," because of course we also filled it with message. But there we tried only to increase the quantity of sound within each syllable; we were not concerned with whether those syllables became more important to the message and therefore in need of greater emphasis. Remember that a message may permit infinite shadings of emphasis, whereas meter admits of only three: stress, unstress, and the semistress that occurs in a hovering accent. So we must notice what happens when the dynamic shifting patterns of message stress are superimposed upon the mechanical ones of meter.

SUBSTITUTIONS AND INVERSIONS. As we have said, anyone can get his meter regular; the trick is to get it irregular in the right places. Now, what happens when we insert a word that is too big for the meter?

$$\text{Ĭ walkéd | wĭth Bíll | fŏr míles |}$$

$$\text{Ĭ walkéd | wĭth Bíl-|lў fŏr míles |}$$

Oddly enough, when we insert an extra syllable, the line speeds up. What happens when we leave out a syllable?

$$\text{The sedge is wither'd from the lake,}$$

$$\text{Ănd nó | wĕe bírds | căn síng |}$$

$$\text{The sedge is wither'd from the lake,}$$

$$\text{Ănd nó | ˘ bírds | ˘ síng |}$$

The metronome inside each of us prolongs the second "birds" and "sing" to compensate for the missing off-beats; the line moves more slowly. It does not matter whether you think of these tricks as the insertion and omission of syllables, or whether you would rather refer to the substitution of anapests and double spondees for iambs; what *is* important is that you notice the effect.

From our experiment with sound you can infer what happens when a sense word is placed in the unstress or off-beat position:

$$\text{Wĕ sáw | thĕ wát-|ĕr frésh | ănd cóol |}$$

$$\text{Wĕ sáw | blùe wàt-|ĕr frésh | ănd cóol |}$$

If the quantities are long enough, or the word is very important to the message, there will develop a hovering accent. Notice what happens when we do the opposite—place a function word in the stress or down-beat position:

Ĭ wan-|derĕd slów-|lў pást | thĕ crówd |

Ĭ wan-|derĕd lóne-|lў ăs | ă clóud |

The resultant foot (it is called a pyrrhic) is quickened, and depending on the message, one or both of the stressed words on either side will become lengthened, and hence more emphatic. Notice the tumbling effect which Dryden secures from a series of pyrrhic fourth feet:

> Of these the false Achitophel was first;
> A name to all succeeding ages curst:
> For close designs and crooked counsels fit,
> Sagacious, bold, and turb*ulent* of wit,
> Restless, unfix'd in prin*ciples* and place,
> In pow'r unpleas'd, impat*ient of* disgrace;
> A fiery soul, which, working out its way,
> Fretted the pigmy bod*y to* decay:
> And o'er-inform'd the ten*ement* of clay.

Is the message reinforced by the slow careful start and the sudden toppling?

Combining these two tricks *inverts* the foot: The emphatic syllable is placed in the unstress position, and the unstressed syllable in the stress position.

Ĭ stróve | wĭth nóne;| fŏr nóne | wăs wórth | mў strífe,|

Natŭre | Ĭ lóved,| ănd néxt | tŏ Nát-|ŭre, Árt |

The inversion of feet is one of the commonest tricks in English poetry. It is especially frequent in the first foot of a line, but occurs often in the second or fourth, sometimes in the third or fifth.

> *Restless,* unfix'd in principles and place
>
> My heart *aches, and* a drowsy numbness pains
>
> How weary, stale, *flat and* unprofitable
>
> To be, or not to be: *that is* the question
>
> Bright star, would I were steadfast as *thou art*

Sometimes too there are multiple inversions within a single line:

> *Striding* the blast, or heaven's *cherub*in hors'd

> *Irrecovera*bly dark, *total* Eclipse

The inverted foot introduces great variation into the rhythm: all the examples we have chosen occur in iambic pentameter lines, and so the meters are all identical; but you need only read them aloud to discover how greatly they differ in rhythm.

SOME SPECIAL PROBLEMS.   You have seen how spectacularly the message can modify the regularity of meter, and you should have little hesitation now in emphasizing the words which your analysis of sense and attitude has shown to be important. Such words, you may be reasonably sure, were placed carefully into the position which would supply the desired rhythmic effect.

But we hope, too, that we have scared you away from prosy reading; by now you should be interested in preserving the meter where possible. A couple of tips are in order at this point. The first is that when you are reading poetry—especially British poetry—you will probably have to sharpen your unstressing. You can expect the frequent insertion of one unstressed syllable into a foot; if you find two or three extra ones, suspect your pronunciation. Let us take a very familiar example: chances are you pronounce the Shakespearean heroine's name as "Jul-i-ette"—$2\frac{1}{2}$ beats; but here are some sample lines:

> I came to talk of. Tell me, daughter Juliet

> We follow thee. Juliet, the County stays

> It is the east, and Juliet is the sun

> Ah, Juliet, if the measure of thy joy

You can see that it is almost a monosyllable, "Jul-y't"; if you will dig out a copy of the play you will notice that "Romeo" is also nearly "monosyllabic"—shorter than "Ro-me-o" or even "Rom-yo." This principle extends to many word endings which you customarily "drawl" in conversation—*-iate, -ion, -ious, -erable,* etc. Such words as "the" and "of" sometimes cannot even be counted in the scansion; they have been elided into the following syllable, even though they are not spelled "th'" and "o'." You will have to cut them very short. But do not mistake us: we are not advising that immedj't adopsh'n of a "British" acc'nt is necess'ry—far from it; we are, however, warning that you may have to tighten your unstressing when reading poetry.

Just to make matters more confusing, remember that in Shakespeare and Milton the terminal ending *-ed* is usually pronounced as a separate syllable, a practice maintained by some poets almost down to the present day. But the trouble is that such later poets may not have been consistent in their spelling, or their editors may have dislik'd the sight of apostrophes. In other words, if the line will not scan, try pronouncing the terminal *-ed*.

There is also the problem of archaic pronunciations. When we mentioned them earlier, in connection with rhyme, we advised you to retain modern pronunciations except for broad comic effect. But when such advice is applied to meter, the results may be altogether jarring.

I have no joy of this *contract* tonight	*R.&J.*
Upon my *secure* hour thy uncle stole	*Ham.*
His means of death, his *obscure* burial	*Ham.*
I'll wipe away all trivial fond *records*	*Ham.*
About the *Supreme* throne	"On Time"
In *profuse* strains of unpremeditated art	"Skylark"

Some of these work well enough if you supply a hovering accent; but our point is that Shakespearean and Miltonic adjectives, and sometimes verbs, shift their accents under certain fixed conditions, and only your ear can tell you that you should retain the shift, or compromise with a hovering accent, or crash through with a modern pronunciation.

Message and Line

Listen to a number of recordings of poets reading poems. Notice that however bad a reader he is, however painful his violations of the elementary principles of oral interpretation, the poet preserves the rhythm and *the structure of his line.* We oral interpreters are often so busy with the *grammatical* structure of the *sentence* that we have no time to wonder why a poem should be written in *lines* of five beats, or four beats, or whatever. The poet knows that the line is the primary unit of rhythm, that the rises and falls, the turns and returns, are functions of sound, of rhythm, and not necessarily of sense. The tremendous complexity which has been woven into the sound pattern will be meaningless if all we attend to is subject-verb-object.

And so our major advice, for prosy and singsong reader alike, is: *hold that line!*

The singsong reader is unaware—and the prosy reader overly aware—of the fact that English poetry, especially that which is written in an even number of beats, tends to split down the middle. Does the following line sound familiar?

Once upon.   A midnight dreary.   While I pon.   Dered weak and weary.

Four lines for the price of one. This invisible caesura—this break—may be a heritage of Anglo-Saxon alliterative poetry; at any rate, it bobs just below the surface of any line, and if the poet or the reader is careless (as we think Wordsworth was careless in "The Daffodils"[5]) the lines will fall apart. *Hold that line!*

Of course few poets write exclusively in sticks of eight or ten syllables, but they need some such basic "stick" as a measure of variation. They may place the message so that it breaks some lines and links others. Part of the music comes from the care with which these thought groups are placed into the line. Robert Bridges has analyzed a musical passage of Milton according to the number of syllables on either side of the break:

Harmonious numbers; as the wakeful Bird	5 + 5
Sings darkling, and in shadiest Covert hid	3 + 7
Tunes her nocturnal Note. Thus with the Year	6 + 4
Seasons return, but not to me returns	4 + 6
Day, or the sweet approach of Ev'n or Morn[6]	1 + 9

The passage shows that you can expect the break—the caesura—at any point in the line.

So now we have two subpatterns to preserve: the grammatical and rhetorical unit (the thought group), and the metrical unit, the line. To break the line carelessly is at least as irritating, and ultimately as destructive of the meaning, as to break the thought group carelessly.

Where the two subpatterns clash, they pose a problem serious enough to merit a special section. Let us turn to it now.

Enjambment

Enjambment—a run-on line—occurs when the grammatical sense is obviously incomplete at the end of a line:

[5] Turn to page 182 and notice how often the thought-groups end precisely in the middle of the line.

[6] The lines are *Paradise Lost*, iii, 38–42; the analysis is from Robert Bridges, *Milton's Prosody*, Oxford, 1921, 44.

> Let me not to the marriage of true minds
> Admit impediments.

> My heart aches, and a drowsy numbness pains
> My sense,

Obviously you cannot pause in the middle of a thought group; and yet you must preserve the line. Fortunately the poet has already faced—and usually has solved —the problem; in all but a very small number of run-on lines at least one of three aids has been provided.

First, the line end concludes an idea unit, even though the thought group is incomplete. Accordingly you can pause very slightly, just as you might after any idea unit; your problem is to indicate in your inflection that the major thought is incomplete.

> I wandered lonely as a cloud
> That floats . . .

> . . . Like to the Pontic Sea,
> Whose icy current and compulsive course
> Ne'er feels retiring ebb, but keeps due on
> To the Propontic and the Hellespont,
> Even so my bloody thoughts, with violent pace,
> Shall ne'er look back, ne'er ebb to humble love,
> Till that a capable and wide revenge
> Swallow them up.

You are not finished until "up," but every line end marks an idea unit.

Second, the line end is marked by a word that is important enough to emphasize strongly, though it may not be the core of the line; while emphasizing this word, particularly by increasing its duration, you can easily "rest" for a moment, and at the same time build the impetus for the run-on.

> My heart aches, and a drowsy numbness pains
> My sense

> . . . Him the Almighty Power
> Hurl'd headlong flaming from th' Ethereal Skie
> With hideous ruin and combustion down
> To bottomless perdition, there to dwell

> In Adamantine Chains and penal Fire,
> Who durst defie th' Omnipotent to Arms.

Third, the line end is marked by a word which is at least important enough, and which contains sufficient *quantity,* that you can prolong it slightly, even though you do not emphasize it otherwise with pitch and stress; you can, in short, treat it as a unique word. Rhyme words especially may have to be handled in this way.

> . . . he stood and call'd
> His Legions, Angel Forms, who lay intrans't
> Thick as Autumnal Leaves that strow the Brooks
> In Vallombrosa, where th' Etrurian shades
> High overarch't imbowr;

Even here, where the inverted feet "Thick as" and "High ov-" make the problem doubly difficult, you will find that you can prolong the end words sufficiently to mark the lines, and yet not so noticeably as to spoil the magnificent cadence.

Ninety-nine times in a hundred, then, an enjambment will almost read itself —if you do not get in the way. And the hundredth? You may as well know the worst.

> Perhaps the self-same song that found a path
> Through the sad heart of Ruth, when, sick for home,
> She stood in tears amid the alien corn;
> The same that oft-times hath
> Charm'd magic casements, opening on the foam
> Of perilous seas, in faery lands forlorn.

It may well be that the sheer magic of these last two lines is so great that no one will care how you read "hath." Even harder is the next one, and in the context of *Antony and Cleopatra,* in which it is delivered by an abrupt and taciturn soldier, it must be almost impossible:

> The barge she sat in, like a burnish'd throne,
> Burn'd on the water. The poop was beaten gold;
> Purple the sails, and so perfumed that
> The winds were love-sick with them. The oars were silver,

Which to the tune of flutes kept stroke, and made   5
The water which they beat to follow faster,
As amorous of their strokes. For her own person,
It beggar'd all description: she did lie
In her pavilion—cloth-of-gold of tissue—
O'er-picturing that Venus where we see   10
The fancy outwork nature. On each side her
Stood pretty dimpled boys, like smiling Cupids,
With divers-colour'd fans, whose wind did seem
To glow the delicate cheeks which they did cool,
And what they undid did.

If you can read this, you can probably read anything. There are some helps—
"made" in line 5, "see" in line 10, and "seem" in line 13 are important enough
that they can be prolonged; but how you get over "that," in line 3, is beyond
us. A dramatic hesitation, while you grope for words? No; in this speech smooth-
ness is all.

Now that you know the worst, and are assured that it is infrequent—perhaps
you can encounter a run-on line with some confidence. There is no need to turn
it into prose; almost always you can find reason either to pause for an instant or
to prolong the end word ever so slightly.

UNCONVENTIONAL STRUCTURE

In the preceding sections we have said again and again that the important
thing in poetry is the rhythm, which we defined as the interplay of meter, sound,
and message. To simplify matters, we restricted our discussion of meter to the
conventional syllable-accent prosody.[7] But there is a fairly large body of poetry
which is not based on those standard metrical patterns, and lest you feel unduly
baffled by it, we add here a sketchy account of some other possibilities.

Before we start, here is a general tip: if you cannot find a standard metrical
pattern, preserve the sound, the line length, and the message, and you will have
retained a large part of the rhythm.

A very few poems are written in *quantitative* verse, which attempts to reproduce in English the meters of classical Greek; such meters had no stresses, but

---

[7] For three different and provocative explanations of poetic rhythm, see Wallace A. Bacon and Robert S.
Breen, *Literature as Experience,* McGraw-Hill, 1959, pp. 180–212. Cornelius C. Cunningham, *Making Words
Come Alive,* Brown, 1951, chap. VIII. John Dolman, *The Art of Reading Aloud,* Harper, 1956, chaps. 5–7.

instead had patterns of long and short syllables. You need a classical education to understand such patterns, but maybe you can sense them.

ROSE-CHEEKT LAURA, COME

Rose-cheekt Laura, come,
Sing thou smoothly with thy beauty's
Silent music, either other
Sweetly gracing.

Lovely forms do flow
From concent divinely framèd;
Heav'n is music, and thy beauty's
Birth is heavenly.

These dull notes we sing
Discords need for helps to grace them;
Only beauty purely loving
Knows no discord.

But still moves delight,
Like clear springs renew'd by flowing,
Ever perfet, ever in them-
Selves eternal.

> —Thomas Campion (1602)

For practical purposes such rare successes should be considered tours de force, but if they hang together for you, by all means read them.

Perhaps equally small is the number of poems which take either of the extremes possible in *qualitative* verse: some form patterns of the number of syllables in the line and ignore the number and placement of the stresses; some form patterns of the stresses in the line, and ignore the unaccented syllables. The extremes are so rare—even in the work of such poets as Marianne Moore and Gerard Manley Hopkins—that they are probably not important in themselves; but because a large body of modern poetry is closer to one or the other than is our conventional prosody—which combines stress- and syllable-counting—we should mention them.

Stress-counting, *accentual* verse, is a variant of Anglo-Saxon poetry, which has probably always lain close to the surface ever since it "disappeared" in the fifteenth century. Anglo-Saxon poetry counted only the heavy beats, of which there were four to a line, two on each side of a heavy caesura; the unaccented syllables did not count; and the line was held together rhetorically and alliteratively. Fortunately, you have a far sounder practical knowledge of this poetry than your two-week survey of *Beowulf* and *Piers Ploughman* led you to suspect. You may not remember this:

> In a somer seson • whan soft was the sonne
> I shope me into shroudes • as I a shepe were
> In habite as an heremite • unholy of workes
> Went wyde in this world • wondres to here.

But you do remember this:

> Christmas is coming, the goose is getting fat,
> Please to put a penny in an old man's hat;
> If you haven't got a penny, a ha'penny will do,
> If you haven't got a ha'penny, God bless you.

Two beats on either side of the line—and if you decide that "God bless you" has three beats, you prepare the pattern by giving three beats to "old man's hat." Now, minimize the break in the middle:

> Is the night chilly and dark?
>
> The night is chilly but not dark.

If you can remember the drum-beats you heard in Mother Goose, or in ROTC, or the ones you may be tapping on the table as you read this next poem, you need not be afraid of accentual verse.

THE WINDHOVER
TO CHRIST OUR LORD

I caught this morning, morning's minion, king-
    dom of daylight's dauphin, dapple-dawn-drawn Falcon, in
      his riding
    Of the rolling level underneath him steady air, and striding
High there, how he rung upon the rein of a wimpling wing
In his ecstasy! then off, off forth on swing,   5

As a skate's heel sweeps smooth on a bow-bend: the hurl
    and gliding
Rebuffed the big wind. My heart in hiding
Stirred for a bird,—the achieve of, the mastery of the thing!

Brute beauty and valor and act, oh, air, pride, plume, here
10   Buckle! AND the fire that breaks from thee then, a billion
Times told lovelier, more dangerous, O my chevalier!
   No wonder of it: sheer plod makes plough down sillion
Shine, and blue-bleak embers, ah my dear,
    Fall, gall themselves, and gash gold-vermillion.[8]
            —Gerard Manley Hopkins (1877)

> Read this silently to get the drift of it, and then try it aloud.
> Notice where the sense demands emphasis:
>
>   I caught this morning, morning's minion, king-
>
> Notice the rhyme scheme: a b b a, a b b a, c d c d c d. The
> first line gives us a pretty good idea of the beat; and the son-
> net form confirms our hunch. Until we find clues to the con-
> trary, we can assume that this is a "standard" sonnet.
>
>   dom of daylight's dauphin, dapple-dawn-drawn Falcon
>
>   in his riding
>
> The third line is harder; Hopkins marks "under-" but as we
> read it, we cannot decide whether there is a sort of hovering
> effect on "level-under-," as there was on "dapple-dawn-drawn,"
> or whether the stress goes on "steady." How do you make the
> line go?
>   Line 10 throws us, too; if we have to stress "AND"—and
> why else would it be set in block caps?—we have a hexameter
> line, though we like the effect. Do you think this boisterous
> rapture could be caught in a more conventional rhythm?

Lest we have frightened you in spite of reassurance, let us point out that
you have just been studying what is as close to one extreme in English poetry
as you are likely to find. More usually Hopkins and his successors today use
accentual verse as a sort of counterpoint on conventional forms. "God's Grandeur," page 283, and "In My Craft or Sullen Art," page 283, reveal many more

[9] Reprinted by permission of Willis Kingsley Wing. © 1955, by Robert Graves. Originally appeared in
The New Yorker. Included in his *Collected Poems,* published by Doubleday & Co. and Gassell & Co.

successive inverted and substituted feet than premodernist poetry would have permitted, but otherwise they may be scanned in the conventional manner.

Accordingly we suggest that if a modern poem does not yield readily at first to conventional scansion, after considerable allowance has been made for substitutions and inversions, you apply heavy stress to the important words, and try to find a "drum-beat" rhythm in them.

Syllable-count verse is not nearly as mechanical as our name for it would imply; indeed, it appears most often under the guise of free verse. You are not expected to count the syllables, any more than you would in *Paradise Lost;* but the practice sometimes helps verify what your ear has told you about the patterning of the thought groups, or cadences. Ordinarily such poetry uses punctuation and line ends to force us to pause in the right places; the sticks of sound so produced will be patterned in length. Perhaps Amy Lowell's "Patterns" is as familiar an example as any.

Insofar as free verse is free, it of course escapes all pattern; but *insofar as it escapes pattern it is not poetry.* You will find a fair amount of prose masquerading as free verse—but a beginning course in oral interpretation is hardly the place to try to explain the difference, if indeed we could explain it. Generally, however, you should look for patterns in the length of the thought groups, the cadences; you should find that they are of nearly the same length, or are fairly clear multiples of a basic unit. Notice the syntactical patterns, parallel grammatical structures. Watch for such sound patterns as alliteration, assonance, and consonance. And, hardly unimportant, look for economy.

We cannot improve upon the advice we gave you earlier: preserve the message, exploit the sound patterns, and hold that line.

EXERCISES AND ASSIGNMENTS

1. In each of the following poems the meter is fairly prominant. How is such effect obtained? Do the sound patterns reinforce or soften the metrical message? Is the rhythm appropriate to such meaning as you extract with the tools of Chapter Three?

   a.

   ### WHEN A MAN HATH NO FREEDOM
   When a man hath no freedom to fight for at home,
   Let him combat for that of his neighbors;
   Let him think of the glories of Greece and of Rome,
   And get knock'd on the head for his labors.

To do good to mankind is the chivalrous plan,
And is always as nobly requited;
Then battle for freedom wherever you can,
And if not shot or hang'd, you'll get knighted.
—George Noel Gordon, Lord Byron (1820)

b.

Why So Pale and Wan

Why so pale and wan, fond lover?
Prithee, why so pale?
Will, when looking well can't move her,
Looking ill prevail?
Prithee, why so pale?

Why so dull and mute, young sinner?
Prithee, why so mute?
Will, when speaking well can't win her,
Saying nothing do't?
Prithee, why so mute?

Quit, quit for shame! this will not move,
This cannot take her;
If of herself she will not love,
Nothing can make her:
The devil take her!
—Sir John Suckling (1646)

c.

I'm Through with You Forever

The oddest, surely, of odd tales
Recorded by the French
Concerns a sneak thief of Marseilles
Tried by a callous Bench.

His youth, his innocency, his tears—
No, nothing could abate
Their sentence of "One hundred years
In galleys of the State."

Nevertheless, old wives affirm,
And annalists agree,
He sweated out the whole damned term,
Bowed stiffly, and went free.

Then come, my angry love, review
    Your sentence of today.
"Forever" was unjust to you,
    The end too far away.

Give me four hundred years, or five—
    Can rage be so intense?—
And I will sweat them out alive
    To prove my impenitence.[9]
              —Robert Graves (1957)

d.

THE DRAGOONS' CHORUS

Now is not this ridiculous—and is not this preposterous?
A thorough-paced absurdity—explain it if you can.
Instead of rushing eagerly to cherish us and foster us,
They all prefer this melancholy literary man.
    Instead of slyly peering at us,
    Casting looks endearing at us,
Blushing at us, flushing at us—flirting with a fan;
They're actually sneering at us, fleering at us, jeering at us!
    Pretty sort of treatment for a military man!
          —W. S. Gilbert, *Patience* (1881)

e. "Love Not Me for Comely Grace," p. 36; "Mock On, Mock On," p. 41; "The Cold Familiar Faces," p. 38; "The Major-General's Song," p. 252.

f. "There Is a Garden in Her Face," p. 42; "Invictus," p. 187; "I Wandered Lonely as a Cloud," p. 182; "Because I Could Not Stop for Death," p. 281.

2. In which of the following poems does the message suggest that there should be a change in the rhythm? Of such poems, which have such a change? How is the change, if any, managed?

a.

ARIEL'S SONG

Full fadom five thy Father lies,
Of his bones are Corrall made:
Those are pearles that were his eyes,
Nothing of him that doth fade,
But doth suffer a Sea-change
Into something rich, and strange:
Sea-Nimphs hourly ring his knell.
    Ding dong.
Hearke, now I heare them; ding-dong bell.
          —William Shakespeare,
          The Tempest (1611)

[9] Reprinted by permission of Willis Kingsley Wing. © 1955, by Robert Graves. Originally appeared in *The New Yorker.* Included in his *Collected Poems,* published by Doubleday & Co. and Gassell & Co.

b.

THE SECOND COMING

Turning and turning in the widening gyre
The falcon cannot hear the falconer;
Things fall apart; the centre cannot hold;
Mere anarchy is loosed upon the world,
The blood-dimmed tide is loosed, and everywhere
The ceremony of innocence is drowned;
The best lack all conviction, while the worst
Are full of passionate intensity.

Surely some revelation is at hand;
Surely the Second Coming is at hand.
The Second Coming! Hardly are those words out
When a vast image out of *Spiritus Mundi*[10]
Troubles my sight: somewhere in sands of the desert
A shape with lion body and the head of a man,
A gaze blank and pitiless as the sun,
Is moving its slow thighs, while all about it
Reel shadows of the indignant desert birds.
The darkness drops again; but now I know
That twenty centuries of stony sleep
Were vexed to nightmare by a rocking cradle,
And what rough beast, its hour come round at last,
Slouches towards Bethlehem to be born?[11]

—William Butler Yeats (1921)

c.

AT THE ROUND EARTH'S IMAGIN'D CORNERS

At the round earth's imagin'd corners, blow
Your trumpets, angels, and arise, arise
From death, you numberless infinities
Of souls, and to your scatt'red bodies go;
All whom the flood did, and fire shall o'erthrow,
All whom war, dearth, age, agues, tyrannies,
Despair, law, chance, hath slain, and you whose eyes
Shall behold God, and never taste death's woe.

But let them sleep, Lord, and me mourn a space,
For, if above all these, my sins abound,
'Tis late to ask abundance of Thy grace,
When we are there; here on this lowly ground,
Teach me how to repent; for that's as good
As if Thou hadst seal'd my pardon with Thy blood.

—John Donne (1633)

[10] *Spiritus Mundi:* Yeats believed that all history, past and future, was contained in a sort of racial subconscious, a "spirit of the world," which could be reached via mysticism.

[11] From W. B. Yeats, *Collected Poems,* Definitive Edition. Copyright 1956 by The Macmillan Company and used with their permission.

  d. "The World Is Too Much with Us," p. 62; "Since There's No Help," p. 68; "Satan's Defiance," p. 96; "Ozymandias," p. 101.

  e. "The Patriot," p. 78; "Death Be Not Proud," p. 97; "On First Looking into Chapman's Homer," p. 197; "To His Coy Mistress," p. 99.

3. Each of the following poems has been praised for the vividness of its imagery—an aspect of message which you previously would have analyzed only with the techniques of Chapters Two and Three. How do meter and line length, rhyme and other sound patterns reinforce the meaning of each? Is the verse structure appropriate to the message in each? Which has the loosest structure; which the tautest?

  a.

TEARS, IDLE TEARS

Tears, idle tears, I know not what they mean,
Tears from the depth of some divine despair
Rise in the heart, and gather to the eyes,
In looking at the happy Autumn-fields,
And thinking of the days that are no more.

Fresh as the first beam glittering on a sail,
That brings our friends up from the underworld,
Sad as the last which reddens over one
That sinks with all we love below the verge;
So sad, so fresh, the days that are no more.

Ah, sad and strange as in dark summer dawns
The earliest pipe of half-awaken'd birds
To dying ears, when unto dying eyes
The casement slowly grows a glimmering square;
So sad, so strange, the days that are no more.

Dear as remember'd kisses after death,
And sweet as those by hopeless fancy feign'd
On lips that are for others; deep as love,
Deep as first love, and wild with all regret;
O Death in Life, the days that are no more.
   —Alfred, Lord Tennyson, *The Princess* (1847)

  b.

BECAUSE I COULD NOT STOP FOR DEATH

Because I could not stop for Death,
He kindly stopped for me;
The carriage held but just ourselves
And Immortality.

We slowly drove, he knew no haste,
And I had put away
My labor, and my leisure too,
For his civility.

We passed the school where children played
Their lessons scarcely done;
We passed the fields of gazing grain,
We passed the setting sun.

We paused before a house that seemed
A swelling of the ground;
The roof was scarcely visible,
The cornice but a mound.

Since then 'tis centuries; but each
Feels shorter than the day
I first surmised the horses' heads
Were toward eternity.

—Emily Dickinson (1890)

c.

SONNET LXXIII

That time of year thou mayst in me behold
When yellow leaves, or none, or few, do hang
Upon those boughs which shake against the cold,
Bare ruin'd choirs, where late the sweet birds sang.
In me thou see'st the twilight of such day
As after sunset fadeth in the west,
Which by and by black night doth take away,
Death's second self, that seals up all in rest.
In me thou see'st the glowing of such fire,
That on the ashes of his youth doth lie,
As the death-bed whereon it must expire,
Consum'd with that which it was nourish'd by.
This thou perceiv'st, which makes thy love more strong,
To love that well which thou must leave ere long.

—William Shakespeare (1595?)

d. "Mock On, Mock On," p. 41; "Sailing to Byzantium," p. 44; "Ozymandias,"
p. 101; "To His Coy Mistress," p. 99; "Bells for John Whiteside's Daughter,"
p. 103.

4. Each of the following poems is written in sonnet form. Account for the differences
in their effects. "The World Is Too Much with Us," p. 62; "Since There's No
Help," p. 68; "Ozymandias," p. 101; "God's Grandeur," p. 283; "Death Be Not
Proud," p. 97; "The People," p. 85; "On First Looking into Chapman's Homer,"
p. 197; "The Windhover," p. 275.

5. Compare the following poems with "The Windhover," p. 275, and with "I Hear
an Army," p. 73. In what ways are each close to the conventional structure of
poetry; in what ways does each differ?

a.

IN MY CRAFT OR SULLEN ART

In my craft or sullen art
Exercised in the still night
When only the moon rages
And the lovers lie abed
With all their griefs in their arms,
I labor by singing light
Not for ambition or bread
Or the strut and trade of charms
On the ivory stages
But for the common wages
Of their most secret heart.

Not for the proud man apart
From the raging moon I write
On these spindrift pages
Nor for the towering dead
With their nightingales and psalms
But for the lovers, their arms
Round the griefs of the ages,
Who pay no praise or wages
Nor heed my craft or art.[12]
                    —Dylan Thomas (1939)

b.

WHEN I HEARD THE LEARN'D ASTRONOMER

When I heard the learn'd astronomer,
When the proofs, the figures, were ranged in columns before me,
When I was shown the charts and diagrams, to add, divide, and measure
    them,
When I sitting heard the astronomer where he lectured with much
    applause in the lecture-room,
How soon unaccountable I became tired and sick,
Till rising and gliding out I wander'd off by myself,
In the mystical moist night-air, and from time to time,
Look'd up in perfect silence at the stars.
                    —Walt Whitman (1865)

c.

GOD'S GRANDEUR

The world is charged with the grandeur of God.
    It will flame out, like shining from shook foil;
    It gathers to a greatness, like the ooze of oil
Crushed. Why do men then now not reck his rod?
Generations have trod, have trod, have trod;

And all is seared with trade; bleared, smeared with toil;
And wears man's smudge, and shares man's smell: the soil
Is bare now, nor can foot feel, being shod.

And for all this, nature is never spent;
There lives the dearest freshness deep down things;
And though the last lights off the black West went
Oh, morning, at the brown brink eastward, springs—
Because the Holy Ghost over the bent
World broods with warm breast and with ah! bright wings.[13]
—Gerard Manley Hopkins (1877)

d.

THE EXPRESS

After the first powerful plain manifesto
The black statement of pistons, without more fuss
But gliding like a queen, she leaves the station.
Without bowing and with restrained unconcern
She passes the houses which humbly crowd outside,
The gasworks and at last the heavy page
Of death, printed by gravestones in the cemetery.
Beyond the town there lies the open country
Where, gathering speed, she acquires mystery,
The luminous self-possession of ships on ocean.
It is now she begins to sing—at first quite low
Then loud, and at last with a jazzy madness—
The song of her whistle screaming at curves,
Of deafening tunnels, brakes, innumerable bolts.
And always light, aerial, underneath
Goes the elate metre of her wheels.
Steaming through metal landscape on her lines
She plunges new eras of wild happiness
Where speed throws up strange shapes, broad curves
And parallels clean like the steel of guns.
At last, further than Edinburgh or Rome,
Beyond the crest of the world, she reaches night
Where only a low streamline brightness
Of phosphorus on the tossing hills is white.
Ah, like a comet through flame she moves entranced
Wrapped in her music no bird song, no, nor bough
Breaking with honey buds, shall ever equal.[14]
—Stephen Spender (1933)

[13] From *Poems of Gerard Manley Hopkins,* 3rd ed., edited by W. H. Gardner. Copyright 1948 by Oxford University Press, Inc. Reprinted by permission.
[14] Copyright 1934 by The Modern Library, Inc. Reprinted from *Collected Poems 1928–1953,* by Stephen Spender, with permission of Random House, Inc.

e.

THE SOCIAL STRUCTURE OF EARLY MASSACHUSETTS

Settlers of Massachusetts
    Were of two sets:
Those by Grace of God elected;
    Those rejected.

One good way to tell the sainted
    From the tainted
Was that those whose prayers were heeded
    Had succeeded.

As a rule it therefore followed
    That the hallowed
Were the favored upper classes,
    Not the masses.

Quite a number of the lowly
    Acted holy,
Hoping they had been elected
    Unsuspected.

Others reasoned, after learning
    Hell-fire burning
Was to be their fate forever:
    Now or never.

They were the common people, which is
Why so many turned out witches.[15]
      —Gilman M. Ostrander (1958)

f. "Sailing to Byzantium," p. 44; "A Glass of Beer," p. 76; "Bells for John Whiteside's Daughter," p. 103; "Arms and the Boy," p. 183.

---

[15] Reprinted from *American Heritage,* the Magazine of History, February, 1958, by permission of the publishers.

TOWARD REFINEMENT OF EXPRESSION

Visibility

YOU CANNOT SPEAK, even as an accomplished ventriloquist, without visible movement. Speech entails motor response. Speech itself is a response, reflecting the complexity of the instrument that produces it. It is mental as well as visibly physical, and it involves the entire organism. That is why psychologists call speech a total response: a response which is an exactly coördinated activity of the whole organism. Remember what was said about piano playing in the first chapter? The pianist's fingers skillfully manipulate the keyboard only to the degree that his entire behavior is properly coördinated toward the particular music he is playing. If totally integrated response is important to the pianist, how intensely important is such response to the oral reader who in himself is not only performer but instrument as well!

Try the following experiment: Stand in front of your mirror; relax as much as comfortable standing up will permit; look as angelic and as sweet tempered as you can. Now, without changing your angelic demeanor shout as convincingly as you can:

Fire, run for your lives!

What happened? Describe the visible changes in your posture, your face. What differences did you feel in your arms, torso, and legs? Repeat it, and see if you can really make it sound convincing without the changes you perceived.

Try a reverse experiment: Again before your mirror assume a posture and expression that you feel accurately suggest the utmost terror. Without any relinquishing of any of your tensions, say, so as to convey peace and quiet pleasure:

Isn't it peaceful tonight?

In each case, you had to modify your total tensions to make the words suggest appropriate meaning. If you didn't alter your total behavior, your voice completely belied the words. In each case the muscles of lips, tongue, jaw, and throat were immediately concerned with managing intelligible articulation, but these muscles in turn necessarily partook of the general tensions of the rest of the body. Sudden spasmodic contraction of the abdominal muscles was necessary to produce the shout. Your legs tightened and your toes took a firmer "grip" in order to support the intensified activity in your torso, and so on. Compare the tensions which accompany a satisfactory reading of "Isn't it peaceful tonight?" with those necessary for shouting "Fire . . .," etc.

All of which is to say that the caliber or essential quality of your utterance is determined by the total response of which it is a part. This totality becomes actually audible. Why, for instance, when you are talking on the telephone, can you tell that the person at the other end is just out of bed, or excited, or tired, etc., without his saying so? In ordinary social intercourse our total manner of utterance frequently reveals far more than our actual words intend. Moreover, sometimes we develop physical mannerisms—twiddling with a button, scratching the nose, looking at everything except the persons addressed, or any of a thousand possibilities—which have nothing to do with our intended message but which nevertheless will not only detract from it but may arouse disapproval for it even to the point of antagonism.

Since you know that speech entails visible movement, that speech in the history of mankind has been preponderantly face to face, and that man finds meaning in what he sees, whether the meaning is intended or not, the visible aspects of speech hold inescapable importance for you in your interpretative reading. You must induce in yourself the response you want to evoke from your listeners. To do this you will not only induce in yourself the total tensions requisite to effective utterance, but you will control all your visible behavior in such manner that everything your listeners see you do will corroborate, clarify, or intensify what they hear you say. You will avoid any visible action which will mislead your audience to get a meaning which you did not intend.

Let us shift our point of view a little and look at the visible aspects of oral reading skill from another angle. It is quite clear that this book is about the effective reading aloud of *literature*—that literature which is known as belles lettres, the literature that, along with music, painting, etc., is one of the fine arts. The pianist looks upon his concert performance, and his audience judges it, as a fine art. Great music requires—and fairly frequently gets—great performance. Great literature (other than drama) merits, but rarely gets, great rendition. The oral reader need be no less artist than the performing musician. He could be as great an artist if, granting comparable endowment, he spent comparable time and effort in developing his oral reading art.

Fundamental to art is arrangement, organization, design. A work of art is a complete fusion of elements into a total unit of pattern or design which is the very "meaning" of that work of art. To the degree that any element is extraneous to the design, the design suffers and the whole work falls short as art. The oral reader's rendition of literature entails his being seen as well as heard. His visible behavior, therefore, is inescapably a major element of his work of art and must be fused into and become a very part of the total design. We cannot neglect the visible elements of the oral reading design.

GENERAL BEARING

Apparel

Clothes may not make the man, but they may mar the reader. Since an audience reacts to the mere sight of a speaker, it is only common sense for the speaker to avoid an appearance which will impede his communication. You, as oral reader, will do well even as a student in your interpretation class to observe the canons of good taste in dress, cleanliness, appropriateness, unobtrusiveness.

Appropriateness and unobtrusiveness are the key words here. These must be determined by the total situation. In the classroom follow the dress standards of your peers, avoiding extremes which will distract. If you are asked to read at a party, dress appropriately for that particular party. If you want a rule: *Look your unobtrusive best!* If your reading is to be part of a formal program, the degree of formality will clearly dictate appropriate dress. Should you some day achieve sufficient fame to earn solo professional billing, appropriateness may even mean white tie and tails—something less might be distractingly conspicuous.

Look your unobtrusive best for each particular occasion.

Should you read "in costume"? If there is absolutely no doubt in your own mind that character or period costume is unquestionably the most appropriate apparel, our answer is "maybe." Otherwise, "never." Would dressing in a costume of mid-eighteenth century Germany improve Van Cliburn's playing of a Bach concerto? Think carefully of your purpose.

Posture

Along with what you are wearing your audience will react to the way you carry yourself—your walk and your posture. These constitute your general bearing. Are you poised or not? If your audience considers that you lack poise you have a difficult hurdle at the outset. So you had better cultivate poise.

The evidence by which an audience recognizes poise is complete but dynamic physical balance. A superb example is a champion diver balanced on his toes and the balls of his feet on the very edge of a high diving board, preparatory to making a successful championship back jackknife. There is nothing static about his poise: it is fluid, it is dynamic, it is balanced, it is, if you will, beautifully dignified. Poise itself is a fusion. When you walk between two points you cover a certain distance, expend a certain amount of energy, during a certain period of time. Poise requires a nice balance or fusion of these elements: just enough energy to produce the optimum movement to carry you the precise distance. Too much or too little of any one of these elements destroys the balance which is discerned as poise. Fidgeting, jerkiness, undue haste, slouching, poorly placed center of gravity—each diminishes poise and contributes to confusion.

Adopt a bearing that suggests comfortable dignity. Stand tall with ears and sternum high. Get your center of gravity where it requires the least muscular tension to maintain it. Avoid the ramrod stiffness of standing at military "attention." Be ready for easy and immediate movement. If there is a lectern before you, remember it was not put there to hold you up. Avoid slumping on it with elbows or forearms.

Holding the Book

How are you going to manage the book or manuscript during your oral reading? After all there are but two feasible possibilities: you will hold it or you will put it on a support of some kind. Which procedure will be most effective? Reading a story to a small intimate group may best be managed by holding your book, whereas reading even the same story to a large audience may be more effective if you use a lectern or reading stand. In the classroom one student may prefer to hold his book, but another will feel more at home if his book is held for him. Sometimes students feel a reluctance to try to use a stand simply because they have never done it. Where the situation readily permits the use of a reading stand we strongly recommend it. The chief reason for such recommendation is that it gives you greater freedom. If you are reading from unbound manuscript, you can manage separate sheets more unobtrusively if they are on a stand. If the book from which you are to read is a very large volume, by all means put it on a stand. Why? How comfortable would you feel listening to and watching a reader holding a very large and heavy book?

Movement

A popular song of many years ago expressed the whole philosophy of bodily movement in a single line, "Every little movement has a meaning all its own." Every movement your audience sees you make will evoke some response or other. Even lack of visible movement is significant and will evoke response. Therefore it is only common sense to direct all activity toward appropriate meaning. Let us examine the general messages which your visible behavior can convey.

To make clear to whom the words are addressed (or who is speaking to whom). Let us imagine that you are going to read aloud Dickens' *A Christmas Carol.* You deem it fitting to make some introductory comment. This you will do extemporaneously, looking your audience squarely in the eyes: you are saying *your* words to *your* listeners. They know this because of the words themselves and because they see you looking at and talking to them directly. Having made your introduction and opened your book, you are ready to begin. As a cue to your audience that your next words will be read from the text, look very deliberately at the text, shift your posture just enough to indicate you are now the reader (storyteller), then look up at your audience and tell them the first two sentences. (Turn to page 118.) Then glance back at the text, and while your eyes are on it read "The register of his burial was signed by the clergyman," then look at your audience again and finish the sentence looking your audience squarely in the eyes. And so proceed.

Of course, if your audience is more than one person you cannot look everybody in the eye simultaneously, but you can establish a communicative eye contact first with one, and then with another in another part of the room in such a way that every person listening, though he be one of a large audience, will feel you are speaking directly to everybody. He, together with everybody else in the audience, can see that you are.

We have been very explicit in the last two paragraphs. However, do not infer that the specific eye contacts we suggested are the only correct ones. By your whole bearing in general and by your eyes in particular you make it unmistakably clear that the opening paragraphs of *A Christmas Carol* are addressed directly to your audience to whom you are bringing Dickens, the omniscient author.

But what are you going to do with words like these?

LET ME CONFESS

Let me confess that we two must be twain,
Although our undivided loves are one:
So shall those blots that do with me remain,
Without thy help, by me be borne alone.
In our two loves there is but one respect,
Though in our lives a separable spite,
Which though it alter not love's sole effect,
Yet doth it steal sweet hours from love's delight.
I may not evermore acknowledge thee,
Lest my bewailèd guilt should do thee shame,
Nor thou with public kindness honour me,
Unless thou take that honour from thy name.
   But do not so: I love thee in such sort,
   As, thou being mine, mine is thy good report.
—William Shakespeare, Sonnet XXXVI (1609)

It is perfectly clear that these words are not addressed directly to the reader as was the case with "Marley was dead to begin with." They were written to be read and heard, but they are addressed to an absent lover. If you maintain the same kind of direct contact and seem to be addressing your audience as "thee" they will be embarrassed and you should be. Here you will not look your audience in the eye when you look away from the book. You must seem to be seeing with your "mind's eye," not with a physical optical focus. Maybe you can suggest this addressing of one not present by looking at the book the whole time. However, it can probably better be suggested, for instance, by looking at the book, say, for the first three words, then looking away toward the horizon as if to think aloud the remainder of the first line and all of the second. You are reading *for* your audience but you make it clear that the words are not addressed directly to them.

In the following excerpt two men are speaking to each other. You must show when Cassius is speaking and that he is speaking to Brutus. This you can do by looking up, say, 40 or 45 degrees to your right and seeming to see Brutus a few feet away facing you. When Brutus replies to Cassius, look 40 or

45 degrees to your left and seem to see Cassius frowning at you. Read the dialogue aloud and make it clear by your visible action who is speaking and who is listening. Thus the directions in which you look up from your book and the focus of your eyes can help inform your audience who is speaking to whom. Determining who is speaking to whom is a nice problem and is not always as easily solved as in the foregoing examples. We shall say more about it later.

BRUTUS AND CASSIUS

CASSIUS[1]

    That you have wronged me doth appear in this:
    You have condemned and noted Lucius Pella
    For taking bribes here of the Sardians;
    Wherein my letters, praying on his side,
    Because I knew the man was slighted off,—

BRUTUS

    You wronged yourself to write in such a case.

CASSIUS

    In such a time as this it is not meet
    That every nice offence should bear his comment.

BRUTUS

    Let me tell you, Cassius, you yourself
    Are much condemned to have an itching palm,
    To sell and mart your offices for gold
    To undeservers.

CASSIUS

    I, an itching palm!
    You know that you are Brutus that speaks this,
    Or, by the gods, this speech were else your last.

BRUTUS

    The name of Cassius honours this corruption,
    And chastisement doth therefore hide his head.

CASSIUS

    Chastisement!

BRUTUS

    Remember March, the Ides of March remember.
    Did not great Julius bleed for justice' sake?
    What villain touched his body, that did stab,

---

[1] Of course you will not read aloud "CASSIUS," "BRUTUS," etc.

And not for justice? What, shall one of us,
That struck the foremost man of all this world
But for supporting robbers, shall we now
Contaminate our fingers with base bribes,
And sell the mighty space of our large honours
For so much trash as may be graspèd thus?
I had rather be a dog and bay the moon,
Than such a Roman.
    —William Shakespeare, *Julius Caesar* (1599)

To mark transitions. A good speaker organizes his material carefully by using a well-designed outline. The body of his speech is organized into carefully thought out main heads and each main head is carefully developed. As he completes the presentation, he will probably bridge the end of one main division and the beginning of the next by some transitional phrase such as "This leads us to my next point," "So much for this, now let's look at the other side of the picture," or "Now how does this fit with . . .," etc., and as he says it, he is likely to change his posture, shift his weight, or even take a step or two. If he is an effective speaker he will do this even if he is reading his speech. This helps his audience to *see* that a transition is taking place.

Now narrative is frequently made up of episodes. When reading narrative you can show the ending of one episode and the beginning of the next by appropriate transitional movement. A shifting of weight from one foot to the other, a step or two, will wordlessly say, "We have finished this part; now let's go on to the next." If you are reading sitting down, you can shift your posture, cross or uncross your feet, change the manner of holding your book, etc. The degree of formality of the occasion must be kept in mind, of course.

Read the following allegory. Where should you make visible transitions?

ALLEGORY OF MAN AND GADGETS

Once upon a time there was a rich man who had so many slaves he didn't know what to do—and even if he had known, he wouldn't have had time to do it.

He divided his servants into companies and set captains over them; captains into corps and set officials over them. These were the only ones of his servants whom he would see personally.

Even so, the deputies were so numerous and the problems of managing the slaves to the best purpose so complex, just by virtue of the size of the establishment, that the rich man was forced to spend all his time advising, or hearing, or ordering his deputies.

The king had heard about this man's wealth. He said to himself: "Surely so rich a man with so many servants will have accomplished some great or attractive thing in his life. I shall go and see what it is."

Finding, however, that the man had built no temple, nor ever journeyed to learn the ways of other people, never written a poem, or a book about the beauties of the king's law, the king was disappointed and perplexed.

"And you," he reproached the man, "you have so many servants to do all else for you."

The man bowed respectfully and replied: "Sire, I have so many slaves that I am slave of my slaves."

Now there's Joe Doakes just down the street—you know him as well as I do. Cuts his lawn with a power mower, shaves with an electric razor, opens his garage doors with a beam from his car's headlights, gets his news by radio-clock that wakes him and tunes in the station every morning at the right hour, stokes his furnace by thermostat that turns on the oil burner at 6 a.m. regularly and slows down its operation at 11 p.m.

What with air conditioning, automatic egg beater, dish washing machine, deep freeze, the Doakeses are the most mechanized family unit on the street. But as Mrs. Doakes was telling her spouse just the other day: "We don't seem to have as much time as we used to for going out to see people, or talking, or reading—I do play the piano a bit, still, but . . ."

But . . . they have so many time savers that they haven't got a moment left over—after they've taken the car for a check-up at the service station and explained to the repairman what the television does just when they want it most.

But why go on? This, too, is an allegory, with just enough truth in it to sharpen up a challenge: Are you a man's man, or a gadget's gadget?

—Carlyle Morgan, editorial in
Christian Science Monitor (October 18, 1958)

The first three paragraphs are the opening unit of the story. "The king" introduces a new element and the next unit. The silence between the third and fourth paragraphs should be longer than that between any two of the first three, and if the silence is filled with a transitory shift of position the audience will be on the lookout for the new development.

The next transition is between the seventh and eighth paragraphs. The silent passage from "I am slave to my slaves," to "Now there's Joe Doakes just down the street" should be longer and have even a greater transitional movement than the first one.

The words "But why go on?" may well be accompanied by a concluding transitional shrug.

To clarify ideas. Any visible bodily movement whose intention, consciously or unconsciously, is to help convey a message is a gesture.

You are asked how to get to the fire escape. You say, "Go through that door there and turn to the left," and you point to a particular door as you say the words "that door there" and flick your hand to the left as you say "turn to the left."

You say, "There was about an inch and a half left in the bottle," and you indicate the amount between your thumb and index finger; or "The fish was eighteen inches long," and visibly estimate the length between your hands; or "A spiral staircase is one that goes like this," and with your index finger describe a helix in the air; or shake your head during "I just can't see it"; or touch your chest with your fingers on "Do you mean me?" etc., etc., etc.

Gestures can clarify ideas by indication of places, by description of shapes, sizes, and actions, by suggestion of concepts and attitudes.

Say each of the following three or four times, using a different clarifying gesture each time. Select what seems to you the particular movement which gives the greatest clarity to each.

Go south to Center Street and turn west.

He is eight years old and comes up to here on me.

The tea table was possibly thirty inches in diameter.

It slithered along like a snake.

The tundra stretched away as far as eye could see.

Let's be perfectly frank and put our cards on the table.

I'm going to reject the whole business.

I should worry; it means nothing to me.

Note there is a certain literal quality about movement which helps to clarify ideas.

To reveal feelings. Just as movement can aid intellectual grasp, so can it reveal feeling, mood, emotive response. What we shall call intellectual and emotive gestures differ from each other in energy, speed, and compass, and the latter tend to be less literal than the former. During intellectual pursuits bodily movement tends to be highly localized toward those motions essential to the pursuit. During emotional states bodily activity tends to become general. For instance, as you write, unemotionally, your visible activity is largely confined to the minimum of movement necessary for writing. However, when you were first learning to write it was an emotional experience and your whole organism was generally involved. You may have hooked your toes on the rung of your chair, bit your tongue, nodded your head from side to side as you made the letters—indeed, tensed all your voluntary muscles. As intellectuality increased, that is, as you gained control, you eliminated those tensions which the act of writing did not need. Even now, however, if your writing becomes emotional, you will find yourself gripping your pen harder, tensing your muscles generally. Compare your bodily activity in copying information from a book in the library and writing an important exam for which you are not well prepared.

(Which is the more intellectual and which the more emotional of the following activities: (1) threading a needle by an expert seamstress or (2) threading a needle by a clumsy husband who finds he must sew on a button while his wife is away?)

Following this pattern, intellectual gestures are largely confined to the agents making them, whereas emotive gestures are part of a more generalized activity. Of course, a given movement may at once clarify an idea and reveal a feeling. For example, "Wring the towel out like this" can be clarified by going through the appropriate descriptive motions of wringing out a wet cloth. But in "I would take the greatest pleasure in wringing the scoundrel's neck" hatred for the scoundrel can be revealed by using basically the descriptive gesture used formerly, but exaggerating it: using more energy, greater tension; slowing up the action; and lengthening the opposing arcs described by the hands. Note that in the intellectual movement your elbows may remain fairly close to your sides, whereas in the emotive gesture you may raise your elbows almost shoulder high in order to get a greater purchase on the scoundrel's neck and twist it right in two. Moreover, you will probably discover that increased tension has gone clear to your toes.

More energy throughout the body in general, wider compass and either slower or faster movement in the gesturing agents in particular tend to characterize gestures which reveal feeling.

There will seem to be exceptions. The curl of a lip into a recognizable sneer can be an eloquent movement to reveal feeling and certainly it requires fewer ergs than to describe with appropriate action a circular staircase, but the psychological nature of the former carries an emotive strength which the latter lacks.

Try each of the following with four or five emotive gestures and select what you feel is the most revealing for each. Is it easier to find more reasonably appropriate emotive gestures for a given situation than it is to find intellectual gestures? Why?

> I loathe the very sight of him.
>
> Don't scrape your finger nails on the blackboard!
>
> It doesn't make a particle of difference to me.
>
> Scat! Get out of here quick.
>
> I shall welcome your suggestion.
>
> I am completely all in.

Try preceding the last sentence with a very deep and prolonged sigh. What visible movements can you add to this further to reveal utter fatigue—mental as well as physical?

To disclose character. Posture, general stance, amount and nature of movement can help to disclose character.

Standing still, fully but not stiffly erect, with no visible movement beyond necessary articulation, will help establish Othello's assured and quiet but powerful dignity in the opening lines of his great defense:

> **Most potent, grave, and reverend signiors,**
> **My very noble and approved good masters:**
> **That I have ta'en away this old man's daughter,**
> **It is most true:**

A general slumping of the weight on the heels, a drooping of the shoulders, a listless hanging of the hands help listeners to realize the dejected and cowardly frustration of Bernard Shaw's Dauphin when Joan says she wants to see him sitting on the throne and he replies

> **What is the good of sitting on the throne when the other fellows**
> **give all the orders? However!** [*he sits enthroned, a piteous figure*]
> **here is the king for you! Look your fill at the poor devil.**
> **—*Saint Joan* (1924)**

The reader can suggest character by his total behavior. That is, he reveals character through his symbolic action.

Ad lib lines which might be spoken by each of the following characters and speak them with visible behavior which suggests the characters.

Ebenezer Scrooge   Lucy of "I Love Lucy"
Santa Claus   Aunt Jemimah
Marshal Dillon   Portia
Huckleberry Finn   Queen Elizabeth I

Having tried to point out the general messages which visible behavior can help to convey, let us review them in the light of some of the problems they present.

Who is speaking to whom? Turn to page 83 and read again what is said about social intent. Although an author is always writing for those who he hopes will read him, he may use various devices for addressing his readers.

He may address them directly in his own person as most essayists do. See "Allegory of Man and Gadgets," page 296. The storyteller often does this. In order to accentuate this directness he may even apostrophize his absent "audience" as Dickens sometimes did with "gentle reader."

When you read such material to an audience, remember you are speaking for the author directly to your hearers. Make them feel personally addressed; look them in the eye and let them see that you are aware of their response.

He may address his readers still very directly but also by assuming the role of someone other than himself, as Poe does in "The Tell-Tale Heart." This calls for a careful study of the text to discover the character, the personality, of the person whose role the author has assumed. When you read such material address your audience very directly and use such behavior—visible as well as audible— as will suggest the personality of the author's imagined mouthpiece. This may call for modified posture, characteristic gesture, as well as appropriate dialect and vocal quality.[2] With this in mind read the excerpt from *Seidman and Son* by Elic Moll on page 146.

He may address his audience—not directly—but through the ears of an imagined listener (reader), as Shakespeare does in "Let Me Confess." If, in reading these aloud, you address your audience directly you will embarrass them. Your audience must sense the apostrophe—the addressing of someone not actually present. You can achieve this by seeming to recall in your mind's eye the person to whom the words are addressed.

He may address his audience through the conversation of imagined characters.

[2] In the event that the question of distinctions between *interpretation, impersonation* and *acting* arises here, you will find it discussed in Chapter Ten, p. 379.

The dramatist uses this method almost entirely. He wants his audience to hear and see his characters speaking their allotted lines to each other. Turn back to the Brutus-Cassius conversation on page 295. Shakespeare is here concerned not with revealing himself but with revealing two characters in heated conversation.

He may combine any or all of these procedures as a novelist may do. In other words, you must study the text very carefully in order to answer the question, "Who is speaking to whom?"

DO NOT BE MISLED BY QUOTATION MARKS!

Who, exactly, and how many persons are speaking in the following passage?

GOSSIP

Well, let me tell you, Mrs. McGarrity, Those three mean no good, I can tell you. You can't trust one of them. They didn't know I was in the next booth and I couldn't help hearing their gossip. Mrs. Flint said, "You can't trust that McGarrity woman," that's just what she said, and Pamela Wearweather said, "You're absolutely right, Eudora. I told her confidentially about Mabel making a mess of things and she went right straight to Angelique here and told her everything. Didn't she, Angelique?" And Mrs. Gruber spoke up and said,—I just wish you could have heard her —she spoke right up and said, "She certainly did, and you should have heard what she said about you, Pamela; she said, 'You are as big a trouble maker as that Hennessy woman.'" That's what Angelique Gruber said you said Mrs. McGarrity; that you said, "Pamela Wearweather is as big a trouble maker as that Hennessy woman." That's me, Mrs. McGarrity! Well, I nearly died, and I would have got up right then and there and told them what I thought of them, but Mrs. Wearweather said, "Take my advice and don't tell either of them anything," and Angelique Gruber said, "They're the worst busybodies I know," meaning you and me, Mrs. McGarrity. You should have heard Eudora Flint then! She said, "I wouldn't trust either of them as far as I could sling a bull by the tail." Now what do you think of that, Mrs. McGarrity?

Who is speaking and who is addressed? Read it aloud so that the speaker-hearer relationship is perfectly clear.

You see that in spite of all the quotation marks, the quotation marks within quotation marks, only one person is speaking and only one person is addressed. Mrs. Hennessy does all the talking. She quotes Mrs. Flint, Mrs. Wearweather,

Mrs. Gruber and she also quotes Mrs. Gruber quoting Mrs. McGarrity, and Mrs. McGarrity listens to all of it but never says a word. Four persons are quoted but only one person speaks.

In contrast to this, when Dickens quotes Scrooge or Bob Cratchit *et al.* in *A Christmas Carol* he wants whoever reads the story or whoever hears it read to get the "feel" of each character *speaking;* he wants his "audience" to imagine they are hearing Scrooge, Bob Cratchit, etc. Dickens wants only to be the medium of transmission between his audience and his characters. Therefore, when you read aloud what Scrooge and Cratchit said, you become (for Dickens) the medium of transmission between the author's intended speakers and your audience.

Careful attention to this matter will save you the "bellowcutionary" error so frequently heard when readers speak the quoted lines in the following poem as if the child in question were speaking them.

LITTLE BOY BLUE

The little toy dog is covered with dust,
    But sturdy and staunch he stands;
The little toy soldier is red with rust,
    And his musket molds in his hands.
Time was when the little toy dog was new,
    And the soldier was passing fair;
And that was the time when our Little Boy Blue
    Kissed them and put them there.

"Now don't you go till I come," he said,
    "And don't you make any noise!"
So, toddling off to his trundle bed,
    He dreamt of the pretty toys;
And, as he was dreaming, an angel song
    Awakened our Little Boy Blue—
Oh! the years are many, the years are long,
    But the little toy friends are true!

Ay, faithful to Little Boy Blue they stand,
    Each in the same old place,
Awaiting the touch of a little hand,
    The smile of a little face;
And they wonder, as waiting the long years through
    In the dust of that little chair,

What has become of our Little Boy Blue,
  Since he kissed them and put them there.
                              —Eugene Field (c. 1885)

This poem at best is pretty sentimental, but it is still widely used. When a reader "renders" it and assumes the role of the child in the quoted speech the whole thing becomes sheer bathos.

To mark transitions. The chief problem here is magnitude: how big a bridge is necessary at any given transition? When is a transition big enough to require visible symbolization? When it indicates a definite break in story, mood, or thought.

Remember, such breaks are part of the structure of literature; they must be very evident and they must be bridged. The bigger the break, the bigger the bridge.

BIG TRANSITIONS.   Good examples of big breaks requiring big bridges are to be found between chapters of a novel; between acts and often between scenes of a play. Dickens divides *A Christmas Carol* into five chapters which he calls "staves." Here following in order are the endings and the beginnings of these staves:

STAVE ONE

. . . And being, from the emotion he had undergone, or the fatigues of the day, or his glimpse of the Invisible World, or the dull conversation of the Ghost, or the lateness of the hour, much in need of repose, went straight to bed, without undressing, and fell asleep upon the instant.

STAVE TWO
THE FIRST OF THE THREE SPIRITS

When Scrooge awoke, it was so dark, that looking out of bed, he could scarcely distinguish window from opaque walls of his chamber. He was endeavoring to pierce the darkness with his ferret eyes, when the chimes of a neighboring church struck the four quarters. . . .

. . . He was conscious of being exhausted, and overcome by an irresistible drowsiness; and, further, of being in his own bedroom. He gave the cap a parting squeeze, in which his hand relaxed; and had barely time to reel to bed, before he sank into a heavy sleep.

STAVE THREE
THE SECOND OF THE THREE SPIRITS

Awaking in the middle of a prodigiously tough snore, and sitting up in bed to get his thoughts together, Scrooge had no occasion to be told that the bell was again upon the stroke of One. . . .

. . . Scrooge looked about him for the Ghost, and saw it not. As the last stroke ceased to vibrate, he remembered the prediction of old Jacob Marley, and lifting up his eyes, beheld a solemn phantom, draped and hooded, coming, like a mist along the ground, toward him.

STAVE FOUR
THE LAST OF THE SPIRITS

The Phantom slowly, gravely, silently, approached. When it came near him, Scrooge bent down upon his knee; for in the very air through which the spirit moved it seemed to scatter gloom and mystery. . . .

. . . Holding up his hands in one last prayer to have his fate reversed, he saw an alteration in the Phantom's hood and dress. It shrunk, collapsed, and dwindled down into a bedpost.

STAVE FIVE
THE END OF IT

Yes! and the bedpost was his own. The bed was his own, the room was his own. Best and happiest of all, the Time before him was his own, to make amends in! . . .

Here we have four chapter breaks: each break must be made, but in each case, there must be a transitional bridge from the end of one stave to the beginning of the next. You may choose to cut stave numbers and their titles, and communicate the break wholly with transitional movement.

Note that these passages from one stave to the next are by no means equal. From Stave One to Stave Two and from Two to Three there is an actual lapse of time, and in each case one episode is concluded and another begun. From Three to Four and from Four to Five there is no lapse of time. From Three to Four there is no break in the action. Here the break is a subtle psychological one. Dickens might have concluded Stave Four with

"Scrooge looked about him for the Ghost, and saw it not," because certainly the Phantom introduces a new episode. But such a break would have lessened the relentlessness of the cumulative events. The disappearance of the second spirit accentuates the striking of the clock; as Scrooge becomes aware of the ominous final stroke he recalls Marley's prophecy and immediately he sees the most awesome of the three spirits. He has no time further to prepare himself; he must face what is relentlessly coming. But the Phantom *does* introduce a new episode. Listeners (and readers) must be made aware of that, and also be given opportunity to gird up their loins to take what is coming. A certain psychological breather is necessary.

A pause after "toward him," filled with a subtle increase in muscular tension and a turning of the page in such manner as to say, "It's coming and you can't escape it," effectively prepares for and enhances the ominous mystery of "The Phantom slowly, gravely, silently, approached."

Again, from Four to Five the physical action is continuous, but there is a big break, or better, a big change, in spirit, mood, tone, tempo. After "bedpost" just enough pause to show that the episode is concluded and with "Yes! and the bedpost was his own," a sudden change of tensions to happy relief, to recognition that salvation is possible: an actual standing taller, weight on the balls of the feet ready for action, a lifting of the sternum, a look which tells, "Best and happiest of all, the Time before him was his own, to make amends in!"

Practice these transitions until you can completely communicate the appropriate breaks between staves and the visible bridges which properly hold them together.

Transitions between acts (and usually between scenes) of a play more often than not require verbal, audible, as well as visible, bridging. This will be further dealt with in Chapter Eleven.

Big transitions may occur without such labeling as chapters, parts, acts, or scenes. In "The Young King" (see page 365) there are four big transitions. None of them is verbally labeled; they are indicated simply by increased spacing. Each one must be eloquently made by pause and visible action.

LESSER TRANSITIONS.   In skillful prose the ending of a paragraph and the beginning of the next indicates a transition. However, such interparagraph transitions may not be big enough to need visible movement to help make them clear.

Turn again to "The Young King." There are seven numbered paragraphs before the first big transition. The transition from

(1) to (2) can be achieved vocally, but can be helped by raising your eyes from the book and looking directly at your audience as you say, "And, indeed, it was the hunters who had found him." There is no break here. However, thinking takes a different turn between (2) and (3). A pause here need be very slight, but a shifting of weight with "Such, at least" will help indicate the change in psychological direction. (4) and (5) follow closely, ending with a general statement about the boy's love of beauty. (6) takes a new tack, bringing us from the generality in (5) to his specific concern in (6). The pause before (6) should be small and a visible shift with "But what had occupied him most" will help to make clear the change from general to specific. (7) brings the first episode to a conclusion. Such transition as there is between (6) and (7) is a subtle one and can be managed vocally.

To clarify ideas. Here we are concerned chiefly with intellectual gesture. When visible movement *will help* describe an object, locate a place, illustrate an action, etc., use it. We have italicized *will help*. It would be obviously silly to indicate the size and shape of a baseball in reading: "Jimmy looked longingly at the baseball in the window," because such movement—descriptive of a baseball as it may be—distracts. "Baseball" is not the idea. However, the sentence, "A baseball is this size" will be very greatly helped with appropriate descriptive gesture.

"He caught a trout that was fully eighteen inches long" might be made clearer (and more emphatic) by indicating an estimated foot and a half between the hands. Even though this visible estimate may miss eighteen inches by an inch or two, it may add clarity.

"If you go straight ahead two blocks and then turn to your right" will be clarified if you accompany "straight ahead" with a forward movement of your right hand, and "turn to your right" with a hand movement to the right. In so doing you are saying the same thing visibly as well as audibly. Simultaneous appeal to two senses makes a stronger appeal than either one separately.

The foregoing are examples of pretty literal intellectual gesture. Intellectual gestures need not be always so literal.

Eric Knight, in his delightful story, *The Flying Yorkshireman,* in describing one of Sam's early flights says,

> . . . He felt quite uncomfortable, somehow, but he thought that only natural. Then he turned over to look down at the floor. Very slowly he began revolving his body. And the minute he did that all feeling of awkwardness left him.

In this passage the reader must have very direct contact with his audience. "Then" can be clarified—it introduces a very important development—with an appropriate manual emphasis, finishing the movement with the palm more up than vertical. Then as you read, "Very slowly he began revolving his body," turn your hand over with the palm down, synchronizing the movement through the whole sentence, so that by the time you say the word "body" your palm is down. This will clarify "slowly" and at the same time illustrate Sam's turning over. Accentuate "And the minute he did that" with an emphatic stretching of the fingers on the word "minute"; clarify "all feeling of awkwardness left him" by an inclusive movement of your hand away from your body—three or four inches are plenty—on the word "all" and easily dropping your hand to where gravitation will take it, on "left him."

This may seem very mechanical indeed. It is mechanical. But it is psychological as well. There is no communication whatsoever without mechanics. Practice the foregoing excerpt until you do it effectively, so that your classmates perceiving you get a single message through both eyes and ears. Note that with a continuous visible movement you have clarified six ideas: You have (1) subtly but effectively called attention to an important development ("Then"); (2) illustrated Sam's turning face down; (3) showed that he did it slowly ("Very slowly he began revolving his body."); (4) emphasized the importance of that instant ("minute"); (5) indicated that every bit of his awkwardness ("all") (6) was conquered ("left him"). Do you find that as you build this into a single act of communication your bodily movement tends to improve your vocal utterance?

So often the manner of doing is quite as important as the doing itself. As was the case of "slowly" above. Practice the following, using visible movement that is not a literal illustration of taking hold of the boy's shoulder, but which clarifies the firmness and gentleness of the action:

He placed his hand on the boy's shoulder—firmly, but, Oh, so gently.

You may expect an increase toward literalness in intellectual gestures when they are a part of dialogue. Very often, a character's words are incomplete without appropriate movement. It is always a bit disturbing, for instance, to see someone read Hamlet's advice to the players, "Nor do not saw the air too much with your hand, thus," and never give the slightest hint what "thus" means.

To reveal feelings. Emotive or affective gesture, as we have pointed out, has as its purpose the revealing of attitude, of feeling. Here are gestures which are least literal. An emotive gesture may be literal—remember the neck wringing example—but its affectiveness lies more in its general manner of performance than in its literalness. In the sentence, "In his fury, he pounded the table with a clenched fist," the attitude which produced the action is quite as important as the action itself. Indeed, the action has no point aside from its motive. If, as you read that sentence, you actually pound a table with a clenched fist, you will not only be very literal, you will be melodramatic. The essence of melodrama is action which eclipses the motive which produced it. If, as you read the sentence, you bring your clenched fist up breast high and clench it so that you can feel the tensions throughout your entire arm and with some increase of tension even in your torso, a short downward stroke of three or four inches will reveal the generating attitude and will avoid distracting melodramatic literalness.

Most affective gestures are much less intense. A lift of an eyebrow, a smile, a shake of the head, a shrug of the shoulder, a manual rejection or acceptance of an idea—each can reveal a feeling. The problem is clearly stated in the questions:

Can I better communicate this feeling by using an emotive gesture?

What movement will be most communicative?

We have said it is important for you to induce in yourself the response you want to invoke in your hearers. If you do this with abandon, your own feeling will tend to lead you to certain overt activities. Note what they are. What are your urges to physical tensions as you read?

These should be good cues to the gestures you will ultimately use. Time and again we find students, as they are reading, showing impulses toward movement but "pulling their punches" so that the movement never comes off as an affective gesture. We have no better advice in this matter than to say: while you are practicing *obey the impulse*. It may at first come off a bit crudely, but if it comes off, you have something to refine. Crude oil precedes high octane, and what a lot of refining between the two!

A word or two about refinement. Affective gesture has a very respectable lineage. We have certain basic physiological responses in common with all motile life. It is evident in so simple an organism as the jellyfish. It recoils upon inimical stimuli; it approaches beneficial objects (in its case, food); it adjusts to unavoidable situations which, though possibly uncomfortable, are not bad enough to destroy it.

We withdraw from danger; we go after what we want; and we put up with what we cannot help, or arrange things the best we can. We drop things we do not want, and in order to drop something we open a hand downward. We take hold of something by closing a hand on it and drawing it to us. We arrange things with many movements—relinquishing, clutching, pushing, pulling, etc. These basic movements carry over and become gestures when we are dealing with ideas, attitudes, policies, etc. We can reject or accept ideas, or we can temporize and try for compromise.

Use visible rejection activity to reveal feeling with each of the following utterances:

> Nuts to you, brother!
>
> I will have none of this exile and this stranger.
>
> Away, slight man.
>
> That's neither here nor there: It doesn't make sense.
>
> This policy is out of the question.
>
> Let me not name it to you, you chaste stars!

How many different affective gestures can you devise for each one? Note that though you have a wide latitude for variety, all appropriately affective gestures you have used belong to the rejection activity.

Devise various affective gestures for the following:

> Let me hear your proposition.
>
> I like this idea very much.
>
> I am willing to accept all truth.
>
> > Now, sir, be judge yourself
> > Whether I in any just term am affined
> > To love the Moor.
>
> This is my platform. You have heard exactly what I stand for. I shall welcome any suggestion or support which will further the principles I have enunciated.
>
> I shall hang on to this doctrine with all the tenacity of which I am capable.

By way of exploration, work with a group of three or four of your classmates and see how wide a variety of affective movements the group can discover for each of the foregoing utterances. Such experimentation will increase your awareness of both importance and scope of the visible aspects of oral reading.

We must not leave this discussion without reëmphasizing the importance of totality. A half-done or incomplete gesture can be as distracting and frustrating as inept lack of movement.

To disclose character. Our problem here is visibly to suggest character and yet remain reader; to disclose character with adequate variety of movement and gesture within the limits imposed by the reading situation. If your text is on a reading stand your area of movement is strictly limited, but your hands are relatively free for great variety and subtlety of gesture. If you hold your book, you can move over a wider area, but the necessity for holding the book limits gesture. If you have memorized the text and "read" without book or stand, you have wide latitude indeed—you are limited only *by what you can make convincing.* Within the limits imposed any posture, movement, or gesture which will convincingly reveal character is good. If you are reading a story put into the mouth of an eccentric character and the entire story is in his words, you can do a pretty complete job of assuming his general bearing, his movement within the available area, his peculiar mannerisms. If within the same text you must suggest two or more characters, you cannot give to each such complete visible characterization that the change from one to another becomes cumbersome or distractingly apparent. Transition from one character to another should be as fully credible as the behavior which suggests a given character. Go as far as you convincingly can but do not go so far that you cannot get convincingly back.

EXERCISES AND ASSIGNMENTS

Managing the Book

Turn to "Allegory of Man and Gadgets," p. 296. Work in groups of three or four classmates. Read it aloud sitting down, holding the book. Read it standing up, holding the book. Read it using a reading stand. Make each reading as effective as you can.

To Make Clear Who Is Speaking to Whom

1. Using the Dickens selections in Chapter Four, pp. 160–161, establish unmistakably direct contact with an audience.
2. Read Edmund's speech, "Memories," p. 190, and make your listeners "see" and feel Tyrone's presence. Note that Edmund would not look at his father during the entire reminiscence, but he would look at him directly on the first line of his speech, and when he says "—that last, eh?" and "Want to hear mine?" and possibly on "—if you want to put it that way."

3. Read aloud the following scene making the speakers visibly distinct. Make the letter reading clear.

MRS. MALAPROP AND CAPTAIN ABSOLUTE

MRS. MAL.: Your being Sir Anthony's son, Captain, would itself be a sufficient accommodation; but from the ingenuity of your appearance, I am convinced you deserve the character here given of you.

ABS.: Permit me to say, madam, that as I never yet have had the pleasure of seeing Miss Languish, my principal inducement in this affair at present, is the honor of being allied to Mrs. Malaprop; of whose intellectual accomplishments, elegant manners, and unaffected learning, no tongue is silent.

MRS. MAL.: Sir, you do me infinite honor! I beg, Captain, you'll be seated. *(They sit)* Ah! few gentlemen, now-a-days, know how to value the ineffectual qualities in a woman! Few think how a little knowledge becomes a gentlewoman!—Men have no sense now but for the worthless flower of beauty!

ABS.: It is but too true, indeed, ma'am;—yet I fear our ladies should share the blame—they think our admiration of beauty so great, that knowledge in them would be superfluous. Thus, like garden-trees, they seldom show fruit, till time has robbed them of the more specious blossom.—Few, like Mrs. Malaprop and the orange-tree, are rich in both at once!

MRS. MAL.: Sir, you overpower me with good breeding. *(Aside)* He is the very pineapple of politeness! You are not ignorant, Captain, that this giddy girl has somehow contrived to fix her affections on a beggarly, strolling, eavesdropping ensign, whom none of us have seen, and nobody knows anything of.

ABS.: Oh, I have heard the silly affair before.—I'm not at all prejudiced against her on that account.

MRS. MAL.: You are very good and very considerate, Captain. I am sure I have done everything in my power since I exploded the affair; long ago I laid my positive conjunctions on her, never to think on the fellow again:—I have since laid Sir Anthony's preposition before her; but, I am sorry to say, she seems resolved to decline every particle that I enjoin her.

ABS.: It must be very distressing, indeed, ma'am.

MRS. MAL.: Oh! it gives me the hydrostatics to such a degree.—I thought she had persisted from corresponding with him; but, behold this very day, I have interceded another letter from the fellow; I believe I have it in my pocket.

ABS.: *(Aside)* Oh, the devil! my last note.

MRS. MAL.: Ay, here it is.

ABS.: *(Aside)* Ay, my note indeed! O the little traitress Lucy.

MRS. MAL.: There, perhaps you may know the writing. *(Gives him the letter)*

ABS.:   I think I have seen the hand before—yes, I certainly must have seen this hand before—

MRS. MAL.:   Nay, but read it, Captain.

ABS. *(reads):   My soul's idol, my adored Lydia!*—Very tender indeed!

MRS. MAL.:   Tender! ay, and profane too, o' my conscience.

ABS. *(reads):   I am excessively alarmed at the intelligence you send me, the more so as my new rival*—

MRS. MAL.:   That's you, sir.

ABS. *(reads):   Has universally the character of being an accomplished gentleman, and a man of honor.*—Well, that's handsome enough.

MRS. MAL.:   Oh, the fellow has some design in writing so.

ABS.:   That he had, I'll answer for him, ma'am.

MRS. MAL.:   But go on, sir—you'll see presently.

ABS. *(reads):   As for the old weather-beaten she-dragon who guards you*—Who can he mean by that?

MRS. MAL.:   Me, sir!—me!—he means me!—There—what do you think now?—but go on a little further.

ABS.:   Impudent scoundrel!—*(Reads)   it shall go hard but I will elude her vigilance, as I am told that the same ridiculous vanity which makes her dress up her coarse features, and deck her dull chat with hard words which she don't understand*—

MRS. MAL.:   There, sir, an attack upon my language! what do you think of that?—an aspersion upon my parts of speech! was ever such a brute! Sure, if I reprehend anything in this world, it is the use of my oracular tongue, and a nice derangement of epitaphs.

ABS.:   He deserves to be hanged and quartered! Let me see—*(Reads)*—*same ridiculous vanity*—

MRS. MAL.:   You need not read it again, sir.

ABS.:   I beg pardon, ma'am.—*(Reads)   does also lay her open to the grossest deceptions from flattery and pretended admiration*—an impudent coxcomb!—*so that I have a scheme to see you shortly with the old harridan's consent, and even to make her a go-between in our interview.*—Was ever such assurance!

MRS. MAL.:   Did you ever hear anything like it?—he'll elude my vigilance, will he—yes, yes! ha! ha! he's very likely to enter these doors; —we will try who can plot best!

ABS.:   So we will, ma'am—so we will! Ha! ha! ha! a conceited puppy, ha! ha! ha!—Well, but Mrs. Malaprop, as the girl seems so infatuated by this fellow, suppose you were to wink at her corresponding with him for a little time—let her even plot an elopement with him —then do you connive at her escape—while I, just in the nick, will have the fellow laid by the heels, and fairly contrive to carry her off in his stead.

MRS. MAL.:   I am delighted with the scheme; never was anything better perpetrated!

—R. B. Sheridan, *The Rivals* (1775)

4. Establish the presence of Iago and Roderigo.

IAGO AND RODERIGO

IAGO: How now, Roderigo!

ROD.: I do not find that thou deal'st justly with me.

IAGO: What in the contrary?

ROD.: Every day thou daff'st me with some device, Iago; and rather, as it seems to me now, keep'st from me all conveniency that suppliest me with the least advantage of hope. I will indeed no longer endure it; nor am I yet persuaded to put up in peace what already I have foolishly suffered.

IAGO: Will you hear me, Roderigo?

ROD.: Faith, for I have heard too much, for your words and performance are no kin together.

IAGO: You charge me most unjustly.

ROD.: With nought but truth. I have wasted myself out of my means. The jewels you have had from me to deliver to Desdemona would half have corrupted a votarist: you have told me she hath received them and returned me expectations and comforts of sudden respect and acquaintance; but I find none.

IAGO: Well; go to; very well.

ROD.: Very well! go to! I cannot go to, man; nor 'tis not very well: by this hand, I say 'tis very scurvy, and begin to find myself fopped in it.

IAGO: Very well.

ROD.: I tell you 'tis not very well. I will make myself known to Desdemona: if she will return me my jewels, I will give over my suit and repent my unlawful solicitation; if not, assure yourself I will seek satisfaction of you.

IAGO: You have said now.

ROD.: Ay, and said nothing but what I protest intendment of doing.

IAGO: Why, now I see there's mettle in thee; and even from this instant do build on thee a better opinion than ever before. Give me thy hand, Roderigo: thou hast taken against me a most just exception; but yet, I protest, I have dealt more directly in thy affair.

ROD.: It hath not appeared.

IAGO: I grant indeed it hath not appeared, and your suspicion is not without wit and judgment. But, Roderigo, if thou hast that in thee indeed, which I have greater reason to believe now than ever, I mean purpose, courage and valour, this night show it: if thou the next night following enjoy not Desdemona, take me from this world with treachery and devise engines for my life.

ROD.: Well, what is it? is it within reason and compass?

IAGO: Sir, there is especial commission come from Venice to depute Cassio in Othello's place.

ROD.:   Is that true? Why then Othello and Desdemona return again
to Venice.

IAGO: O, no; he goes into Mauritania, and takes away with him the
fair Desdemona, unless his abode be lingered here by some accident:
wherein none can be so determinate as the removing of Cassio.

ROD.:   How do you mean, removing of him?

IAGO: Why, by making him uncapable of Othello's place; knocking
out his brains.

ROD.:   And that you would have me to do?

IAGO: Ay, if you dare do yourself a profit and a right. He sups tonight with a harlotry, and thither will I go to him: he knows not
yet of his honorable fortune. If you will watch his going thence,
which I will fashion to fall out between twelve and one, you may
take him at your pleasure: I will be near to second your attempt,
and he shall fall between us. Come, stand not amazed at it, but go
along with me; I will show you such a necessity in his death that
you shall think yourself bound to put it on him. It is now high supper time, and the night grows to waste: about it.

ROD.:   I will hear further reason for this.

IAGO: And you shall be satisfied.

—William Shakespeare, *Othello* (1622)

5. Go back to "The Proposal: II," p. 110, and rework it carefully in order to show
relative positions of characters.

To Mark Transitions

1. Read "Fast-Fish and Loose-Fish," p. 161, making the transitions visibly clear. Be
careful to address your listeners directly.
2. Re-do "Memories," p. 190. Where are transitional movements needed?
3. How many transitions are there in "The Illumination," p. 224?

To Clarify Ideas

1. Study Victor Hugo's description of Waterloo. Following the description, draw
the battlefield on paper. Then read it aloud using a reading stand and illustrate
the "A" with clear explanatory gestures. Work at it until visible and audible descriptions are fused into a single message.

WATERLOO

Those who would get a clear idea of the battle of Waterloo have
only to lay down upon the ground in their mind a capital A. The left
stroke of the A is the road from Nivelles, the right stroke is the road
from Genappe, the cross of the A is the sunken road from Ahan to
Braine-l'Alleud. The top of the A is Mount Saint Jean, Wellington is
there; the left-hand lower point is Hougomont, Reille is there with

Jerome Bonaparte; the right-hand lower point is La Belle Alliance, Napoleon is there. A little below the point where the cross of the A meets and cuts the right stroke, is La Haie Sainte. At the middle of this cross is the precise point where the final battle-word was spoken. There the lion is placed, the involuntary symbol of the supreme heroism of the Imperial Guard. The triangle contained at the top of the A, between the two strokes and the cross, is the plateau of Mount Saint Jean. The struggle for this plateau was the whole of the battle. The wings of the two armies extended to the right and left of the two roads from Genappe and from Nivelles; D'Erlon being opposite Picton, Reille opposite Hill. Behind the point of the A, behind the plateau of Mount Saint Jean, is the forest of Soignes. As to the plain itself, we must imagine a vast undulating country; each wave commanding the next, and these undulations rising toward Mount Saint Jean are there bounded by the forest.

Both generals had carefully studied the plain of Mount Saint Jean, now called the plain of Waterloo. Already in the preceding year, Wellington, with the sagacity of prescience, had examined it as a possible site for a great battle. On this ground and for this contest Wellington had the favorable side, Napoleon the unfavorable. The English army was above, the French army below.

—Victor Hugo, *Les Misérables* (1862)

2. Memorize the following selection and then tell it, using explanatory gestures.

A Pinhole Camera

Get a cardboard box—shoe box will do nicely. Glue the lid on so that the box is light-tight. Take a sharp knife and cut off about three inches from one end. Discard the smaller portion. Cover the open end of your "camera" with a piece of architect's tracing paper. A sheet of onion-skin paper will do. It is less sturdy than the tracing paper. Glue the paper tightly around the sides of the open end so that no light can get in except through the translucent—but not transparent—tracing paper. This is your film. Find the center of the closed end. This you can do by drawing diagonals from the opposite corners. The point of intersection of the diagonals will be the center. Pierce the point of intersection with a pin. Rotate the pin so as to smooth the inside edge of the pinhole. The pinhole is your lens.

Light a candle. Go into a dark room. Set the lighted candle on a table or dresser; hold the "camera" between you and the candle, with the pinhole nearest and on a level with the candle flame. You will be facing the tracing paper. You will find a "picture" of the candle flame upside down on the tracing paper.

3. Read "Hamlet to His Mother," p. 360. Imagine there are two full-length portraits hanging on the wall. Make the positions of the Queen and of the portraits visibly clear.

To Reveal Feeling

1. The Dauphin Charles has just asked Joan why she cannot mind her own business and let him mind his. She has been urging him to stand up to his responsibilities, and she replies to him:

> Minding your own business is like minding your own body: it's the shortest way to make yourself sick. What is my business? Helping mother at home. What is thine? Petting lapdogs and sucking sugarsticks. I call that muck. I tell thee it's God's business we are here to do: not our own. I have a message to thee from God: and thou must listen to it, though thy heart break with the terror of it.
>
> —George Bernard Shaw, *Saint Joan* (1924)

Ask the questions visibly. Reject the "muck" visibly. Emphasize "Tell thee" visibly, and so on.

2. George Washington is encouraging the men at Valley Forge against defection:

AT VALLEY FORGE

What I fight for now is a dream, a mirage, perhaps, something that's never been on this earth since men first worked it with their hands, something that's never existed and will never exist unless we can make it and put it here—the right of free-born men to govern themselves in their own way.—Now men are mostly fools, as you're well aware. They'll govern themselves like fools. There are probably more fools to the square inch in the Continental Congress than in the Continental army, and the percentage runs high in both. But we've set our teeth and trained our guns against the hereditary right of arbitrary kings, and if we win it's curfew for all the kings of the world.—It may take a long time. . . . It may not be worth the doing. When you deal with a king you deal with one fool, knave, madman, or whatever he may be. When you deal with a congress you deal with a conglomerate of fools, knaves, madmen and honest legislators, all pulling different directions and shouting each other down. So far the fools and knaves seem to have it. That's why we're stranded on this barren side-hill, leaving a bloody trail in the snow and chewing the rotten remains of sow-belly on which some merchant has made his seven profits.—So far our government's as rotten as the sow-belly it sends us. I hope and pray it will get better. But whether it gets better or worse, it's your own, by God, and you can do what you please with it—and what I fight for is your right to do what you please with your government without benefit of kings.—It's for you to decide, Master Teague—you, your son, and the rest of you. . . . If you desert they may catch you and they may not, but the chances are they won't. . . . Make your own decision. But if we lose you—if you've lost interest in this cause of yours—we've lost our war, lost it completely, and the men we've left

lying on our battle-fields died for nothing whatever—for a dream that
came too early—and may never come true.

—Maxwell Anderson, *Valley Forge* (1934)

Read that speech so that the intensity and the fluctuation of feeling are made
apparent.

3. Kurt Müller, a member of the anti-Nazi underground has killed a man who has
   discovered his identity; he is telling his three children goodbye:

KURT MÜLLER

Now let us get straight together. The four of us. Do you remember
when we read *Les Misérables?* Do you remember that we talked about
it afterward and Bodo got candy on Mama's bed? . . .

Well. He stole bread. The world is out of shape we said, when there
are hungry men. And until it gets in shape, men will steal and lie and—
. . . kill. But for whatever reason it is done, and whoever does it—
you understand me—it is all bad. I want you to remember that. Whoever does it, it is bad. . . . But you will live to see the day when it will
not have to be. All over the world, in every place and every town, there
are men who are going to make sure it will not have to be. They want
what I want: a childhood for every child. For my children, and I for
theirs. . . . Think of that. It will make you happy. In every town and
every village and every mud hut in the world, there is always a man
who loves children and who will fight to make a good world for them.
And now good-bye. Wait for me. I shall try to come back for you. . . .
Or you shall come to me. At Hamburg, the boat will come in. It will
be a fine, safe land—I will be waiting on the dock. And there will be
the three of you and Mama and Fanny and David. And I will have or-
dered an extra big dinner and we will show them what our Germany
can be like—[3]

—Lillian Hellman, *Watch on the Rhine* (1941)

Make it evident that Kurt is trying to impress what he says indelibly on the minds
of his children.

4. A middle-class shareholder is demanding money owed him by the eighty-year-old and chair-ridden president of a shaky shipping concern:

OLD ENGLISH

Now you look here! You owe me three hundred pounds; you've owed it to me for thirteen years. Either you pay me what you owe me at once, or I call this meeting and make what I know public. You'll very soon find out where you are, and a good thing too, for a more unscrupulous—you'll do no good for yourself by getting into a passion. At your age, and in your condition, I recommend a little prudence. Now just take my terms quietly, or you know what'll happen. I'm not to be intimidated by any of your brass. You've said you won't pay me, and I've said you shall. I'm out to show you who's master. . . . Oho! Bluster it out, do you? You miserable old turkey-cock! You apoplectic old image! I'll have you off your boards—I'll have you in the gutter. You think in your dotage you can still domineer. Two can play at that game. By George!

—John Galsworthy, *Old English* (1924)

In addition to showing the imagined Old English that he has met his match, show your actual audience that, twice during the speech, the old man has reacted violently.

To Disclose Character

1. Everybody knows Huckleberry Finn. Here is the opening of his story. Learn it. See how completely you can show a Huck Finn by your general bearing, movement, and gesture. When you feel you can do a good total job without the book, read it aloud from the book using as much of your former visible message as you convincingly can.

HUCK FINN

You don't know about me without you have read a book by the name of *The Adventures of Tom Sawyer;* but that ain't no matter. That book was made by Mr. Mark Twain, and he told the truth, mainly. There was things which he stretched, but mainly he told the truth. That is nothing. I never seen anybody but lied one time or another, without it was Aunt Polly, or the widow, or maybe Mary. Aunt Polly—Tom's Aunt Polly, she is—and Mary, and the Widow Douglas is all told about in that book, which is mostly a true book, with some stretchers, as I said before.

Now the way that the book winds up is this: Tom and me found the money that the robbers hid in the cave, and it made us rich. We got six thousand dollars apiece—all gold. It was an awful sight of money when it was piled up. Well, Judge Thatcher he took it and put it out at interest, and it fetched us a dollar a day apiece all the year round—more than a body could tell what to do with. The Widow Douglas she took me for her son, and allowed she would sivilize me; but it was rough living in the house all the time, considering how dismal regular and decent the widow was in all her ways; and so when I couldn't stand it no longer I lit out. I got into my old rags and my sugar-hogshead again, and was free and satisfied. But Tom Sawyer he hunted me up and said he was going to start a band of robbers, and I might join if I would go back to the widow and be respectable. So I went back.

—Mark Twain, *Huckleberry Finn* (1884)

Summary

1. Here is a story written in highly conversational narrative. It is told in the first person, the narrator reporting two simultaneous conversations interlarded with her own comment. Work on this story until you can satisfactorily suggest the character of the narrator and still make perfectly clear the conversations she is reporting. Here is a *tour de force* for a reader.

PRAY EMPLOY MAJOR NAMBY

I am a single lady—single, you will please to understand, entirely because I have refused many excellent offers. Pray don't imagine from this that I am old. Some women's offers come at long intervals, and other women's offers come close together. Mine came remarkably close together—so, of course, I cannot possibly be old. Not that I presume to describe myself as absolutely young, either; so much depends on people's points of view. I have heard female children of the ages of eighteen or nineteen called young ladies. This seems to me to be ridiculous—and I have held that opinion, without once wavering from it, for more than ten years past. It is, after all, a question of feeling; and shall I confess it? I feel so young!

I live in the suburbs, and I have bought my house. The major lives in the suburbs, next door to me, and *he* has bought his house. I don't object to this of course. I merely mention it to make things straight.

Major Namby has been twice married. His first wife—dear, dear! how can I express it? Shall I say, with vulgar abruptness, that his first wife had a family? And must I descend into particulars, and add that they are four in number, and that two of them are twins? Well, the words are written; and if they will do over again for the same purpose, I beg to repeat them in reference to the second Mrs. Namby (still alive), who has also had a family, and is—no, I really cannot say, is likely to go on having one. There are certain limits in a case of this kind, and I think I have reached them. Permit me simply to state that the second Mrs. Namby has three children at present. These, with the first Mrs. Namby's four, make a total of seven. The seven are composed of five girls and two boys. And the first Mrs. Namby's family all have one particular kind of constitution, and the second Mrs. Namby's family all have another particular kind of constitution. Let me explain once more that I merely mention these little matters, and that I don't object to them.

My complaint against Major Namby is, in plain terms, that he transacts the whole of his domestic business in his front garden. Whether it arises from natural weakness of memory, from total want of a sense of propriety, or from a condition of mind which is closely allied to madness of the eccentric sort, I cannot say, but the major certainly does sometimes partially, and sometimes entirely, forget his private family matters, and the necessary directions connected with them, while he is inside the house, and does habitually remember them, and repair all omissions, by bawling through his windows, at the top of his voice, as soon as he gets outside the house. It never seems to occur to him that he might advantageously return indoors, and there mention what he has forgotten in a private and proper way. The instant the lost idea strikes him—which it invariably does, either in his front garden, or in the roadway outside his house—he roars for his wife, either from the gravel walk, or over the low wall—and (if I may use so strong an expression) empties his mind to her in public, without appearing to care whose ears he wearies, whose delicacy he shocks, or whose ridicule he invites. If the man is not mad, his own small family fusses have taken such complete possession of all his senses that he is quite incapable of noticing anything else, and perfectly impenetrable to the opinions of his neighbors. Let me show that the grievance of which I complain is no slight one, by giving a few examples of the general persecution that I suffer, and the occasional shocks that are administered to my delicacy, at the coarse hands of Major Namby.

We will say it is a fine warm morning. I am sitting in my front room, with the window open, absorbed over a deeply interesting book. I hear the door of the next house bang; I look up, and see the major descending the steps into his front garden.

He walks—no, he marches—half way down the front garden path, with his head high in the air, and his chest stuck out, and his military cane fiercely flourished in his right hand. Suddenly, he stops, stamps with one foot, knocks up the hinder part of the brim of his extremely curly hat with his left hand, and begins to scratch at that singularly disagreeable-looking roll of fat red flesh in the back of his neck (which scratching, I may observe, in parenthesis, is always a sure sign, in the case of this horrid man, that a lost domestic idea has suddenly come back to him). He waits a moment in the ridiculous position just described, then wheels round on his heel, looks up at the first-floor window, and, instead of going back into the house to mention what he has forgotten, bawls out fiercely from the middle of the walk:

"Matilda!"

I hear his wife's voice—a shockingly shrill one; but what can you expect of a woman who has been seen, over and over again, in a slatternly striped wrapper as late as two o'clock in the afternoon—I hear his wife's voice answer from inside the house:

"Yes, dear."

"I said it was a south wind."

"Yes, dear."

"It isn't a south wind."

"Lor', dear."

"It's a sou'-east. I won't have Georgina taken out to-day." (Georgina is one of the first Mrs. Namby's family, and they are all weak in the chest.) "Where's nurse?"

"Here, sir."

"Nurse, I won't have Jack allowed to run. Whenever that boy perspires he catches cold. Hang up his hoop. If he cries, take him into my dressing-room and show him the birch rod. Matilda!"

"Yes, dear."

"What the devil do they mean by daubing all that grease over Mary's hair? It's beastly to see it—do you hear?—beastly! Where's Pamby?" (Pamby is the unfortunate work-woman who makes and mends the family linen.)

"Here, sir."

"Pamby, what are you about now?"

No answer. Pamby, or somebody else, giggles faintly. The major flourishes his cane in a fury.

"Why the devil don't you answer me? I give you three seconds to answer me, or leave the house. One—two—three. Pamby! what are you about now?"

"If you please, sir, I'm doing something—"

"What?"

"Something particular for baby, sir."

"Drop it directly, whatever it is. Nurse!"

"Yes, sir."

"Mind the crossings. Don't let the children sit down if they're hot. Don't let them speak to other children. Don't let them get playing with strange dogs. Don't let them mess their things. And above all, don't bring Master Jack back in a perspiration. Is there anything more before I go out?"

"No, sir."

"Matilda! Is there anything more?"

"No, dear."

"Pamby! Is there anything more?"

"No, sir."

Here the domestic colloquy ends, for the time being. Will any sensitive person—especially a person of my own sex—please to imagine what I must suffer as a delicate single lady, at having all these family details obtruded on my attention, whether I like it or not, in the major's rasping martial voice, and in the shrill answering screams of the women inside? It is bad enough to be submitted to this sort of persecution when one is alone; but it is far worse to be also exposed to it—as I am constantly—in the presence of visitors, whose conversation is necessarily interrupted, whose ears are necessarily shocked, whose very stay in my house is necessarily shortened by Major Namby's unendurably public way of managing his private concerns.

Only the other day, my old, dear, and most valued friend, Lady Malkinshaw, was sitting with me, and was entering at great length into the interesting story of her second daughter's unhappy marriage engagement, and of the dignified manner in which the family ultimately broke it off. For a quarter of an hour or so our interview continued to be delightfully uninterrupted. At the end of that time, however, just as Lady Malkinshaw, with tears in her eyes, was beginning to describe the effects of her daughter's dreadful disappointment on the poor girl's mind and looks, I heard the door of the major's house bang as usual; and looking out of the window in despair, saw the major himself strut half-way down the walk, stop, scratch violently at his roll of red flesh, wheel round so as to face the house, consider a little, pull his tablets out of his waistcoat-pocket, shake his head over them, and then look up at the front windows, preparatory to bawling as usual at the degraded female members of his household. Lady Malkinshaw, quite ignorant of what was coming, happened, at the same moment, to be proceeding with her pathetic story, in these terms:

"I do assure you, my poor dear girl behaved throughout with the heroism of a martyr. When I had told her of the vile wretch's behavior, breaking it to her as gently as I possibly could; and when she had a little recovered I said to her—"

("Matilda!")

The major's rasping voice sounded louder than ever, as he bawled out that dreadful name, just at the wrong moment. Lady Malkinshaw started as if she had been shot. I put down the window in despair; but the glass was no protection to our ears—Major Namby can roar through a brick wall. I apologized—I declared solemnly that my next door neighbor was mad—and I entreated Lady Malkinshaw to take no notice, and to go on. That sweet woman immediately complied. I burn with indignation when I think of what followed. Every word from the Namby's garden (which I distinguish below by parentheses) came, very slightly muffled by the window, straight into my room, and mixed itself up with her ladyship's story in this inexpressibly ridiculous and impertinent manner:

"Well," my kind and valued friend proceeded, "as I was telling you, when the first natural burst of sorrow was over, I said to her—"

"Yes, dear Lady Malkinshaw," I murmured, encouragingly.

"I said to her—"

("By jingo, I've forgotten something! Matilda! when I made my memorandum of errands, how many had I to do?")

" 'My dearest, darling child,' I said—"

("Pamby! how many errands did your mistress give me to do?")

"I said, 'my dearest, darling child—' "

("Nurse! how many errands did your mistress give me to do?")

" 'My own love,' I said—"

("Pooh! Pooh! I tell you, I had four errands to do, and I've only got three of 'em written down. Check me off, all of you—I'm going to read my errands.")

" 'Your own proper pride, love,' I said, 'will suggest to you—' "

("Gray powder for baby.")

—" 'the necessity of making up your mind, my angel, to—' "

("Row the plumber for infamous condition of back kitchen sink.")

—' "to return all the wretch's letters, and—' "

("Speak to the haberdasher about patching Jack's shirts.")

—" 'all his letters and presents, darling. You need only to make them up into a parcel, and write inside—' "

("Matilda! is that all?")

—" 'and write inside—' "

("Pamby! is that all?")

—" 'and write inside—' "

("Nurse! is that all?")

" 'I have my mother's sanction for making one last request to you. It is this—' "

("What have the children got for dinner today?")

—" 'it is this: Return me my letters, as I have returned yours. You will find inside—' "

("A shoulder of mutton and onion sauce? And a devilish good dinner too.")

The coarse wretch roared out those last shocking words cheerfully, at the top of his voice. Hitherto, Lady Malkinshaw had preserved her temper with the patience of an angel; but she began—and who can wonder?—to lose it at last.

"It is really impossible, my dear," she said, rising from her chair, "to continue any conversation while that very intolerable person persists in talking to his family from his front garden. No! I really cannot go on—I cannot, indeed."

Just as I was apologizing to my sweet friend for the second time, I observed, to my great relief (having my eye still on the window), that the odious major had apparently come to the end of his domestic business for that morning, and had made up his mind at last to relieve us of his presence. I distinctly saw him put his tablets back in his pocket, wheel round again on his heel, and march straight to the garden gate. I waited until he had his hand on the lock to open it; and then, when I felt we were quite safe, I informed dear Lady Malkinshaw that my detestable neighbor had at last taken himself off, and, throwing open the window again to get a little air, begged and entreated her to oblige me by resuming the charming conversation.

"Where was I?" inquired my distinguished friend.

"You were telling me what you recommended your poor darling to write inside her inclosure," I answered.

"Ah, yes—so I was. Well, my dear, she controlled herself by an admirable effort, and wrote exactly what I told her. You will excuse a mother's partiality, I am sure—but I think I never saw her look so lovely —so mournfully lovely, I should say—as when she was writing those last lines to the man who had so basely trifled with her. The tears came into my eyes as I looked at her sweet pale cheeks; and I thought to myself—"

("Nurse! which of the children was sick, last time, after eating onion sauce?")

He had come back again!—the monster had come back again, from the very threshold of the garden gate, to shout that unwarrantable, atrocious question in at his nursery window!

Lady Malkinshaw bounced off her chair at the first note of his horrible voice, and changed towards me instantly—as if it had been my fault—in the most alarming and most unexpected manner. Her ladyship's face became awfully red; her ladyship's head trembled excessively; her ladyship's eyes looked straight into mine with an indescribable fierceness.

"Why am I thus insulted?" inquired Lady Malkinshaw, with a slow and dignified sternness which froze the blood in my veins. "What do you mean by it?" continued her ladyship, with a sudden rapidity of utterance that quite took my breath away.

Before I could remonstrate with my friend for visiting her natural irritation on poor innocent me: before I could declare that I had seen the major actually open his garden gate to go away, the provoking brute's voice burst in on us again.

"Ha, yes?" we heard him growl to himself, in a kind of shameless domestic soliloquy. "Yes, yes, yes—Sophy was sick, to be sure. Curious. All Mrs. Namby's step-children have weak chests and strong stomachs. All Mrs. Namby's own children have weak stomachs and strong chests. *I* have a strong stomach *and* a strong chest. Pamby!"

"I consider this," continued Lady Malkinshaw, literally glaring at me, in the fulness of her indiscriminate exasperation—"I consider this to be unwarrantable and unladylike. I beg to know—"

"Where's Bill?" burst in the major from below, before she could add another word. "Matilda! Nurse! Pamby! Where's Bill? I didn't bid Bill good-bye—hold him up at the window, one of you!"

"My dear Lady Malkinshaw," I remonstrated, "why blame *me?* What have I done?"

"Done?" repeated her ladyship. "Done?—all that is most unfriendly, most unwarrantable, most unladylike, most—"

"Ha! ha! ha-a-a-a!" roared the major, shouting her ladyship down, and stamping about the garden in fits of fond paternal laughter. "Bill, my boy, how are you? There's a young Turk for you! Pull up his frock—I want to see his jolly legs—"

Lady Malkinshaw screamed and rushed to the door. I sank into a chair, and clasped my hands in despair.

"Ha! ha! ha-a-a-a! What calves the dog's got! Pamby! look at his calves. Aha! bless his heart, his legs are the model of his father's! The Namby build, Matilda: the Namby build, every inch of him. Kick again, Bill—kick out, like mad. I say, ma'am! I beg your pardon, ma'am!—"

"*Ma'am?* I ran to the window. Was the major actually daring to address Lady Malkinshaw, as she passed indignantly, on her way out, down my front garden? He was! The odious monster was pointing out his—his, what shall I say?—his *undraped* offspring to the notice of my outraged visitor.

"Look at him, ma'am. If you're a judge of children, look at him. There's a two-year-older for you! Ha! ha! ha-a-a-a-! Show the lady your legs, Bill—kick out for the lady, you dog, kick out!"

—Wilkie Collins (c. 1862)

2. Demonstrate your grasp of Chapter Eight by effective reading of "The Illumination" by Jessamyn West, p. 224.

ADDITIONAL EXERCISES

Prose: "The Evil Eye," p. 80; "The Proposal II," p. 110; "To Know What to Do," p. 144; "Seidman's Success," p. 146; "The First Round," p. 188; "Lincoln's Inn at Night," p. 188; "The Bar of England," p. 160; "Small Aunt Cecily," p. 205.

Poems: "I Hear an Army," p. 73; Harry's Address at Harfleur," p. 175; "The Major General's Song," p. 252; "When a Man Hath No Freedom," p. 277.

Audible Subtlety

WE HAVE ALREADY pointed out that the written record of our language represents the language itself no more fully than a map records every detail of its territory. Textual distortions, such as spaces between words in English texts, tend to lead the unwary reader into actually distorting the language when he reads aloud. Moreover, those aspects of language which are not visibly represented in texts are likely to be overlooked and lead one to assume "if it isn't in the text, it isn't in the language." This has led to such foolish assumptions as, "It's what you say that matters; not how you say it." In language the *how* and the *what* are parts of an indivisible whole. You cannot say a *what* without a *how*. Furthermore, a single text which visibly would suggest a single *what* may become any one of a number of what's by reading it aloud—that is, by turning the text into language. This can be accomplished by using a variety of how's.

Turn back to page 132 in Chapter Four. You were asked to read aloud five times the sentence, "She will be here next week," and to give each reading a different but specific meaning. You did this by using five different how's. In reality, did not the *how* in each case produce a different *what* out of the single visible "sentence"? So, in the five separate utterances we have five distinct how's and five distinct what's. (Maybe it would be better to say "five separate *how-what's* or *what-how's*.") Note the differences; although they are not represented by visible symbols in the text, they are nonetheless part of the very essence of language. Since they are differences which listeners hear and are therefore auditorily produced, we must examine still more closely the audible aspects of oral reading.

ORAL READING AND SINGING

In order better to understand the audible aspects of oral reading, let us look at the differences between speaking and singing. Though each of us does both with the same instrument, the audible results have marked differences.

Singing

In our culture the voice, when singing, follows a pitch design built upon a predetermined pitch scale and proceeds from one pitch to another on the steps or intervals of that scale. The shortest pitch interval we call a half-tone. The pitches on a piano are arranged in half-tone steps.

Furthermore, each pitch struck is held for an appreciable length of time, and the length of time a given pitch is held is part of a predetermined time scheme. A good coloratura soprano, even when she is singing a cadenza, will hit each note accurately and separately. These aspects of singing can be quite accurately symbolized in print.

As Joseph Was A-Walking

As   Jos—eph   was   a — walk — ing,   he   heard an an — gel   sing: This
He   nei—ther   shall be   born — ed   in   house nor in   the   hall,   Nor

night   shall be   the   birth — night   of   Christ,   the heav'n-ly   King;   This
in   a   King's   pal — ace,   but   in   an ox - en's   stall;   Nor

—American folk carol

Oral Reading

In our culture the voice when speaking may proceed from pitch to pitch in a continuous glide without stopping on any intermediate pitch. A given utterance may begin or end anywhere *within* a half-tone span. What time pattern there is, is much less rigid than in singing and it is not predetermined. Utterance is not molded into a set time scheme; its time sequence is the result of its significance. These aspects are difficult to symbolize in print. Using a modified musical staff, where each line and space represents a range of a half-tone, we might crudely illustrate thus:

All Men Are Brothers

Note that there is neither time signature nor key signature. It cannot be played on the piano.

We are more keenly aware of pitch variation in singing because we are listening for it as such and are displeased when we hear a singer violate the scale, that is, sing sharp or flat. We hear pitch and time variations in good speech not as pitch and time variations, but as meanings—as what's. We become conscious of them as pitch and time only when they are structural distortions of the language, that is, when they fail to carry intended messages, or when we are deliberately studying the phonation process in speech.

Here we authors face *our* biggest problem in communicating with *you:* we cannot actually use language in communicating with you; we cannot talk to you from these pages; we can only supply visible symbols which are excruciatingly silent! With the indispensable help of your teacher, we hope you are supplying adequate sound for the passages we ask you to read aloud.

In Chapter Four we called attention to the sense aspects of sound. Maybe the obverse can help us now: examining the sound aspects of sense.

SOUNDS ESSENTIAL FOR SENSE

Most persons are aware that consonants and vowels are sound units of our language, but relatively few are aware that consonants and vowels constitute not more than 75 per cent of the basic sound units of English—17/23 to be exact. We are especially concerned with the other 6/23, because, though they are as definitely parts of our language structure as vowels and consonants, unfortunately we have no popular symbols for them.

Linguistic analysis tabulates the following sound units of English:

> 24 consonants
> 9 vowels
> 1 semivowel
> 1 juncture
> 4 stresses
> 4 pitches
> 3 terminal glides

This makes a total of forty-six sound units. And remember, these are *basic* units, each one of which may have sound variations within its own limits.

In order to write more intelligibly about the units which most concern us we shall adopt the symbols which have been worked out by students of language structure. However, we shall try to use as few new symbols as possible. We shall get along without phonetic alphabet symbols, for example, and the juncture sign.[1]

---

[1] Phonetic symbols, like [i], [æ], [ɔ] and [t], [o], [ʃ], are signs used to indicate vowels and consonants of English. Each sound—vowel or consonant—is represented by a single symbol (in contrast to the many ways of spelling the *ee* sound, for example), and each symbol represents only one sound (in contrast to the many sounds which the letter *a,* for example, can indicate in spelling.)

The juncture + helps to show the subtle sound distinctions between such similar sounds as those found in the pairs of italicized words in the following sentences:

I *scream* for *ice cream.*
He has *an aim* to make *a name* for himself.
Let *me choose* my track-*meet shoes.*
It was ironic that the man told to *unarm* had lost *an arm.*

Each pair has the same string of vowels and consonants.

Stress is accent, or degree of vocal force, given to a syllable. The symbols for the four stresses are

    ˊ Primary stress
    ˄ Secondary stress
    ˋ Tertiary stress
    ˘ Weak (lightest) stress

For example:

The tăll máil-màn ĭs ă bíg chàp.

As a matter of economy we can eliminate ˘ with the understanding that unmarked words and syllables receive the least degree of stress. Study the following sentences and practice reading them aloud with the indicated stresses; then read them to someone who has not read this discussion and ask him what each sentence means.

1. Shĕ will be here nêxt wèek.

2. She wíll bè here nèxt wèek.

3. Shĕ will be hére nèxt wèek.

4. Shĕ will be hêre nèxt wéek.

5. Shĕ will be hĕre nèxt wèek.

Do the meanings you get correspond to those suggested on page 132?

In normal effective speech vocal pitch fluctuates through a certain range. We pointed out in Chapter Four that within this range there are four significant bands or partial ranges. They are called "significant" bands because, in effective speech, changing from one to another changes meaning. The following diagram recapitulates:

High

Normal Speech Pitch Range

4	
3	
2	Pitch most often used
1	

Low

The symbols for terminal glides are not new (see Chapter Four). Recall that the principle audible symbol for indicating completeness, finality, is a vocal inflection falling toward the lower level of your speech pitch range—1. Obversely, a level or rising vocal inflection symbolize there is something to follow—either in explicit words or in implied idea.

In speaking you finish a word cluster, insofar as pitch is concerned, in one of three ways: with rising intonation / ↗ /, with level intonation / → /, or with falling intonation / ↘ /. These pitch *directions* are of great importance to sense. You must become keenly aware that some of the most subtle shades of meaning in English are conveyed by stress and pitch, neither of these vocal subtleties being symbolized in ordinary print. Lacking this awareness, many persons have erroneously concluded, if they have thought about it at all, that stress and intonation, i.e., changes in accent and pitch, are merely frills superimposed upon the language—the "frills of elocution." Unfortunately, such judgment is not without empirical foundation.

Much oral reading is, and has been, of two kinds—either dull and relatively meaningless or pompous or offensively "arty." Both kinds violate the structure of English and therefore vitiate meaning. The dull reader (much too often a professor) fails to use requisite vocal symbols because he does not realize that *changes in pitch are fully as much a part of the very fabric of language as vowels, consonants, and spoken words are.* The "yellowcutionist" fails by arbitrary overuse of vocal symbols; he *does* superimpose frills upon the language. The first bores, the second embarrasses us.

Since we cannot speak without accent, intonation, etc., it will help us to write about them if we can supply written symbols for them.

We can symbolize the four significant pitch bands by underlining and overlining the text:

A line placed a space below the text will represent the lowest or number 1 of the four pitch bands.

A line immediately below the text, pitch band 2.

A line immediately above, pitch band 3.

A line a space above, pitch band 4.

For example:

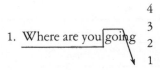

2. I had my pie for lunch.
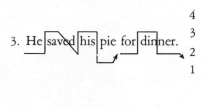

4
3
2
1

In contrast to

3. He saved his pie for dinner.

4
3
2
1

4. What a mess

4
3
2
1

5. "I an itching palm"

4
3
2
1

With the meaning, "Do you mean to stand there and say I have an itching palm?"

6. O no you don't.
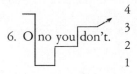

4
3
2
1

The straight lines, remember, represent a small range of pitch, not a single tone of pitch; e.g., in sentence 1 "you" will probably be a shade lower in pitch than "where are," but all three words are within pitch range 2.

What differences in sense do the following markings suggest?

1. Where are you going

2. Where are you going

3. Where are you going

4. Where are you going

5. Where are you going

Would you have any difficulty in stressing the foregoing as follows?

1. Where are you going

2. Where are you going

3. Whére aȓe you goìng

4. Whȇre aȓe yôu goìng

5. Whére aȁe you góing

Now try reading each of the stress-marked sentences with two or three variations of pitch but without changing the stress pattern. Note that there are
not many possibilities if the sentence is to remain English. Stress and pitch
patterns are closely linked.

We need one more set of symbols to make our text structure more closely
represent the language structure. In Chapter Four we pointed out the importance of relative lengths of silences.

| will represent a break between two relatively closely related ideas.
|| will represent a break between less closely related ideas, but ideas that still be-
long to the same thought sequence.
will represent a break long enough to indicate breaks between thought se-
quences.

For example:

Marley|was dead||to begin with # There is no doubt whatever about
that # The register of his burial|was signed by the clergyman||the
clerk|| the undertaker||and the chief mourner # And Scrooge's name|was
good upon 'Change|for anything he chose to put his hand to # Old
Marley|was as dead as a door-nail #

If we use all three kinds of markings (for stress, pitch, and pause) and you
study and apply them closely, we can together achieve an increased subtlety in
our communication.

Work over the following sentences carefully by yourself. When you think
you are reading them pretty accurately, analyze their several meanings and compare your readings with those of your classmates. With careful practice, you
should find that all of you working independently, will arrive at very similar
readings.

1. A black|bird|is not necessarily a|black|bird #

2. A|black|bird|is not necessarily a black|bird #

3. John||said his sister||is|loony #

4. John|said his|sister is|loony #

5. What do you think I'll|do||this or|that #

6. What do you|think|I'll do||this|or that #

7. What do|you|think I'll do||this or that #

8. What # do you think I'll do this or that #

9. What # do you think I'll do this or that #

10. What # do you think I'll do this or that #

11. What do you think # I'll do this or that #

12. What do you think # I'll do this or that #

13. What do you think I'll do this or that #

We have tried to make it perfectly clear that articulated sound (which enables us to recognize what we call words) is only part of language and that other aspects, stress, pitch, etc., are vital structural elements.

Indeed the subtleties of language, the nice distinctions, the fine shades of meaning, are best conveyed and perceived via nuances of pitch-stress. (We hyphenate the words in order to emphasize the fact that what we have called "pitch" and "stress" are but aspects of a single process.) Any intelligible "word" sequence can be given different meanings through different pitch-stress patterns. Normal speakers, for the most part, achieve these subtleties in their own language without being fully aware of it.

Even the dullest lecturer will automatically suggest the contrast between "square" and "cube" in the following sentence with a pitch-stress difference:

Today || I shall explain the difference | between ⌈square root| and

cube |root. #

He does not say

—between square root and cube root.

or

—between ⌈square |root| and ⌈cube |root.

or

—between square ⌈root| and cube ⌈root, etc.

In our normal spontaneous use of language our intent induces tensions which produce appropriate pitch-stress patterns; after all, we are then concerned with our own meaning. When we are reading aloud, however, we are concerned with someone else's meaning. This calls for such study as we have suggested in Chapters One and Two *and* a certain *awareness of how our language really operates* in effective communication. We are laboring this matter of pitch-stress in order to help you achieve indispensable awareness. Experience with class after class has made the authors aware that many students have a difficult time indeed just learning to hear themselves.

RATE OF UTTERANCE ESSENTIAL TO SENSE

Study carefully the next two selections, bearing in mind all that has been said thus far, and practice reading them until you feel you have achieved real excellence.

THE PIPER AND THE CHILDREN

And ere he blew three notes (such sweet
Soft notes as yet musician's cunning
Never gave the enraptured air)
There was a rustling that seemed like a bustling
Of merry crowds justling at pitching and hustling,
Small feet were pattering, wooden shoes clattering,
Little hands clapping, and little tongues chattering;
And, like fowls in a farmyard when barley is scattering,
Out came the children running.
All the little boys and girls,
With rosy cheeks and flaxen curls,
And sparkling eyes and teeth like pearls,
Tripping and skipping, ran merrily after
The wonderful music with shouting and laughter.

—Robert Browning, "The Pied Piper" (1845)

MOONLIGHT AND MUSIC

How sweet the moonlight sleeps upon this bank!
Here will we sit, and let the sounds of music
Creep in our ears. Soft stillness and the night
Become the touches of sweet harmony.
Sit, Jessica. Look how the floor of heaven

Is thick inlaid with patens of bright gold.
There's not the smallest orb which thou behold'st
But in his motion like an angel sings,
Still quiring to the young-eyed cherubins:
Such harmony is in immortal souls;
But whilst this muddy vesture of decay
Doth grossly close it in, we cannot hear it.
—William Shakespeare,
The Merchant of Venice (1596)

Now read each one aloud to the very best of your ability and time each reading. Which selection took longer?

Did you find that the second took a few seconds longer than the first? We have found that what we consider to be good reading of these passages takes about forty seconds for the Shakespeare selection and thirty-five for the Browning passage. Yet the Browning passage has 14 lines, 97 words, and 139 syllables compared with 12 lines, 94 words, and 123 syllables in the Shakespeare excerpt. A good reading rate for the Browning is appreciably faster than an equally good rate for the Shakespeare.

Why?

Deliberately slow down the first and speed up the second. In each case, what does the inappropriate rate do to the sense?

The second selection says more than the first, although it uses fewer words and syllables; its words carry more weight; it gives you more to think about. You can expand it into an extensive philosophical paraphrase because of its implications. You cannot expand the first selection very far; the whole event is explicitly related and leaves little indeed to inference. This illustrates the important principle that, with a given reader-audience situation, the harder it is to grasp the sense, the slower you will read. Put another way, relative amounts of "thinking" which words require for their proper understanding determine the relative rates at which they should be read.

VOCAL TEXTURE AS SENSE

Each one of us has a voice peculiarly his own—a unique composite of pitch range, partials, and resonance. We have little difficulty in recognizing each

other by our vocal texture. Each of us has vocal limits beyond which he cannot go, but each of us within his unique vocal boundaries is capable of producing an astonishing variety of "sound effects." We can produce tones which
may be severally described as smooth, rich, harsh, nasal, de-nasal, breathy, strident, metallic, thin, piping, sonorous, hollow, mellow, throaty, whining, etc.,
etc., etc. Most of these adjectives have a certain exasperating vagueness about
them, and yet if you were asked to say a few words using vocal textures which
could be described with these adjectives, you would find that, with practice,
you could do it. Try it on this sentence:

Never before was there a time like this.

Using the check list of adjectives which follows below (add others of your
own choosing) say each of the following sentences with as many different vocal
textures as you can and have your classmates check each reading against the
adjectives they think are most accurately descriptive.

Not a single one of them ever returned.

O, come now; you will have to do better than that.

I tell you, this is the end.

You will do exactly what you're told.

Stop it. See if you can stop it.

You have no idea how delighted I am.

Check List of Adjectives

breathy _____	de-nasal _____	dull _____	harsh _____
hollow _____	mellow _____	metallic _____	nasal _____
piping _____	rasping _____	rich _____	smooth _____
sonorous _____	strident _____	thin _____	throaty _____
whining _____	_____ _____	_____ _____	_____ _____
_____ _____	_____ _____	_____ _____	_____ _____

Compare lists. Where you find general agreement examine your performance
to discover just how you did it. What did you do to yourself to induce the

tensions that produced the texture? How did you achieve the sound which your classmates described as "rich"? As "harsh"? As "nasal"? Etc.? Was your "metallic" reading interpreted as "strident"?

On "readings" where your classmates' judgments varied widely, explore (discuss) the variations to see if you can discover the reasons for them.

Note that, unlike descriptions of pitch and stress, descriptions of vocal texture are for the most part value judgments. This gives us an important clue to the role vocal texture plays in the use of language.

If one's normal vocal texture is generally rated with adjectives which indicate adverse judgment he should seek voice training to reduce or eliminate the factors producing the unpleasantness. Since adequate consideration of voice training as such would take us beyond the scope of this work, we must assume that you normally have acceptable vocal texture.

Value judgments reflect attitudes, feelings, states of mind, etc. When you scold you put "harshness" into your vocal texture; when you comfort the bereaved there is an increase of "mellowness"; when you attempt withering sarcasm a "metallic" quality may creep in, and so on. Your intent or "feeling" at the moment is an essential part of your "sense" and it tends to induce a bodily set which produces a vocal texture which, in turn, reveals your intent or feeling to your listeners. You do this quite as a matter of course in spontaneous utterance. But reading aloud is not spontaneous utterance, though reading aloud *well* must simulate spontaneity. This calls for a high degree of control.

In order to turn literature into appropriately communicative language, you study the text to discover as nearly as you can the whole sense, which includes attitude, feeling, state of mind, intent. Having arrived at the sense, you must consciously supply utterance which will wholly convey it. Vocal texture is the medium by which you must convey much of the emotive burden of sense.

If you could make the sense of a literary text as total within yourself as is the sense of your own spontaneous utterance, your vocal texture *might* take care of itself—as the "think the thought" school of elocution advocated. Such control is much easier advocated than accomplished. We have learned, however, that deliberately assuming tensions which accompany a given "feeling" helps to bring on that feeling. Therefore, an important aid to instigating the "thought for thinking" is deliberately to supply an appropriate vocal texture to the utterance of the required words.

Without the context of the entire situation, see how much emotive sense you can give to each of the two separate utterances of the following, by deliberately assuming vocal textures which fit the italicized descriptions: first with *delighted satisfaction,* second with *sneering sarcasm.*

However did you think of it? There isn't anything that would have pleased me more.

Work on those two utterances carefully until you can persuasively convey delight and sarcasm. Try each one out on your family or close friends and ask them what it means. Write out as precisely as you can a description of your total behavior for each and suggest a situation for which it would be appropriate.

Work out the next two sentences in similar manner, first suggesting *excited and eager urging,* then *disgusted impatience:*

For heaven's sake hurry up! We've got to get out of here.

First *reverent admiration,* second *terrified awe:*

What a view! We are standing on the brink of the infinite.

First *harsh threatening,* second *plaintive wheedling:*

Go home and don't loiter on the way.

How infinite are the possibilities of subtleties of sense in human utterance! No wonder a great teacher[2] told a great actor[3] who had requested coaching that it would take six weeks to learn to read one of Hamlet's soliloquies!

Atmosphere

Every great piece of literature—indeed, every work of art—is conceived within a particular framework, and that framework gives to it a pervading spirit or "atmosphere." Even so long a work as Dickens' *A Tale of Two Cities,* with all its variety and nuance, is always enveloped in the atmosphere of the French Revolution; even in London the guillotine casts its shadow. The witches "set the stage" for *Macbeth,* and hovering evil is always present. Fantasy and foolery make everything in *A Midsummer Night's Dream* delightfully credible. Since atmosphere is the all-pervading spirit of a piece of literature, it must be maintained in oral reading. Variety of vocal texture must not violate atmosphere. One of the reasons you "can't" read the quoted lines in "Little Boy Blue" (see

[2] Alfred Ayres.
[3] E. H. Sothern.

page 303) with a childlike vocal texture is that such texture does violate atmosphere. We pointed out, with the illustration of "The Patriot" (page 178), that you may not be able fully to determine how the first line of a selection should be read until you have read the last line. Atmosphere is not always wholly revealed at the outset. To read the first sentence of "The Patriot" with gaiety and exuberance, as the sentence by itself might well suggest, would be grotesque. Although your audience may not know the details which are to follow, a tone of *bitter recollection* on "It was roses, roses all the way," etc., properly prepares your audience for what is to come. Mark the words *properly prepares.* This *preparation* has two important aspects: (1) To help establish atmosphere so that subsequent responses in your listeners will not produce frustrating conflict (nobody likes to be misled, even inadvertently); (2) to arouse expectation and to channel the listener's response so that he partly anticipates the solution; and when he is given the solution he partly expected his pleasure is augmented by a sense of personal triumph. Herein lies not only one of the excellences of reading aloud well but also one of its rewarding joys: the arousing of anticipatory impulses which only the whole reading will satisfactorily allay or resolve.

So the vocal texture of your first utterance in reading is a very important business.

Note the openings of *A Christmas Carol* and *The Young King:*

Marley was dead, to begin with. There was no doubt whatever about that.

It was the night before the day fixed for his coronation, and the young King was sitting alone in his beautiful chamber.

Both seem to be statements of fact, nothing unusual, mere introduction. Why not read them with the same vocal texture? Because if you do, you fail, at least in one, to induce the particular and subtle hunger in your readers which is necessary for their exquisite satisfaction.

The "fare" in the two stories is very different. One is laid in good old solid London. Its characters are very real, down-to-earth persons. One of them dreams fantastic dreams, but just such dreams as he ought to dream. All the characters are enveloped in the Spirit of Christmas, whether they like it or not. It is a "face-the-facts" business, and it is really a very happy one ultimately. The opening words call for a vocal texture which reveals unequivocal matter-of-factness and at the same time says, "That's as it should be and you need have no fear that everything won't work out all right."

The other story is laid—who knows where? Its characters are rather embodiments of ideas and attitudes than flesh and blood persons. They do not even have proper names, only titles. The chief character here also dreams dreams—the kind he should dream. But over it all there is the mystery of enchanting allegory, a pervading spirit of "otherwhereness." Its opening words call for a vocal texture which not only says "Once upon a time," but also "You should listen to this with reverent respect because of what is to follow." You must introduce each with a quality that suggests the atmosphere of the whole and therefore will not be misleading and that will subtly arouse the proper expectancy.

To tell you in exact detail *how* to do this is impossible. However, you can learn to do it. Study the whole text carefully until you "get" the atmosphere. With the critical help of classmates and teacher, work on the opening lines until you can introduce that atmosphere. Practice the whole text, trying to get all the variety and nuance the author was striving for. Your teacher at this stage is indispensable.

Idealization

No one would contend that in "real life" anyone ever actually talked like Romeo or Othello. Yet when we see either of them in the theatre we are disappointed if he does not "sound real," and if, when we read his lines aloud, either to ourselves or to someone else, we do not give them a "reality" we miss the great satisfaction which comes from giving life (form) to literature. The problem is not to drag Romeo or Othello down to the humdrum real life of "please-pass-the-butter," but to infuse life with the "golden cadence" reality of poetry. This takes some doing!

Say the following in as convincingly a conversational way as you can:

Hey, talk some more, sweetie-pie.

Say it two or three times and note exactly how it sounds. Now, with the same vocal texture, pitch variation, etc., say this line:

O, speak again, bright angel!

It just won't do, will it? Spoken in "real life" fashion, the words seem absurdly flat. On the other hand, you can "moan" the words in a maudlin "arty" way so that they will be embarrassing or even positively nauseous. But if you're going to give Romeo an acceptable reality you must say those words so that they sound altogether appropriate—above humdrum and below bombast. Again we cannot tell you exactly how to do it. We can tell you it calls for a more exalted manner—a more resonant vocal texture, impeccable articulation; that you must induce in yourself an attitude and totality of tension that will produce this idealization; and we can quote Hamlet, "Now this overdone or come tardy off . . . cannot but make the judicious grieve," but *you* must find the psychophysical behavior which will give the words "reality." The idealization we are talking about is a kind of amplification, a speaking on a bigger scale. In other words, idealization in a text requires idealization in utterance.

Although the manner of utterance of "Hey, talk some more, sweetie-pie" is inadequate for "O, speak again, bright angel," it may help to start reading the second with the sound of the first and then try to magnify the manner until it seems adequate for Romeo. This may help to avoid spurious elocution.

Here is a magnificent sentence:

> Where wast thou when I laid the foundations of the earth? Declare, if thou hast understanding.

This was God's devastating query to Job, who had been complaining about his multiple misfortunes. Consider the speaker; consider the cosmic import. To the very best of your ability give it the utterance that it merits. Give it the dignity, the sonority, the amplitude that its meaning demands. Listen to other members of the class speak the sentence. What were the characteristics of the most effective utterances?

Now, in the same, amplified manner—dignity and sonority—say

> Where were you when I poured the concrete for the cellar? Speak up if you have any sense.

If you really managed to do it, it was pretty awful, was it not? Now give the second sentence the colloquial utterance it merits. Compare the two carefully in rate, stress, intonation, physical bearing.

Imagine yourself haled into court on the false charge that you coerced a girl to run away with you; given the opportunity to tell your story you begin with these words:

> May it please the court, your Honor, and ladies and gentlemen of the jury, it is true that I eloped with this man's daughter; it is also true that I have married her. This is the sum total of my offense.

Say it with serious dignity, and with the perfect assurance that you are not guilty of any crime. Work at it until it sounds "real."

Now, with the foregoing as basic pattern, say the following:

> Most potent, grave, and reverend signiors,
> My very noble and approved good masters:
> That I have ta'en away this old man's daughter,
> It is most true: true, I have married her:
> The very head and front of my offending
> Hath this extent, no more.
> —William Shakespeare, *Othello* (1604)

Magnify your utterance until you can convey to listeners as well as to yourself a satisfactory reality of Othello.

Both passages have a common basic idea; but Shakespeare, through his choice of words, achieves an idealization of that idea which clothes it with far greater power than can be achieved with the pedestrian words of the other. Reading Othello's defense requires commensurate idealization in utterance, otherwise you say Othello's words but you do not speak his language.

CLIMAX

Sometimes, in a series of ideas, each idea has the same importance as every other idea in the sequence. The intent behind such sequence is simply to make clear the several ideas in it, as in the following sentence:

She bought bread, fruit, and cake, nothing more.

Sometimes the intent is an increasing magnitude, each subsequent idea having a greater importance by virtue of the preceding ideas—as in saying the foregoing sentence to mean, "She bought not only bread, but also fruit, and even cake."

She bought bread, fruit, and cake. Think of it!

Note that in the first example, "bread," "fruit," and "cake" all follow a similar vocal pattern, whereas in the second "fruit" takes off from where "bread" finished, and "cake" goes higher than "fruit." There is a "climbing." (The Greek word *klimax* means ladder or staircase.) There is more than a succession of ideas, there is a cumulative importance, each idea gaining importance from its predecessor, and this climbing must be conveyed vocally.

Climaxes are not always so simple, but the principle always applies. Here is a more complex one:

1. No sail from day to day, but every day
2. The sunrise broken into scarlet shafts
3. Among the palms and ferns and precipices;
4. The blaze upon the waters to the east;
5. The blaze upon his island overhead;
6. The blaze upon the waters to the west;
7. Then the great stars that globed themselves in Heaven,
8. The hollower-bellowing ocean, and again
9. The scarlet shafts of sunrise—but no sail.

— Alfred, Lord Tennyson, *Enoch Arden* (1864)

In line 3, there is a simple nonclimactic sequence in "palms," "ferns," "precipices," but a climax begins with the fourth line. Line 5 adds a climactic idea; line 6 builds on line 5; lines 7 and 8 together build on line 6, and the climax reaches its highest point on the word "again." Lines 4, 5, and 6 call for similar vocal patterns, but if they are all read with identical pitch changes—within the same key, as it were—the cumulative power is missed; there is no climax. Lines 5, 6, and 7 and through "ocean" in line 8, repeat the basic pattern in line 4, but each successively in a slightly higher "key" and with subtly increasing intensity. "East," "overhead," "west," and "ocean" should have rising terminal endings (you may manage with level ones but certainly not falling ones), and the next succeeding stressed word after each should take up about where its predecessor left off. Each of the next most important words— "blaze," "blaze," "Then," "again," respectively—actually introduces a new and higher key. The whole nine lines, therefore, call for a wider total pitch range than you normally use in ordinary conversation. You must start low enough, and make each modulating rise small enough so that you do not become shrill at the top of the climax.

Here is an attempt to illustrate this climax visually. Read from the bottom up. Each indentation to the right indicates a higher key—a higher step in the climax.

again The scarlet shafts of sunrise—
The hollower-bellowing ocean, and
Then the great stars that globed themselves in Heaven,
The blaze upon the waters to the west;
The blaze upon his island overhead;
The blaze upon the waters to the east;
Among the palms and ferns and precipices;
The sunrise broken into scarlet shafts
No sail from day to day, but every day

The remaining three words, "but no sail," are not part of the climax; indeed, vocally they descend and return us relentlessly to "no sail from day to day."

Here is a still more complex and difficult climax: Othello has decided upon vengeance. Iago suggests he may change his mind, and Othello replies:

Never, Iago. Like to the Pontic sea,
Whose icy current and compulsive course
Ne'er feels retiring ebb, but keeps due on
To the Propontic and the Hellespont;
Even so my bloody thoughts, with violent pace,
Shall ne'er look back, ne'er ebb to humble love,
Till that a capable and wide revenge
Swallow them up.
—William Shakespeare, *Othello* (1604)

The climax begins in the first line with "Like to the Pontic sea," and like a wave that begins quietly far from shore, relentlessly gathers momentum and increases in height until it fairly crashes in "Swallow them up." From "Like" to "up," through all the fluctuations of intonation and stress necessary to reveal the niceties of meaning, there must be a gradual rise in pitch, a crescendo, an increasing intensity, without a single falling terminal ending. If the climbing is too rapid, or if you start too high, you may get as far as you are able to go before the climax is concluded—you are stranded and Othello has disappeared in your ineptitude. It will take a good octave; if you start in the middle of your vocal register you will never make it.

CONTEXT DIRECTS UTTERANCE

We hope by this time that the ordinarily unprinted aspects of language—rate, stress, intonation, and vocal texture: that is, the *how*'s of utterance—are appearing in their true significance within the very structure of language and that written words, especially if they have very little written context, can be translated into many meanings in language. The words "why this" will convey some meaning to you but it will be pretty vague. You can say them in dozens of ways, some of which may convey very definite ideas, others may be nonsensical noise. You can supply many meanings by *how* you say them. As soon as those words are written into sentences, they acquire more specific meanings and the possible number of sensible utterances is reduced.

Of all the dozens of possibilities under the sun, why this?

How is perfectly clear, but *why* this?

You can't tell which? Why, this.

Read each sentence aloud. The words "why this" require three different kinds of utterance. The *how* of each utterance is determined by the meaning of the whole sentence. In other words, each sentence is a context which directs, or should direct, how "why this" is to be said. In a given sentence you cannot say "why this" any old way. Contexts set limits to utterance and those limits are conventionally determined by the structure of language.

Look at the third of the illustrative sentences above. True, it is a meager context; you can supply any one of a good many implications: you can enrich its context by utterance. But note carefully that every implication you give it requires a precise utterance. You can no more convey specific implication by your oral reading if you violate the sound structure of language than you can write sense if you destroy the word order of English. The following words spoken (if you are able to manage it) as follows

$$\text{You } | \text{can't } || \text{ tell } | \text{why this } \#$$

do not make any more sense than these:

Tell you can't which? This, why.

In "You can't tell which? Why, this," there is a word choice and a word order, conventionally evolved, which establishes a context and sets a limit to utterance. Any implication or nice shade of meaning you can bring to it calls for specific utterance, also conventionally evolved, within those limits.

Suppose the text is fuller and therefore leaves less to inference?

> Do you mean to stand there and say to me that you are so stupid you
> can't tell which? Why, this, of course, you dumb ox!

This fuller context specifically prescribes the utterance of "why this."

It is the business of authors to supply texts with adequate contexts. One of
the criteria for excellence in writing is fullness of context. Excellent writing demands excellent reading. Precision calls for precision. Literature, therefore, sets
severe vocal limits for its proper utterance. We encouraged vocal experiment in
Chapter Five in order to help you achieve necessary abandon and, indeed, to help
you discover your own possibilities and extend your range. Beware of becoming
enamored of vocal achievement to the point that you rely on vocal tricks.

SKIRTING THE OBVIOUS

The difference between the good reader and the merely passable reader lies
chiefly in the former's ability to avoid belaboring the obvious and to find—*in
the context*—the specific directives for precise utterance. Many a line *can* be read
as if it merely presented information, and a passable reader is content to read it
that way. But the good reader becomes vaguely dissatisfied during rehearsal and
suddenly sees that this "merely informative" phrase or sentence is really redundant, that the information has already been implied in the context. Is the author
merely padding? The good reader seeks an answer which will justify a variant
reading—one which will make the offending sentence pull its due weight in the
selection.

> Juan and Haidee were not married, but
> The fault was theirs, not mine; 'tis unfair,
> Chaste reader, in any way to put
> The blame on me, unless you wish they were.
> If then you'd have them wedded, please to shut
> This book which treats of the erroneous pair,
> Before the consequences become too awful—
> 'Tis dangerous to read of loves unlawful . . .
> —George Noel Gordon, Lord Byron,
> *Don Juan* (1820)

> The last line can be read merely to present the information
> that reading about illicit love is dangerous. But surely this is al-
> ready implicit in the context—why else shut the book? How

else could the consequences become awful? If the line is to do more than repeat what has already been said, there must be an implication which has been missed. What is the key word? Byron is addressing the reader, he is warning him about certain dangers of *reading,* "read" must be the key word. Emphasizing "read" makes the line imply "illicit love is so touchy a subject that *even reading* about it is dangerous, especially if the reader is squeamish and 'would have them wedded.' " The line now adds something new. It calls for precisely emphatic utterance of "read."

This of course is merely another aspect of the principle we stressed in Chapter Two—that the chief difference between a good reader and a poor one lies in the former's ability to track down and to communicate the new developments, the nice implications in what he is reading. Search for new ideas in lines which seem redundant. Sometimes reading is so careless that the reader imposes by implication a repetition of an idea. Turn to page 372 and read the entire Prodigal Son story; be sure to make "kid" a key word.

THE PITFALLS OF ONOMATOPOEIA

Onomatopoeic words—words made with sounds that resemble or suggest their referents—tempt some readers to indulge in vocal tricks. Many students have been mistaught "to bring out the onomatopoeic quality of each onomatopoeic word." Result: spurious reading.

When Edgar Allan Poe wrote

> How they tinkle, tinkle, tinkle,
>   In the icy air of night!
> While the stars that oversprinkle
> All the heavens, seem to twinkle
>   With a crystalline delight;
>   —*The Bells* (1849)

he was playing with sound. So was Robert Southey when he wrote about

> thumping and plumping and bumping and jumping
> And dashing and flashing and splashing and clashing

of the Cataract of Lodore. English is rich in onomatopoeic words and sometimes they are fun to play with. In "The Bells" and "The Cataract of Lodore" Poe and

Southey were fairly wallowing in onomatopoeia. If a person elects to read them aloud he will have to wallow too and do his best to make the words *sound* like their referents. However, we are of the opinion that one should think twice before asking an audience to listen to such acoustic *tours de force,* except as illustrations of the offensive lengths to which onomatopoeia can be carried. Even then a few lines will be a-plenty.

Unquestionably there are occasions when full onomatopoeic quality of a word should be utilized, but they are relatively rare. For instance, out of the total number of times you have had occasion to speak of a cuckoo clock or bird, how many times was it essential to your sense to mimic the clock or bird in your pronunciation of "cuckoo"? Even such apparently complete onomatopoeia as "Cocka-doodle-do" will not always be fully onomatopoeic in utterance. If you are reading to little children a story which has the following sentence,

> The rooster stretched his wings and wakened the neighborhood with a lusty "Cocka-doodle do,"

you probably should sound just as much like a rooster crowing as you can. But if you were reading a story to adults, what would you do with the following passage?

> Having lived all his life in the city, he missed the comfortable noises of heavy traffic. Crowing of roosters had been romantic to read about; the actual cocka-doodle-do which now waked him at four-thirty in the morning was becoming intolerable.

The complete onomatopoeia of the first example would be not only grotesque but offensive in the second.

Remember, the word gets its precise meaning from its context; so far as oral reading is concerned a word's context is the entire work in which the word is used. Onomatopoeic utterance which violates atmosphere should be scrupulously avoided.

EXERCISES AND ASSIGNMENTS

Sounds Essential for Sense

1. In the light of this discussion, rework the following: "The Sins of the Fathers," p. 144; "Seidman's Success," p. 146; "International Obligations," p. 148; the translations of the Iliad excerpt, pp. 153–156.

2. In the mid-seventeenth century popular opinion in England opposed a state church. John Milton reflects the opinion in the following sonnet. Study the text, dig out its sense, and then turn it into appropriate "language." Beware of misleading terminal endings!

SONNET XVI

(1652)

Cromwell, our chief of men, who through a cloud
Not of war only, but detractions rude,
Guided by faith and matchless fortitude
To peace and truth thy glorious way hast plowed,
And on the neck of crownèd fortune proud
Hast reared God's trophies and his work pursued,
While Darwen stream with blood of Scots imbrued,
And Dunbar field resounds thy praises loud,
And Worcester's laureate wreath; yet much remains
To conquer still; peace hath her victories
No less renowned than war, new foes arise
Threatening to bind our souls with secular chains:
Help us to save free conscience from the paw
Of hireling wolves whose gospel is their maw.

Rate of Utterance

1. Read "At Valley Forge," p. 317. At what point should rate of utterance increase? Why? At what other points should the rate change?
2. Examine carefully and describe the appropriate rate of utterance of the "Old English" excerpt, p. 319.
3. J. B. Priestley is an English writer who spent a year (1935–1936) on the American desert. Here are three paragraphs he wrote about Boulder Dam. See if you can catch and convey Priestley's admiration. What does it do to your reading rate? Where, how, and why should the rate fluctuate?

BOULDER DAM

That is worth traveling weeks to see. It is like the beginning of a new world, that world we catch a glimpse of in one of the later sequences of Wells' film, "Things to Come," a world of giant machines and titanic communal enterprises. Here in this Western American wilderness, the new man, the man of the future, has done something, and what he has done takes your breath away. When you look down at that vast smooth wall, at its towers of concrete, its power stations, at the new lakes and cataracts it has created; and you see the men who have made it all moving far below like ants or swinging perilously in midair as if they were little spiders; and you note the majestic order and rhythm of the work—you are visited by emotions that are hard to describe, if only because some of them are as new as the great dam itself.

. . . .

Some Americans I met grumbled to me about the cost of the dam, and dropped the usual hints about nest-feathering. I was a visitor and it was not for me to tell them they were wrong, even though I have the privilege of paying American taxes myself while not being granted any other privilege of the ordinary American citizen. But if any of the dollars taken from me went towards paying the cost of Boulder Dam, I am more than satisfied, I am proud and delighted. The Colorado River must not be allowed to do what it likes. Imperial Valley cannot exist in constant danger of flood or drought. The electric power that is carried over the hundreds of miles of desert to the coast will light up the faces of Chaplin and Garbo for us. There may come a season soon when all the water in Boulder Canyon will be urgently needed.

So much for utility. But Boulder Dam is something more than a vast utilitarian device, a super-gadget. Enchanted by its clean functional lines and at the same time awed by its colossal size, you might be tempted to call it a work of art; as if something that began with utility and civil engineering ended somewhere in the neighborhood of Beethoven's "Ninth Symphony." There is no doubt whatever that it is a thing of beauty, and that the impression it makes on any sensitive observer is not unlike that made by a massive work of art. But if you feel that language is being abused here, and hold that nothing so impersonal as a dam can be a genuine work of art, then you have to find some new way of accurately describing this new creation.[4]

4. Turn to the Iliad translations, pp. 153–156: Can you read them all effectively at the same rate? Account for the necessary differences.

ADDITIONAL EXERCISES

Prose: "I Am Born," p. 145; "The Fall of Hickman," p. 188; "Memories," p. 190.

Poems: "Sailing to Byzantium," p. 44; "Lament," p. 149; "Rustum Eyes the Drudge," p. 150; "The Jabberwocky," p. 255; "The Second Coming," p. 280; "The Express," p. 284.

Vocal Texture

1. Here are two episodes from Stephen Vincent Benét's *Western Star,* very different in mood. The first is largely soliloquy; get Raleigh's analytical resentment. Convey the half-delirious terror in the second.

SIR WALTER RALEIGH IN THE TOWER
Raleigh, in the Tower
Watched while the sun went down in palest gold,
An Autumn sunset, Winter coming on.
He stroked his beard and there was grey in it.

[4] From *Midnight on the Desert,* Harper, 1937.

They let him write and read and talk and walk,
Play chemist and discover an elixir,
Ponder an endless History of the World.
They let him do all things, except his will.

"And now," he thought, "the ships set out again,
Kit Newport leads them on, the same Kit Newport
That brought the Spanish carrack in for me,
—Set out for the Virginia that was mine,
Goodspeed and *Susan Constant* and *Discovery*—
And here am I, a leopard in a cage,
Prisoned and tweaked at by a stuttering king
With a fool's cunning and a potboy's heart,
A sort of show for greasy citizens
Walking their wives, on Sundays.
                                   'Ay—see, see!—
Nay, to the left—the grizzled one in black
Taking the air by the high window there—
'Tis Raleigh—atheist Raleigh—sold his soul
To devils for a heap of heathen gold,
Cozened the Queen, conspired against the King
And left his gulls to die in far Virginia.
God keep us all! I'm glad I've seen the man.
Yes, Jacky, we will view the lions, now.'

And yet I was the man. I was the man.
Ere the dice fell against me, I was he.
And, if they find the glory and the gold,
My ghost has been before.
                               It maddens me.
I had the whole adventure in my hands,
The patent and the money and the men,
And yet they died.
                       They died at Roanoke,
Vanished as though the wood had taken them,
In some wild Irish tale.
                             The ship returned
—Delayed, of course—delayed—always delayed—
And, where there had been men, there were no men,
Only the name carved out upon the tree,
Croatan.
They called and cried but there was still no sound,
Only the wild-beast silence of the forest,
The forest that had never heard of men.

They try again. Well, let them try again.
I will not envy where I may not rule.

I have my huge Guianas waiting for me,
My maps, my plans, my gilded emperor,
Ruling the treasures of ten Mexicos,
I have my prison.
                              God, three little ships!
You'd think that even this oatcake of a king
Would give three little ships to Walter Raleigh!
Had I but half what he admits these men,
I'd pour such riches in his greedy lap
He'd swoon above them, lovesick, like a girl,
The El Dorado's treasure, the pure gold.
And I will have it though I die for it.
What's dying but a kind of gilded sleep,
A rattle given to a fretful child
To keep it quiet, a poor, drowsy draught
Common to any tapster, but the last
And best refreshment of the noble mind
That has known all, endured all, suffered all
And now would quit the crosses of its flesh,
The daily spites, the yearly injuries,
The trammels of court favor and disfavor,
And ruin, and the sour smiles of kings,
For the great freedom without bound or name?

And yet, I cannot die within a cage.
'I cannot die and this unconquered.'
And that was Tamburlaine in Marlowe's play,
I would I had not thought of that.
                              A king!
A king who cannot even make a verse
But Baas and blethers Scots—and keeps me here.

Roanoke, Roanoke,
Good seaman, bring me news of Roanoke.
For I was once concerned with Roanoke
And thought to be a god at Roanoke."

He sighed and turned away from the last light,
Fading into the darkness, like his fame.

                                   (1943)

At Jamestown men were dying; here is Benét's account of one of the deaths:

DEATH AT JAMESTOWN

There were never Englishmen left in a foreign country
In such misery as we.
If there were conscience in men, it would bleed their hearts
To hear the pitiful outcries of our sick men.

(Water, my lads! Will no man bring me water?
Will no man come? I thought we were all friends.
Good lads, you'll not desert me in this den?
Nay, but I am not dead yet, though I ail
And cannot keep my watch. Go, tell the ancient,
I cannot keep my watch. There's water here
But, when I reach for it, it flees away,
Like the damned gold we came so far to find.
And there was something that I wish to say
If I could think of it. 'Tis hard to think,
And I am back upon the tossing ship
Or seeing the dead face of Edward Brookes,
Suddenly stricken on that rocky isle
Where we went hunting. Nay, do not grin at me,
With that chopfallen mouth of blank surprise!
We all die. Did you not know we all die?
Why, then you're no Virginia man, my lad,
Not to know that.

              Nay, nay, it is not true
I harmed the wench, and those who say it lie,
Lie in their throats most foully—nor was I
The one who stabbed the sutler. It hath done
Much injury to my name. That I avouch.
But I was born a gentleman.

                      O Christ,
Sweet Christ, a little water for my thirst!
I will give gold for water. See my gold,
Yellow as buttercups in Leicestershire
In the sweet Spring—I'll ride the pony home
For Brother is afraid of it and cries—
Nay, uncle, I repent me my misdeeds
And will amend. I swear I will amend,
Although the wench was eagerer than I,
But do not leave me here, tied down and bound
Upon this narrow bed of burning gold
With not one drop of water for my lips
And the thick tide of fever—

                   Ale, I say!
Call Billy Tapster that he bring us ale,
And we will revel till the night's worn out
And bright day pales the candle—

                      Nay, bend closer!
I tell you, I was born in Leicestershire
And my name is—it was—it matters not.
But, when you go there, tell them how I died,
Lonely and desolate in a far land.)

And it was mid-September and no hope,
For half of them were dead, and the living gaunt
Life-sickened shadows, dragging weary limbs
Mechanically to the rotten bulwarks,
Staring into the forest with dull eyes,
Knowing they had to watch for something there
But half-forgetting what.[5]

(1943)

2. Read Chapter 38 of the Book of Job. Give it all the dignity you can command; suggest its cosmic bigness.
3. King Claudius in *Hamlet* is not a *petty* villain. Read the following speech so as to reveal his stature as a character.

CLAUDIUS' PRAYER

O, my offence is rank, it smells to heaven:
It hath the primal eldest curse upon't,
A brother's murther. Pray can I not,
Though inclination be as sharp as will.
My stronger guilt defeats my strong intent,
And like a man to double business bound,
I stand in pause where I shall first begin,
And both neglect. What if this cursèd hand
Were thicker than itself with brother's blood,
Is there not rain enough in the sweet heavens
To wash it white as snow? Whereto serves mercy
But to confront the visage of offence?
And what's in prayer but this twofold force,
To be forestallèd ere we come to fall,
Or pardoned being down? Then I'll look up:
My fault is past. But O, what form of prayer
Can serve my turn? 'Forgive me my foul murther?'
That cannot be, since I am still possessed
Of those effects for which I did the murther,
My crown, mine own ambition and my queen.
May one be pardoned and retain th'offence?
In the corrupted currents of this world
Offence's gilded hand may shove by justice,
And oft 'tis seen the wicked prize itself
Buys out the law; but 'tis not so above:
There is no shuffling, there the action lies
In his true nature, and we ourselves compelled
Even to the teeth and forehead of our faults
To give in evidence. What then? What rests?

[5] From *Western Star,* by Stephen Vincent Benét, Rinehart & Company, Inc., copyright, 1943, by Rosemary Carr Benét.

Try what repentence can. What can it not?
Yet what can it when one can not repent?
O wretched state! O bosom black as death!
O limèd soul, that, struggling to be free,
Art more engaged! Help, angels! Make assay!
Bow, stubborn knees, and, heart with strings of steel,
Be soft as sinews of the new-born babe!
All may be well.
                    —William Shakespeare, *Hamlet* (1600)

4. Hamlet is torn by grief for his father's death, love for his mother, horror at her incest. Note climax after climax. Pay special attention to the central idea.

HAMLET TO HIS MOTHER

Look here, upon this picture, and on this,
The counterfeit presentment of two brothers.
See what a grace was seated on this brow;
Hyperion's curls, the front of Jove himself,
An eye like Mars, to threaten and command;
A station like the herald Mercury
Newlighted on a heaven-kissing hill:
A combination and a form indeed,
Where every god did seem to set his seal
To give the world assurance of a man.
This was your husband. Look you now, what follows.
Here is your husband, like a mildewed ear,
Blasting his wholesome brother. Have you eyes?
Could you on this fair mountain leave to feed,
And batten on this moor? Ha! have you eyes?
You cannot call it love, for at your age
The heyday in the blood is tame, it's humble,
And waits upon the judgement; and what judgement
Would step from this to this? Sense sure you have,
Else could you not have motion; but sure that sense
Is apoplexed: for madness would not err,
Nor sense to ecstasy was ne'er so thralled
But it reserved some quantity of choice
To serve in such a difference. What devil was't
That thus hath cozened you at hoodman-blind?
Eyes without feeling, feeling without sight,
Ears without hands or eyes, smelling sans all,
Or but a sickly part of one true sense
Could not so mope. O shame! where is thy blush?
Rebellious hell,
If thou canst mutine in a matron's bones,
To flaming youth let virtue be as wax

And melt in her own fire. Proclaim no shame
When the compulsive ardour gives the charge,
Since frost itself as actively doth burn,
And reason pandars will.
                    —William Shakespeare, *Hamlet* (1600)

5. Puck asks one of the fairies, "How now, spirit! whither wander you?" And the
spirit replies in part:

> Over hill, over dale,
>   Thorough bush, thorough brier,
> Over park, over pale,
>   Thorough flood, thorough fire,
> I do wander everywhere,
> Swifter than the moon's sphere;
>   —William Shakespeare,
> *A Midsummer Night's Dream* (1596)

Note the climax. Can you build it through a full octave?

6. Build the climax in this speech which Macbeth addresses to the witches:

> MACBETH TO THE WITCHES
> I conjure you, by that which you profess,
> Howe'er you come to know it, answer me.
> Though you untie the winds and let them fight
> Against the churches; though the yesty waves
> Confound and swallow navigation up;
> Though bladed corn be lodged and trees blown down;
> Though castles topple on their warders' heads;
> Though palaces and pyramids do slope
> Their heads to their foundations; though the treasure
> Of nature's germens tumble all together,
> Even till destruction sicken: answer me
> To what I ask you.
>   —William Shakespeare, *Macbeth* (1605)

Exactly where does the climax begin? What is its highest point?

7. In the scene immediately preceding the foregoing speech, there are climaxes within
a climax. It is easy to read the list of hellish ingredients without climax—simply
cataloguing the items, and repeating the unison refrain. You will greatly increase
the dramatic power of the scene if you read the speech of each witch as a climax
which reaches its highest point in the unison "Double, double," etc. The Second
Witch should begin her speech a "rung" above the beginning of the First Witch's
speech so that the second "Double, double" is climactic to the first. Diagrammed,
the entire climax would look like this

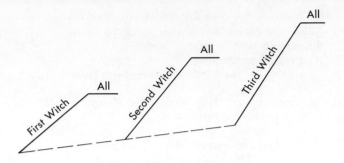

FIRST WITCH

Round about the cauldron go.
In the poisoned entrails throw.
Toad, that under cold stone
Days and nights has thirty-one
Sweltered venom sleeping got,
Boil thou first i' th' charmèd pot.

ALL

Double, double, toil and trouble;
Fire burn and cauldron bubble.

SECOND WITCH

Fillet of a fenny snake,
In the cauldron boil and bake;
Eye of newt and toe of frog,
Wool of bat and tongue of dog,
Adder's fork and blindworm's sting,
Lizard's leg and howlet's wing,
For a charm of pow'rful trouble,
Like a hell-broth boil and bubble.

ALL

Double, double, toil and trouble,
Fire burn and cauldron bubble.

THIRD WITCH

Scale of dragon, tooth of wolf,
Witch's mummy, maw and gulf
Of the ravined salt-sea shark,
Root of hemlock digged i' th' dark,
Liver of blaspheming Jew,
Gall of goat and slips of yew
Slivered in the moon's eclipse,
Nose of Turk and Tartar's lips,

> Finger of birth-strangled babe
> Ditch-delivered by a drab,
> Make the gruel thick and slab.
> Add thereto a tiger's chaudron,
> For th' ingredients of our caudron.

ALL
> Double, double, toil and trouble,
> Fire burn and cauldron bubble.

8. Turn back to "The Man with a Hoe," p. 186. Work for climax. Get the climax in lines 3 and 4. Build into effective climax the *"who"* series beginning in line 5 and running through line 10.

In the second stanza, bring out the overall climax of the "is" series, lines 11 and 15. Note the climaxes within the climax; the "to" series, lines 12–14 and the single line 17. Bring out the cumulative power in the "more" series, lines 19–21.

Stanza three: Build the "what" series, lines 22–26 and bring out the two internal climaxes, one in line 24 and the other in lines 25 and 26. Get the climactic strength of line 30.

Examine carefully the last two stanzas for climax.

We hope you will be asked to read "The Man with the Hoe" for an oral examination.

ADDITIONAL EXERCISES

Prose: "The House of Usher," p. 72; "The Proposal: I," p. 364; "The Proposal: II," p. 110; "I Am Born," p. 145; "Seidman's Success," p. 146; "Style and the Man," p. 157; "Memories," p. 190.

Poems: "The Patriot," p. 78; "To His Coy Mistress," p. 99; "Lines Composed on Westminster Bridge," p. 178; "If It Were Done," p. 156; "The Rural Walk," p. 159; "Arms and the Boy," p. 183; "Mending Wall," p. 222.

Summary

1. The following selection provides fertile ground for experiment. For example:
   a. Is there any danger that Gwendolen will seem cold-blooded and undesirable? How can you forestall this impression?
   b. Do the characters speak in the same rhythm?
   c. How can Jack's floundering through his fourth speech be made extremely funny? Is there any danger of overdoing it?
   d. Is there any abrupt change of attitude during Gwendolen's long fourth speech? Where?
   e. Is Gwendolen's seventh speech—about metaphysical speculation—really just one long word? Is there a change of pace in it?

f. Does Gwendolen give serious consideration to the name "Jack" in her ninth speech? Is it more, or less, funny if she does?

g. Where is the center in Gwendolen's line, "It produces absolutely no vibrations"? Does her pitch rise or fall?

THE PROPOSAL: I

JACK: Charming day it has been, Miss Fairfax.

GWENDOLEN: Pray don't talk to me about the weather, Mr. Worthing. Whenever people talk to me about the weather, I always feel quite certain that they mean something else. And that makes me so nervous.

JACK: I do mean something else.

GWENDOLEN: I thought so. In fact, I am never wrong.

JACK: And I would like to be allowed to take advantage of Lady Bracknell's temporary absence. . . .

GWENDOLEN: I would certainly advise you to do so. Mamma has a way of coming back suddenly into a room that I have often had to speak to her about.

JACK *(nervously)*:   Miss Fairfax, ever since I met you I have admired you more than any girl . . . I have ever met since . . . I met you.

GWENDOLEN: Yes, I am quite aware of the fact. And I often wish that in public, at any rate, you had been more demonstrative. For me you have always had an irresistible fascination. Even before I met you I was far from indifferent to you. . . . We live, as you know, Mr. Worthing, in an age of ideals. The fact is constantly mentioned in the more expensive monthly magazines, and has reached the provincial pulpits I am told: and my ideal has always been to love some one of the name of Ernest. There is something in that name that inspires absolute confidence. The moment that Algernon first mentioned to me that he had a friend called Ernest, I knew I was destined to love you.

JACK: You really love me, Gwendolen?

GWENDOLEN: Passionately! . . .

JACK: But you don't really mean to say that you couldn't love me if my name wasn't Ernest?

GWENDOLEN: But your name is Ernest.

JACK: Yes, I know it is. But supposing it was something else? Do you mean you couldn't love me then?

GWENDOLEN *(glibly)*:   Ah! that is clearly a metaphysical speculation, and like most metaphysical speculations has very little reference at all to the actual facts of real life, as we know them.

JACK: Personally, darling, to speak quite candidly, I don't much care about the name of Ernest. . . . I don't think that name suits me at all.

GWENDOLEN: It suits you perfectly. It is a divine name. It has a music of its own. It produces vibrations.

JACK: Well, really, Gwendolen, I must say that I think there are lots of other much nicer names. I think, Jack, for instance, a charming name.

GWENDOLEN: Jack? . . . No, there is very little music in the name Jack, if any at all, indeed. It does not thrill. It produces absolutely no vibrations. . . . I have known several Jacks, and they all, without exception, were more than usually plain. Besides, Jack is a notorious domesticity for John! And I pity any woman who is married to a man called John. She would probably never be allowed to know the entrancing pleasure of a single moment's solitude. The only really safe name is Ernest.

JACK: Gwendolen, I must get christened at once—I mean we must get married at once. There is no time to be lost.[6]

—Oscar Wilde, *The Importance of Being Earnest* (1895)

2. We have already referred to the atmosphere of the following story. In studying it for oral reading, write an analytical account of the oral reading problems you encounter.

THE YOUNG KING

(1)   It was the night before the day fixed for his coronation, and the young King was sitting alone in his beautiful chamber. The lad— for he was only a lad—had flung himself back on the soft cushions of his embroidered couch, lying there, wild-eyed and open mouthed, like some young animal of the forest newly snared by the hunters.

(2)   And, indeed, it was the hunters who had found him, coming upon him almost by chance, as bare-limbed and pipe in hand, he was following the flock of the poor goatherd who had brought him up, and whose son he had always fancied himself to be. The child of the old King's only daughter by a secret marriage with one much beneath her in station, he had been, when but a week old, stolen away from his mother's side, and given into the charge of a common peasant and his wife, who lived in a remote part of the forest, more than a day's ride from the town. Grief, or the plague, or, as some suggested, a swift Italian poison administered in a cup of spiced wine, slew, within an hour of her wakening, the white girl who had given him birth, and as the trusty messenger who bare the child across his saddle-bow stooped from his weary horse and knocked at the rude door of the goatherd's hut, the body of the Princess was being lowered into an open grave that had been dug in a deserted church-yard.

(3)   Such, at least, was the story that men whispered to each other. Certain it was that the old King, when on his death-bed, whether moved by remorse for his great sin, or merely desiring that the kingdom should not pass away from his line, had had the lad sent for, and had acknowledged him as his heir.

---

[8] If a longer reading is desired, "The Proposal: II," p. 110, which in the original is a direct continuation of this excerpt, may be added.

(4)   And it seems that from the very first moment he had shown signs of that strange passion for beauty that was destined to have so great an influence over his life. Those who accompanied him to the suite of rooms set apart for his service, often spoke of the cry of pleasure that broke from his lips when he saw the delicate raiment and rich jewels that had been prepared for him, and of the almost fierce joy with which he flung aside his rough leathern tunic and coarse sheepskin cloak. He missed, indeed, at times the fine freedom of his forest life, but the wonderful palace seemed to him to be a new world freshfashioned for his delight.

(5)   All rare and costly materials had certainly a great fascination for him, and in his eagerness to procure them he had sent away many merchants to buy stained ivory, moonstones and bracelets of jade, sandalwood and blue enamel and shawls of fine wool.

(6)   But what had occupied him most was the robe he was to wear at his coronation, the robe of tissued gold, and the ruby-studded crown, and the sceptre with its rows and rings of pearls. Indeed, it was of this that he was thinking to-night, as he lay back on his luxurious couch. He saw himself in fancy standing at the high altar of the cathedral in the fair raiment of a King, and a smile played and lingered about his boyish lips.

(7)   When midnight sounded from the clock-tower he touched a bell, and his pages entered and disrobed him with much ceremony. A few moments after they had left the room, he fell asleep.

And as he slept he dreamed a dream, and this was his dream:

He thought that he was standing in a long, low attic, amidst the whirr and clatter of many looms. The meagre daylight peered in through the grated windows, and showed him the gaunt figures of the weavers bending over their cases. Pale, sickly-looking children were crouched on the huge cross-beams. Their faces were pinched with famine, and their thin hands shook and trembled. Some haggard women were seated at a table sewing. The air was foul and heavy, and the walls dripped and streamed with damp.

The young King went over to one of the weavers, and stood by him and watched him. And the weaver looked at him angrily, and said, "Why art thou watching me? Art thou a spy set on us by our master?"

"Who is thy master?"

"Our master! He is a man like myself. Indeed, there is but this difference between us—that he wears fine clothes while I go in rags, and that while I am weak from hunger he suffers not a little from overfeeding."

"The land is free, and thou art no man's slave."

"In war, the strong make slaves of the weak and in peace the rich make slaves of the poor. We must work to live, and they give us such mean wages that we die. We toil for them all day long, and they heap up gold in their coffers, and our children fade away before their time, and the faces of those we love become hard and evil. We tread out the grapes, and another drinks the wine. We sow the corn, and our own board is empty. We have chains, though no eye beholds them; and are slaves, though men call us free."

"Is it so with all?"

"It is so with all, with the young as well as with the old, and the women as well as with the men. The merchants grind us down, and we must needs do their bidding. The priest rides by and tells his beads, and no man has care of us. Through our sunless lanes creeps Poverty with her hungry eyes, and Sin with his sodden face follows close behind her. Misery wakes us in the morning, and Shame sits with us at night. But what are these things to thee? Thou art not one of us. Thy face is too happy." And he turned away scowling, and threw the shuttle across the loom, and the young King saw that it was threaded with a thread of gold.

And a great terror seized upon him. "What robe is this that thou art weaving?"

"It is the robe for the coronation of the young King; what is that to thee?" And the young King gave a loud cry and woke, and lo! he was in his own chamber, and through the window he saw the great honey-coloured moon hanging in the dusky air.

And he fell asleep again and dreamed, and this was his dream:

He thought that he was lying on the deck of a huge galley that was being rowed by a hundred slaves. On a carpet by his side the master of the galley was seated. He was black as ebony, and his turban was of crimson silk. In his hands he had a pair of ivory scales.

The slaves were naked, but for a ragged loin-cloth, and each man was chained to his neighbour. The hot sun beat brightly upon them, and the Negroes ran up and down the gangway and lashed them with whips of hide. They stretched out their lean arms and pulled the heavy oars through the water.

At last they reached a little bay, and began to take soundings.

As soon as they had cast anchor and had hauled down the sail, the Negroes went into the hold and brought up a long rope-ladder, heavily weighted with lead. The master of the galley threw it over the side, making the ends fast to two iron stanchions. Then the Negroes seized the youngest of the slaves, and knocked his gyves off, and filled his nostrils and his ears with wax, and tied a big stone round his waist. He crept wearily down the ladder, and disappeared into the sea. A few bubbles rose where he sank. Some of the other slaves peered curiously over the side. At the prow of the galley sat a shark-charmer, beating monotonously upon a drum.

After some time the diver rose up out of the water, and clung panting to the ladder with a pearl in his right hand. The Negroes seized it from him, and thrust him back.

Again and again he came up, and each time that he did so he brought with him a beautiful pearl. The master of the galley weighed them, and put them into a little bag of green leather. The young King tried to speak, but his tongue seemed to cleave to the roof of his mouth.

Then the diver came up for the last time, and the pearl that he brought with him was fairer than all the pearls of Ormuz, for it was shaped like the full moon, and was whiter than the morning star. But his face was strangely pale, and as he fell upon the deck the blood gushed from his ears and nostrils. He quivered for a little, and then he was still. The Negroes shrugged their shoulders and threw the body overboard.

And the master of the galley laughed, and, reaching out, he took the pearl, and when he saw it he pressed it to his forehead and bowed. "It shall be for the sceptre of the young King."

And when the young King heard this he gave a great cry, and woke, and through the window he saw the long grey fingers of the dawn clutching at the fading stars.

And he fell asleep again, and dreamed, and this was his dream: He thought that he was wandering through a dim wood, hung with strange fruits and with beautiful poisonous flowers. The adders hissed at him as he went by.

On and on he went, till he reached the outskirts of the wood, and there he saw an immense multitude of men toiling in the bed of a dried-up river. They swarmed up the crag like ants. They dug deep pits in the ground and went down into them. Some of them cleft the rocks with great axes; others grabbled in the sand.

From the darkness of a cavern Death and Avarice watched them, and Death said, "I am weary; give me a third of them and let me go."

But Avarice shook her head. "They are my servants."

And Death said to her, "What hast thou in thy hand?"

"I have three grains of corn; what is that to thee?"

"Give me one of them to plant in my garden; only one of them, and I will go away."

"I will not give thee anything," and she hid her hand in the fold of her raiment.

And Death laughed, and took a cup, and dipped it into a pool of water, and out of the cup rose Ague. She passed through the great multitude, and a third of them lay dead. A cold mist followed her, and the water-snakes ran by her side.

And when Avarice saw that a third of the multitude was dead she beat her breast and wept. "Thou hast slain a third of my servants, get thee gone. There is war in the mountains of Tartary, and the kings of each side are calling to thee. What is my valley to thee, that thou should'st tarry in it? Get thee gone, and come here no more."

"Nay, but till thou hast given me a grain of corn I will not go."

But Avarice shut her hand and clenched her teeth. "I will not give thee anything."

And Death laughed, and took up a black stone, and threw it into the forest, and out of a thicket of wild hemlock came Fever in a robe of flame. She passed through the multitude, and touched them, and each man that she touched died. The grass withered beneath her feet as she walked.

And Avarice shuddered, and put ashes on her head. "Thou art cruel, thou art cruel. There is famine in the walled cities of India, and the cisterns of Samarcand have run dry. There is famine in the walled cities of Egypt, and the locusts have come up from the desert. Get thee gone to those who need thee, and leave me my servants."

"Nay, but till thou hast given me a grain of corn, I will not go."

"I will not give thee anything."

And Death laughed again, and he whistled through his fingers, and a woman came flying through the air. Plague was written upon her forehead, and a crowd of lean vultures wheeled round her. She covered the valley with her wings, and no man was left alive.

And Avarice fled shrieking through the forest, and Death leaped upon his red horse and galloped away, and his galloping was faster than the wind.

And out of the slime at the bottom of the valley crept dragons and horrible things with scales, and the jackals came trotting along the sand, sniffing up the air with their nostrils.

And the young King wept: "Who were these men, and for what were they seeking?"

"For rubies for a king's crown."

And the young King started, and, turning round, he saw a man habited as a pilgrim and holding in his hand a mirror of silver.

And he grew pale. "For what king?"

"Look in this mirror, and thou shalt see him."

And he looked in the mirror, and, seeing his own face, he gave a great cry and woke, and the bright sunlight was streaming into the room, and from the trees of the garden the birds were singing.

And the Chamberlain and the high officers of State came in and made obeisance to him, and the pages brought him the robe of tissued gold, and set the crown and the sceptre before him.

And the young King looked at them, and they were beautiful. More beautiful were they than aught that he had ever seen. But he remembered his dreams, and he said to his lords: "Take these things away, for I will not wear them."

And the courtiers were amazed, and some of them laughed, for they thought that he was jesting.

But he spoke sternly to them again, "Take these things away, and hide them from me. Though it be the day of my coronation, I will not wear them. For on the loom of Sorrow, and by the white hands of Pain, has this my robe been woven. There is Blood in the heart of the ruby, and Death in the heart of the pearl." And he told them his three dreams.

And when the courtiers heard them they looked at each other and whispered, "Surely he is mad; for what is a dream but a dream, and a vision but a vision? They are not real things that one should heed them. And what have we to do with the lives of those who toil for us? Shall a man not eat bread till he has seen the sower, nor drink wine till he has talked with the vinedresser?"

And the Chamberlain spake to the young King, and said, "My lord, I pray thee set aside these black thoughts of thine, and put on this fair robe, and set this crown upon thy head. For how shall the people know that thou art a king, if thou hast not a king's raiment?"

And the young King looked at him. "Is it so, indeed? Will they not know me for a king if I have not a king's raiment?"

"They will not know thee, my lord."

"I had thought that there had been men who were kinglike, but it may be as thou sayest. And yet I will not wear this robe, nor will I be crowned with this crown, but even as I came to the palace so will I go forth from it."

And he bade them all leave him, save one page whom he kept as his companion, a lad a year younger than himself. Him he kept for his service, and when he had bathed himself in clear water, he opened a great painted chest, and from it he took the leathern tunic and rough sheepskin cloak that he had worn when he had watched the goats on the hillside. These he put on, and in his hand he took his rude shepherd's staff.

And the little page opened his big blue eyes in wonder, and said, "My lord, I see thy robe and thy sceptre, but where is thy crown?"

And the young King plucked a spray of wild briar that was climbing over the balcony, and bent it, and made a circlet of it, and set it on his own head.

"This shall be my crown."

And thus attired he passed out of his chamber into the Great Hall where the nobles were waiting for him.

And the nobles made merry, and some of them cried out to him, "My lord, the people wait for their king, and thou showest them a beggar," and others were wroth and said, "He brings shame upon our state, and is unworthy to be our master." But he answered them not a word, but passed on, and went down the bright staircase, and out through the gates of bronze, and mounted upon his horse, and rode towards the cathedral.

And the people laughed, "It is the King's fool who is riding by."

And he drew rein and said, "Nay, but I am the King." And he told them his three dreams.

And a man came out of the crowd, and spake bitterly to him, and said, "Sir, knowest thou not that out of the luxury of the rich cometh the life of the poor? By your pomp we are nurtured, and your vices give us bread. To toil for a hard master is bitter, but to have no master to toil for is more bitter still. Thinkest thou that the ravens will feed us? And what cure hast thou for these things? Wilt thou say to the buyer, 'Thou shalt buy for so much,' and to the seller, 'Thou shalt sell at this price?' I trow not. Therefore go back to thy Palace and put on thy purple and fine linen. What hast thou to do with us, and what we suffer?"

"Are not the rich and the poor brothers?"

"Aye, and the name of the rich brother is Cain."

And the young King's eyes filled with tears, and he rode on through the murmurs of the people.

And when he reached the great portal of the cathedral, the soldiers thrust their halberts out and said, "What dost thou seek here? None enters by this door but the King."

And his face flushed with anger, "I am the King." He waved their halberts aside and passed in.

And when the old Bishop saw him coming in his goatherd's dress, he rose up in wonder from his throne, and went to meet him, and said to him, "My son, is this a king's apparel? And with what crown shall I crown thee, and what sceptre shall I place in thy hand? Surely this should be to thee a day of joy, and not a day of abasement."

"Shall Joy wear what Grief has fashioned?" And he told him his three dreams.

And when the Bishop had heard them he knit his brows, and said, "My son, I am an old man, and in the winter of my days, and I know that many evil things are done in the wide world. The beggars wander through the cities, and eat their food with the dogs. Canst thou make these things not to be? Is not He who made misery wiser than thou art? Wherefore I praise thee not for this that thou hast done, but I bid thee ride back to the Palace and make thy face glad, and put on the raiment that beseemeth a king, and with the crown of gold I will crown thee, and the sceptre of pearl will I place in thy hand. And as for thy dreams, think no more of them. The burden of this world is too great for one man to bear, and the world's sorrow too heavy for one heart to suffer."

"Sayest thou that in this house?" The young King strode past the Bishop, and climbed up the steps of the altar, bowed his head in prayer and the priests in their stiff copes crept away from the altar.

And suddenly a wild tumult came from the street outside, and in entered the nobles with drawn swords and nodding plumes. "Where is this dreamer of dreams? Where is this King, who is apparalled like a beggar—this boy who brings shame upon our State? Surely we will slay him, for he is unworthy to rule over us."

And the young King bowed his head again, and prayed, and when he had finished his prayer he rose up, and turning round he looked at them sadly.

And lo! through the painted windows came the sunlight streaming upon him, and the sunbeams wove round him a tissued robe that was fairer than the robe that had been fashioned for his pleasure. The dead staff blossomed, and bare lilies that were whiter than pearls. The dry thorn blossomed, and bare roses that were redder than rubies. Whiter than fine pearls were the lilies, and their stems were of bright silver. Redder than male rubies were the roses, and their leaves were of beaten gold.

He stood there in the raiment of a king, and the gates of the jewelled shrine flew open, and from the crystal of the many-rayed monstrance shone a marvellous and mystical light. He stood there in a king's raiment, and the Glory of God filled the place.

And the people fell upon their knees in awe, and the nobles sheathed their swords and did homage, and the Bishop's face grew pale, and his hands trembled. "A greater than I hath crowned thee," and he knelt before him.

And the young King came down from the high altar, and passed home through the midst of the people. But no man dared look upon his face, for it was like the face of an angel.

—Oscar Wilde (1890)

3. The following parable is one of the world's masterpieces. We referred to it when we were discussing emphasis. Read the whole of it now. Get the subtle emphases; suggest a reality of persons in son and father, but remember that only one person speaks.

The Parable of the Prodigal Son

. . . And he said, A certain man had two sons; and the younger of them said to his father, Father, give me the portion of goods that falleth to me. And he divided unto them his living. And not many days after, the younger son gathered all together, and took his journey into a far country, and there wasted his substance with riotous living. And when he had spent all, there arose a mighty famine in that land; and he began to be in want. And he went and joined himself to a citizen of that country; and he sent him into his fields to feed swine. And he would fain have filled his belly with the husks that the swine did eat; and no man gave unto him. And when he came to himself, he said, How many hired servants of my father's have bread enough and to spare, and I perish with hunger! I will arise and go to my father, and will say unto him, Father, I have sinned against heaven, and before thee, and am no more worthy to be called thy son: make me as one of thy hired servants. And he arose, and came to his father. But when he was yet a great way off, his father saw him, and had compassion, and ran, and fell on his neck, and kissed him. And the son said unto him, Father, I have sinned against heaven, and in thy sight, and am no more worthy to be called thy son. But the father said to his servants, Bring forth the best robe, and put it on him; and put a ring on his hand, and shoes on his feet: And bring hither the fatted calf, and kill it; and let us eat, and be merry: For this my son was dead, and is alive again; he was lost, and is found. And they began to be merry. Now his elder son was in the field: and as he came and drew nigh to the house, he heard music and dancing. And he called one of the servants, and asked what these things meant. And he said unto him, Thy brother is come; and thy father hath killed the fatted calf, because he hath received him safe and sound. And he was angry, and would not go in: therefore came his father out, and entreated him. And he answering said to his father, Lo, these many years do I serve thee, neither transgressed I at any time thy commandment: and yet thou never gavest me a kid, that I might make merry with my friends: But as soon as this thy son was come, which hath devoured thy living with harlots, thou hast killed for him the fatted calf. And he said unto him, Son, thou art ever with me, and all that I have is thine. It was meet that we should make merry, and be glad: for this thy brother was dead, and is alive again; and was lost, and is found.

—The Bible

TO JOIN YOUR HEARERS

Enter the Audience

THE TITLE OF THIS chapter may seem strange after all the references we have made to your "listeners," "hearers," "audience," etc. Everything that has been said has been aimed at your doing a good job of reading *to* somebody, but now it is time to take a much closer look at the "somebody" you read to. We must look at this from a number of angles.

YOUR ROLE AS READER

Even during your practice sessions before the class, when you were striving for proper word grouping, emphasis, vocal texture, etc., and the audience seemed relatively unimportant, you must have sensed that your job did not end with adequate translation of the text. Something more was needed. You were forced, by the mere fact that there *was* an audience, to enter into some sort of personal relationship with that audience. And when you reflect that your future audiences will come to hear, not *Macbeth,* but your *reading* of *Macbeth,* you will see that you cannot long pretend to be merely an impersonal transmitter of someone else's material. Even more than your classmates, your future audiences will demand that you give something of yourself.

Now it is easy to warn you not to "put on an act," to advise you to "be natural" or to "be yourself." But in so doing we beg the question. Granted, in appearing arty, or in overwhelming us with the intensity of your communion with the immortals, you are obviously putting on an act; but in a deeper sense you are putting on an act even when you "be yourself." Each of us is a complex of a myriad of different selves, most of them perfectly sincere. The "you" who talks to your parents is different from the "you" who talks to your best friend, and the "you" revealed to us in class is not the "you" we see in the snack bar or tuck shop or rathskeller. Every social relationship evokes in you a unique series of responses—a particular personality, a particular role.

The propriety of your role as an oral reader may be tested by the same criteria as those applied to the judgment of any role. One of the first is that the role lie within your capabilities; when you say you feel false or insincere, you generally mean that the role which has been forced upon you is hard for you to play. Second, the role should fit the situation and shift with shifting circumstances. Again, it must accord with what observers have a right to expect: not only must it be consistent enough for them to identify it, but it should invite them to adopt roles that are easy for *them*. (If you appear inordinately dedicated, or if, at the opposite extreme, you present us the awkward grinning stereotype of the "nice guy," you catch us unawares, and force us into roles we do not wish to play. We come neither as adoring disciples nor as personal counselors.)

In other words, although every reading will be unique, in general you must select a role—a "you"—that allows you to perform efficiently, consistently, and "sincerely" the functions which your own purpose and the rightful expectations of your audience have dictated. Those functions, as we conceive them, are as follows.

The Reader Is a Transmitter of the Text

This has been the burden of the past nine chapters; here we need only reëmphasize our belief that no amount of charm will absolve you of the responsibility to make the objective message clear, to reflect accurately the tone and attitude and mood, and to render immediately and persuasively the sensuous detail and the personalities of the persons involved in the action. Although these tasks may be modified somewhat by the functions that follow, they are basic; they constitute the bare minimum without which any reading is almost certainly unacceptable.

The Reader Is a Transmitter of an Art Object

As we suggested in Chapters Five and Six, you must draw attention to the skill with which the text has been constructed. Your listeners should be able to trace the design, with its balances, contrasts, and climaxes; they must detect the implications of the symbols and dramatic ironies; they must relish the sound and rhythm.

In a later section on Empathy and Aesthetic Distance we shall show that emphasis upon structural elements will prevent your listeners from becoming so deeply involved in the material that they react as if it were real life. More immediate, if you emphasize those elements and show *your* appreciation of them, you prevent your audience from *comparing* your reading with real life; you never allow them to think you are trying to *be* Marc Antony or Satan or the "I" who wandered lonely as a cloud.

The Reader Is a Member of the Audience

This is implied when we advise you to avoid anything that draws conscious attention to your performance as "performance." Here is the basis for the strictures against impersonation as contrasted with interpretation, the defense or refutation of which have occupied so many theoreticians for so many years.[1]

The point is that even when presenting a "dramatic monologue," wherein your own personality seems to be completely submerged in that of the character, you must appear before your audience not so much as one who *does* but as one who *shares*.

You establish your membership in the audience at the very outset by the way in which you acknowledge the presence of the others; you retain your membership, first, by an appearance of spontaneity—creating "the illusion of the first time," and second, by your evident awareness of your listeners' response. You can seem surprised by the surprising details, you can seem apprehensive when the hero is in danger, you can appear baffled or nonplussed or delighted—you can and should show the reactions you would have if you were indeed encountering the ideas and events for the first time. You deliberately assume the responses you want to evoke in your audience. Furthermore, you can tease your audience—show them how delighted you are when you and the author succeed in tricking them or console them for having been tricked.

Ordinarily, of course, you will not interpolate verbally; but your visible and audible behavior can clearly indicate such unstated comments as "What do you think of that?" "I wonder how they'll get out of this mess!" "Aha, you think such-and-such is going to happen, don't you!" "I know you're excited,

---

[1] Despite all the pages written to the contrary, these two words do not have concrete and specific referents—a statement implicitly proved at every speech contest or festival where participants enter "interpretative reading" and/or "impersonation" events (maybe we should add "declamation"). Judges, teachers, students go round and round on the matter and arguments are perennial. We feel that trying to prescribe oral reading skill in opposing terms of "interpretation" and "impersonation" is futile; it puts the cart before the horse and leads to unsupportable arbitrariness and woeful disregard for listeners. After all, what on earth is oral reading skill for but to enable a person effectively to read a text to listeners? Isn't it, then, an inescapably sound principle that a reader should orally present the chosen text in *whatever manner will most completely communicate his comprehension of the text?*

but you'll just have to wait until I choose to tell you!" "We must have great compassion for this person," "This is a despicable business"—and countless others. Subject always to the demands of your text, reveal your reactions and in general show that you are one of the group (audience) which is composed of friends you can trust. One final tip that most beginners need: when reading the conclusion, let your manner say clearly, "This is the end, and it is as it should be."

The Reader Is a Leader of the Audience

The foregoing suggestions must be tempered by the fact, among others, that you have prepared the material and your audience has not. Although you are one of them, for this particular occasion you are the authority. However spontaneous your presentation, it must always be apparent that you have things under complete control. However worried your audience becomes about the outcome of what you are reading, they must never become worried about your ability to handle the matter. Do not violate their confidence by mispronunciation, apology, apparent lack of confidence in yourself.

The Reader Is the Creator of an Art Object

Since this function embraces the others, the discussion here should summarize the preceding sections. Indeed, it should summarize the entire book, because as an artist you must create your own mood and attitude and tone, your own balances and harmonies, your own rhythm—your own work of art: you must exploit the potentialities of the elements you find in the text, in your audience, in your personality, and fuse them into a single unity.

These five functions of the *reader-cum-audience* may suggest that the role is discouragingly complex. But remember that frequently two or more functions may be filled simultaneously; even more important, they may be filled in rapid succession. Just as you can easily "fade" one attitude into another, you can at one moment "see" the sensuous detail, at the next "become" one of the characters, and a moment later signal to the audience that neither is to be taken at face value.

AUDIENCE AS RECEIVER

Since there can be no communication without reception, a receptor is an indispensable part of communication machinery. Everyone knows this, but not everyone appreciates the fact that communication is not fully complete until the sender has received satisfactory evidence from the receiver that the message has been received. The response which tells the sender "message received," "Roger," etc., communication engineers call "feedback." A schematic representation may help to make the communication cycle in oral reading more vivid to you.

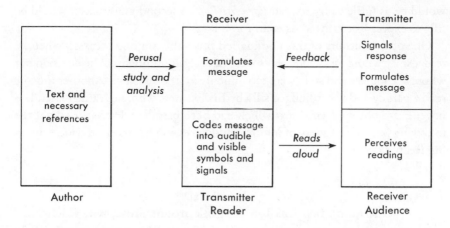

The structure of the receptor, along with the entire structure of the communication machine, determines what is, indeed, what *can* be, received. As a reader, therefore, you had better have some pretty accurate knowledge of the structure of your audience.

Occasion Structures Audience

You know very well that the situations in which persons function direct their behavior. The behavior of a group dressed in jeans and pedal pushers at a "hoe-down" or beach party differs greatly from the behavior of the same persons formally attired at an annual prom. Think of your own classmates as they behave in class, at a funeral, in an assembly, in a committee, at the college inn. People actually see things differently on different occasions and under different circumstances. What you read and how you read it must be fully consonant with the occasion. This comes close to being an absolute. Even in the familial intimacy of your own home you would not read aloud a joke you found in the daily paper if one of the family lay at death's door. Your reading of the same joke at another time might be received with delight.

Your classroom situation permits wide latitude in texts and manners, but even here there are circumscriptions of assignment—and of appropriateness.

Composition and Background Structure Audience

Not only is the question "What is appropriate to the occasion?" pertinent; you must answer also "What can my specific audience properly receive?"

High school students, Boy Scouts, church members, school faculty, etc.—the situation which brings together persons of each such category will impose its limits, but so will the background and caliber of the assembled members. It would be as futile to try to read *Paradise Lost* to second graders as it would be silly to expect Rotarians to listen to *Little Women.*

One of the authors of this book failed miserably on one occasion when he read a story whose ideas and events were entirely appropriate to the occasion but whose vocabulary and style were too difficult for the audience. Another time he read a parody and was adjudged silly by his listeners who, he learned later, had never heard of the original text which had been parodied. He has tried out the following on a wide variety of informal audiences and has received widely differing feedbacks.

THE BALLET

One night, heppens I'm hengink arount Moscowitz's delicatessen wit loose ents, when a friend iss hendink me a free pess to de bellet. I'm knowink nodding from bellet, but—I'm in de mood and de price iss right. So, gredually I'm arrivink de teatre and hup iss goink de coitin.

On to de stage iss comink oud, dencing on tippy toes, gredually a goil, dressed foity degrees younger den spreeng, in noddink but a seemple blue crepe de cheney. Her foist name iss Premiere. In beck, each laig iss looking like she's cerrying New England boiled dinner.

She's ronnink here, she's ronnink dere. She's afraidt sometink. I'm sayink to mineself, what's mekkink de goil so noivous, when soddenly comes jumpink on de stage a fella. He's wearink noddink but a stale leopard. De boy's name iss Adagio.

Soddenly de goil Dansuesy iss seeink Adagio, so she's hidink. So help me, on de stage iss not one steeck foiniture. But she's hidink. Behind nottink! Adagio iss lookink. In de exect middle on de stage she's stendink yet, but he's not seeink her, de dope!

Soddenly he's seeink Dansuesy. He's mekink terrific jump at de goil. He vants. She's jumpink avay. She dun't vant. He's leapink wit jumpink wit grebbink. He vants! She's ronnink wit leapink wit dodgink. She dun't vant! So he starts chasink de goil at eight toity-five. I'm leavink at ten twenty-five. I'm not knowink how he came oudt.

—Anon.

A withering response of sickly bewilderment came from a remotely rural audience; an exhilaratingly hilarious response came at an after-performance party for guests and leading performers of a British ballet company. Why?

How an audience will receive your reading, therefore, depends on what it is structured to perceive. Everybody's perception is conditioned by his background —what he has experienced, what he "knows."[2] Recall your study of "On First Looking into Chapman's Homer," page 197. Can you remember your first "perception" of the sonnet? As you probed the text, familiarized yourself with the allusions, pondered what Keats was getting at, you broadened your background and deepened your perception. At the outset, you (as Keats' audience) found you had some "receptor" deficiencies. Study of the text reduced them and improved your perception.

Now carry this principle to your preparation for reading this sonnet to a specific audience.

No situation is static: occasions can be modified; listeners can be primed. Audience's perception—and hence reception—can be extended during particular occasions, sometimes within astonishing limits. Every good salesman knows this. You have an opportunity, within limits, to remove certain deficiencies in your listeners' backgrounds by supplying necessary information in introductory comment. For instance, you have been asked by your literature teacher to come prepared to read a sonnet to the class. You like Keats' sonnet on Chapman's Homer, and moreover, you feel that you learned to read it pretty well in your interp class. You know most of the students in the lit class have never even heard of Chapman. Furthermore, some of them think that "literature" is just another academic chore, certainly not an adventure in the "realms of gold." From your own experience, you know such lack of background will limit their perception. Their receiving apparatus needs priming, so, how about prefacing your reading with something like this:

I have chosen a sonnet by John Keats: "On First Looking into Chapman's Homer." I selected it because I like it; I like the idea that one

[2] You will enjoy reading the following: Chaps. III and IV, "The Hanover Institute Demonstration in Perception," and "The Deeper Meaning of Vision" in Earl C. Kelley, *Education for What Is Real*, Harper, 1947; chap. 14, "The Perceiver" in Gardner Murphy, *Personality, A Biosocial Approach to Origin and Structure*, Harper, 1947; J. Samuel Bois, *Explorations in Awareness*, Harper, 1957.

can get a real thrill of discovery from exploring literature. Keats got a thrill when he discovered and read a translation of Homer's work by George Chapman.

In less than twenty seconds you have extended your listeners' background sufficiently to increase their perception in listening to "On First Looking into Chapman's Homer." Note also that you adjusted the occasion itself.

Size Structures Audience

Whereas consideration of composition and caliber of audience will direct your choice of texts, size of audience will dictate magnitude of manner. Two extremes will illustrate what we mean.

Think of a situation where your audience is a single person—a close friend with whom you enjoy sharing things of interest. You have discovered the following sonnet. It was used in Chapter 3, page 85.

THE PEOPLE

The people is a beast of muddy brain,
    That knows not its own force, and therefore stands
    Loaded with wood and stone; the powerless hands
    Of a mere child guide it with bit and rein;
One kick would be enough to break the chain;
    But the beast fears, and what the child demands,
    It does; nor its own terror understands,
    Confused and stupefied by bugbears vain.
Most wonderful! with its own hand it ties
    And gags itself—gives itself death and war
    For pence doled out by kings from its own store.
Its own are all things between earth and heaven;
    But this it knows not; and if one arise
    To tell the truth, it kills him unforgiven.

> —Thomaso Campanella (1622),
> Trans. J. A. Symonds (1878)

You were impressed with its contemporary significance and astonished to learn its original was written more than three hundred years ago. You want to read it to your friend so that he will get its ironic impact as you did. You will read it to him, therefore, as skillfully as you can.

Consider another situation where your audience is a thousand persons assembled to hear the finalists in an oratory contest. You are one of the finalists and your subject is "The People Must Think!" In the treatment of that subject you read the sonnet bitingly to drive home its point. Here again, you will want to read it as skillfully as you can. But how different the two readings!

	First Reading	Second Reading
	Visible Behavior	
Apparel	wholly unimportant	your dignified best
Posture	probably sitting	certainly standing
Movement and gesture	very little; likely to be limited to facial expression	maybe 1 or 2 cleanly emphatic gestures to drive home such points as "with its own hand," "But this it knows not"
Attention to audience	personal rapport with friend requires no eye contact during reading	will drive important points home by looking squarely at audience while uttering words which carry those points
	Audible Behavior	
Volume	slightly more than that used in conversation; emphasis will call for this increase	enough to enable 1000 persons comfortably to hear; this volume will be increased for emphasis
Rate	a bit slower than ordinary conversation	much slower; pauses longer
Range and change of pitch	range about the same as normal conversation; fluctuation less abrupt	wider range; more sustaining of pitch
Vocal texture	pretty conversational; colored by your particular response to sonnet	oratorical—not to be confused with bombastic; your best sonority
Articulation and enunciation	probably more precise, sharper than your conversational wont. The poem calls for incisive clarity (but not pedantry)	magnified; fewer neutral vowels; vowels of key words lengthened

How would your friend receive it if you read it to him exactly as you read it to the thousand? What feedback could you expect from the thousand if you read it to them precisely as you did to your friend?

The size of audience calls for proportionate "largeness" in transmission of messages.

Oral reading skill requires careful adaptation to and control of occasion; adjustment to composition and background, and size of audience; awareness of perception as a participating function of communication.

EMPATHY AND AESTHETIC DISTANCE

Empathy

We now look at audience response from still another angle.
Observe the following figure.

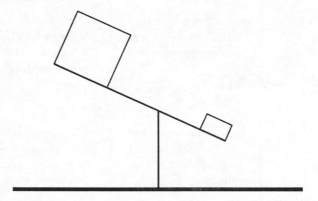

What do you see?
How do you like it.

What do you want to do to it? Exactly: pull the left side down where you feel it belongs.[3] You want to do something to it because it has done something unpleasant to you. Are you able to describe that something? It is easy to say that it is ugly, that it is unbalanced, that it violates the principle of first-degree leverage—in short, that it offends you, but in so saying you have not explained really *why* you want to pull the left side down. A small child would have no such desire. Probably adults could be found in certain cultures

---

[3] We have seen students literally squirm when this figure has been drawn on the blackboard. Some of them have pushed up with their right and pulled down with their left shoulders; others have used their hands to correct the "error," and a few, when the figure has been left on the board, have pleaded that it be erased. Even if you rationalize that the left side is an empty box and the right a cube of lead, you still dislike it.

who would not be offended in any way by the picture and would therefore
have no inclination to pull the left side down—a further illustration that perception is conditioned by experience. The figure seems to violate what you
have experienced and therefore you do not like it. Note that this still does not
describe what you, thanks to your background, are doing when you look at it.

You are implicitly *reproducing* it without being aware of it. You are unconsciously taking on tensions which "imitate" the figure. Thanks to your experience, these imitative tensions are unpleasant, and you say, "The figure is
wrong, it is unbalanced, I don't like it." What you do not like is what is going on in you, but not being fully aware of the tensions as such, you project
your response to the figure. This fundamental human tendency implicitly and
unconsciously to reproduce an object of perception is an aspect of what is
called *empathy*.

Empathy is at work when you rise at a forward pass in a football game,
when you strain with jumpers and pole vaulters, or even lift a leg with hur-
dlers. You hold your breath when a soprano sustains high C; stretch upwards
before a great church spire; take an expansive breath when viewing a sweeping panorama from a high summit; laugh with Jacques; suffer with Hamlet;
weep with Lear.

Next time you attend a movie which is packed full of suspense and tense
action, sit far enough forward so that the greater part of the audience is behind you. After you have seen the show through, remain for the next run.
During the tense and particularly exciting scenes, turn round and watch the
audience. (If the procedure seems gauche, rationalize it as "scientific research.")
Note how many of the spectators are visibly reproducing what they are looking
at. Look for those who are enjoying it most; see if you can find any who are
downright disliking it; are any of them bored?

Those who will report, "It was a top-notch show," enjoyed their emphatic
participation in—their unconscious own reproduction of—the performance.
Should any report, "I hated it; it was just too painful to be borne," their empathic participation was too acutely realistic for enjoyment. Any who were
"bored stiff" lacked empathic participation; they were completely "unmoved."

Bear in mind that everyone who listens to you read is, in one degree or another, an incipient "empathizer" to your reading. His particular empathy will
result from *his* perception of your reading. Your objective, then, can be stated:
inducing proper empathy in your audience, neither too much nor too little
and just the right kind.

The right kind establishes a relationship of enjoyment which has been called
aesthetic distance.

Aesthetic Distance

Just at the close of World War II, an RAF navigator, on leave from active duty which had entailed many missions over Germany, was visiting a large city in the western United States. One night his host took him for a skyline drive along the hills overlooking the city, which afforded an excellent view of the entire valley in which the city lies. The mountain air was crystalline clear; the heart of the city was a blaze of colored light. The host stopped the car and with considerable home-town pride pointed to the brilliant display. The following conversation ensued:

"Isn't that a beautiful sight?"
"No."
"You don't think that's beautiful?"
"Not at all."
"Why not?"
"It looks too much like a city I have just bombed."

Another instance: One of the authors was crossing the Atlantic during the war. He enjoys ship travel. One night late, he was standing alone in the very prow of the great liner which was blacked out behind him. Like a double-bladed plow, the ship cut through the black water, turning it into two great phosphorescent surges. Ahead was the vast, silent and strangely luminous blackness of the sea. Here was great beauty; he experienced an exhilaration, an exultation of spirit. In the midst of this tremendous empathic uplift, he thought suddenly, "What would I do if I should see the white wake of a torpedo rushing directly at the ship?" In that instant a scene of thrilling magnificence was not only shattered, it became menacing and "ugly."

A third case: The same author had the opportunity of seeing two very different productions of John Van Druten's play, *There's Always Juliet;* one was in a traditional proscenium-arched theatre, the other in a very small theatre-in-the-round. The first was a satisfactory performance, the second downright embarrassing. The torrid lovemaking up on the stage, framed by the proscenium, was credible make-believe; comparable amorous cavorting at our very feet and witnessed closely from all angles was too real, too near—it was positively clinical.

Each of the foregoing cases illustrates two kinds of empathy, one producing enjoyment, one dislike. The enjoyment is of a particular kind; it has been labeled aesthetic enjoyment, that is, enjoyment involving the higher senses. It has been described as perception of beauty, pleasurable appreciation of excellence, pleasurable recognition of skill, etc. It entails a peculiar aloofness, a certain detachment on the part of the perceiver. He sort of "stands off" to enjoy the object, as it were. If he becomes too closely, too realistically involved, either directly or through past experience, the "beauty" is lacking, as in the case of the RAF visitor. This calls to mind a rancher who lived near Bryce Canyon, Utah, that amazing labyrinth of colored sandstone monoliths. A visitor, awed by what he called its weird majesty said to him, "My, it must be a thrill to live where you can see all this beauty every day;" to which the rancher replied, "Humph! Damnedest place to lose cattle in you ever saw!" The rancher lacked the detachment necessary for aesthetic pleasure.

When the perceiver sees something in the object which is inimical to him, he becomes too closely involved, he loses detachment, and if there was beauty there before, it tends to dissolve, aesthetic pleasure ceases, as was the case in the prow of the ship. An electrical storm can be a beautiful thing until it threatens damage to the beholders.

Hence the term "aesthetic distance." Sometimes this "distance" is purely psychological as in the first of the three foregoing cases. Sometimes an actual physical distance is necessary for establishing the necessary detachment, as in the third case. A large painting seen from three or four feet may seem an ugly daub, but viewed from twenty-five or thirty feet it may become a part of a profoundly aesthetic experience.

Very recently (summer, 1959) audiences in some of our great metropolitan centers thrilled to the Bolshoi Ballet. Some of the performances at the Metropolitan Opera House were photographed from the stage. Some spectators who saw both the live performance and the movies report an interesting thing: a certain grotesque quality in some of the movies that was lacking in the actual performance. Here is a beautiful example of the role of aesthetic distance. The ballet was not designed to be seen from such close range as the stage where the cameras were placed. Exaggeration of make-up, and indeed of movement, necessary for spectators in a great theatre becomes unpleasantly apparent when seen too close.

Does this help explain why effective readings of Campanella's sonnet to a single person and to a thousand, respectively, are entirely inappropriate if reversed?

Oral reading skill calls for appreciation of the functions of empathy and aesthetic distance.

Turn to the selection "Death at Jamestown," page 357. You must bring to this selection an empathy for suffering, for terrific thirst, for delirium, for terror, but always within you there must be an objective, aesthetic satisfaction in your reproduction, your creation. Never for a moment do you actually suffer, feel agonizing thirst, or experience delirium. You are narrating for Benét. You do not die the moment you have read "Lonely and desolate in a far land," but you are keenly aware that the speaker you have been quoting has died, and you are fully ready to go on with Benét's narrative as you sense his comment: "And it was mid-September and no hope."

All this you must convey to your audience, be it one person or a thousand, so that he or they, perceiving your good works, will catch the suffering, the thirst, the delirium, the death, the commentary—and all with aesthetic satisfaction.

If your audience is bored, your reading is probably flabby: you are too inert; you have failed to induce in your audience and in yourself proper empathy. If, on the other hand, your audience is embarrassed because you are overdoing it, you have destroyed aesthetic distance.

HOW FAR SHOULD I GO?

The answer to the question of how far you should go is: *As far as your audience will follow.*

Let us try to make that generality specific with further specific reference to "Death at Jamestown."

Your audience must grasp at once the retrospective sentiment of the first five lines. Here is the collective and poignant memory of the survivors at Jamestown. The lines are addressed directly to the reader, and this directness must be passed on from you to your audience.

To make sure that "pitiful outcries of our sick men" will be appreciated, Benét constructs the dying speech of one of the sick men. You must make a visible transition after the fifth line which will make clear that something new is coming. With "Water, my lads!" your audience must realize at once that they are listening to the words of one of the sick men. Moreover, they must "feel" they are overhearing those words as he said them. And here is the crux of the matter. You must say the words so that they really *suggest* the way you think they might have sounded. If your suggestion is strong enough, it will induce the appropriate empathy in your listeners and they will satisfactorily complete the picture in their several imaginations. They will apprehend along with you the thirst, the terror, the delirious transitions, the fevered hallucinations, the desperate appeals, the last clear realization of futility, and finally, the mortal fading in the words "Lonely and desolate in a far land."

If your audience does not "get" all these things, your own empathy has not gone far enough in the re-creation of the dying man's speech. If, on the other hand, your audience gets the uncomfortable feeling that "He's laying it on pretty thick," or looks away or fidgets in embarrassment, you have lost your audience. You have either gone too far with your re-creation or it is faulty.

A visible transition after "in a far land," must tell your audience: "There we have had a concrete example." And as you address them directly with "And it was mid-September," they know they are being addressed with straight narrative and author's commentary and they appreciate the lines:

> Life-sickened shadows dragging weary limbs
> Mechanically to the rotten bulwarks.

We cannot be completely explicit, since we cannot know every situation in which you might appropriately read "Death at Jamestown." Each situation will have its unique appropriateness. We can, however, suggest that if your audience is small and the situation intimate, you would be wise to sit down to read. You will find a quiet intensity needed. If your audience is large and you are on a platform, you will certainly want to stand and a lectern is almost mandatory. Your whole rendition must be magnified. The cry

> O Christ,
> Sweet Christ, a little water for my thirst!

may seem to fill the auditorium and rend the hearts of your listeners. But note: they must feel their hearts rent by the dying man's cry; they must *not* feel that *you* are rending their ears with your profane shouting.

You will have to learn from feedback from listeners whether or not they are with you. With practice and paying attention to audience behavior you can learn to tell whether you are succeeding. Rapt, undivided attention indicates you and your audience are together. Inattention, coughing, whispering signal boredom. Increase your apparent attention to your audience. Remember, attention begets attention. Intensify your suggestion in such ways as your material and the situation indicate. The following techniques, singly or in combination, may help to get the desired response: stepping up volume, magnifying manner, exaggerating implications, increasing realism.

Wry smiles, furtive glances at each other, refusal to look at you, or looks of frank disfavor warn of overdoing. Your suggestion may be too strong. You may be too loud, too realistic, too "emotional." You cease to be a sharer and become a bombarder. Increased restraint is the order of the moment. A deliberate but subtle increase of emphasis on structural elements—contrast, balance, parallelism, metaphorical figures, rhyme, rhythm, etc.—will help restore aesthetic distance. Remember what has been said about form as a function of meaning. Recognition of excellence in structure is one of the chief sources of aesthetic satisfaction.

We used the word "suggests" a few paragraphs back. What is a suggestion? This is a nice question, and so important for the oral reader that it requires an answer. Maybe we can illuminate our definition with two examples from the theatre.

Some years ago one of the authors saw a number of performances of each of two plays, *Saint Joan* and *The Wandering Jew*. The plays have this in common: the chief character in each is burned at the stake. In every performance of the former, the audience perceived the burning of Joan in satisfyingly terrible silence. In every performance of the other, the burning elicited nervous titters or audible comment.

After her condemnation, Joan was dragged from the trial room and the visible stage was left completely empty. We heard the rumble of the crowd and then we saw coming through the great window and lighting the opposite wall the red glare of the fire.

The Wandering Jew was bound to a stake center stage, piled about with what seemed to be faggots which were apparently lighted and we saw the Wanderer writhe to his apparent death amidst what seemed to be very real flames. It was a most realistic incineration.

Both burnings were suggestions. The first was enough to set our imaginations working and each member of the audience could complete the burning to his aesthetic satisfaction. The second was so realistic as to be unbearable as a reality. Nothing was left to the imagination, and in order to make the thing tolerable, spectators had to remind themselves that it was not as real as it looked and after all the actor had to play another performance the next night, so he was really quite all right. The first had tremendous empathic impact but permitted us to maintain our aesthetic distance. The second had tremendous empathic impact but destroyed aesthetic distance.

Suppose a third case. What would have happened if the scene in *Saint Joan* had ended merely with the passing of sentence? The sentence would have suggested quite clearly that she was to be burned, but it would not have been powerful enough to bring home to us the terror of the burning, and her later speeches in the mystic epilogue would have been denied some of their suggestive power.

And now for a specific definition: *Suggestion is the deliberate inducing in an audience of a particular idea, impulse, or empathic response through the stimulus of oral reading.* Does this help in further determining how far you should go?

EXERCISES AND ASSIGNMENTS

1. Discuss severally the last round of readings with your classmates in light of the five audience-relationship functions.
   a. What were the excellencies and the shortcomings in the sheer transmissions of the texts?
   b. How did the readers show their appreciation of form?
   c. How well did the readers maintain their status as sharers with the class rather than performers before the class?
   d. Did you lose confidence in any of the readers? If so, what were the reasons?
   e. Was the whole of each reading a satisfactory experience? Why or why not?
2. Describe an ideal situation for the reading of each of the following selections:

How to Be Efficient with Fewer Violins

The following is a report of a Work Study Engineer—a Specialist in Method Engineering—after a visit to a symphony at the Royal Festival Hall in London:

For considerable periods the four oboe players had nothing to do. The number should be reduced and work spread more evenly over the whole of the concert, thus eliminating peaks of activity.

All the twelve violins were playing identical notes; this seems unnecessary duplication. The staff of this section should be drastically cut. If a larger volume of sound is required, it could be obtained by electronic apparatus.

Much effort was absorbed in the playing of demi-semi-quavers; this seems to be an unnecessary refinement. It is recommended that all notes should be rounded up to the nearest semi-quaver. If this were done, it would be possible to use trainees and lower-grade operatives more extensively.

There seems to be too much repetition of some musical passages. Scores should be drastically pruned. No useful purpose is served by repeating on the horns a passage which has already been handled by the strings. It is estimated that if all redundant passages were eliminated the whole concert time of two hours could be reduced to twenty minutes and there would be no need for an intermission.

The conductor agrees generally with these recommendations, but expresses the opinion that there might be some falling-off in box-office receipts. In that unlikely event it should be possible to close sections of the auditorium entirely, with a consequential saving of overhead expenses, lighting, attendance, etc. If the worst came to the worst, the whole thing could be abandoned and the public could go to the Albert Hall instead.

—Anonymous memorandum circulating in London, 1955
Harper's Magazine (June, 1955)

Preview of Stellar Travel

Man is taking his first hesitant, exciting, faltering steps into space with rockets and this is sparking a race into the fabulous unknown. Take time, for example.

When man starts traveling several hundred thousand miles per second strange things are expected to start happening. At such high speeds time begins to "stretch," and as velocity approaches the speed of light, time might even appear to stand still.

As one accelerates away from earth, earthly things fade. The four seasons become longer, minutes and hours become longer. The traveler himself will eat less often, sleep less, and even the pulse beat will slow down.

But here complications set in, for most people choose to manage their activities on "old" theories, facts, and supposed laws with which they have been familiar. But after considerable "time" with "space" physicists this reporter has come to the conclusion that if man is ever to travel among the stars, either in theory or actuality, he must rid himself of his inbred prejudices against novelties of the universe.

Even now there is a great need for the kind of thinking that can transcend earth-bound existence. It is difficult, for example, to convince people that our system of measuring time by the earth's motion around the sun can have no meaning outside of our own solar system.

For instance, light takes a million years or so to travel from here to the next big assembly of stars, or spiral galaxy. Yet, according to the men who are supposed to know, a space traveler may be able to get there in his lifetime. And the reason (simple, they say) is that what seems like a million years to one here on earth does not necessarily seem like a million years to another out in space (and here is the catch) if he travels fast enough.

(If you are still with me, let's go on.) If a man would travel from here to Andromeda, to the observer on earth he would seem to take more than a million years. And when he goes to Andromeda, returns and comes back he will find that the earth has got older by more than two million years. Yet he accomplished it all in his own lifetime.

So, many people are now asking if a week-end trip into space would turn the years back. If a person took a trip into space, would he return younger, fresher, and gayer? You would think that it would be possible to get a yes or no answer to this. But, no sir! Several of the top physicists in New York took this reporter on a universe grand tour on the subject without ever committing themselves.

However, one expert was willing to go part way out on the limb and it seems that, in "simplest terms," time would literally "slow down" for the person traveling in space at very high—but by no means improbable—speeds. As a result, a person traveling at two-thirds the speed of light would find upon his return from a trip to the star Sirius, brightest in our galaxy, that the journey had taken him five or six years less than his 18-year absence recorded on earth.

Now then, if you took the same trip would you come back five or six years younger? Relatively yes, when compared with an earth counterpart. Whether you would be older biologically is the hotly debated question.

But before all of this can happen to you, you will be happy to know that considerable research must be conducted into the necessary factors which will make your trip comfortable—not to say possible.[4]

—Harry C. Kenney, *Christian Science Monitor* (October 18, 1958)

3. Here are four selections: a familiar essay, a chapter from a novel, a biblical commentary, and a short story. Study them carefully. What differences in treatment do they require? How would you specifically polarize your audience's attention for proper listening to each?

Maine Speech (October, 1940)

I find that, whether I will or no, my speech is gradually changing, to conform to the language of the country. The tongue spoken here in Maine is as different from the tongue spoken in New York as Dutch is from German. Part of this difference is in the meaning of words, part in the pronunciation, part in the grammar. But the difference is very great. Sometimes when a child is talking it is all one can do to translate until one has mastered the language. Our boy came home from school the first day and said the school was peachy but he couldn't understand what anybody was saying. This lasted only a couple of days.

For the word "all" you use the phrase "the whole of." You ask, "Is that the whole of it?" And whole is pronounced hull. Is that the hull of it? It sounds as though you might mean a ship.

For lift, the word is heft. You heft a thing to see how much it weighs. When you are holding a wedge for somebody to tap with a hammer, you say: "Tunk it a little." I've never heard the word tap used. It is always tunk.

Baster (pronounced bayster) is a popular word with boys. All the kids use it. He's an old baster, they say, when they pull an eel out of an eel trap. It probably derives from bastard, but it sounds quite proper and innocent when you hear it, and rather descriptive. I regard lots of things now (and some people) as old basters.

A person who is sensitive to cold is spleeny. We have never put a heater in our car, for fear we might get spleeny. When a pasture is sparse and isn't providing enough feed for the stock, you say the pasture is pretty snug. And a man who walks and talks slowly or lazily is called mod'rate. He's a powerful mod'rate man, you say.

When you're prying something with a pole and put a rock under

---

[4] Reprinted by permission from The Christian Science Publishing Society.

the pole as a fulcrum, the rock is called a bait. Few people use the word "difference." When they want to say it makes no difference, they say it doesn't make any odds.

If you have enough wood for winter but not enough to carry you beyond that, you need wood "to spring out on." And when a ewe shows an udder, she "bags out." Ewe is pronounced yo.

The ewe and yo business had me licked at first. It seemed an affectation to say yo when I was talking about a female sheep. But that was when I was still thinking of them as yews. After a while I thought of them as yos, and then it seemed perfectly all right. In fact, yo is a better-sounding word, all in all, than yew. For a while I tried to pronounce it half way between yew and yo. This proved fatal. A man has to make up his mind and then go boldly ahead. A ewe can't stand an umlaut any more than she can a terrier.

Hunting or shooting is called gunning. Tamarack is always hackmatack. Tackle is pronounced taykle. You rig a block and taykle.

If one of your sheep is tamer than the others, and the others follow her, you say she will "toll" the others in. The chopped clams which you spread upon the waters to keep the mackerel schooling around your boat, are called toll bait. Or chum bait. A windy day is a "rough" day, whether you are on land or sea. Mild weather is "soft." And there is a distinction between weather overhead and weather underfoot. Lots of times, in spring when the ground is muddy, you will have a "nice day overhead."

Manure is always dressing, never manure. I think, although I'm not sure, that manure is considered a nasty word, not fit for polite company. The word dung is used some but not as much as dressing. But a manure fork is always a dung fork.

Wood that hasn't properly seasoned is dozy. The lunch hour is one's nooning. A small cove full of mud and eelgrass is a gun hole. When a pullet slips off and lays in the blackberry bushes she "steals away a nest." If you get through the winter without dying or starving you "wintered well."

Persons who are not native to this locality are "from away." We are from away ourselves, and always shall be, even if we live here the rest of our lives. You've got to be born here—otherwise you're from away.

People get born, but lambs and calves get dropped. This is literally true of course. The lamb actually does get dropped. (It doesn't hurt it any—or at any rate it never complains.) When a sow has little ones, she "pigs." Mine pigged on a Sunday morning, the ol' baster.

The road is often called "the tar." And road is pronounced rud. The other day I heard someone call President Roosevelt a "war mongrel." Statute is called statue. Lawyers are busy studying the statues. Library is liberry. Chimney is chimley.

Fish weir is pronounced fish ware. Right now they're not getting anything in the wares.

Hoist is pronounced hist. I heard a tall story the other day about a man who was histed up on the end of a derrick boom while his companions accused him of making free with another man's wife. "Come on, confess!" they shouted. "Isn't it true you went with her all last year?" For a while he swung at the end of the boom and denied the charges. But he got tired finally. "You did, didn't you?" they persisted. "Well, once, boys," he replied, "Now hist me down."

The most difficult sound is the "a." I've been in Maine, off and on, all my life, but I still have to pause sometimes when somebody asks me something with an "a" in it. The other day a friend met me in front of the store, and asked, "How's the famine comin' along?" I had to think fast before I got the word "farming" out of his famine.

The word dear is pronounced dee-ah. Yet the word deer is pronounced deer. All children are called dee-ah, by men and women alike.

The final "y" of a word becomes "ay." Our boy used to call our dog Freddie. Now he calls him Fredday. Sometimes he calls him Fredday dee-ah; other times he calls him Fredday you ol' baster.

Country talk is alive and accurate, and contains more pictures and images than city talk. It usually has an unmistakable sincerity which gives it distinction. I think there is less talking merely for the sound which it makes. At any rate, I seldom tire listening to even the most commonplace stuff, directly and sincerely spoken; and I still recall with dread the feeling that occasionally used to come over me at parties in town when the air was crowded with loud intellectual formations— the feeling that there wasn't a remark in the room that couldn't be brought down with a common pin.[5]

—E. B. White, *One Man's Meat* (1940)

THE YANKEE'S FIGHT WITH THE KNIGHTS

Up to the day set, there was no talk in all Britain of anything but this combat. All other topics sank into insignificance and passed out of men's thoughts and interest. It was not because a tournament was a great matter; it was not because Sir Sagramor had found the Holy Grail, for he had not, but had failed; it was not because the second (official) personage in the kingdom was one of the duellists; no, all these features were commonplace. Yet there was abundant reason for the extraordinary interest which this coming fight was creating. It was born of the fact that all the nation knew that this was not to be a duel between mere men, so to speak, but a duel between two mighty magicians; a duel not of muscle but of mind, not of human skill but of superhuman art and craft; a final struggle for supremacy between the two master enchanters of the age. It was realized that the most prodigious achievements of the most renowned knights could not be worthy of comparison with a spectacle like this; they could be but child's play, contrasted with this mysterious and awful battle of the gods. Yes, all

[5] From *One Man's Meat* by E. B. White. Copyright, 1940, by E. B. White. Reprinted by permission.

the world knew it was going to be in reality a duel between Merlin and me, a measuring of his magic powers against mine. It was known that Merlin had been busy whole days and nights together, imbuing Sir Sagramor's arms and armor with supernal powers of offense and defense, and that he had procured for him from the spirits of the air a fleecy veil which would render the wearer invisible to his antagonist while still visible to other men. Against Sir Sagramor, so weaponed and protected, a thousand knights could accomplish nothing; against him no known enchantments could prevail. These facts were sure; regarding them there was no doubt, no reason for doubt. There was but one question: might there be still other enchantments, *unknown* to Merlin, which could render Sir Sagramor's veil transparent to me, and make his enchanted mail vulnerable to my weapons? This was the one thing to be decided in the lists. Until then the world must remain in suspense.

So the world thought there was a vast matter at stake here, and the world was right, but it was not the one they had in their minds. No, a far vaster one was upon the cast of this die: *the life of knight-errantry.* I was a champion, it was true, but not the champion of the frivolous black arts, I was the champion of hard unsentimental common-sense and reason. I was entering the lists to either destroy knight-errantry or be its victim.

Vast as the show-grounds were, there were no vacant spaces in them outside of the lists, at ten o'clock on the morning of the 16th. The mammoth grand-stand was clothed in flags, streamers, and rich tapestries, and packed with several acres of small-fry tributary kings, their suites, and the British aristocracy; with our own royal gang in the chief place, and each and every individual a flashing prism of gaudy silks and velvets—well, I never saw anything to begin with it but a fight between an Upper Mississippi sunset and the aurora borealis. The huge camp of beflagged and gay-colored tents at one end of the lists, with a stiff-standing sentinel at every door and a shining shield hanging by him for challenge, was another fine sight. You see, every knight was there who had any ambition or any caste feeling; for my feeling toward their order was not much of a secret, and so here was their chance. If I won my fight with Sir Sagramor, others would have the right to call me out as long as I might be willing to respond.

Down at our end there were but two tents; one for me, and another for my servants. At the appointed hour the king made a sign, and the heralds, in their tabards, appeared and made proclamation, naming the combatants and stating the cause of quarrel. There was a pause, then a ringing bugle-blast, which was the signal for us to come forth. All the multitude caught their breath, and an eager curiosity flashed into every face.

Out from his tent rode great Sir Sagramor, an imposing tower of iron, stately and rigid, his huge spear standing upright in its socket and grasped in his strong hand, his grand horse's face and breast cased in steel, his body clothed in rich trappings that almost dragged the ground—oh, a most noble picture. A great shout went up, of welcome and admiration.

And then out I came. But I didn't get any shout. There was a wondering and eloquent silence for a moment, then a great wave of laughter began to sweep along that human sea, but a warning bugle-blast cut its career short. I was in the simplest and comfortablest of gymnast costumes—flesh-colored tights from neck to heel with blue silk puffings about my loins, and bareheaded. My horse was not above medium size, but he was alert, slender-limbed, muscled with watchsprings, and just a greyhound to go. He was a beauty, glossy as silk, and naked as he was when he was born, except for bridle and ranger-saddle.

The iron tower and the gorgeous bedquilt came cumbrously but gracefully pirouetting down the lists, and we tripped lightly up to meet them. We halted; and tower saluted, I responded; then we wheeled and rode side by side to the grand-stand and faced our king and queen, to whom we made obeisance. The queen exclaimed:

"Alack, Sir Boss, wilt fight naked, and without lance or sword, or—"

But the king checked her and made her understand, with a polite phrase or two, that this was none of her business. The bugles rang again; and we separated and rode to the ends of the lists, and took position. Now old Merlin stepped into view and cast a dainty web of gossamer threads over Sir Sagramor which turned him into Hamlet's ghost; the king made a sign, the bugles blew, Sir Sagramor laid his great lance in rest, and the next moment here he came thundering down the course with his veil flying out behind, and I went whistling through the air like an arrow to meet him—cocking my ear the while, as if noting the invisible knight's position and progress by hearing, not sight. A chorus of encouraging shouts burst out for him, and one brave voice flung out a heartening word for me—said:

"Go it, slim Jim!"

It was even bet that Clarence had procured that favor for me—and furnished the language, too. When that formidable lance-point was within a yard and a half of my breast I twitched my horse aside without an effort, and the big knight swept by, scoring a blank. I got plenty of applause that time. We turned, braced up, and down we came again. Another blank for the knight, a roar of applause for me. This same thing was repeated once more; and it fetched such a whirlwind of applause that Sir Sagramor lost his temper, and at once changed his tactics and set himself the task of chasing me down. Why, he hadn't any show in the world at that; it was a game of tag, with all the advantage on my side; I whirled out of his path with ease whenever I chose, and once I slapped him on the back as I went to the rear. Finally I took the chase into my own hands; and after that, turn, or twist, or do what he would, he was never able to get behind me again; he found himself

always in front at the end of his maneuver. So he gave up that business and retired to his end of the lists. His temper was clear gone now,
and he forgot himself and flung an insult at me which disposed of mine.
I slipped my lasso from the horn of my saddle, and grasped the coil in
my right hand. This time you should have seen him come!—it was a
business trip, sure; by his gait there was blood in his eye. I was sitting
my horse at ease, and swinging the great loop of my lasso in wide cir-
cles about my head; the moment he was under way, I started for him;
when the space between us had narrowed to forty feet, I sent the snaky
spirals of the rope a-cleaving through the air, then darted aside and
faced about and brought my trained animal to a halt with all his feet
braced under him for a surge. The next moment the rope sprang taut
and yanked Sir Sagramor out of the saddle! Great Scott, but there was
a sensation!

Unquestionably, the popular thing in this world is novelty. These
people had never seen anything of that cowboy business before, and
it carried them clear off their feet with delight. From all around and
everywhere, the shout went up:

"Encore! encore!"

I wondered where they got the word, but there was no time to cipher
on philological matters, because the whole knight-errantry hive was
just humming now, and my prospect for trade couldn't have been better. The moment my lasso was released and Sir Sagramor had been assisted to his tent, I hauled in the slack, took my station and began to
swing my loop around my head again. I was sure to have use for it as
soon as they could elect a successor for Sir Sagramor, and that couldn't
take long where there were so many hungry candidates. Indeed, they
elected one straight off—Sir Hervis de Revel.

Bzz! Here he came, like a house afire; I dodged: he passed like a flash,
with my horse-hair coils settling around his neck; a second or so later,
fst! his saddle was empty.

I got another encore; and another, and another, and still another.
When I had snaked five men out, things began to look serious to the
ironclads, and they stopped and consulted together. As a result, they
decided that it was time to waive etiquette and send their greatest and
best against me. To the astonishment of that little world, I lassoed Sir
Lamorak de Galis, and after him Sir Galahad. So you see there was
simply nothing to be done now, but play their right bower—bring
out the superbest of the superb, the mightiest of the mighty, the great
Sir Launcelot himself!

A proud moment for me? I should think so. Yonder was Arthur,
King of Britain; yonder was Guenever; yes, and whole tribes of little
provincial kings and kinglets; and in the tented camp yonder, renowned
knights from many lands; and likewise the selectest body known to
chivalry, the Knights of the Table Round, the most illustrious in Chris-
tendom; and biggest fact of all, the very sun of their shining system

was yonder couching his lance, the focal point of forty thousand adoring eyes; and all by myself, here was I laying for him. Across my mind
flitted the dear image of a certain hello-girl of West Hartford, and I
wished she could see me now. In that moment, down came the Invinci-
ble, with the rush of a whirlwind—the courtly world rose to its feet
and bent forward—the fateful coils went circling through the air, and
before you could wink I was towing Sir Launcelot across the field on
his back, and kissing my hand to the storm of waving kerchiefs and
the thunder-crash of applause that greeted me!

Said I to myself, as I coiled my lariat and hung it on my saddle-horn,
and sat there drunk with glory, "The victory is perfect—no other will
venture against me—knight-errantry is dead." Now imagine my astonishment—and everybody else's, too—to hear the peculiar bugle-call
which announces that another competitor is about to enter the lists!
There was a mystery here; I couldn't account for this thing. Next, I
noticed Merlin gliding away from me; and then I noticed that my lasso
was gone! The old sleight-of-hand expert had stolen it, sure, and slipped
it under his robe.

The bugle blew again. I looked, and down came Sagramor riding
again, with his dust brushed off and his veil nicely re-arranged. I trotted
up to meet him, and pretended to find him by the sound of his horse's
hoof's. He said:

"Thou'rt quick of ear, but it will not save thee from this!" and he
touched the hilt of his great sword. "An ye are not able to see it, because of the influence of the veil, know that it is no cumbrous lance,
but a sword—and I ween ye will not be able to avoid it."

His visor was up; there was death in his smile. I should never be
able to dodge his sword, that was plain. Somebody was going to die
this time. If he got the drop on me, I could name the corpse. We rode
forward together, and saluted the royalties. This time the king was disturbed. He said:

"Where is thy strange weapon?"

"It is stolen, sire."

"Hast another at hand?"

"No, sire, I brought only the one."

Then Merlin mixed in:

"He brought but the one because there was but the one to bring.
There exists none other but that one. It belongeth to the king of the
Demons of the Sea. This man is a pretender, and ignorant; else he had
known that that weapon can be used in but eight bouts only, and then
it vanisheth away to its home under the sea."

"Then is he weaponless," said the king. "Sir Sagramor, ye will grant
him leave to borrow."

"And I will lend!" said Sir Launcelot, limping up. "He is as brave
a knight of his hands as any that be on live, and he shall have mine."

He put his hand on his sword to draw it, but Sir Sagramor said:

"Stay, it may not be. He shall fight with his own weapons; it was his privilege to choose them and bring them. If he has erred, on his head be it."

"Knight!" said the king. "Thou'rt overwrought with passion; it disorders thy mind. Wouldst kill a naked man?"

"An he do it, he shall answer it to me," said Sir Launcelot.

"I will answer it to any he that desireth!" retorted Sir Sagramor hotly.

Merlin broke in, rubbing his hands and smiling his lowdownest smile of malicious gratification:

" 'Tis well said, right well said! And 'tis enough of parleying, let my lord the king deliver the battle signal."

The king had to yield. The bugle made proclamation, and we turned apart and rode to our stations. There we stood, a hundred yards apart, facing each other, rigid and motionless, like horsed statues. And so we remained, in a soundless hush, as much as a full minute, everybody gazing, nobody stirring. It seemed as if the king could not take heart to give the signal. But at last he lifted his hand, the clear note of the bugle followed, Sir Sagramor's long blade described a flashing curve in the air, and it was superb to see him come. I sat still. On he came. I did not move. People got so excited that they shouted to me:

"Fly, fly! Save thyself! This is murther!"

I never budged so much as an inch till that thundering apparition had got within fifteen paces of me; then I snatched a dragoon revolver out of my holster, there was a flash and a roar, and the revolver was back in the holster before anybody could tell what had happened.

Here was a riderless horse plunging by, and yonder lay Sir Sagramor, stone dead.

The people that ran to him were stricken dumb to find that the life was actually gone out of the man and no reason for it visible, no hurt upon his body, nothing like a wound. There was a hole through the breast of his chainmail, but they attached no importance to a little thing like that; and as a bullet wound there produces but little blood, none came in sight because of the clothing and swaddlings under the armor. The body was dragged over to let the king and the swells look down upon it. They were stupefied with astonishment naturally. I was requested to come and explain the miracle. But I remained in my tracks, like a statue, and said:

"If it is a command, I will come, but my lord the king knows that I am where the laws of combat require me to remain while any desire to come against me."

I waited. Nobody challenged. Then I said:

"If there are any who doubt that this field is well and fairly won, I do not wait for them to challenge me, I challenge them."

"It is a gallant offer," said the king, "and well beseems you. Whom will you name first?"

"I name none, I challenge all! Here I stand, and dare the chivalry of England to come against me—not by individuals, but in mass!"

"What!" shouted a score of knights.

"You have heard the challenge. Take it, or I proclaim you recreant knights and vanquished, every one!"

It was a "bluff" you know. At such a time it is sound judgment to put on a bold face and play your hand for a hundred times what it is worth; forty-nine times out of fifty nobody dares to "call," and you rake in the chips. But just this once—well, things looked squally! In just no time, five hundred knights were scrambling into their saddles, and before you could wink a widely scattering drove were under way and clattering down upon me. I snatched both revolvers from the holsters and began to measure distances and calculate chances.

Bang! One saddle empty. Bang! another one. Bang—bang, and I bagged two. Well, it was nip and tuck with us, and I knew it. If I spent the eleventh shot without convincing these people, the twelfth man would kill me, sure. And so I never did feel so happy as I did when my ninth downed its man and I detected the wavering in the crowd which is premonitory of panic. An instant lost now could knock out my last chance. But I didn't lose it. I raised both revolvers and pointed them—the halted host stood their ground just about one good square moment, then broke and fled.

The day was mine. Knight-errantry was a doomed institution. The march of civilization was begun. How did I feel? Ah, you never could imagine it.

And Brer Merlin? His stock was flat again. Somehow, every time the magic of fol-de-rol tried conclusions with the magic of science, the magic of fol-de-rol got left.

—Mark Twain,
A Connecticut Yankee at the Court of King Arthur (1889)

NO PLACE AT THE INN

There was no place for them in the inn. There are no words in the whole Gospel of Luke upon which the minds of Christians have dwelt more meditatively and more tenderly than upon these. Out of what is stated here the scene shapes itself again as vividly to the imagination as though it were beheld by actual eyes: a little town in darkness, a jostling crowd of people arriving here and pressing ahead of one another for harborage, Joseph and Mary of Nazareth coming wearily to the end of their long road; no room for them in the rude village inn, and nothing to do then but to find a corner in a stable where Mary could come to rest. Christian poets have caught the strange and wistful wonder of it all, as in Phillips Brooks's "O Little Town of Bethlehem," G. K. Chesterton's "There Fared a Mother Driven Forth," and Joyce Kilmer's "There Was a Gentle Hostler."

Of course the picture as Luke gives it cannot be pressed too far, as though we could identify persons and their motives in a Bethlehem that was. But one reason why it lays such a hold upon the mind and heart is that the crowded inn of the story becomes also an eternal parable of the human soul. Therefore in that everlastingly present sense, why was there—why is there—no room in the inn for the Christ child who is at its doors?

In the first place, simply because of other guests who would have got there first. In the imagined scene at Bethlehem, if Mary and Joseph had come earlier to the inn, they doubtless would have been received. If they were turned away, it was not that there was any ill will against them, but simply because the innkeeper was so harried with other people that he had no patience to look at any more. His house was a caravansary and those who had happened to arrive first had filled it up. These travelers from Nazareth had come late, the inn was crowded, they could not get in; and that was all there was to that. Just so casually, through the near drift of circumstances, and not through any particularly hostile will, may Jesus be excluded from the inn of our hearts. We have merely filled all the space we have with other guests. We do not mean to be irreligious, but our thoughts and feelings are so occupied with other matters that religion cannot find a place. We too are like a caravansary where the first come are the first served. In this world with its noisy and demanding clamor the crowd of common thoughts and common interests has poured in upon us and taken possession of our time and our attention, and when Christ comes with his infinite gift for the enrichment of our souls, there is no room for him in the inn.

In the second place, it might be said that the reason why there was no room in the inn for Mary and Joseph and for the Christ child who was to be born was because nobody knew that they were coming, and did not recognize their importance when they came. If the one who had charge of the inn had dreamed who Mary's child would be, he would have found means to welcome him. Like most of the rest of us, he would have been flattered at the idea of welcoming greatness. If someone could only have told him that here was the world's Savior, that here was the One by whose name every little town and place he touched should be made significant forever, then he would have rearranged his guests and sent some of them to find lodgings elsewhere, that Mary the mother of Jesus might come in. But he did not know. That is the way it always is. We never do know when the great possibilities of God are at our doors unless we have taken the pains to keep our spirits sensitive. The mystery waiting to bring to us the birth of a redeeming Savior may be at our doors, and all that we shall see will be some ordinary stranger whom we shall wave away, saying, "There is no room in my inn."

There is another course of thought along which we might be led concerning the theme which has been suggested. When the reality of Christ is at our doors, what may be the signs of his presence?

In the first place, the note of his coming will be joy. When anything happens in life that is or might be joyous, then we need to understand that the reality of Jesus may be coming near. Love has come to a man and a woman, or some great friendship has begun, or new opportunities open into a work which gives happier self-expression than has been known before. If a man chooses, he may take these things self-confidently, as if he himself had deserved them and created them. Or he may realize with a sense of wonder how widely life seems to be expanding beyond anything which he himself could have brought to pass. A child is born into a human home, and a man and woman may treat that great gift with a natural but shallow pride, and with no more than that. On the other hand, they may let the birth of that little child unlock for them the larger sense of the mystery and wonder of life. They may know that it is God who is giving himself to them, and then they will want to widen all the ways of their recognition so that most fully the heavenly blessing may come in.

In the second place, the sign that Jesus may be near us is when we stand in the presence of innocence. The curse of our world is not so apt to be its evil as its disillusionment. We can fight evil and gain strength in the battling with it, as long as we know unmistakably that evil is evil, and as long as we believe in the beauty and worthwhileness of good. But our danger is that we may grow cynical. We see so much of compromise that we may doubt whether there is any such thing as purity of motive and an unspoiled heart. To cleanse us from that cynicism our consciousness needs to dwell upon every fine act that we may hear of, especially those acts which are all the finer because they are simple and unpretentious—the faithfulness of mothers to their little children, the capacity of innumerable people to suffer for the sake of those they love, the integrity which makes men forego advantages in business which they might have gained through crooked paths, the idealism of young people who, notwithstanding many things which we call unconventional, still keep the cleanness of their hearts. Then it will be seen that human life is not the poor thing which sometimes it seems, but rather that there is a divine gift standing outside the doors, nearer than some of us imagine, ready always to come in and take up its abode with us.

In the third place, it may be a sign that Jesus is drawing near when we are moved with any impulse that is generous. And the most real generosity is not that which is expressed in material gifts. Rather it means to have the quick imagination which sees what others need before they have to tell us. It means to be generous with sympathy and with trust, and to follow every impulse which breaks through self-centeredness to make one eager and outgoing. When any man or woman does that, something wonderful will happen. Through the door which love has opened from within, Christ enters from without. Those who are trying to make their human affections beautiful learn that these are not human only, but divine. The spirit of Jesus comes to find room within the inn, and when once through the open doors he has really entered, then less and less can anything alien to his spirit continue dwelling there.[6]

—*The Interpreter's Bible,* Vol. 8 (1952)

GOD'S AGENTS HAVE BEARDS

One hot June night after having simultaneously eaten two hundred and fifty peanuts and read two hundred and fifty pages of *The Three Musketeers* by Dumas—which is at the average rate of one peanut a page—I slammed the book shut, stood up to face my father, and announced: "I want to meet God."

Every beautiful, dark-haired, book-loving member of my amazing family, gathered as usual around the dining-room table, stopped reading. Everyone, that is, except my father, who instead of reading had been composing music. For over two hours the only sounds in the room had been the turning of pages, the cracking of brittle peanut shells in the learned, book-salted mouths of my impassioned family, and the scratching of my father's goose quill on the stiff white music paper before him on the dining-room table. Now everyone stared at me in horror, and there was a ghastly stillness that was broken finally, as expected, by waves of hacking laughter from my tubercular uncle, Amos.

"The boy has gone crazy all of a sudden," he said, simultaneously laughing, gasping, coughing, retching, and finally breaking into tears.

"Amos," my father said, "close your mouth to senseless laughter. Boys who express interest in God should not be laughed at unless, of course, they express immoderate interest in God." Then he turned to me. "What are you reading?" he asked gently. My father was the gentlest man alive. Sweetness, kindness, and goodness dripped all over him like the warm wax on a great luminous candle.

"*The Three Musketeers,* by Alexandre Dumas," I said. "A very exciting if poorly written book."

My father shook his head. "Very interesting," he said. "Extremely interesting."

Uncle Amos let some more laughter, coughing, and mockery escape from his bitter lungs again. "The boy is *meshugeh*-mad," he insisted. "Here he is quietly reading *The Three Musketeers* by Alexandre Dumas, as generations of us have done each in our turn, and all of a sudden he stands up and says he wants to meet God—and at the same time he gives a book review! Did you ever hear of such a thing before in

---

[6] By Walter Russell Bowie in *The Interpreter's Bible,* Vol. 8. Copyright 1952 by Pierce and Smith. By permission of Abingdon Press.

your whole history of book reading? May I cackle like a jackal full of moldy *potato-kugel* if I ever did!"

"Sure, I've heard of such a thing," my father said. He was quiet and kind, but it was clear that he was thinking hard about this sudden and unlooked for family crisis.

"Well, I haven't, and if you ask me the boy has suddenly gone crazy from eating too many peanuts," Uncle Amos almost shouted. "That's what he is, crazy from too many peanuts!"

"He's a philosopher," my father said. "Everyone knows it. Otherwise would the very first word he ever enunciated at the age of eleven months and two weeks and three days have been 'why'?"

"He's crazy like a bedbug suffering dyspepsia from the sour blood of an anemic grandmother." Uncle Amos cried.

"Oh, be quiet," my father said. "This emergency calls for some important concentration. Let me think."

Everyone obeyed my father. We were all as quiet as the corpse at a funeral. Nobody cracked peanuts, nobody read, nobody even dared breathe. Except me. I dared do everything with my father.

But this time I was really frightened. The many-mouthed spider of superstition had me in its mandibles. It bit me at page 249. Of course, I had known for a long time what a profound theological upheaval was taking place in my superstitious heart. Every time I walked across town to the great haunted-looking house of Mr. Vladimir Rasputin for my weekly violin lesson, I used to make a deal with fate. "If the toes of my right shoe come out even with the cross lines on the cement sidewalk for ten consecutive steps," I used to say, "I'll have a good lesson and Mr. Rasputin won't spit in my eyes and yell: 'Ai, vut a demnt goot-far-nahtting boy you are. Ai, you are dr-riving me cr-razy!' " I hoped very hard that my toes would come out even. If sometimes after the fifth or sixth or seventh step the toes would not coincide, once, with the concrete lines, I'd start all over again. Other times I'd try to cheat fate by lengthening or shortening my pace. But if by hook or crook the toes refused to come out even then I *didn't* have a good lesson.

I had been cogitating on the problem for months. And now, on the eve of going to summer school to skip the sixth grade, I had suddenly realized, on page 249, that perhaps there really was a dark, long-bearded man in the sky who could not be cheated no matter how hard you tried. In that case something had to be done about it right away since summer school started next day, and I had to pass at all costs. Being the official philosopher of the family I always proceeded to logical conclusions. That was why I suddenly felt imbued with a cosmic urge to meet God face to face, if there was such a thing. A grown man of ten has tremendous responsibilities!

So now with the others I waited small and tense for the answer of my gentle and wonderful father.

He was a delight to look at as he pulled his short goatee and con-centrated. He was short and stocky, but powerfully built, with broad shoulders that always drove clothing clerks slightly daft. His huge shock of coal-black hair was somewhat interspersed with strands of gray, and his small beard was the same color. By contrast, his forehead was snow-white and high and intelligent. His eyes were a bright danc-ing blue and his mouth was the gentlest mouth in the whole wide world. I imagined that women would love to kiss that mouth very ten-derly. From him there somehow exuded a soft melancholy perfume that was like the fragrance of old and precious books in a bright sunny garden of lilies of the valley.

Finally my father said: "Well, little children, I have decided. The boy's interest in God is not immoderate."

He got up and put on his hat. "Come outside with me," he said, beckoning.

We went out of doors into the warm brilliance of the June evening and began to walk in utter silence.

After we had walked around the block twice without saying a word, my father said: "Now tell me all over again so I'll be sure."

"Pa," I said, "I want to meet God."

We walked around the block once more.

"How do you mean you want to *meet* God? You mean you want proof that there is a God?"

"Excuse me, Pa," I said. "I don't go for secondhand things. I'm a philosopher. I want to meet God personally, face to face."

My father looked amazed. He was wonderful. He didn't say a word. Of course, I knew he wouldn't take me by the left ear and twist my head around. But sometimes if you did something wrong, or, what was worse, something foolish, he would laugh at you in a gentle kind way. This time my father did not even laugh in a gentle way.

We took another walk around the block, then we sat down under a huge elm on the soft sweet grass of June, far away from the lights.

"Do you see the stars up there?" my father asked.

"Yes, Pa," I said. "I see them."

"There's millions," my father said.

"I know it," I said.

"They move exactly on schedule," he said. "They never change."

"Like a clock," I said. This was an old routine.

"Suppose," my father went on, "there was no traffic system to keep the cars downtown moving right. They'd bump into each other all the time."

"Yes," I said.

"Well, there's a traffic system that keeps the stars moving the same way. It's God."

I thought for a while.

"Maybe," I said, "they don't bump each other because they are so far apart. Maybe once upon a time there used to be more of them, closer together. So they destroyed each other and what's left has all the room it needs. That's why, maybe, they don't bump now."

My father pulled up some grass by the roots and meditated. I did the same.

After a while he said: "Yes, that's possible. It could be like that."

He pulled up some more grass. Then he said: "I want to tell you a story. Once a great idol-worshiping and terrible king told a rabbi that unless this rabbi could produce his God, face to face, in court the very next day, the rabbi's head would roll in the streets. The rabbi said: 'Sure, O great king, but first come on outside in the warm sunshine. I want to show you something.' The king humored the old fellow and went outside. 'Take a look at the sun, O great king,' said the rabbi. The king tried to look. It was a pretty hot sun because this was over in Asia somewhere where the sun's heat is something awful. 'I can't look at the sun,' said this mighty king. 'It hurts my eyes.' 'Well, how in heaven's name do you expect to see God face to face?' said the rabbi, 'if you can't even look at the sun which is only one of the *many* things God has made?' So next day," my father said, "that rabbi was made a vizier or some such almighty thing and from then on until the day he died that king never let the anti-Semites hurt the Jews."

I was pretty quiet for a kid my size.

"Do you get the moral?" my father said.

"Sure," I said. "I get the moral all right, but it doesn't satisfy me."

"It doesn't satisfy you?" my father asked.

"No, Pa," I said.

"Well, why not?"

"Because, Pa, doesn't it say somewhere in the Bible that the old prophets used to speak with God face to face?"

"Yes, it does say that," my father admitted.

"Then why can't I see God, too, face to face, Pa?" I asked.

My father took me by the hand and we got up from the soft green grass and began to walk home. Before we reached the house my father said:

"I'm going to tell you something. But I don't want you to breathe it to a soul, especially not to Uncle Amos." My father wasn't afraid of Uncle Amos. He just didn't like to keep telling him he was wrong all the time.

"Sure, Pa," I said. "I can keep a secret just as good as the next fellow."

"Then," my father said, lowering his voice to a whisper, "if you really want to see God face to face, you can."

"I can?"

"Yes, you can, if you keep asking God long enough and hard enough and God is sure you really mean it."

"You're not kidding me just because I'm only ten years old, are you, Pa?" I said.

"No," my father said. "I never kid anyone—unless it's your mother once in a while."

We started to climb the stairs. "There's something else you should know if you're going to meet God," my father whispered. "Sometimes God's too busy seeing somebody else; then he sends his personal representative. Will that be OK?"

I thought a while.

"Sure, Pa," I said. "I guess that will be OK—so long as I know it *is* his representative."

"You'll know when the time comes," my father said. "But remember, not a word of this to anyone."

"Not a word, Pa," I said.

The next morning at nine o'clock I went down to Union Street School and signed up for summer school. You attended summer school for six weeks and if you passed you skipped a whole grade. That meant a whole year saved.

I was the most ambitious kid in town and I knew that I knew more than anybody else, but I was scared stiff of flunking. That's why I usually came out first in my class. I was so scared of not passing that I worked hard enough to be considered the most brilliant and promising boy in the history of the school system. But being the most promising and brilliant boy in the school system still didn't stop me from being scared to death.

Each day on my way to school I prayed to God to let me pass. "Dear God," I said, "just think of the disgrace to my whole book-reading family if I don't pass the sixth grade in six weeks. My mother will say, 'Oh, it was too hard for him,' but you and I know it isn't too hard. Uncle Amos will laugh his head off and that isn't too good for his consumption because every time he laughs the blood comes out. So, for the sake of my poor book-devouring family let me pass to my just reward, the seventh grade, O God!" I said it over and over. That was one prayer.

I had a second. "O God," I said, "don't let me waste my valuable time praying to you if you aren't real. Let me see you face to face like the old prophets in the Bible. Just one look, O God!"

I kept repeating this every day. I knew them so well that I was even able to say them under my breath during class.

But I didn't see God. This frightened me all the more since I began to think that maybe God was really there and that he was keeping under cover, out of shame because he had already decided to flunk me. The more frightened I became the harder I studied and I got 100 per cent in all my preliminary exams. But I was still afraid of flunking because the final exam was still to come. I thought that if God was really there, it would be more fun for him to tantalize me with 100 per cent in the beginning but with a zero in the end. So I kept praying, harder every day.

What made it worse, Miss Regan, my teacher, was fifty-two years old, quite beyond the hopeful stage. Everyone whispered how she once had been in love with a man who, on his way to marry her, had been killed in a railroad wreck. She was skinny and sharp-jawed and always scowled at the kids from way down deep in her rich brown eyes. I felt she was just the type to conspire with God against me.

In fact, the entire summer was vaguely metaphysical.

At length, I took the final examination and was told to report the following morning to find out if I'd passed or not.

That morning I started out for school earlier than usual. I wanted to give myself and God a good last chance. I crossed the South Street bridge, praying hard all the way. As I turned on Washington Street and headed for school, I said: "O God, in just three minutes I'm going to turn the corner at Union where the traffic light is broken and walk into school. You've got just three minutes, O God, to save me and my family from a terrible everlasting disgrace. Incidentally, O God," I said, "those three minutes are important to you, too, because if you don't show yourself to me, then I'll have to stop believing in you, and that means I'll have to stop believing in my father, too, because he said I would see you if I only prayed hard and long enough. So, please God, let me see you now—this minute!"

I stopped walking—scared stiff. If I didn't see God I knew I had flunked. If I saw God—what would I do or say? After all, I had never met God before; he was a perfect stranger to me. But there wasn't a soul on the street, not even a sparrow.

I started walking again, very slowly. Ahead of me was the corner of Washington and Union. Once I turned that it was all over.

"O God," I said, "maybe I've been asking too much. Maybe you're too busy, like my father said. If you are, O God, why not send your representative? Any old representative will do."

I came to the corner.

"O God," I said. "I'm going to turn the corner now. Send a representative. Let him be right around the corner. Let him have a long black beard. Please, God, please!"

I took a deep breath, clenched my fists, and turned the corner.

There *was* a man there. He *did* have a long black beard.

I didn't know what to do. I just stared wildly at him. When he saw how excited I was, he smiled to me and asked me in Jewish:

"What time is it, son?"

I knew it was just nine o'clock because the school bell was ringing.

"It's nine o'clock, O mighty sir," I replied in my best chosen Jewish. Of course, I knew he was checking up on the time so he could tell God what time he had done his job.

He stroked his long black beard, hoisted to his shoulder a huge pack that looked as though it contained carpets, and walked away. I didn't know what to do, so I simply bowed from the waist and watched him until he had turned the corner. Then I went inside.

Sure enough I had passed the sixth grade. I was number one in my class. Miss Regan smiled for the first time in six weeks and said I was the most brilliant and promising boy in the school system. She said I would have a happy future, but that I must be careful of trains.

That night at home I joined my amazing book-devouring family. In the center of the dining-room table was a fresh, five-pound sack of peanuts. In front of each member of the family was a plate for shells. From the shelf I took down *The Three Musketeers* and opened it to page 251.

On the way to my place at the table I stopped and whispered to my father as he scratched musical notes with his goose quill on a shiny sheet of paper.

"I passed, Pa," I said.

My father nodded his head sweetly.

"I expected you would," he said.

I paused for a while and my father waited patiently.

"I also saw His personal representative today," I said. "He had a long black beard and asked me what time it was."

My father nodded again.

"I expected you would," he said, pulling at his short goatee.

"You two, there, what are you gloating about?" Uncle Amos cried from his couch in the corner. He alone was not reading; he had already read every book in the world in three or four different languages. "If it's something we should know, tell us and stop gloating secretly like two kittens with a bellyful of well-spiced gefüllte fish," he said.

My father smiled to me and I smiled to him. "It's nothing, Amos," he said gently. "The boy tells me he has passed the sixth grade in six weeks, that's all."

"Well, why shouldn't he pass?" Uncle Amos grumbled. "Haven't generations of us passed the sixth grade—like maggots through the small eyes of a sieve?"

I waited for the family's applause to die down. Then I went to my place at the table and began to read and eat peanuts.

It was still an exciting if poorly written book. But I felt somewhat superior to Alexandre Dumas. He, too, had undoubtedly passed the sixth grade, but had God's personal representative with a long black beard smilled at *him?*[7]

—Emmanuel Winters, *Harper's Bazaar* (1943)

4. Of the longer selections in this book, which you have studied and practiced, which ones did you enjoy working on most? Which ones do you feel you read best? Which ones gave you the most difficulty? Why?

5. What is the most embarrassing performance (of any kind) that you have witnessed? Describe specifically the reasons for your embarrassment.

[7] Reprinted by permission of the author.

ADDITIONAL EXERCISES

Prose: "The Evil Eye," p. 80; "The Death of Victoria," p. 101, "The Lord Chancellor," p. 152; "Fast Fish and Loose Fish," p. 161; "The Illumination," p. 224; "You'll Come Back," p. 235; "Allegory of Men and Gadgets," p. 296; "At Valley Forge," p. 317.

Poems: "Hotspur's Answer," p. 81; "For a Dead Lady," p. 262; "The Windhover," p. 275; "I'm Through with You Forever," p. 278; "At the Round Earth's Imagined Corners," p. 280; "Because I Could Not Stop for Death," p. 281; "Sonnet LXXIII," p. 282, "The Social Structure of Early Massachusetts," p. 285; "Brutus and Cassius," p. 295; "Sir Walter Raleigh in the Tower," p. 355; "Death at Jamestown," p. 357.

TO END AND TO BEGIN

Perennial Questions

FROM HERE ON you will be making more and more of your own assignments. Since you will be "on your own," we now bring this volume full circle with a quotation from Chapter One:

> The range open to you is two-dimensional: the literature you read and your "reading" of the literature. The scope of the first is the whole field of English letters, including translations from other languages. The scope of the second is determined by your purpose, talent, and industry.

LITERATURE TO READ

For fullfilling class assignments beyond the book we made certain suggestions to help you "find" material. Now you have almost finished with assignments for your present course. (We sincerely hope you will have—and will seize—opportunity for taking advanced courses.) Hereafter, you will have wider latitude in choosing what you will read aloud, which brings us back to your first question.

What Shall I Read?

Your area of choice will have two limits: the first, and by all odds the most important, is the extent of your own experience in the "realms of gold"; the second, though less important, is by no means negligible; it has to do with your wise consideration of specific audience.

CONSIDER YOUR OWN KNOWLEDGE OF LITERATURE. We have specifically advised that you read something you like; the very best way to have extensive choice is to have a lot of things that you like, and the very best way to have a lot of things that you like is to "travel extensively in the realms of gold." Do not waste time by sheer hunting for something to read aloud. Read widely for the fun of it, for enlightenment, for the thrill of discovery, for the very humanity of it. You will be surprised how often you find yourself wanting to share your reading experience with someone else: a news item, a story, an essay, a poem, a scene in a novel or from a play, a religious treatise, a philosophical argument. Read, READ, *READ!* Not with the idea of finding something to read aloud, but to avail yourself of as much experience as you can. There is no place on earth or any moment of recorded time to which you cannot travel if you make the written word your ship! Moreover, every book that was ever written offers a voyage of exploration into the mind of him who wrote it.

However, because a trip is available does not mean it is worth taking; some trips are sterile; others are pregnant with new experience, with adventure. Many minds that have produced books are hardly worth exploration; others invite repeated journeys. While you follow a tawdry tale you deprive yourself of rewarding exploration. So, since your time is limited, even if you live to be three-score years, it seems only common sense to strive for such discrimination in selection as offers real satisfaction in retrospect. Deliberately set out to read a few of the recommended "greats," and follow Professor John Erskine's advice:

> The method I should advise in reading great books is a simple one. I should try, first of all, not to be awed by their greatness. Then I should read without any other preparation than life has given me—I should open the pages and find out how much they mean to me. If I found my experience reflected in some parts of the book and not in others, I shouldn't worry about those blind spots. They may be the fault of the book in those places—it may be out of date. But it is more prudent of me to suppose, which is just as likely, that my own experience is perhaps a little thin in the regions those parts of the book dealt with. To find out which is so, I should read the book a second time, and a third.
>
> When we encounter these dead spots in books supposed to be masterpieces, and when we are humble enough to explain them by some insufficiency in ourselves, the impulse is to go for help to other books, to works of criticism. It is much more profitable to go directly to life. I won't say that no aid can be had from other people; I couldn't believe that and keep on teaching literature, or even write these papers. But the best teachers

of literature, in my opinion, try to suggest the experience which such passages are designed to reflect; they remind their hearers of experience mislaid for the moment; they can't impart it. . . .

It is advisable to sample as many of the great books as we can, for the first ones we come to may not be those which reflect us most completely. But once we have found our author, we have only to read him over and over, and after a while to read out from him, into the authors who seem kindred spirits. When the reader has found himself in two great authors, he is fairly launched.

But the books should be read over and over. Until we have discovered that certain books grow with our maturing experience and other books do not, we have not learned how to distinguish a great book from a book.

—*The Delight of Great Books* (1935)

As you thus increase your own reading store, you will have not the slightest need to rush to a bibliography of selections to "find" something to read aloud. Hardly a week will go by but you will have read something you *want* to read to someone else. Your store for reading aloud becomes ever greater. Your recognition of things to be read is a facet of your skill in reading aloud.

Again from the first chapter:

Obviously, you will have neither reason nor occasion to read aloud by far the greater part of what you read silently to yourself. Even so, as you increase your oral reading skill, you will find more and more literature that seems to be unfulfilled without appropriate utterance; you will find your mind's ear hearing that utterance even as you read silently. Furthermore, it is axiomatic that increasing ability to do brings with it more frequent opportunity for doing.

CONSIDER THE INTERESTS AND CAPACITIES OF YOUR AUDIENCE.   In very informal situations, and especially oral reading situations of your own making, this really is not a problem. But when you are invited to "give a reading," you must choose from your increasingly plentiful store.

The first difficulty here lies in avoiding two seductive extremes: "Give them what they want" and "Give them what they ought to want." Since the second is generally less attractive to beginning students, we need only remark to the small self-confident minority that "Listen to this because it's good for you" is a didactic, if not snobbish, attitude, and that didacticism has spoiled many a work of art. We shall therefore concentrate instead upon the first, and apparently more attractive, option.

The view that "the customer is always right" has proved so successful in large-volume business and accords so well with a popular but sentimental view of democracy that it probably would have spread into arts and other disciplines even without the further impetus given it by the "entertainment industry"—radio, TV, Broadway, Hollywood and the "press"—all of which pride themselves upon being Big Business, though they are still "artistic" enough to cater to "the public" instead of to the "customer." So the formula becomes revised to "Give the public what it wants." Now of course no working democracy can afford to assume that the majority is always right; it can assume only that in the long run the majority of those who are qualified to judge will judge wisely.[1]

By assuming that everyone in the "public" is equally qualified to judge, many in the entertainment industry have claimed, as you know, to have been forced to appeal to the lowest common denominator. History pretty well proves that the public *does not* know what it wants, until someone has the courage and the originality to show it what it wants—and then the rest of the industry scurries to follow the new "trend." If, like Hollywood during the 1920's, 1930's, and 1940's, for example, you surrender your standards to the audience-as-customer, you can hardly avoid repeating Hollywood's pattern. The point is, not only that sooner or later a competitor will meet your audience on his own terms, and reveal by the integrity of his performance the shallowness of your own, but in the meantime you forfeit your self-respect.

Admittedly, in our culture the signs of escapism and sentimentality can easily blur the very real advances made in popular taste. Nevertheless, if you look closely you can see evidence of a widespread desire for satisfaction more lasting than that provided by the slick, the sentimental, and the sensational. Consider the tremendous sales of classical recordings, or the popularity of magazines devoted to form and design; compare the movies that won "Academy awards" during the 1930's (you can often see them on TV) with those which win them today; compare even the dance routines of today's musical comedies with those of twenty years ago; study the implications of the huge market for highbrow

---

[1] Democracy further assumes that no one can accurately predict the qualifications which will prove most relevant to a given act of judgment, and so it tries to stock as many and as varied qualifications as it can. We might add that insofar as this course has helped to sharpen your ability to analyze and synthesize, or to broaden and deepen your sensitivity to experience embodied and reported in literature, insofar as it has strengthened your appreciation of form, or enabled you to make finer discriminations, and insofar as it has trained you to detect and to use subtler shades of expression, it may contribute quite as much to our democracy as will a comparable course in physics or mathematics. Quite a number of persons know how to make an H-bomb; but what a sad time we are having learning how to avoid using one! So much for the "fripperies" of oral reading.

paperbacks. Since we believe that there is a surprisingly strong popular yearning for the better, we would reverse the neat advice, "Tell it to Sweeney; the Stuyvesants will understand." If you tell it well to the Stuyvesants, you'll find that Sweeney will not only try very hard to keep up, but that he will understand far more than you expected.

The problem is a vexed one and authorities disagree, but we think that a reader is mistaken, on the one hand, to read only to where he thinks the heads of his audience should be, or on the other hand, to limit himself to what he is sure everyone in the audience will like. The compromise we suggest is not to aim at the average—and certainly not at a hypothetical average—but rather at the more sophisticated, the more mature, the more sensitive in the particular audience you are preparing to face.

So much for the literature you read. Let us turn to how you read it.

YOUR READING OF THE LITERATURE

In order more specifically to recapitulate the steps in preparation for reading aloud, let us assume you have been invited (or assigned) to read something you have not carefully studied. Your generic question is How Shall I Prepare? This at once suggests specific questions.

How Shall I Study?

Start with the text you are going to read. Do not dash off to the library to see what critics have said about it, or even worse, what biographers and historians have said about the author. Note that we do not advise that you *never* go to criticism and biography—undoubtedly reading history and criticism will impel you to further and profitable reading. What we are saying, emphatically, is that *by far the most important clue to the meaning of a selection is the selection itself, and consulting critics and biographers should be one of the last steps in your preparation.* Since these assumptions underlie fully half of this text, and since so many other books make contrary recommendation, we suggest you review intensively pages 60–95.

Is it not irrefragably true that no one knows exactly how the author felt or what he meant except, possibly, the author himself? Experience is a sensory-neuromuscular (and to take care of what we know but have a hard time proving) spiritual modification within a person. Experience lies below or transcends the level of words. It can be verbally symbolized from "What is man that Thou

art mindful of him," to "Rowley, Powley, gammon and spinach," to *"E=MC²."*
It can be verbally induced: George Chapman's translation of Homer changed
John Keats, who symbolized his experience in a great sonnet—and indeed gave
himself a new experience in the very writing of it. We can study the sonnet and
induce new and rich experience in ourselves—but it is not Keats' experience. Experience can be discussed: the discussion becomes an experience in itself; it does
not repeat the original experience.

If W. H. Auden, say, could explain completely in an essay what he "meant"
in one of his poems, why read the poem? We should scrap it and read the essay.
An artist does not merely *tell* something, he *builds* something. His telling is a
structure in itself and if we are going to understand it, we had better begin our
study with the thing built.

The critic is of course merely an experienced reader (not necessarily an oral
reader) and can sometimes help us to *see* the thing built. But as long as we let
him do our thinking for us we are unlikely to learn how to think for ourselves.
All in all, it seems wiser, and in the end more rewarding—and therefore more
efficient—to plumb the thing itself to the depths of our own ability before we
seek aid from commentary.

The following should help recall the steps presented in Chapters One, Two,
and Three.

1. Read the selection sympathetically and silently in order to gain a general
impression. Do not worry about the details yet, and skim over the tough spots.
Now ask yourself what feelings have been evoked in you; try to find a word
(sadness, joy, longing, mystery, despair, etc.) or a loose sentence that roughly
describes those feelings. You have tentatively identified the mood.

2. Reread the selection in similar fashion, and ask yourself what kind of person is writing, and, more important, what tone he is adopting toward you. If you
cannot come up with an answer, do not worry.

3. Now dig in. Carefully read the selection as often as is necessary to establish
clearly "what is being said." Consult a dictionary of at least collegiate size for the
meanings of all words about which you are in the least uncertain; here we emphatically include those "familiar" words which you have met often but which
do not seem to fit the context. Write out in your own words a paraphrase of
all the difficult or puzzling passages; then check your paraphrase against the
original to insure that you have accounted for every word. Finally, in your own
words, condense the original into less than one-third of its length; check this
précis against the original to insure that you have accounted for all major ideas.
By now you should have a pretty clear idea of the sense.

4. Study the selection carefully for evidence of attitude—i.e., roughly, bias or

slanting. Study the word choice: why were those words used instead of the words you used in your précis or in your paraphrase? Note which details have been emphasized, and which omitted; be especially suspicious of "unnecessary" repetition, and of quick changes of subject.

5. Now, in the light of what you have discovered from the emotion-packed ideas, test your early hunches about the mood and tone of the person talking.

At this point, or perhaps as early as point (4), you are ready to begin rehearsing the selection if it is short and relatively simple. Longer and more complex selections may require at least a preliminary examination of structure before you attempt to practice aloud. If necessary, review Chapters Five and Six which discuss the main problems of structure.

6. If there are characters in the selection, determine not only the kind of persons they are, and their relationship to each other, but their function: why is such-and-such a person needed in the story at all?

7. Break the selection up into units or sections, each of which contains a significant piece of action (e.g., the argument about selling the farm, the decision to sell, the sale, etc.) or accomplishes a major part of the writer's task (e.g., the description of the farm, the tirade against bombs, the contrast between Tom and Jerry, etc.). In the mere attempt to make these divisions you have probably answered the crucial questions: what must be accomplished in this part? Why does this part belong?

8. Within each unit, look for sources of conflict: what ideas are contrasted? How does one of them gain a victory? What characters are struggling? What does each character in the unit desire at this point? What part does he play in promoting or obstructing whatever is accomplished in the unit?

9. Determine the point of greatest intensity within the selection, and within each of the units. Trace the rise and fall of tension throughout the selection.

10. Look for balance within the units and within the entire selection. What ideas can be "paired off" as having approximately equal importance? What events? Characters? Peaks of intensity? Units?

11. Now reread the selection to see if everything "fits" and to be sure you know how it has been put together.

*Now is the time for some research into the life and other works of the author—*especially if, as far as you have gone, everything does *not* quite fit. Focus this research in the direction the textual difficulties indicate. Sometimes some relevant fact about the author will supply the clue to the difficulty—the missing link, without which the selection will not hang together.

Read through the following poem and then without reading beyond it, analyze it carefully and decide what you make of it.

A WARSONG OF THE HUNS
O Rome it is three leagues off yet,
But we'll get there ere the sun doth set!
There will be a dreadful fight,
Perhaps by day, perhaps by night!
    Blood and gore
    For evermore!

We'll dip our hands in Roman blood,
As they lie sweltering in the mud!
Instead of horseflesh we will eat
The Romans' raw and bleeding meat!
    Blood and gore
    For evermore!

We'll march away and shout hurray
For we'll have won the war today!
For triumph we will eat for joy
A very young and tender boy!
    Blood and gore
    For evermore![2]

—Beatrice Aspland (1938)

Disturbing, is it not? The poem is right, and yet it is completely wrong. Is it a problem of tone? Are we to take it seriously? Or what? But our puzzlement disappears—the poem clicks into focus—the moment one fact is supplied: the author was eleven and a half years old.

If you had had that fact *before* you studied the poem, you might easily have dismissed it as possessing less merit than it does; you would have been looking for less than was written. It is really surprising how knowledge of biographical data can obstruct as well as expand perception. How often does the too-early learning of an unsavory, but irrelevant, biographical event misdirect and impede understanding! Hence our advice: In preparation for reading a text aloud, read about the author *after* you have read *him* to the depth of your own critical and analytical ability. Make your own careful study of the text direct you to relevant study of biography and criticism.

There is a further advantage to such textually directed study. If your audience is a very sophisticated one, it will not be amiss for you to be able to

---

[2] From *Ego 3,* by James Agate, London, George G. Harrap and Company, Ltd., 1938.

match their general sophistication. Focus your critical and biographical research, not merely to gain facts for an impressive introduction (beware of putting on a show of learning), but to find out what the audience probably knows, so that you can better control their reactions. You should certainly know what is generally known. Look for clarifications of references in your material to events contemporaneous with your author.

How Shall I Practice?

The tasks you do best, the games at which you excel, are those which you have learned well. In Chapter One we called attention to the importance of practice, and every chapter since Chapter Two has called for your reading aloud— always with definite goals in mind. We hope by this time you have established a basic pattern for practicing. We suggest the following principles to keep in mind:

1. Avoid practicing in a very small room. Your empathic response to a small room will "cramp your style." Find a room that will permit you to feel free in it.

2. When you feel that you are developing your "expression" pretty well, rehearse for the particular occasion. Construct the situation in your imagination to the best of your ability and practice to achieve the total behavior (audible and visible) which will evoke in yourself the feedback which informs you that you have done justice to your text. In short, strive in rehearsal to do the thing just as you would like to do it when the audience is really there. Do not hesitate to go over and over—*and over*—the rough spots.

3. Remember always to make clear who is talking to whom. Read directly to your imagined audience those passages directly addressed by the author to the reader. If you are to make clear that characters are addressing each other, imagine carefully their relative positions and as you speak for each, look up enough from your book to seem to address the space where the listener's head would be. In switching from character to character, do not scoop down into the script between speeches; instead, follow this pattern: finish the first character's speech; immediately give the visible response of the character who is to reply; then, if necessary, glance down *in character* at the text to make sure of the words and then give the reply while "looking at" the first speaker. As a matter of principle, it makes for better reading of dialogue to get the words from the book *during* speeches rather than *between* them. If you happen to muff a reaction, bluff the matter through, even in rehearsal: pantomime the change into the right reaction before you give the lines. You can go back at the next transition and rework it. This kind of practice will help you to avoid drawing undue attention to your mistakes.

4. Make transitions visible—the larger the transition, the bigger the bridge. Relinquish the tensions of the unit just completed—thought, episode, chapter, etc.—and assume the tensions of the ensuing one, during a silence of appropriate length. This will permit your listeners needed relaxation and will lead them to gird up their empathic loins for what is to come. This is essential for clarity.

5. Time your later rehearsals carefully. If they exceed your time limit, cut some material; do not try to read faster.

6. If possible, have a "dry run" in the room or auditorium where you are scheduled to read.

7. Lastly, unless you are an experienced reader, be chary of tape-recording your rehearsals. Since the sound-recorder does not present the accompanying visible behavior, beginners tend to listen too intently to sheer acoustic variation and try to repair "mistakes" by experimenting with mere vocal tricks. Beginners in oral reading would be wise to use the tape recorder only under the careful supervision of a competent teacher.

By the time you get to the point where you feel you are about ready for your audience, you may find you know your text by heart and may, therefore, well ask the next logical question.

Shall I Use the Book?

Well, the word *reading* suggests the presence of a text. If your audience is expecting you to use a book, you had better use your book. Even if you know your text by heart and feel you do not need it, answer very carefully this question: "Will my audience react unfavorably to my memorization?" One of the most devastating bits of feedback one of the authors ever received followed his verbatim presentation of a half-hour story without the book. The remark was: "O, you're wonderful! How do you ever manage to remember all that?" He still cringes at the very recollection.

The use of the book helps to make your reading less obviously a "perform-ance." It helps to align you with your audience. Some famous readers can re-peat their readings without texts, but they use the book in order to maintain the reading situation. (Some of you may have earned enviable reputations for giving certain selections "from memory" and are asked at parties to "read such-and-such for us." By all means accede to the request. Here the performance ele-ment is of great importance; it is the performance the audience wants, and actual reading of the text would spoil the show.)

Fairly close attention to the book before a small audience helps to establish and maintain aesthetic distance. Before a large audience, you must be freer from the book; too close attention to it becomes a barrier rather than an aid. Because formality tends to increase with the size of audience, as does the need for magnification of manner, aesthetic distance may be more easily sustained without the book before a large audience than before a small, intimate one. But even so, "reading without the book" is a risky business. More risky than a generation ago. Fashions change. So, consider the matter carefully:

The advantages of using the book are, briefly, that you remind your listeners that the words are not your own and you avoid the suggestion "I'm doing this for real." You more easily maintain aesthetic distance. Also, the presence of the book gives you the comfortable assurance that the material will not vanish.

The chief disadvantage is that necessary eye contact is a bit more difficult to manage. Just as you must avoid burying your nose in the book, so must you avoid bobbing your head like a thirsty chicken.

The dangers of reading by rote are that you focus attention upon yourself; you become more the performer who does, and less the friend who shares. You are more vulnerable because you minimize the author's collaboration. Finally, you may become more concerned with recalling the words than with uttering them, to say nothing of the possibility of your going blank altogether.

Generally, then, we advise you to read from the book. Further, we advise the use of lectern or reading stand whenever the situation warrants. In this regard, remember that when you are invited (or assigned) to read, you have the right and the responsibility tactfully to suggest such improvements in the physical arrangements as are reasonably feasible.

While we are on this matter of using the book, here is a very important suggestion:

Keep your script clean. Do not try to indicate the pauses, the emphases, the inflections, etc. There are already enough black marks on the page to keep you busy.

No system of markings whatever | can indicate all the nuances of expression. ||| (It is impossible | even in musical notation.) ||| Moreover, | if you rely on such markings, || your reading | will sound "mechanical" || even if you are lucky enough | to avoid confusing yourself. |||

Such marks tend to become signals for mere gaps, stresses, pitch changes, etc., rather than symbols of meaning.[3] Late in rehearsal, when you have discovered chronic danger spots—spots that seem invariably to give you trouble—

---

[3] Phoneticians and linguists require marks for visibly recording phonetic and linguistic analysis of utterance. The oral reader requires understanding of meaning for persuasive utterance.

you may find a lightly penciled warning helpful. You may need, say, a Q at the bottom of some right-hand pages to remind you that on the top of the next page is a quick cue—a quick change of speaker. In more than three-way dialogue, an occasional arrow ($\nwarrow$, $\uparrow$, $\nearrow$) preceding a speech may help to keep you straight.

But the basic point is a sound one: use as few markings as possible. Markings of this kind are crutches and crutches are for cripples. When you "must" use marks, make them with an easily erasable soft black pencil. (Persons who ink up other persons' books—and especially library books—should be hanged by the thumbs!)

There is one kind of marking that is essential. If words or passages are to be omitted, the "cuts" must be indicated. If the cut is but a few words, it can be indicated by drawing a line through them:

"Curse the scoundrel," ~~he hissed.~~

(If the book you are using is borrowed, it may be wiser to enclose the cut words in brackets. The line through makes for easier reading, the brackets for easier erasure.) An extensive cut is most efficiently indicated by running a peripheral line around it. If it includes facing pages, clip those pages together.

Except in poetry, many of the "he said's" and "remarked John's" after the first necessary indications can be cut.

An extensive discussion of "what and how to cut" belongs in an advanced course. In some colleges it *is* an advanced course. This book will not pursue the matter further.

What Shall I Wear?

As the occasion for your reading approaches, you must face the question of what to wear.

Sir John Gielgud gave a very successful reading program of selections from Shakespeare's works to large audiences across the country. Audiences and critics were enthusiastic. He wore a black tuxedo, appropriate attire for an evening lecture for which admission is charged. Sixteenth century costume would have been ridiculous; a business suit—certainly in cosmopolitan centers—would have been a violation of accepted social usage.

We have earlier pointed out that maybe under very unusual circumstances "costume" might be appropriate. If you are a male and have been asked to read selections from Charles Dickens on February seventh, when Dickensians forgather to eat roast beef and Yorkshire pudding and to toast the "immortal memory" of their favorite author, you might enhance the effectiveness of your reading for that occasion by dressing and making up like Charles Dickens. (By the way, we might mention here that Dickens, in his time, was almost as famous for his reading of his works as he was for authoring them.)

Bearing in mind that your audience will accept any behavior which induces in them satisfactory empathy and through which they can retain their aesthetic distance, the answer to question 4 can be succinctly stated:

Choose clothing appropriate to the occasion, clothing that will not violate the audience's reasonable expectations, that is not in itself a distraction. Your ultimate criterion, then, is the reaction of the audience you face. Your own experience will enable you to predict their probable response: for example, they are likely to be embarrassed if you wear "stage costume," they will be nonplussed if your clothing is more formal than the occasion demands, they will resent the too informal. Girls should avoid large or glittering jewelry and grotesque make-up; boys must beware of looking starched or boiled, or, at the other extreme, as if they have crawled out from under a car.

How Do I Start Out?

Your communication with your audience really begins the moment they first notice you and continues until their attention turns to someone else. So you can never "stop and start over"; you can never divorce your grimaces, your apologetic grins, your sighs of relief, from the actual performance. Your immediate job is evoking appropriate anticipation—or, if you like, it is one of public relations. Your problem is essentially to lead your listeners from the mood with which they first look at you to the mood necessary for appreciation of the opening lines of your material. This can be accomplished by your manner.

1. The way you conduct yourself before you are announced. Show an interest in whatever preliminary proceedings there are. You cannot assume the role of dedicated reader until you have established common ground, some amiable personal relationship with your audience.

2. The way you approach your reading position. Take your place purposefully with easy, affable, and confident dignity. Open your book to the proper place and then look at your audience to get the feedback which signals their state of readiness.

3. The way you first address them. If you discover pockets of inattention, a friendly introductory statement ostensibly explaining why you are reading will help polarize attention and properly adjust their mood. If you have been ade-

quately announced and you find your silent communication has put your audience into the desired mood, introductory comment may be quite superfluous. If there are aspects of your selection—references or special circumstances, knowledge of which is essential to proper perception—you may have to phrase the necessary explanation very carefully. This, of course, must have been carefully prepared for.

With your audience where you want them, nothing remains but for you to keep them that way until you have finished! Be alert to feedback from them and make such adjustment in your reading as their response indicates is necessary.

And, as a final warning: Do not be upset by untoward events. Astonishing things can happen. Here are some of the contingencies your authors have met: in a private home, a crash of breaking crockery in the kitchen; in a gymnasium doubling as an auditorium, a folding chair collapsing under too great a burden; at a high school assembly, a string of low-flying jets following each other at sixty-second intervals; in a college theatre during a reading of *Hamlet,* a dog (indeed a very large dog) strolling inquisitively onto the stage. These things are unusual but it is surprising how usual unusual things can be. Disconcerting as such things may be, you can prevent their being wholly disruptive— sometimes by apparently unperturbed waiting for restoration of attention, sometimes by good-natured and adroit recognition of them. Indeed, your appropriate response to unexpected disturbance can strengthen and improve the empathic bond between you and your audience.

LOOKING FORWARD

As our final word, let us reiterate that when anyone is willing to listen to you read what someone else has written, he is not hearing the author speak, he is hearing you, and he has a right to expect two things:

1. That you will do justice to the text—that you will not violate the text, and
2. That you will effectively reveal your understanding of the text.

And remember, if listeners come to hear you read—say, *Hamlet*—they will come not just to hear *Hamlet* but to hear *you read Hamlet*. You will always be unique; glory in that uniqueness.

Since we started on a musical note, let us finish on one. The following parting advice was given recently to his master class in violin at the University of California, Los Angeles, by Jascha Heifetz:

I don't want any imitations. Perhaps the easiest and best way to learn in the beginning is to copy, to imitate. But I want you to play like you, to copy yourself as it were. I will try to show you basic things, then you have to go on and develop yourself, your own personality.

Follow what's in the music; unless you can think of an awfully good reason for changing something, play what is printed. . . . And, above all, be your own severest critic. Never find excuses for yourself, the violin, or the strings. Say you're culpable and see if you can find out what's the matter. Never be satisfied with yourself.[4]

[4] Quoted by Beverly Somach, *New York Times*, September 6, 1959.

APPENDIX

Improving Your Vocal Instrument

WE HOPE WE HAVE made unmistakably clear that the underlying purpose of this book has been to supply a guide for a course whose objective is to help students to increase skill in reading aloud. Although the overall purpose of such a course has not been voice improvement, we believe you cannot have made any appreciable gains from Chapters Four, Five, Seven, Eight, and Nine without making some vocal improvement.

We have avoided the discussion of voice improvement as such because we did not want to focus attention on voice to the neglect of its symbolic function. That was one of the sins that brought the old-time "elocution" into disrepute. Indeed, declamation contests and "festivals" where both teachers and "declaimers" listen primarily to voice are still discouragingly frequent. It is a pity to have message drowned in voice, but this happens easily when "voice improvement" is made the first objective in speech training; it is easy to become enamored of voice to the detriment of message. Nevertheless, adequate voice is essential; an excellent instrument is a priceless possession.

In Chapter One, we called attention to the importance of instruments: the pianist can buy a good instrument; the oral reader *is* his instrument. We have tried implicitly to show that the reader has a compensating advantage: the increasing of pianistic skill does not improve a piano, but increasing oral reading skill does improve the reader's instrument. We—you and the authors— have failed each other if this fact has not emerged in your experience. Also, we have failed each other if you are not aware of greater potential and are not desirous of making your instrument better still. But we believe that a thorough disquisition on voice lies outside the scope of a beginning course in "oral reading skill." The following suggestions may help to point the way to further study.

I. Whenever you read aloud, your voice—along with all of you—should evoke appropriate empathy by:

1. Being comfortably produced. Your phonation should give you an essentially pleasing sensation.

2. Being easily audible. Your listeners should not have to strain to hear you. Indeed, they should not be consciously aware of the process of hearing at all.

3. Having a texture always appropriate to the text. Quality should fluctuate so that it is always adequately symbolic of meaning. If at any time vocal texture distracts from its symbolic function, voice is malfunctioning.

II. Increase your awareness of your vocal instrument by:

1. Improving your personal hygiene—physical and mental. A flaccid or sluggish organism is a poor instrument. Keep it tuned up.

   a. Work hard. Set out deliberately to achieve the satisfaction that comes from doing a job well.

   b. Get adequate rest. Give your body full opportunity to eliminate and replace fatigue products. Learn to relax. This takes considerable doing. Lie down on a firm bed and start relaxation with your hands. Have someone help you; have him lift a hand and drop it back on the bed. Keep at it until your arm is responding only to the pull of gravity and you can invariably recognize the sensation of relaxation. Repeat with the legs, and then with the head. The ability to lie down and *consciously* relax to the point where you feel that but for your restraining skin you would ooze out over the bed like molasses is a tremendously valuable hygienic asset.

   c. Eat wisely. For the average American today eating unwisely is inexcusably stupid.

   d. Make time for and take wholesome recreation. Many college students in their zeal for academic accomplishment exclude from their time budgets intelligently planned programs for recreation. One should seek recreation that complements his job: the sedentary worker needs physical exercise; the manual laborer needs diversified activity, and both need recreationally intellectual stimulation.

   e. Refuse to worry about what you cannot help; get rid of the worry about what you can help by helping it. This may sound utterly banal, but it is important and it can be done.

2. Ascertaining whether you have any vocal habits which evoke unpleasant empathy. Three common vocal "unpleasantnesses" are these:

   a. Breathiness. This is caused by expelling more air than is necessary for good phonation. It is inefficient as well as unpleasant. If you cannot sustain a full, rich "ah" for at least twenty seconds you are probably wasting breath. Hold a lighted candle as near to your mouth as you can without endangering your nose and in a full, rich voice say

A long, lonely wail ran along the ravine.

The candle flame should scarcely flicker.

   b. Nasality. Most whiners are nasal. (See section on *Resonance,* page 439.)

   c. Harshness. More often than not this is the result of hypertension.

3. Find out if your voice is placed where it belongs. Each of us has a physiological structure which establishes an ultimate limit to vocal range. For instance a good tenor cannot become a good basso and he will waste his time to try. Each of us speaks, therefore, within a physiologically determined pitch range. However, none of us uses the whole of it and most of us do not use enough of it. The level at which one generally speaks is called one's *habitual pitch* and it may not be "placed" within the vocal range to the best advantage. You know that if you go too high you squeak; if you go too low you rumble. Each of us has an *optimum pitch* at which he can produce the most satisfactory sound—for himself as well as for listeners. Your optimum pitch should be the basis for your habitual pitch. Usually it is about one-third—maybe a little less—from the bottom of your pitch range. Locating it may require considerable trial-and-error experimentation, but it is worth the search.

    Drop your jaw, relax your face muscles so that the lower jaw will drop of its own weight, take a comfortable breath and say "ah" or "aw," whichever comes more easily. Then slowly lower the pitch until you reach the bottom of your range—until you run out of voice. Take another good comfortable breath and start again, this time raising the pitch until you run out at the top. Now run up and down your vocal range a number of times and see if you can locate the spot at which your phonation seems to be richest, the spot where phonation is most comfortable to produce and pleasant to listen to. It may be that this pitch is very near the first sound you made. Your teacher can help you. If your habitual pitch and optimum pitch are pretty much the same, all well and good; if not, your habitual needs replacing.

4. Extend your vocal control.

   a. Breathing. Lie flat on your back on the floor with your hands clasped behind your head, elbows touching the floor. Relax as much as the position will allow. Exhale as completely as you can and then inhale slowly and fully. Note that you seem to be breathing with your abdominal wall: as you inhale your abdomen lifts; as you exhale, it sinks. Practice this "abdominal" breathing at frequent intervals until you are fully aware of the sensation of it.

Stand up with your back against a wall, hands behind head, finger and elbows touching the wall. Repeat your abdominal breathing. Now fill your lungs and exhale very slowly and evenly. *Do not tighten the muscles in neck and throat.* Note that your abdominal wall is slowly pushing in. Extend your exhalation evenly through a period of fifteen seconds or more.

Place your hands on your sides with the tips of your middle fingers at the top of the pelvic bone and the upper palms over the lower ribs. Breathe deeply and easily and note that the rib cage expands along with the expanding abdomen. Practice inhaling fairly rapidly and exhaling slowly and evenly.

Now take a deep breath, open your mouth by relaxing your lower jaw, say "ah" on your optimum pitch as loudly as you can without strain, and continue the phonation evenly through twelve or fifteen seconds without faltering and without diminishing the volume. Are the abdominal muscles slowly and steadily pushing in?

Repeat the foregoing exercise saying the following jingle instead of "ah."

> A dillar a dollar, a ten o'clock scholar,
> What makes you come so soon?
> You used to come at ten o'clock,
> And now you come at noon.

Do it on one breath without faltering or weakening tone or volume. This is an exercise for developing and getting the feeling of complete control. You will rarely have to say so much on one breath. While you were working on Chapter Four, you should have learned to inhale often. Keep your lungs comfortably filled for reading: do not "pack" the air in and do not say so much on one exhalation that you weaken or strain phonation. Either error will immediately evoke discomfort in listeners, because one suggests explosion, the other threatens collapse.

b. Power. Put your hand on your abdomen and cough. Note the sudden contraction of the abdominal muscles. That contraction exerts pressure on the viscera, which in turn exert pressure on the partition between the abdominal and thoracic cavities, which partition shoves against the lungs, thus supplying the expulsive force for the cough. (The source of the expulsive power was in the contraction of the abdominal muscles.) Place your hand over the upper abdomen, inhale deeply and while you are saying a prolonged "ah"—keeping the jaw and throat relaxed—push your abdomen sharply and quickly five or six times with your hands. The sudden pressures cause a staccato increase in vocal volume. This illustrates the importance of the abdominal muscles as the chief source for vocal power, though not the *sole* source. The "diaphragm" (and that is the first time we have used the word) is not the source of vocal power, but it plays a vital role in vocal control because you can control the rate of its movement. It contracts to produce inhalation and relaxes during phonation. Muscular power depends on contraction of muscle. Phonation occurs during exhalation. Since the diaphragm is relaxing during phonation it *cannot* be the *source* of expulsive power for speech. So much for the diaphragm.

When you shout (a football game gives an excellent opportunity for socially acceptable practice in shouting) make the abdominal muscles supply the power. Avoid tensing the neck muscles. Trying to get vocal power by tensing the neck and throat may result in hoarseness and even temporary loss of voice.

Have you ever watched a dog pant and noted its abdominal activity? If you have difficulty developing the necessary kinesthetic awareness of the role of the abdominal muscles in producing vocal power, mimic the dog. Open the mouth by relaxing the jaw, keep the throat fully open and make the abdominal wall produce the panting by rapid succession of contraction and relaxation. When you can do it easily try phonating on every exhalation.

c. Resonance. The popularity of bathroom singing is by no means due solely to the protective privacy of the locale: your voice sounds better in there because the small room with its hard walls becomes a "resonator." When sound issues into or passes through an enclosed or nearly enclosed body of air it is modified. Take a glass tumbler and speak into it. Try using pitchers of various sizes. Note the acoustic effects. Place an empty milk bottle in the sink and let water trickle into it from the faucet. Listen to the sounds as the bottle fills. Compare that sound with the same trickle of water running into a sauce dish. In both cases the actual vibrations set up on the water surfaces are similar, but in the bottle the sound is "enriched" by the resonance set up in the air in the bottle.

Your pharynx (the open part of your throat), your nasal passages, and your mouth are resonators which modify and amplify the sound initiated by your vocal cords. Put your lips lightly together and hum a scale extending three or four notes above and below your optimum pitch. Increase the volume. You can feel the resonant vibration in a tingling of the lips.

You cannot do much about changing the basic range of vibrations set up between the vocal cords. You *can* do a great deal about modifying, enriching, and amplifying the sound as it passes through your resonators. The most important of these resonators is your mouth— a miraculous organ capable of modifying vocal vibration in infinite variety. To illustrate its resonating ability, form the vowel "ah" *silently* and then very gradually and still *silently* round your lips until you are forming the vowel "oo"; while you are doing this strike your forehead just above the hairline sharply and repeatedly with your knuckles. You should find a narrow range of vowel positions which audibly amplify the vibrations you set up in your skull. What you can do with your mouth determines in good measure what happens in your nose and throat.

Good vocal quality requires resonation *from all the resonators in proper proportion.* (Remember, the resonators cannot "resonate" without adequate vibration from the vocal cords. They cannot make "voice" out of the excessive wind of a breathy voice.) If too much sound is going through the nose unpleasant nasality results; if too little, voice lacks "brilliance," is "dull." This is a complex business and oftener than not the person with a nasal voice (or indeed, breathy, harsh, grating, etc.) does not know it until he is told. Too often he is never told.

Your vocal instrument merits intensive study; we hope your introduction to oral reading will prompt such study which, we feel, should properly begin when one has gained an appreciation of the symbolic function of voice in speaking. You may gain much from the following texts:

Anderson, V. A., *Training the Speaking Voice,* Oxford Press, 1942.
Eisenson, Jon, *The Improvement of Voice and Diction,* Macmillan, 1958.
Fairbanks, Grant, *Voice and Articulation Drill Book,* Harper, 1960.
Hahn, E., Lomas, C. W., Hargis, D., Vandraegen, D., *Basic Voice Training for Speech,* McGraw-Hill, 1952.

Van Dusen, C. Raymond, *Training the Voice for Speech,* McGraw-Hill, 1953.
Van Riper, Charles, and Irwin, John V., *Voice and Articulation,* Prentice-Hall, 1959.

The last book in the foregoing list especially offers help to students who have more than ordinary "instrument" deficiencies. All deal in varying degrees with "articulation." You have been articulating ever since you pronounced your first consonant, and you know that you can no more read aloud without articulation than a pianist can play without fingering. We were especially concerned with it when we discussed word clustering and emphasis, but we did not discuss it as such. Certainly your pronunciation (of which articulation is a most important aspect) was modified by varying your message. Perhaps now, after all your articulation in reading for meaning it is safe to consider the complexity of the articulatory process itself. (Remember the centipede who was immobilized by the question, "How ever do you manage to walk with a hundred feet?")

In ordinary conversation your tongue makes well over a thousand precisely coördinated movements a minute. Many persons have more than ordinary articulatory difficulty which requires extra attention and even clinical help. That kind of help lies beyond our present scope. But sometimes you meet a tongue-twister that is very difficult to manage. Try, for example, the following:

The skunk sat on the stump; the stump said the skunk stunk and the skunk said the stump stunk.

Although you do not often run into such concentrated difficulty in oral reading, it is nevertheless worth while to increase your articulatory facility. This can be done with practice. Articulation is a motor process. Practice, however, to be effective for oral reading requires articulation *in context*. Extensive drill on separate words without practicing those words in a variety of contexts will avail very little.

Bearing in mind all you have done by way of analysis, oral practice, and consideration of audience, work on the following story. It will reward you and should prove a delightful experience for a sophisticated audience. This story may easily be divided into sections so that each student in a class may have his own section for articulatory practice.

THE PSYCHOSEMANTICIST WILL SEE YOU NOW, MR. THURBER
JAMES THURBER

I believe there are no scientific investigators that actually call themselves psychosemanticists, but it is surely time for these highly specialized therapeuticians to set up offices. They must not be carelessly confused with psychosomaticists, who study the effects of mental weather upon the ramparts of the body. The psychosemanticists will specialize in the havoc wrought by verbal artillery upon the fortress of reason. Their job will be to cope with the psychic trauma caused by linguistic meaninglessness, to prevent the language from degenerating into gibberish, and to save the sanity of persons threatened by the onset of polysyllabic monstrosititis.

We have always been a nation of categorizationists, but what was once merely a national characteristic is showing signs of malignancy. I shall not attempt to discover the incipient primary lesion, for I am not a qualified research scholar in this field. Indeed, for having had the impudence to trespass thus far I shall no doubt be denounced by the classificationists as a fractional impactionist (one who hits subjects a glancing blow), an unauthorized incursionist, a unilateral conclusionist, and a presumptuous deductionist. Our national predilection for ponderous phraseology has been traced by one authority as far back as the awkward expression "taxation without representation" (unjust impost). It is interesting to note that the irate American colonists of that period in our history would be categorized today as "anti-taxation-without-representationists."

Not long ago, for the most recent instance in my collection, Senator Lyndon Johnson was described by a Washington newspaperman as a pragmatic functionalist, a term that was used in a laudatory sense. It isn't always easy nowadays to tell the laudatory from the derogatory at first glance, but we should be glad that this Democratic leader is not a dogmatic divisionary or an occlusive impedimentarian. The most alarming incidence of verbal premalignancy occurs, of course, in this very area of politics, but let us skip over such worn and familiar doublejointedisms as creeping Socialists, disgruntled ex-employees, ritualistic liberals, massive retaliationists, agonized reappraisalists, unorthodox thinkers, unwitting handmaidens (male), to name only a few out of hundreds, and take a look at excessive prewar anti-Fascism, a colossal (I use the adjective as a noun, in the manner of television's "spectacular") that was disgorged a few years ago. Here the classificatory degradationists brought a time element into what might be called the postevaluation of political morality. The operation of this kind of judgment during and after the Civil War would have thrown indelible suspicion upon all the Northern patriots, including Abraham Lincoln, who wanted Robert E. Lee to take command of the Federal Armies in the field. They would be known today as "overenthusiastic pre-Manassas pro-Leeists."

The carcinomenclature of our time is, to be sure, an agglomerative phenomenon of accumulated concretions, to which a dozen different types of elaborative descriptivists have contributed—eminently the old Communist intellectuals, with their "dialectical materialists," "factional deviationists," "unimplemented obscurantists," and so on, and so on. Once the political terminologists of all parties began to cross-infect our moribund vocabulary, the rate of degeneration became appalling. Elephantiasis of cliché set in, synonym atrophied, the pulse of inventiveness slowed alarmingly, and paraphrase died of impaction. Multiple sclerosis was apparent in the dragging rhythms of speech, and the complexion of writing and of conversation began to take on the tight, dry parchment look of death. We have become satisfied with gangrenous repetitions of threadbarisms, like an old man cackling in a chimney corner, and the onset of utter meaninglessness is imminent.

The symptoms of this ominous condition show up most clearly in the tertiary stage of "controversial figure." The most complicated specimen of this type of modern American is the man of unquestionable loyalty, distinguished public service, and outstanding ability and experience who has nonetheless "lost his usefulness." Actually this victim of verbositosis has not lost his usefulness, his nation has lost it. It doesn't do the national psyche any good to realize that a man may be cut off in the full flower of his usefulness, on the ground that that is not what it is. I trust I have made the urgent need for psychosemanticists apparent, even though I have admittedly become contaminated in the process, and I doubt whether my own psychosemanticist, after treating me, will ever be able to turn to my wife and say cheerfully, "Madam, your husband will write clearly again."

Before visiting my hypothetical psychosemanticist for a brief imaginary interview, I feel that I should get something reassuring into this survey of depressing ailments of the tongue. We have, then, cured, or at least survived, various incipient mouth maladies in the past. There was a moment when "globaloneyism," growing out of the Timethod of wordoggle, seemed likely to become epidemic, but it fortunately turned out to be no worse than a touch of pig Latin or a slight case of Knock, Knock, Who's There? Congress was not prepared to adopt the telescoping of words, which takes both time and ingenuity, and unless an expression becomes absorbed by Congressionalese, it has little chance of general survival. This brings me to what may easily be the direct cause of my being bundled off to the psychosemanticist's before long: the beating the word "security" is taking in this great, scared land of ours. It is becoming paralyzed. This is bound to occur to any forceful word when it loses its quality of affirmation and is employed exclusively in a connotation of fear, uncertainty, and suspicion. The most frequent use of "security" (I hate to add to its shakiness with quotation marks, which have taken on a tone of mockery in our day) is in "security risk," "weakest link in our chain of security," and "lulled into a false sense of security."

Precision of speech and meaning takes a small tossing around in the last of those three phrases. "Lulled" is actually what happens to a nation after it has been argued, tricked, maneuvered, reasoned, coaxed, cajoled, or jockeyed into a false sense of security, but the inflexibility that has descended upon us has ruled out the once noble search for the perfect word and the exact expression. What Eric Partridge calls "a poverty of linguistic resource" is exemplified by the practically exclusive use of two verbs in any public-forum discussion of national security. It is threatened or it is bolstered; I never heard of its being supported, reinforced, fortified, buttressed, or shored up, and only very rarely is it menaced, endangered, or in jeopardy.

The word "insecurity," by the way, seems to have been taken over by the psychiatrists as their personal property. In politics, as in penology, "security" itself has come to mean "insecurity." Take, for example, this sentence: "He was considered a 'maximum security' prisoner because of his police record and was never allowed out of his cell block." Similarly, "security data," means data of the kind calculated to scare the living daylights out of you, if not, indeed, your pants off. I could prove that "maximum," in the case of the prisoner mentioned above, really means "minimum," but I don't want to get us in so deep that we can't get out. The present confused usage of "security" may have originated with the ancient Romans. Anyway, here is what Cassell's Latin Dictionary has to say about *securitas:* "I. *freedom from care.* A. In a good sense, *peace of mind, quiet,* Cic. B. In a bad sense, *carelessness, indifference,* Tac. II. Transf., *freedom from danger, security,* Tac."

A vital and restless breed of men, given to tapping our toes and drumming with our fingers, infatuated with every new crazy rhythm that rears its ugly beat, we have never truly loved harmony, the graceful structure of shapes and tones, and for this blindness and deafness we pay the awful price of continuous cacophony. It gets into language as well as music; we mug melody for the sake of sound effects, and the louder and more dissonant they are, the better we seem to like them. Our national veins have taken in the singing blood of Italy, Wales, Ireland, and Germany, but the transfusion has had no beneficial effect. Great big blocky words and phrases bumble off our tongues and presses every day. In four weeks of purposeful listening to the radio and reading the newspapers I have come up with a staggering list, full of sound and fury, dignifying nothing: "automation," "readability," "humature," "motivational cognition" (this baby turned up in a series of travel lectures and was never defined), "fractionalization," "varietism," "redesegregation," "additive," "concertization" (this means giving a concert in a hall, and is not to be confused with cinematization or televisionization). The colloquial deformity "knowledgeable," which should have been clubbed to death years ago, when it first began crawling about like the late Lon Chaney, has gained new life in recent months. It is a dented derby of a word, often found in the scrawny company of such battered straw hats as "do-gooder," "know-how," "update," "uptake" (I recently uptook the iodine uptake test for thyroidism), and others so ugly and strange I can't decipher them in my notes. One of them looks like "de-egghead," which would mean to disintellectualize or mentally emasculate—a crippling operation approved of by an alarming number of squash-heads, in Washington and elsewhere.

During my month of vigil and research, I heard an able physiologist who has a radio program say, quite simply, "We do not use up all the food we take in." He wasn't allowed to get away with that piece of clarity, however. "Ah," cut in his announcer, for the benefit of those no longer able to understand simplicity, "the utilization factor!" I turned from this station to a droning psychologist, just in time to hear him say, "The female is sometimes the sexual aggressor." Here a familiar noun of mental illness and military invasion was clumsily at work beating in the skull of love with a verbal bung-starter. The sweetheart now often wears the fustian of the sick man and the Caesar. In the evening, I tuned in on one of the space-patrol programs that gleefully exude the great big blockyisms. "Your astrogation bank will tell you!" cried the captain of a space ship to another interplanetary pilot, meaning his navigational instruments. In a fairy tale, an astrogation bank would be a "star panel," but the quality of fairy tale is nowhere to be found in these dime novels of the constellations.

One Sunday morning, my head aching with "kiss-close" and "swivel-chair-it," meaning, I guess, "at kissing distance" and "maul it over in your executive brain," respectively, I stumbled upon a small radio station that had been captured by a man of God, ominous and squealful, who was begging his listeners to live on their knees, not as slaves but as supplicants. This particular fundamentalist, or maybe it is fundamentalitarian, had probably never heard of the great protest "I would rather die on my feet than live on my knees." But these yammering eschatologists, and many of their followers, have even less respect for the glory and grace of English than the unsaved politicians. "Let us cease to sugar-coat, let us cease to whitewash, let us cease to bargain-counter the Bible!" the speaker implored us. He finished second in vulgarity, I regret to say, to a reverend I had heard earlier in the year, who shouted, "I didn't cook up this dish, God cooked it up. I'm just dishing it out to ye!" The line between holiness and blasphemy becomes even thinner when some of the lay testimonialists begin ranting. "I own a shoe store in New Jersey," one of them confessed, "but Jesus Christ is my senior partner."

A recent investigation of the worries and concerns of five thousand selected Americans revealed that we are preoccupied almost wholly with the personal and private, and are troubled only mildly by political anxieties, including the danger of war, the state of civil liberties, and the internal Communist threat. This does not come as a surprise to me, since the nature of our national concern about Communism is proved to be personal by such expressions as "anti-anti-Communists" and "anti-anti-

anti-Communists." The first actually means men who are against men who are against Communists, and the second, when you unravel it, means men who are against men who are against men who are against Communists. In these wonderful examples of our love of formidable elaborationisms, concept and doctrine are put aside, and personalities take their place. What we have left is pure personalism—a specific reactionary who who is against a specific liberal who is against Senator Malone, let us say. The multiplicity of prefixes, another sign of linguistic poverty, was touched with a fine and healthful irony in Quincy Howe's invention of the phrase "ex-ex-Communist." (Many will claim that for their own, but Mr. Howe got to it first.) One would think that Americans would be worried, or at least concerned, by a man who may have ceased to be a man who may have ceased to be a Communist, but the Worry Research I have mentioned showed that this isn't so. We are worried about health, family matters and money, and we have no time for a man who may be lying about lying. Incidentally, a fairly new advertising slogan, "The portable portable," fits neatly into modern jargon: the typewriter that you can carry that you can carry.

While I was exploring the decline of expression in America, I spent a week in a hospital. Medical science has done much for humanity, but not in the area of verbal communication. It should undergo a prefectomy, and have some of its prefixes taken out, I should like to see the "semi" removed from "semi-private," a dispiriting word that originated in hospitals; there must be a less depressing way of describing a room with two or more beds. I am also for taking the "sub" out of "sub-clinical," and starting all over again with the idea in mind of making the word mean something. Incidentally, I discovered at the hospital the difference between "to be hospitalized" and "to become hospitalized." The first means to be placed in a hospital, and the second has two meanings: to get so that you can't stand it in the hospital any longer, and to like it so much there that you don't want to leave.

Lying in bed brooding over these matters, I turned on the radio and heard an American describe another American as "an old-time A.D.A. type of anti-Jeffersonian radical"—a beautiful specimen of bumblery. Sir Winston Churchill, in the exhilarating years of his public life, turned out many phrases as sharp as stilettos—for one example, "squalid gamin." But you can count on your fingers the Americans, since the Thomas Paine of "the summer soldier and the sunshine patriot," who have added bright, clear phrases to our language. If you can bumble an opponent to death why stab him seems to be the general feeling among our politicians, some of whom have got through the twelve years since the war ended with only five adjectives of derogation: naive, hostile, unrealistic, complacent, and irresponsible. All these slither easily, if boggily, into bumblery, and the bumbler is spared the tedious exercising of his mental faculties.

The day I got dressed and was about to leave the hospital, I heard a nurse and an interne discussing a patient who had got something in his eye. "It's a bad city to get something in your eye in," the nurse said. "Yes," the interne agreed, "but there isn't a better place to get something in your eye out in." I rushed past them with my hair in my wild eyes, and left the hospital. It was high time, too.

When and if I find a reputable psychosemanticist, I want to take up with him something that happened to me one night more than two years ago. It may be the basis of my etymological or philological problems, if that's what they are—words, especially big ones, are beginning to lose their meaning for me. Anyway, I woke up one summer night, from a deep dream of peacelessness, only to realize that I had been startled by nothing whatever into a false sense of insecurity. I had a desperate feeling that I was being closed in on, that there was a menace in the woods behind my house or on the road in front of it, watchful, waiting, biding its time. A few weeks later I bought a .38-calibre Smith & Wesson police revolver, which startled my wife into a genuine sense of insecurity. She hid the gun somewhere, and the cartridges somewhere else, and I still don't know where they are. I have often thought of telling my psychosemanticist about it, and I sometimes have the feeling that I did call on him and that the interview went like this:

"Doesn't your wife's hiding the gun worry you?" he asked.

"No," I said.

"It would me," he confessed.

"It would *what* you?" I demanded.

It seemed to disturb him. "*What* would *what* me?" he asked cautiously.

I suddenly couldn't think of a thing. I didn't even know what what was, but I had to say something, so I said something: "Ill fares the land, to galloping fears a prey, where gobbledygook accumulates, and words decay."

About two years ago a wistful attempt was made by some Washington bureau to straighten out the governmentalization of English. Directives were sent to the various departments demanding, among other things, the elimination of "finalize." It was as hopeless as asking a tiny child to drop its popsicle and bathe the St. Bernard. Izationism is here to stay. It appeals to bureaucrats and congressmen because of its portentous polysyllabification. Politicians love it the way they love such expressions as "legislativewise." Lord Conesford, stout defender of the Queen's English, recently paraphrased Churchill's "Give us the tools and we will finish the job" by Washingtonizing it like this: "Supply us with the implements and we will finalize the solution of the matter."

Webster's Unabridged, to my sorrow, recognizes such mastadonisms as "psychologize" and "physiologize" and, a prime favorite of congressmen, "analogize." It was, however, the physiologist I have already mentioned who classified those of us who are still up and about as "the noninstitutionalized." This is a piece of bungalorum calculated to give even the healthiest men a sense of monolithic insecurity. "Non" has an insidious way of creeping into izationisms. A piece of journalism was described on the air not long ago as "absolutely non-fictionalized." This negationization of what once could be described as verbal communication caused a Scot of my acquaintance to ask me, "Have you nothing that is positively American? It seems to me that everything one hears about in America is un-American." This abused and imprecise arrangement of letters seems bound to lose its proud A before long and to end up as "Un-american." President Eisenhower might well add to his imperatives the necessity to speak and write in such a way that we can be understood by the English-speaking peoples as well as the other races of a world that stands in grave need of clarity, accuracy, and sense.

The conspiracy of yammer and merchandising against literate speech reached a notorious height in 1956 with a singing commercial for a certain cigarette which we were told "tastes good like a cigarette should." I have one or two suggestions for the Madison Avenue illiterates in the gray flannel suits. The first is a slogan for a brewery: "We still brew good like we used to could." The second is an ad for some maker of tranquilizing drugs:

Does he seldomly praise you any more? Those kind of husbands can be cured of the grumps with Hush-Up. So give you and he a break. Put Hush-Up in his food. It don't have no taste.

And now, for God's sake, let's go out and get a breath of fresh air.[1]

—James Thurber, *The New Yorker* (1955)

ADDITIONAL EXERCISES

Prose: "Slander," p. 32; "Catherine Dead," p. 88; "Expression of Opinion," p. 104; "Mr. Polly's Decision," p. 107; "Gettysburg Address," p. 138; "The Runaway Slave," p. 215.

Poetry: "There Is a Garden in Her Face," p. 42; "The World Is Too Much with Us," p. 62; "Since There's No Help," p. 68; "I Hear an Army," p. 72; "Hotspur's Answer," p. 80; "Satan's Defiance," p. 96; "Brutus and Cassius," p. 295; "Sir Walter Raleigh in the Tower," p. 355; "Death at Jamestown," p. 357; "Claudius' Prayer," p. 359; "Hamlet to His Mother," p. 360.

INDEX